Legitimising Rejection

Refugees and Human Rights

VOLUME 13

The *Refugees and Human Rights* Series aims to meet the increasing need for literature which probes the nature and causes of forced migration, the modalities and procedures employed when refugees present themselves, and the manner in which the human rights of refugees are, or should be, promoted and protected.

Legitimising Rejection

International Refugee Law in Southeast Asia

By

Sara E. Davies

MARTINUS NIJHOFF PUBLISHERS

LEIDEN • BOSTON
2008

This book is printed on acid-free paper.

Library of Congress Cataloging-in-Publication Data

A C.I.P. record for this book is available from the Library of Congress

ISSN 1387-6031
ISBN 978 90 04 16351 5

PRINTED IN THE NETHERLANDS

For Mum and Dad

Contents

Acknowledgements

I would like to acknowledge those whose help made this book possible.

First, I must thank Lindy Melman and Bea Timmer from Martinus Nijhoff Publishers. Lindy and Bea have been absolutely wonderful to work with and incredibly patient. Bea thank you for always promptly answering my endless emails! I also want to thank the independent reviewer of this manuscript—your advice, critique and encouragement was carefully noted and I hope I have responded to your review with the care that it deserved.

I would like to acknowledge a wonderful scholar and friend, Barbara Sullivan. Barbara's scholarly dedication to detail and intellectual contribution has been invaluable. Thank you Barbara. To Roland Bleiker, a friend who always calls upon me to write with 'rhythm'—I hope I have fulfilled this in some measure. Roland and Barbara, your commitment to academe has been an inspiration. Thank you for always being there and being dear friends.

The School of Political Science and International Studies, University of Queensland provided a great amount of support and intellectual stimulation. Those who particularly cannot go unmentioned are: Stephen Bell, Rachel Parker, Mark Beeson, Richard Shapcott and Gillian Whitehouse. The administration staff: Roslyn Nicol and Anne Webber also deserve a thank you. I want to particularly acknowledge the expert eye that Robyn Lui and Richard Devetak cast over sections of the manuscript.

The School of Justice, Queensland University of Technology deserves a special mention. Here, my colleagues have shown endless interest and support in my research. It is exciting to work in an environment where the importance of research is acknowledged and quality is encouraged. Particular thank you to Roderic Broadhurst, Belinda Carpenter and the QUT Law and Justice Research Centre.

A number of libraries and archives deserve large credit for the completion of this manuscript. If it were not for the staff's dedication to assist me in my endeavors,

I would not have progressed as far as I did on my quest. Thank you to the staff at the Australian National Library—in particular everyone in the 'basement' who were always willing to help me find yet another pile of UN papers. The Library at the Australian Department of Immigration, Multicultural and Indigenous Affairs—thank you for giving me time to delve into the collection. To the Rockefeller Archive Center in Sleepy Hollow, New York for sifting through boxes of files to find me the Bellagio File—thank you Amy Fitch in particular. At the United Nations Palais des Nations Library in Geneva, especially the staff in the General Assembly and Security Council records section—thank you for endless patience with my endless enquiries. Last, but certainly not least, Lee McDonald and all the wonderful archive staff at the UNHCR Archives at UNHCR Headquarters, Geneva. My time there not only produced wonderful discoveries, but also represents one of the most enjoyable times during the research process of this book. Thank you Lee and the archive team for helping me, as we constantly said, 'bring it all together' and your endless patience! In addition, thank you Bela Hovy for being happy to answer my (ignorant) questions on statistics and Diego Rosero, who was at the UNHCR Tokyo Branch Office back in 2003 and helped inspire me to go down this path.

Anthony Burke, Hazel Lang, Nicholas Wheeler, Matt MacDonald, Heather Rae, Louise Tamaschke and Nicola Piper thank you for providing intellectual support and assistance whenever called upon.

This book has indeed been an accomplishment not just for me but also for my family. In every possible way, they have been as much a part of this process as me! Thanks to my puppy Polly who was always ready for a walk when I needed a break! To my brothers (in-law), Tony and James, you are both more dear to me than what the term 'in-law' conveys. Dear Jane and Clair, the best sisters a sibling could ever ask for, you are both everything that is graceful, intelligent, loving and warm.

I have been truly blessed through this journey with the rarity of finding my soul mate, a person who not only provides me with intellectual, but also emotional transcendence. Alex, you have supplied endless encouragement, support and love—I will endeavor for the rest of my life to deserve the constant faith and love that you have in me. Thank you so much for being my best friend, editor, companion, an inspiring scholar, and a wonderful husband. Words cannot describe how grateful I am that you are in my life and I am in yours. You know how much you mean to me and you always will forever more.

I end this section by dedicating this book to my parents, because there is no one else in world that deserves this dedication more than Mum and Dad. It has not just been the physical, emotional and financial support that both of you have always supplied (though incredibly important!), but the essential 'something extra'. It is intangible, yet always present and of great significance: your selfless love. You have always placed us three girls first, regardless of what was going on in your own lives and best of all, you always trust and believe in us, even when we do not. My journey to this publication signifies the selfless love and endless trust that you gave me. You are everything to me Mum and Dad, and so I end this section with two words that only touch upon the deepness of what I want to express to you both: thank you.

Sara Ellen Davies
Brisbane, February 2007

List of Abbreviations

AALCC	Asian African Legal Consultative Committee
ASEAN	Association of Southeast Asian Nations
CPA	Comprehensive Plan of Action
DISERO	Disembarkation Resettlement Offers Scheme
ECOSOC	Economic and Social Committee (Third Committee of the UN General Assembly)
ICEM	International Committee for European Migration
ICRC	International Committee of the Red Cross
IGCR	Inter-Governmental Committee for Refugees
IOM	International Organisation for Migration
ILO	International Labour Office
IRO	International Refugee Organisation
LON	League of Nations
OAU	Organisation of African Unity
ODP	Orderly Departure Programme
ORP	Orderly Return Programme
RASRO	Rescue at Sea Resettlement Offers
RPC	Refugee Processing Centres
TAC	Treaty of Amity and Cooperation
UN	United Nations
UNGA	United Nations General Assembly
UNHCR	United Nations High Commissioner for Refugees
UNICEF	United Nations Children's Fund
UNRRA	United Nations Rehabilitation and Relief Administration
USCR	United States Committee for Refugees

Introduction

During the twentieth century, large movements of asylum seekers and refugees were a familiar sight in Asia. There was a mass flight of Chinese (approximately one million)[1] into Southeast Asia during the second Sino-Japanese war that accompanied the Japanese occupation of Manchuria in 1937.[2] Immediately after the Second World War, ethnic Chinese from Southeast Asia, who had been forced into China during the war, sought to return to the Southeast Asian countries that were their state of origin.[3] Approximately 700 000 nationalist supporters fled China immediately after the Communists seized power in 1949, while the partition between India and Pakistan led to an estimated 8–10 million displaced people.[4] In 1954, one million Vietnamese fled from the North of their country in the wake of the first French-Indochina War. Border conflicts and internal disputes in Afghanistan,

---

1 V. Muntarbhorn, *The Status of Refugees in Asia* (Oxford: Clarendon Press, 1992), p. 4.

2 The first Sino-Japanese war occurred in 1932, when the Japanese seized the Three Eastern Provinces of China and the province of Jehol and this area was proclaimed an independent state from China, and called Manchukuo. H. M. Vinacke, *A History of the Far East in Modern Times* (London: George Allen and Unwin, 1960), p. 514. The Chinese continually contested the Japanese seizure of Manchukuo (which Japan claimed was rightful under the conditions of the release of the land from the Russians in the end of the 1905 Russo-Japanese war). The second Sino-Japanese war broke out, allegedly when Chinese troops opened fire on Japanese troops who were in territory outside of the agreed boundaries in Lukouchiao (Vinacke, *A History of the Far East*, 1960, p. 572). This led to a heightened military occupation of Manchuria by the Japanese with expulsion of Chinese and other incidences such as the fall of Nanking and the Chinese government retreat from Hankow to Chungking in Szechuan province.

3 United Nations Economic and Social Council, *Report of the International Refugee Organization (IRO)*, E/1334, 1949, pp. 38–39. The International Refugee Organisation (IRO) was made responsible for the Chinese population repatriation, and encountered resistance to re-absorb this population from the Philippine government. Burma, Indonesia, Malaysia and Singapore agreed to allow these people to return.

4 Hambro, E. *The Problem of Chinese Refugees in Hong Kong* (Leiden: A. W. Sijthoff, 1955); Vernant, J. *The Refugee in the Post-War World* (London: George Allen and Unwin, 1953), p. 738.

Iran, India, Nepal, Bangladesh, Burma (Myanmar), Pakistan and Tibet,[5] and the civil wars in Indochina all added to the refugee and asylum seeker population from the 1960s to the present day.[6] During the 1980s and 1980s, 2.5 million fled Indochina alone.[7]

At the beginning of the twenty-first century, Asia's refugee population is still the largest of any region in the world.[8] Asia has the highest number of 'persons of concern' who fall under the mandate of the Office of the United Nations High Commissioner for Refugees (UNHCR).[9] It is also estimated that Asia has a large number of people who could claim refugee status but do not do so.[10] These people either do not know they are able to seek refugee status or fear their case for refugee status will not be recognised under the UNHCR's definition of a refugee.[11] As a result, while the UNHCR estimates there are 6,187,800 refugees in Asia, this figure is hardly inclusive.[12] The only region in the world with a comparable problem is Africa.[13]

Across the globe, there are significant variations in the way asylum seekers and refugees are treated. The international community's response to asylum seekers and refugees has, since the League of Nations, primarily focused on the development of international legal rules. The 'magna carta'[14] of international refugee law is the 1951 Convention Relating to the Status of Refugees and 1967 Protocol Relating

5 See Muni, S. D. and Lok Raj Baral (eds.), *Refugees and Regional Security in South Asia* (Delhi: Konark Publishers, Regional Centre for Strategic Studies, Sri Lanka, 1996); Vincent, M. and Birgitte Refslund Sorensen (eds.), *Caught Between Borders: Response Strategies of the Internally Displaced* (London: Pluto Press, Norwegian Refugee Council, 2001).

6 See Chapter 6 in Zolberg, A., Astri Suhrke and Sergio Aguayo, *Escape From Violence: Conflict and the Refugee Crisis in the Developing World* (New York: Oxford University Press, 1989); UNHCR, *The State of the World's Refugees* (New York: Oxford University Press, 2000), p. 102.

7 Robinson, W. C. *Terms of Refuge: The Indochinese Exodus and The International Response* (London: Zed Books, 1998); UNHCR, *State of the World's Refugees*, 2000, p. 102.

8 Asia contains 36 percent of the world's refugees; Africa follows with 25%. UNHCR, *Refugees by Numbers* (2004 Edition), www.unhcr.ch/egi-bin/texis/basics.

9 The UNHCR's definition of 'populations of concern' includes not only those who meet the Office's mandate for the definition of a refugee, but also people granted a humanitarian or comparable status (usually at the request of the UN Secretary-General or the UN General Assembly) and those granted temporary protection. UNHCR, *Refugees by Numbers* (2004 Edition), www.unhcr.ch/egi-bin/texis/basics.

10 USCR, *World Refugee Survey 2002* (Washington: USCR, 2002), p. 11. United States Committee for Refugees (USCR) is an independent research body based in the United States. The USCR releases every year a publication called *World Refugee Survey*—which releases their own independent research into refugee and asylum seeking populations around the world, and individual state responses.

11 USCR, *World Refugee Survey 2002* (Washington: USCR, 2002), p. 11.

12 UNHCR, *Refugees by Numbers* (2004 Edition), www.unhcr.ch/egi-bin/texis/basics.

13 The UNHCR statistics are calculated on a per capita basis, and therefore the impact of the population size of a region is discounted. However, population size is an obvious factor in creating large flows of refugees and this in itself makes the situation in Asia significant. The figure for Asia admittedly includes 3 million Afghan refugees. If this group was excluded, Asia would still have a refugee population only second to Africa. UNHCR, *Refugees by Numbers* (2004 Edition), www.unhcr.ch/egi-bin/texis/basics.

14 Read, J. M. *Magna Carta for Refugees* (New York: United Nations Department of Public Information, 1953); Hathaway, J. *The Law of Refugee Status* (Toronto: Butterworths, 1991).

to the Status of Refugees (hereafter referred to as the 1951 Convention and 1967 Protocol). The 1951 Convention was drafted after the Second World War and established an international agreement for defining, processing and resettling refugees. However, under the 1951 Convention, people needed to demonstrate that they faced persecution at an individual level; groups could not be given refugee status *en masse*. There were also significant time and geographic constraints: states could only grant refugee status to those who demonstrated a fear of persecution due to events in Europe and before 1 January 1951, unless states agreed to abrogate the relevant passages. The 1967 Protocol was introduced as an addendum to the 1951 Convention and was created with the intention of removing the Convention's time and geographic constraints.[15] These international instruments have two main purposes. The first purpose is to create a universal definition of *who* can be properly identified as a person deserving of refugee status. Second, they seek to promote uniformity of response in the way that states provide asylum. This is achieved through setting standards to guide state responses to refugees and asylum seekers.

The majority of Asian states are not party to the 1951 Convention and the 1967 Protocol.[16] Of twenty-nine states in the region, only ten have signed both the Convention and Protocol: Azerbaijan, Cambodia, China, Japan, Kazakhstan, Korea (South), Kyrgyzstan, Philippines, Tajikistan and Turkmenistan. Only five of these have incorporated the instruments into their domestic law: Japan, Kazakhstan, Korea (South), Kyrgyzstan and Tajikistan.[17]

There has also been no concerted attempt in Asia to develop regional instruments that would oblige states to respond uniformly to refugee crises.[18] Other regions, such as Africa[19] and South America[20] have adopted regional refugee mechanisms to complement international refugee law. The vast majority of Asian states are signatories to the Asian-African Legal Consultative Committee (AALCC), which instituted the so-called Bangkok Principles in 1966 and reaffirmed these in 1988

15 UNGA, *Colloquium on the Legal Aspects of Refugee Problems*, Note by the High Commissioner, Executive Committee of the High Commissioner's Programme, Thirteenth Session, 5 May 1965, A/AC.96/INFO.40, Annex 1, p. 1. Rockefeller Foundation Archives, Record Group 1.2, Series 200, Box 484, Folder 4143.

16 The Asian region I identify is composed of twenty-nine states: Afghanistan, Azerbaijan, Bangladesh, Bhutan, Brunei, Cambodia, China, East Timor, India, Indonesia, Japan, Kazakhstan, Kyrgyzstan, Laos, Malaysia, Mongolia, Myanmar, Nepal, North Korea, Pakistan, Philippines, Singapore. South Korea, Sri Lanka, Tajikistan, Thailand, Turkmenistan, Uzbekistan and Vietnam. This selection has come from the UNHCR identification of the Asian region in its Population and Geographic Data Section.

17 One explanation for the accessions by the former Soviet states of Azerbaijan, Kazakhstan, Kyrgyzstan, Tajikistan and Turkmenistan is that in the 1990s especially, accession to international humanitarian and human rights law became central to the recognition and legitimation of new states by the international community; the same applies to Cambodia as all of these states acceded while being administered by a United Nations transnational administration.

18 Battistella, G. and Maruja M. B. Asis, 'Southeast Asia and the Specter of Unauthorized Migration', in Battistella, G. and Maruja M. B. Asis (eds.), *Unauthorized Migration in Southeast Asia* (Quezon City: Scalabrini Migration Center, 2003).

19 Organisation of African Unity (OAU) *1969 Convention governing the specific aspects of refugee problems in Africa.*

20 Organisation of American States (OAS) *1984 Cartagena Declaration on Refugees.*

(see Appendix 4). The Bangkok principles acknowledge the existence of refugees, insist that member states are expected to provide asylum, and uphold the principle of *non-refoulement*.[21] However, an important caveat to the Bangkok principles is that refugees can exercise these rights only where the security of a state is not threatened.[22] Moreover, unlike the regional agreements in Africa and South America, the Bangkok Principles do not create reciprocal regional expectations about how refugees should be treated; the Bangkok Principles are only declaratory and non-binding. They only 'aim *inter alia* at inspiring member states for enacting national legislation for the Status and Treatment of Refugees as a guide to deal with refugee problems'.[23] Thus they serve as a guide to appropriate refugee treatment, but the onus remains upon each state to decide whether or not it will apply them in particular circumstances. Compliance with the Principles is neither enforced nor monitored. As a result, they have had little discernible effect on Asian state practice in relation to refugees.[24]

Southeast Asia has the highest number of refugees seeking asylum from a single UNHCR branch office (Malaysia) and the second highest number of asylum seekers submitting claims for refugee status from any single country (Burma).[25] Furthermore, Southeast Asia hosts a large number of potential asylum seekers, who are forced to live as 'illegal migrants' because these states have no refugee recognition policy and many fear being refused refugee status by the UNHCR. Beyond the limited assistance provided by the UNHCR, there are no agreed procedures and bureaucratic infrastructure in Southeast Asia for determining refugee status.[26] This

---

[21] *Non-refoulement* is a key principle of international law (see Article 33 of the 1951 Convention) and specifies that a person who seeks asylum and is then determined to be a refugee, cannot be returned or *refouled* to the country they originated from. See Lauterpacht, Sir E. and Daniel Bethlehem, 'The Scope and Content of the Principle of *non-refoulement*: Opinion', in Feller, E., Volker Turk and Frances Nicholson (ed.), *Refugee Protection in International Law: UNHCR's Global Consultations on International Protection* (Cambridge: Cambridge University Press, 2003). For a dissenting view on the customary status of *non-refoulement*, see Hailbronner, K., 'Non-refoulement and 'Humanitarian' Refugees: Customary International Law or Wishful Legal Thinking?', *Virginia Journal of International Law*, Vol. 26, No. 4 (1986).

[22] Asian-African Legal Consultative Organisation. *Final Text of the AALCO's 1966 Bangkok Principles on Status and Treatment of Refugees*. AALCO 40th session (New Delhi: 24 June 2001), 5. http://www.aalco.org/Final%20Text%20of%20Bangkok%20Prinicples

[23] Asian-African Legal Consultative Organisation. *Final Text of the AALCO's 1966 Bangkok Principles on Status and Treatment of Refugees*. AALCO 40th session (New Delhi: 24 June 2001), 5. http://www.aalco.org/Final%20Text%20of%20Bangkok%20Prinicples

[24] Muntarbhorn, *The Status of Refugees in Asia*, 1992; Robinson, *Terms of Refuge: The Indochinese Exodus and the International Response*, 1998.

[25] UNHCR, *Trends in Refugee Status Determination 1 January—30 September 2004. Asylum Applications, Refugee Status Determination and Pending Cases in 73 Mostly Developing Countries* (Geneva: UNHCR Population Determination Unit, Population and Geographic Data Section, 2004).

[26] Muntarbhorn, *The Status of Refugees in Asia*, 1992; Jacobsen, K. 'Factors influencing the policy responses of host governments to mass refugee influxes', *International Migration Review*, Vol. 30, No. 3 (Fall 1996), pp. 655–679; Crisp, J., 'Who has counted the refugees? UNHCR and the politics of numbers', *New Issues in Refugee Research*, Working Paper No. 12, June 1999, (Geneva: UNHCR Policy Research Unit); Alexander, M., 'Refugee Status Determination Conducted by UNHCR', *International Journal of Refugee Law*, Vol. 11, No. 2 (1999), p. 251–289; Hovy, B.,

means that most humanitarian relief is provided only on an *ad hoc* basis. Out of the twelve states in the Southeast Asian region,[27] only two—Cambodia (1994) and the Philippines (1981)—have acceded to the 1951 Convention and 1967 Protocol. Neither Cambodia nor the Philippines have incorporated the international instruments into their domestic law.

The Association of Southeast Asian Nations (ASEAN) has not demonstrated any collective interest in creating a regional refugee instrument that would at least provide all members with a common legal or political framework for responding to refugees in the region. However, the need for either a collective ASEAN response to the region's refugee situation or a higher number of state accessions to the international refugee law instruments has been recognised.[28]

The persistent rejection of international refugee law by the large majority of Southeast Asian states has had a number of effects. First, there are large populations of people in each Southeast Asian country who live without access to refugee status and who are usually labelled 'illegal migrants'. These people live difficult lives, choosing not to seek refugee status from the UNHCR in case they are rejected and their presence is made known to the government.[29] Second, the absence of international refugee law places a large burden on the UNHCR to monitor and manage refugee flows, while conducting its own refugee status determinations whenever possible.[30] Third, it has created an impetus for the region's asylum seekers to seek refugee status outside the region, for instance in Europe, the US and Australia, whenever possible. Clearly, the question of why most Southeast Asian states have

'Statistics on Forced Migration', *Migration Information Source*, 1 September 2002. http:/www.migrationinformation.org/Feature/print.cfm; Wickramasekera, P., 'Asian Labour Migration: Issues and Challenges in an Era of Globalization', *International Migration Papers* No. 57 (Geneva: International Labour Office, 2002), p. 8, 21–23; Refugees International, 'Protecting Burmese Refugees in Thailand', *Asian News Tribune*, 25 January 2003. http:///www.asiantribune.com/show_news; Jacobsen, K. 'Just Enough for the City: Urban Refugees Make 'Their Own Way', *World Refugee Survey Report 2004* (Washington: United States Committee for Refugees, 2004), pp. 57–65; Martin, V., 'Myanarese Refugees in Thailand: No Freedom, No Choices', *World Refugee Survey Report 2004* (Washington: United States Committee for Refugees, 2004), pp. 82–89; Martin, V., 'Regional Summaries', *World Refugee Survey 2004* (Washington: United States Committee for Refugees, 2004); UN News, 'Malaysia urged by UN agency to protect refugees in crackdown on migrants', *UN News Centre*, 4 March 2005. http://www.un.org/apps/news.

27 Membership to ASEAN was the primary factor for selecting the states analysed in this study: Brunei, Cambodia, Indonesia, Laos, Malaysia, Myanmar, Philippines, Singapore, Thailand and Vietnam. East Timor was included owing to its geographic proximity.

28 See *inter alia*, Muntarbhorn, *The Status of Refugees in Asia*, 1992; Kourula, P., *Broadening the Edges: Refugee Definition and International Protection Revisited* (The Hague: Martinus Nijhoff, 1997), pp. 154–156; Hans, A. and Astri Suhrke, 'Responsibility Sharing', in Hathaway, J. (ed.), *Reconceiving International Refugee Law* (The Hague: Kluwer Law, 1997), pp. 99–101; Nadig, A., 'Forced Migration and Global Processes: Report of the Eighth Conference of the International Association for the Study of Forced Migration, Chiang Mai, Thailand, 5–9 January 2003', *Journal of Refugee Studies*, Vol. 16, No. 4 (2003), p. 364; UNHCR, 'East Asia and the Pacific', in *UNHCR Global Report* (Geneva: UNHCR, 2003).

29 Alexander, M., 'Refugee Status Determination Conducted by UNHCR', *International Journal of Refugee Law*, Vol. 11, No. 2 (1999), pp. 251–289.

30 Communication with Diego Rosero, (then) Senior Legal Officer, UNHCR Tokyo. Date: 27 August 2003.

not acceded to international refugee law is an important political puzzle. This book asks why the majority of Southeast Asian states have not acceded to the two pivotal international refugee law instruments—the 1951 Convention and 1967 Protocol. Moreover, I explore how these states have legitimated their refusal to sign the international refugee law instruments over time.

Existing approaches

There are three major problems with the prevailing identification of 'refugees' in Southeast Asia. First, *who is* considered a 'refugee' in this region is not always easy to determine.[31] Defining a refugee in situations of mass displacement is very difficult. On the one hand, it is evident that a significant number of people leave their homes because their human security is impaired by their state or society.[32] On the other hand, in situations of generalized violence it can be difficult to prove that an individual will be targeted for persecution by their home state. However, proof of individual, targeted persecution is required in order to be granted refugee

[31] See Hugo, G., 'Postwar refugee migration in Southeast Asia: patters, problems, and policies', in Rogge, J. R. (ed.), *Refugees: A Third World Dilemma* (New Jersey: Lowman & Littlefield, 1987); Nakavachara, N. and John R. Rogge, 'Thailand's refugee experience', in Rogge (ed.), *Refugees: A Third World Dilemma*, 1987; Rachagan, S. S., 'Refugees and illegal immigrants: the Malaysian experience with Filipino and Vietnamese refugees', in Rogge (ed.), *Refugees: A Third World Dilemma*, 1987; McNamara, D., 'The Origins and Effects of "Humane Deterrence" Policies in South-east Asia', in Loescher, G. and Laila Monhahan (eds.), *Refugees and International Relations* (New York: Oxford University Press, 1989); Zolberg, A. et al., *Escape From Violence*, 1989, in particular Chapter One, Five and Six; Muntarbhorn, *The Status of Refugees in Asia*, 1992; Hans, A. and Astri Suhrke, 'Responsibility Sharing', in Hathaway, J. (ed.), *Reconceiving International Refugee Law*, 1997; Jackson, I. C. *The Refugee Concept in Group Situations* (The Hague: Martinus Nijhoff Publishers, 1999), in particular Chapter 6, Part D and Chapter 9, Part B; Robinson, *Terms of Refuge: The Indochinese Exodus and International Response*, 1998; Suhrke, A. and Aristide Zolberg, 'Issues in Contemporary Refugee Policies', in Bernstein, A. and Myron Weiner (eds.), *Migration and Refugee Policies: An Overview* (London: Pinter, 1999); Alexander, M., 'Refugee Status Determination Conducted by UNHCR', *International Journal of Refugee Law*, Vol. 11, No. 2 (1999), pp. 251–289; Unger, D., 'Ain't Enough Blanket: International Humanitarian Assistance and Cambodian Political Resistance', in Stedman, S. J. and Fred Tanner (eds.), *Refugee Manipulation: War, Politics, and the Abuse of Human Suffering* (Washington: Brookings Institution Press, 2003); Martin, V., 'Myanarese Refugees in Thailand', *World Refugee Survey Report 2004* (Washington: United States Committee for Refugees, 2004), pp. 82–89; Chapter Four: 'Defining Refugees and Voluntary Repatriation at the United Nations High Commissioner for Refugees' in Barnett, M. and Martha Finnemore. *Rules for the World: International Organizations in Global Politics* (Ithaca: Cornell University Press, 2004); Kent, J., 'Malaysia's Trouble with Migrants', *BBC News*, accessed: 7 April 2005. http://www.news.bbc.co.uk/1/hi/world/asia-pacific/

[32] Human security according to Caroline Thomas is about prioritising the security of the individual and this personal security is only achieved when basic material needs are met and "meaningful participation in the life of the community" and human dignity is realised. Thomas, C., 'Introduction', in Thomas, C. and Peter Wilkin (eds.), *Globalization, Human Security and the African Experience* (Boulder: Lynne Rienner, 1999), p. 3. The UNHDR defines human security as meaning "safety from chronic threats such as hunger, disease and repression" and "protection from sudden and harmful disruptions in the patterns of daily life". United Nations Development Programme, *Human Development Report 1994* (New York: Oxford University Press, 1994), p. 23.

status according to the most widely accepted definition of a refugee contained in the 1951 Convention.

Second, as the 1951 Convention's definition of a refugee is not recognised by the majority of Southeast Asian states,[33] referring to these groups of people as 'refugees' implies a level of recognition that is presently unavailable in the region.[34] In the case of Southeast Asia, the *lack* of refugee status determination procedures results in people automatically being labeled as 'illegal migrants' without consideration for the fact that they may have been *forced* to flee their homeland.

Third, it is clear that the academic literature in this field mainly focuses on *either* refugees or migrants in Southeast Asia. In other words, scholarly approaches have bifurcated into studies of 'refugees'[35] and studies of 'migration',[36] with little

---

33 UNHCR, 'East Asia and the Pacific', *UNHCR Global Report 2003* (Geneva: UNHCR, 2003), pp. 366–387. Also UNHCR individual *Country Operations Plan* for each of the countries in Southeast Asia, Planning Year 2004 (Geneva: UNHCR, 2004).

34 An excellent addition to refugee literature is on human security and how it has the potential to provide a greater academic and policy understanding through identifying the relationship between refugee responses and refugee experiences. Of note, there is no specific mention of Southeast Asia in this volume: Newman, E. and Joanne Van Selm (eds.), *Refugees and Forced Displacement: International Security, Human Vulnerability and the State* (Tokyo: United Nations University Press, 2003).

35 See note 31 for refugee literature pertaining to Southeast Asia. Literature accounting for the existence of individual refugee groups in Southeast Asia is not particularly notable. Aside from the array of work done on Indochinese refugees (which will be further referenced in Chapters 4–7), the most notable is Chantavanich, S. and E. Bruce Reynolds, *Indochinese Refugees: Asylum and Resettlement* (Bangkok: Institute of Asian Studies, Chulalongkorn University, 1988); Muntarbhorn, *The Status of Refugees in Asia*, 1992 and Robinson, *Terms of Refuge: The Indochinese Exodus and the International Response*, 1998. The most recent and original contribution on an individual refugee group in Southeast Asia has been on the experience of Burmese refugees on the borders of Thailand: Lang, H. *Fear and Sanctuary: Burmese Refugees in Thailand* (Ithaca: Cornell University Press, 2002). A notable exception in the general field is South Asia. There are a large volume of, relatively recent, works dedicated towards this specific issue of demarcating the refugee from the illegal immigrant: Muni, S. D. and Lok Raj Baral (eds.), *Refugees and Regional Security in South Asia*, 1996; Alexander, M., 'Refugee Status Determination Conducted by UNHCR', *International Journal of Refugee Studies*, Vol. 11, No. 2 (1999), pp. 251–289; Abrar, C. R. (ed.), *On the Margin: Refugees, Migrants and Minorities* (Dhaka: Refugee and Migratory Movements Research Unit, 2000); Ahmed, S. R. *Forlorn Migrants: An International Legal Regime for Undocumented Migrant Workers* (Dhaka: The University Press Limited, 2000); Chimni, B. S. *International Refugee Law: A Reader* (New Delhi: Sage Publications, 2000); Vijayakumar, V., 'Judicial Responses to Refuge Protection in India', *International Journal of Refugee Law*, Vol. 12, No. 2 (2000), pp. 235–243; Abrar, C. R., 'Legal Protection of Refugees in South Asia', *Forced Migration Review*, Issue 10, pp. 21–23; Farr, G., 'Afghanistan: Displaced in a Devastated Country', in Vincent, M. and Birgitte Refslund Sorensen (eds.), *Caught Between Borders: Response Strategies of the Internally Displaced* (London: Pluto Press, Norwegian Refugee Council, 2001); Khan, G., 'Citizenship and statelessness in South Asia', *New Issues in Refugee Research*, Working Paper No. 47 (Geneva: UNHCR Research Unit, 2001); Giri, T. N. *Refugee Problems in Asia and Africa: Role of the UNHCR* (New Delhi: Manak Publications, 2003).

36 See note 29 for refugee literature pertaining to Southeast Asia. Literature on migrants in Southeast Asia are (*inter alia*): Suhrke, 'The "High Politics" of Population Movements: Migration, State and Civil Society in Southeast Asia', in Weiner, M. (ed.), *International Migration and Security*, 1993; Chan Kwok Bun, et al. (eds.), *Crossing Borders: Transmigration in Asia Pacific*, 1995; Hugo, G., 'Undocumented International Migration in Southeast Asia', in Yen-Fen Tseng, Chilla Bulbeck, Lan-Hung Nora Chiang and Jung-Chung Hsu (eds.), *Asian Migration: Pacific Rim Dynamics*, Monograph 1 (Taiwan: National Taiwan University, Interdisciplinary Group for Australian

account for those who do not fit neatly into *either* category. The literature's apparent acceptance of the categorical difference between 'refugee' and 'migrant' in Southeast Asia has no doubt occurred as a result of problems on the ground, namely that a lack of refugee recognition procedures has lead to asylum seekers being labeled 'illegal migrants' by host countries. The consequence of the absence of refugee status determination procedures throughout Southeast Asia clearly requires further investigation.[37] The separation of the 'migrant' from the 'refugee' is not a clear cut process in this region, which is why terms such as 'illegal migrant' or 'irregular migrant'[38] are often used.

Studies, 1999); Castles, S., 'New Migrations in the Asia-Pacific region: a force for social and political change', *International Social Science Journal*, Volume 48, Issue 156, (1998), pp. 215–228; Castles, S., 'International Migration and the Nation-State in Asia', in Siddique, M. A. B. (ed.), *International Migration in the 21st Century: Essays in Honour of Reginald Appleyard* (Cheltenham: Edward Elgar, 2001); Iguchi, Y., 'Migration Policies in East and South-East Asia in the 21st Century', in OECD, *International Migration in Asia: Trends and Policies* (Paris, Organisation for Economic Co-operation and Development [OECD], 2001); Wickramasekera, P., 'Asian Labour Migration: Issues and Challenges in an Era of Globalization', *International Migration Papers*, Number 57 (Geneva: International Labour Office, 2002); Battistella, G. and Maruja M. B. Asis (eds.), *Unauthorized Migration in Southeast Asia* (Quezon City: Scalabrini Migration Center, 2003); Hugo, G., 'Migration and Development: A Perspective from Asia', *IOM Migration Research Series*, Number 14 (Geneva: International Organization for Migration, 2003); Iredale, R., Fei Guo and Rozario, S. (eds.), *Return Migration in the Asia Pacific* (Cheltenham: Edward Elgar, 2003); also note the *Asian and Pacific Migration Journal*.

37 Recent volumes evaluating refugee protection issues that did not include a single chapter on the question of refugees in Southeast Asia, or Asia more generally include: Zolberg, A. R. and Peter M. Benda (eds.), *Global Migrants, Global Refugees: Problems and Solutions* (New York: Berghahn Books, 2001); Fitzpatrick, J. (ed.), *Human Rights Protection for Refugees, Asylum-Seekers, and Internally Displaced Persons: A Guide to International Mechanisms and Procedures* (New York: Transnational Publishers, 2002); Joly, D. (ed.), *Global Changes in Asylum Regimes: Closing Doors* (Hampshire: Palgrave Macmillan, 2003); Newman, E. and Joanne Van Selm (eds.), *Refugees and Forced Displacement: International Security, Human Vulnerability and the State*, 2003. For more on this see Davies, S. E., 'Start Looking South: The Refugee Convention Fifty Years On', *International Journal of Human Rights*, Vol. 8, No. 3 (Autumn 2004), pp. 355–366. One exception is Stedman, S. J. and Fred Tanner (eds.), *Refugee Manipulation: War, Politics and the Abuse of Human Suffering*, 2003.

38 The closest the literature has come to recognising the uncertain status of many migrants in Southeast Asia is by labelling them 'irregular migrants'. This term has been a starting point for recognising that 'illegal migrants', in particular, need basic rights in their host country. See Ghosh, B. *Huddled Masses and Uncertain Shores: Insights into Irregular Migration* (The Hague: Martinus Nijhoff, 1998); Battistella, G. and Maruja M. B. Asis (eds.), *Unauthorized Migration in Southeast Asia*, 2003. However, the literature has neglected thus far that the term 'irregular migrant' may also include *potential refugees*. See Wickramasekera, P., 'Asian Labour Migration: Issues and Challenges in an Era of Globalization', *International Migration Papers*, No. 57 (Geneva: International Labour Office, 2002), p. 8, 21–23. Therefore, when we refer to migrants we must keep in mind that the literature's concept of legal and illegal migrants may not reflect the political and legal complexities associated with determining the status of such people. Indeed, the fact that most Southeast Asian states have no formal refugee recognition process means that we are potentially mislabelling a group of vulnerable people as 'illegal migrants', on the erroneous assumption that such people have access to mechanisms that will enable them to make their migrant status legal. Noted in Nadig, A., 'Forced Migration and Global Processes Report of the Eighth Conference of the International Association for the Study of Forced Migration, Chiang Mai, Thailand, 5–9 January 2003', *Journal of Refugee Studies*, Vol. 16, No. 4 (2003), p. 364.

In the existing literature, there are four main explanations for Southeast Asia's non- commitment to international refugee law. These are the 'good neighbourliness' argument; the argument that Southeast Asian states cannot bear the economic cost of refugee recognition; the argument that refugees recognised under international refugee law would pose a threat to social cohesion in Southeast Asian states; and the Asian Values argument, which is that Southeast Asian states cannot be expected to recognise international refugee law as the concept is based on Western, as opposed to Asian, values.

First, the good neighbourliness arguments takes as central the non-interference principle of the so-called 'ASEAN way'[39] and the general principle that Southeast Asian states should not interfere in the 'sensitive issues' of neighbouring countries. This argument holds that Southeast Asian states have chosen not to accede to international refugee law because doing so would bind them into positions that could violate the good neighbour principle. Astri Suhrke argues that refugees represent a 'foreign policy complication'[40] which would get in the way of major geopolitical and strategic concerns. Similarly, Chowdry Abrar insists that in that case of South Asia,

> [An] important hindrance towards developing a formal refugee regime in South Asia has been the adherence to the policy of working out political solutions through bilateral negotiation between the host country and the country of origin, with the emphasis on sovereign jurisdiction.[41]

Suhrke and Vitit Muntarbhorn have followed similar lines of argument in explaining Southeast Asian states' apparent reluctance to accede to international refugee law instruments.[42] However, as Suhrke herself noted, 'good neighbourliness' fails to account for the fact that Asian states have often used the presence of refugees within their state to score political points over their neighbours.[43] For instance, Malaysia's initial intake of Muslims from Mindanao between 1972 and 1977 could have been seen as an implicit endorsement of the Muslim struggle in the Philippines. During this period Muslims refugees in Sabah were immediately granted liberal residence rights and, in some circumstance, citizenship.[44] The same could be said

---

39 Acharya, A. *The Quest for Identity: International Relations of Southeast Asia* (Oxford: Oxford University Press, 2000); Muntarbhorn, *The Status of Refugees in Asia*, 1992.

40 Suhrke, 'The "High Politics" of Populations Movements: Migration, State and Civil Society in Southeast Asia', in Weiner, M (ed.), *International Migration and Security*, 1993, p. 180.

41 Abrar, C. R., 'Legal Protection of Refugees in South Asia', *Forced Migration Review*, 10 (April 2001), p. 21.

42 Muntarbhorn, *The Status of Refugees in Asia*, 1992; Suhrke, 'The "High Politics" of Populations Movements: Migration, State and Civil Society in Southeast Asia', in Weiner, M. (ed.), *International Migration and Security*, 1993, p. 180.

43 Suhrke, A., 'Indochinese Refugees: The Law and Politics of First Asylum', *ANNALS of the American Academy of Political and Social Science*, Volume 467 (May 1983), pp. 102–115; Suhrke, 'The "High Politics" of Populations Movements: Migration, State and Civil Society in Southeast Asia', in Weiner, M. (ed.), *International Migration and Security*, 1993, p. 180; Hans, A. and Astri Suhrke, 'Responsibility Sharing', in Hathaway, J. (ed.), *Reconceiving International Law*, 1997, pp. 99–102.

44 Muntarbhorn, *The Status of Refugees in Asia*, 1992, p. 115.

for Malaysia's more recent intake of Acehnese asylum seekers fleeing the separatist struggle in Indonesia.[45] It is clear however, that neither population presented any grave danger to the relationship between Malaysia and either the Philippines or Indonesia (for more on this see Chapter 5). This also suggests there are significant empirical flaws in the 'good neighbourliness' argument for why Asian states have refused to adopt international refugee law.

The second explanation given as to why Asian states have failed to commit to international refugee law is that (as with most developing states) the perceived economic costs of accession are too great. This argument holds that the refugee recognition practices of international refugee law implies heavy financial burdens and developing states lack the wherewithal to bear this burden.[46] This argument is not only evident in the scholarly literature,[47] but has also frequently been invoked by Asian states themselves. For instance, on several occasions when the UNHCR privately invited Asian states to sign the 1951 Convention or 1967 Protocol, governments replied that the financial obligations that accession would create for developing states was too high. Governments in Japan, Laos, Malaysia, Philippines and Singapore all stressed that the 1951 Convention created financial expectations that were higher than developing states could commit to on behalf of refugees.[48] However, other developing states (outside the Asian region) have not regarded the cost factor as crucial; the majority of African states for example have acceded to the 1951 Convention and 1967 Protocol yet only a minority are able to afford any real welfare to their refugee community.[49] The economic cost argument also overlooks the economic function that retaining particular social groups as 'illegal

---

45 UNHCR, 'East Asia and the Pacific', *UNHCR Global Report 2003* (Geneva: UNHCR, 2003), pp. 366–387.

46 Wickramasekera, P., 'Asian Labour Migration: Issues and Challenges in an Era of Globalization', *International Migration Papers* No. 57 (Geneva: International Labour Office, 2002); Jacobsen, K. 'The Forgotten Solution: Local Integration for Refugees in Developing Countries', *UNHCR New Issues in Research*, Working Paper No. 45 (Geneva: UNHCR, 2001); A. H. Richmond, 'International Migration and Global Change', in Chan Kwok Bun, et al. (eds.), *Crossing Borders: Transmigration in the Asia-Pacific*, 1995; Suhrke, 'The "High Politics" of Populations Movements: Migration, State and Civil Society in Southeast Asia', in Weiner, M. (ed.), *International Migration and Security*, 1993.

47 Suhrke, A. and Aristide R. Zolberg, 'Issues in Contemporary Refugee Policies', in Bernstein, A. and Myron Weiner (eds.), *Migration and Refugee Policies: An Overview*, 1999; Castles, S., 'International Migration and the Nation-State in Asia', in M. A. B. Siddique (ed.), *International Migration into the 21st Century: Essays in Honour of Reginald Appleyard*, 2001.

48 UNHCR, Secretary of Foreign Affairs, Republic of Philippines to Deputy High Commissioner, 2 July 1956; Folio 578, 671.1 GEN—1951 Convention, 1949–1969 General; Series 1, Classified Subject Files; Fonds 11, Records of the Central Registry; Archives of the UNHCR for Refugees (hereafter Series 1, Fonds UNHCR 11); UNHCR, Minister Permanent Delegate of Japan to the International Organisations to the Deputy High Commissioner, 3 August 1956; Folio 579, 671.1 GEN; Series 1, Fonds UNHCR 11; UNHCR, Mr E. Schlatter to United Nations Vientiane, Laos, 28 January 1967; Folio 1692, 671.1 GEN; Series 1, Fonds UNHCR 11; W. K. McCoy to UNHCR, Geneva, 'Malaysia—Attitude to Convention', 15 March 1969, Folio 1829, 671.1 GEN; Series 1, Fonds UNHCR 11; W. K. McCoy to UNHCR, Geneva, 'Singapore—Attitude to Convention', 24 March 1969; Folio 1831, 671.1 GEN; Series 1, Fonds UNHCR 11.

49 Oucho, J. O., 'Refugees and Internally Displaced Persons: Africa's Liability for the Next Millenium', in D. Joly (ed.), *Global Changes in Asylum Regimes: Closing Doors*, 2002, p. 154.

immigrants' fulfil. Throughout the region, 'illegal immigrants' fulfil important economic roles. In many cases the state prefers them to remain 'illegal' in order to encourage or coerce them to continue fulfilling those roles.[50] For instance, the most widely used term to describe the economic roles that 'illegal immigrants' fulfil is 3D-jobs. They are: dirty, dangerous and demanding (difficult). The '3D-job' term derives from the Japanese term '3-K' (*katanai, kiken, kitsui*).[51] Another term used in Southeast Asia is 'SALEP'—Shunned by ALl Except the very Poor—which is another indication of the nature of these jobs.[52] Wickramasekera argues that the common description of these jobs as 'undignified labour' demonstrates that this employment is increasingly unattractive to the local urban population in rapidly developing states where opportunities for employment conditions are improving as a result of economic growth.[53] 'Illegal immigrants' conduct important tasks that would otherwise go unfulfilled and creates a powerful incentive for states in Asia to admit immigrants but deny them either refugee status or citizenship. For example, in states such as Malaysia and Thailand, there is immense economic benefit from the work of Vietnamese and Burmese migrants, who work for low wages and in conditions in factory jobs that locals would not generally consider.[54] However, the lack of local interest in these jobs suggests little, if any, correlation between achieving refugee status, securing a labour market for 3D-jobs, and the economic welfare of the receiving state. Even in developed industrialised countries, refugees do not immediately attain an employment status that corresponds to the one they had in their country of origin. In many cases, because of language difficulties and their inability to afford the education required to upgrade skills, recognised refugees in developed and developing states often remain in the 'lower' sections of the employment market for considerable periods of time.[55]

A related economic argument is that developing states are reluctant to recognise refugees because of the economic costs of doing so, particularly in a context where

---

[50] Battistella, and Asis, 'Southeast Asia and the Specter of Unauthorized Migration', in Battistella, G. and Maruja M. B. Asis (eds.), *Unauthorized Migration in Southeast Asia*, 2003.

[51] Wickramasekara, P., 'Asian Labour Migration: Issues and Challenges in an Era of Globalization', *International Migration Papers* (Geneva: International Labour Office, 2002), p. 3; Hugo, G., 'Migration and Development: A Perspective from Asia', *IOM Migration Research Series*, Number 14 (Geneva: International Organization for Migration, 2003).

[52] Bohning, W. R., 'Conceptualizing and Simulating the Impact of the Asian Crisis on Filipino's Employment Opportunities Abroad', *Asian and Pacific Migration Journal*, Vol. 7, Nos. 2–3 (1998), p. 367.

[53] Wickramasekara, P., 'Asian Labour Migration: Issues and Challenges in an Era of Globalization', *International Migration Papers* (Geneva: International Labour Office, 2002), p. 3.

[54] Adi, R., 'Irregular Migration from Indonesia', in Battistella, G. and Maruja M. B. Asis (eds.), *Unauthorized Migration in Southeast Asia*, 2003; Wong, D. T. and Teuku Afrizal Teuku Anwar, '*Migran Gelap*: Irregular Migrants in Malaysia's Shadow Economy', Battistella, G. and Maruja M. B. Asis (eds.), *Unauthorized Migration in Southeast Asia*, 2003; Amarapibal, A., Allan Beesey and Andreas Germershausen, 'Irregular Migration into Thailand', Battistella, G. and Maruja M. B. Asis (eds.), *Unauthorized Migration in Southeast Asia*, 2003.

[55] Heisler, M. O. and Zig Layton-Henry, 'Migration and the Links Between Social and Societal Security', in O. Waever, Barry Buzan, Morten Kelstrup and Pierre Lemaitre (ed.), *Identity, Migration and the New Security Agenda in Europe* (New York: St Martin's Press, 1993), p. 152.

industrialised countries are closing their borders.[56] Karen Jacobsen argues the perception that refugees create more economic costs than benefits does not correspond to the evidence provided by close analysis of a host-state's market, and that 'refugees are often blamed for pre-existing... economic problems'.[57] Even though 'self-settled' refugees can compete with locals for resources, their presence can also lead to 'expanding the capacity and productivity of the RHA [Refugee Hosting Area] economy'.[58] Jacobsen cites a field study on Afghan refugees in Pakistan to demonstrate that the presence of refugees can in fact lead to the stimulation of a local economy.[59] Thus, Jacobsen casts significant doubt on the claim that granting refugee status would damage local economies. In fact, refugees can bring not only new economic resources and social capital, but also financial windfalls from international society for those states willing to provide asylum.[60]

The third explanation for why Asian states have failed to commit to international refugee law is that migrants represent a danger to the already fragile social cohesion of developing countries.[61] The existence of different ethnic groups in the majority of Asian states has a history of causing domestic friction and many states in the region adopt policies that aim to promote social cohesion. Perhaps the best known example is Malaysia's policy of providing child benefits for children born to Malay parents, with the express intention that Malays will come to outnumber the Indian and Chinese populations in Malaysia. In contrast, Singapore has a strict multicultural policy whereby social events and housing communities are purposely constructed in order to encourage inter-racial marriages and communities amongst the Chinese, Indian and Malay populations.[62] The argument has frequently been made that any further introduction of people with different ethnic and politi-

[56] Richmond, A. H., 'International Migration and Global Change', in Chan Kwok Bun, et al. (eds.), *Crossing Borders: Transmigration in Asia Pacific*, 1995, p. 43.

[57] Jacobsen, K., 'The Forgotten Solution: Local Integration for Refugees in Developing Countries', *UNHCR New Issues in Research*, Working Paper No. 45 (Geneva: UNHCR, 2001), p. 12.

[58] Jacobsen, K. 'The Forgotten Solution: Local Integration for Refugees in Developing Countries', *UNHCR New Issues in Research*, Working Paper No. 45 (Geneva: UNHCR, 2001), p. 16.

[59] See Ashraf (1988) quoted in Jacobsen, K., 'The Forgotten Solution: Local Integration for Refugees in Developing Countries', *UNHCR New Issues in Research*, Working Paper No. 45 (Geneva: UNHCR, 2001), pp. 16, 18.

[60] Daniel Unger talks of the enormous financial support that Thailand received when it allowed Cambodian refugees to seek refuge on their territory from donor states. Unger, D. 'Ain't Enough Blanket: International Humanitarian Assistance and Cambodian Political Resistance', in S. J. Stedman and Fred Tanner (eds.), *Refugee Manipulation: War, Politics and the Abuse of Human Suffering*, 2003.

[61] Suhrke, 'The "High Politics" of Population Movements', in Weiner, M. (ed.), *International Migration and Security*, 1993; Weiner, 'Rejected Peoples and Unwanted Migrants in South Asia', in M. Weiner (ed.), *International Migration and Security*, 1993; Afolayan, A. A., 'Issues and Challenges of Emigration Dynamics in Developing Countries', *International Migration*, Vol. 39, No. 4 (2001), p. 17.

[62] I would like to thank a panel of presenters (whose anonymity I will protect according to Chatham House Rules) at the New Zealand Asian Studies Conference held at Auckland University from 22–24 November 2003, where these ethnic practices in Malaysia and Singapore were candidly discussed.

cal backgrounds could exacerbate ethnic tensions causing disintegration within the state.[63] This approach has led to the incarceration of many asylum seekers in camps so that they are physically separated from the local population. Use of the label 'illegal immigrant' in Southeast Asia has certainly enabled the demarcation of irregular migrants as separate from the social community, and enhanced the cohesion of the social community by positioning them as the 'other'.[64]

However, the experience of irregular migrants or, as Jacobsen terms them 'self-settled refugees', does not substantiate the social cohesion argument.[65] First, in the past, social cohesion has been attempted by containing asylum seekers in camps so as to keep them away from the local population. However, this practice has created more danger for both the would-be refugees and local population, as camps have a long history of association with crime, the infiltration of rebel groups, spread of disease and increased insecurity—thus destabilising the social environment.[66] Such problems are much less frequent when refugees are integrated into the local community. Second, the source of societal opposition to refugees is often the perception that they will take over jobs, constrain the economy and over-populate urban centres.[67] Yet, as explained earlier, there is rarely a correlation between these two sets of issues.[68]

According to Jacobsen, dissatisfaction with a refugee population can be a way of expressing resentment that has more to do with government failure than the actual presence of refugees.[69] She argues that hostility to refugees can be ameliorated by programmes designed to increase awareness of the benefits of local integration and points out that studies are rarely carried out on the presence of 'self-settled' refugees in host countries. In light of Asia's experience such studies would appear to be important.[70] Arguably, the breakdown of social cohesion has more to do with internal factors than the presence of refugees. As Jacobsen demonstrates the

---

63 Suhrke, 'The "High Politics" of Population Movements', in Weiner, M. (ed.), *International Migration and Security*, 1993; Weiner, 'Rejected Peoples and Unwanted Migrants in South Asia', in M. Weiner (ed.), *International Migration and Security*, 1993.

64 Castles, S., 'International Migration and the Nation-State in Asia', in M. A. B. Siddique (ed.), *International Migration into the 21st Century: Essays in Honour of Reginald Appleyard*, 2001.

65 Jacobsen, K. 'The Forgotten Solution: Local Integration for Refugees in Developing Countries', *UNHCR New Issues in Research*, Working Paper No. 45 (Geneva: UNHCR, 2001).

66 Jacobsen, K. 'The Forgotten Solution: Local Integration for Refugees in Developing Countries', *UNHCR New Issues in Research*, Working Paper No. 45 (Geneva: UNHCR, 2001).

67 Afolayan, A. A., 'Issues and Challenges of Emigration Dynamics in Developing Countries', *International Migration*, Vol. 39, No. 4 (2001); Jacobsen, K. 'The Forgotten Solution: Local Integration for Refugees in Developing Countries', *UNHCR New Issues in Research*, Working Paper No. 45 (Geneva: UNHCR, 2001).

68 Jacobsen, K. 'The Forgotten Solution: Local Integration for Refugees in Developing Countries', *UNHCR New Issues in Research*, Working Paper No. 45 (Geneva: UNHCR, 2001); Wickramasekara, P., 'Asian Labour Migration: Issues and Challenges in an Era of Globalization', *International Migration Papers* (Geneva: International Labour Office, 2002).

69 Jacobsen, K. 'The Forgotten Solution: Local Integration for Refugees in Developing Countries', *UNHCR New Issues in Research*, Working Paper No. 45 (Geneva: UNHCR, 2001).

70 Jacobsen, K. 'The Forgotten Solution: Local Integration for Refugees in Developing Countries', *UNHCR New Issues in Research*, Working Paper No. 45 (Geneva: UNHCR, 2001), p. 4.

more that 'self-settled' refugees are locally integrated, the less chance there is that the social cohesion of the host state will be destabilised.[71]

Thus, most common explanations as to why the majority of Southeast Asian states have not acceded to international refugee law are flawed in important respects. In addition, all three approaches suffer from two general pitfalls. First, none of them address the relationship between politics and law in international relations. That is, they are not grounded in an understanding of how states relate to law and how law shapes behaviour by enabling and constraining certain types of action. Second, none of these approaches explore the justifications that the region's states themselves offer to explain their reticence; they have not investigated how the general tendency toward rejecting international refugee law shapes the way that Southeast Asian states, international organisations, and interested states outside the region respond to irregular migrants within the region.

A fourth potential explanation suggests that human rights, such as the right to asylum, reflects European values and is divorced from the experiences and interests of Southeast Asian states. From this perspective, Southeast Asian non-compliance with international refugee law is part of a broader pattern of non-compliance with international human rights laws. As a result, literature about the idea of universal human rights has proliferated in recent years.[72] These works focus on the question of whether international human rights law is rooted in the tradition of a Western (in particular European) history and understanding. Since the end of the Cold War, there have been increased attempts to promote the principles of the Universal Declaration of Human Rights (UDHR) into the domestic laws of Asian countries.[73] One of the articles enshrined in the UDHR is Article 14—the right to seek asylum. It was Article 14 that provided the mandate for the establishment of the UNHCR and subsequent international refugee law. In response to these attempts, Southeast Asian states have argued that human rights law was constructed when the majority of Asia was still under colonial rule and therefore there is little contained in the instruments that are of relevance to their situation.[74]

[71] Jacobsen, K. 'The Forgotten Solution: Local Integration for Refugees in Developing Countries', *UNHCR New Issues in Research*, Working Paper No. 45 (Geneva: UNHCR, 2001), pp. 23–25.

[72] *See inter alia:* Donelly, J. *Universal Human Rights in Theory and Practice* (New York: Cornell University Press, 2002); Talbott, W. *Which Rights should be Universal?* (New York: Oxford University Press, 2005).

[73] *See inter alia:* Freeman, Chimni, B. S. 'The Geopolitcs of Refugee Studies: A View from the South', *Journal of Refugee Studies*, Vol. 11, No. 4 (1998), pp. 350–374; Chimni, B. S., 'Protection of Refugees in South Asia: Need for a Legal Framework', in *South Asian Forum for Human Rights Refugee Studies Project* (Kathmandu: SAFHR, 2000); Langlois, A. *The Politics of Justice and Human Rights: Southeast Asia and Universalist Theory* (Cambridge: Cambridge University Press, 2001); Rajagopal, B. *International Law from Below: Development, Social Movements and Third World Resistance* (Cambridge: Cambridge University Press, 2003); Barr, M. D. *Cultural Politics and Asian Values: The Tepid War* (London: Routledge, 2006).

[74] Chimni, B. S. 'The Geopolitics of Refugee Studies: A View from the South', *Journal of Refugee Studies*, Vol. 11, No. 4 (1998), pp. 350–374; Sen, S., 'The Refugee Convention and practice in South Asia: a marriage of inconvenience?', in van Selm, J., *Khoti Kamanga, John Morrison,* Aninia Nadig, Sanja Spoljar-Vrzina, *and Loes van Willigen (eds.), The Refugee Convention at Fifty: A View from Forced Migration Studies* (Lanham: Lexington Books, 2003).

Although this idea that Southeast Asian states' attitude towards international refugee law is part of a broader attitude towards international human rights law has some merit, further investigation is beyond the scope of this book. It is also wroth noting that such claims have been widely criticised. This claim is rejected by scholars such as Michael Freeman. Freeman opposes the 'Asian Values' argument on the ground that 'the human rights question is not properly an issue between East and West at all. It is a question of how governments can be truly responsive to the people they claim to serve'.[75] Other scholars join Freeman in arguing that "there is no distinctly "Asian" perspective, entirely different from Western or other perspectives and unanimously shared by all Asian societies'.[76]

This book does not seek to evaluate the existence of 'Asian values' as opposed to 'Western values' in the area of human rights. However, it is necessary to briefly challenge the fundamental assumption of 'Asian values'. If these states have a general antipathy to the concept of human rights, then surely they would also reject the institutions that enshrine them. Yet this is not the case. Southeast Asian states are quite happy to be members of the United Nations, a condition of membership is, of course, to recognise the UDHR. They seek representation in the Security Council—a forum for international law making; and as this book will show, participate in the UNHCR Executive Committee and conferences held to discuss responses to refugees in their region. Thus, the argument that Southeast Asian states reject human rights and its associated laws because it is contrary to their values does not correlate to their practices. The key focus of this book is to evaluate whether involvement in law formation is the key to these states then participating the application of law. As a result, evaluating whether the underlying argument of Asian Values—that states need to partake in the formation of laws that they are expected to adhere to—will be explored.

Therefore, this book aims to remedy the deficiency of explanation for Southeast Asian states rejection of international refugee law by charting the region's response to it in detail and by locating the politics of law via an examination of the region's response to the Indochinese refugee crisis from 1975–1996. The following section begins this exploration by providing a brief overview of the foundation of international refugee law and then charting the relationship between politics and international refugee law.

[75] Freeman, M., 'Human Rights, Asia and the West' in J. T. H. Tang (ed.), *Human Rights and International Relations in the Asia Pacific Region* (London/New York: Pinter, 1995), p. 24.

[76] Bruun, O. and Michael Jacobsen, 'Introduction', in M. Jacobsen and Ole Bruun (eds.), *Human Rights and Asian Values: contesting national identities and cultural representations in Asia* (Richmond: Curzon, 2000), p. 1.

Explanatory framework

There are two main complaints that Southeast Asian states had concerning international refugee law. First, they believed that the international refugee laws placed the greatest burden on developing states near to the source of a crisis. Second, Southeast Asian states also complained that they had not participated in the drafting of international refugee law and that many non-European concerns were not addressed. The 1951 Convention and the 1967 Protocol were not primarily developed to respond to Asian and African concerns about refugee problems. As James Hathaway argues, the 1951 Convention was primarily concerned with serving the political needs of the West.[77] Even the 1967 Protocol, though important because it removed the time and geographic constraints contained in the Convention, prohibited alternative interpretations of *who* a refugee was and *how* this status could be determined. What is apparent from the drafting procedures of both instruments is that developing states had little role the process of creating these instruments but they were nonetheless expected to just simply *adopt* them. The common perception of the 1951 Convention and 1967 Protocol as Eurocentric is an important starting point for any attempt to understand the relationship between Southeast Asian states and international refugee law. As will be demonstrated in more depth in chapters one and two, in the eyes of Southeast Asian states the 1951 Convention and 1967 Protocol were the direct result of Western states presenting their own narrow understanding of the refugee problem and views about how law should interpret and deal with this problem.[78]

However, while Southeast Asian states have chosen to reject international refugee law they still converse and reason within this paradigm. This is the result of what Rajagopol terms 'radically pluralist interpretations':[79] whilst law provides a common framework of meaning, its application and significance in particular cases can have a variety of interpretations that are ultimately shaped by politics.

In providing a new understanding of the relationship between politics and international refugee law in Southeast Asia, I will argue that although the region's states have formally rejected international refugee law, the law has played an important yet hitherto unrecognised role in the politics of Southeast Asia. The framework that I am using for an exploration of Southeast Asian states relationship to international refugee law instruments is based on the idea that international law has a political-constitutive role. As Koskenniemi argues, 'in law, political struggle is waged on what legal words.... mean, whose policy they will include, and whose they will exclude'.[80] Thus, I will utilise a critical legal approach to understand the

[77] Hathaway, *The Law of Refugee Status*, 1991.

[78] Koskenniemi, M., 'The Politics of International Law', *European Journal of International Law*, Vol. 1 (1990), pp. 4–32.

[79] Rajagopol, B. *International Law from Below: Development, Social Movements and Third World Resistance* (Cambridge: Cambridge University Press, 2003).

[80] Koskenniemi, M., 'International Law in Europe: Between Tradition and Renewal', *The European Journal of International Law*, Vol. 16, No. 1 (2005), p. 119.

relationship between international law and international relations.[81] The central claim of critical legal studies is that there are 'historical processes through which dominant approaches to international law (and international relations) both create and perpetuate social injustices and repressive interests and then make them appear as neutral and objective ontological conditions'.[82] Thus, even though the majority of Southeast Asian states have not formally acceded to the international refugee law instruments, they have a consistent history of justifying their position by reference to the international refugee legal framework. Thus, whilst the legal framework covering refugees can protect those who entered a state without first seeking permission, it can also be used to deny protection. In the majority of cases in Southeast Asia, states insist that many entering do not meet the legal definition of a refugee. They do so by using refugee law to frame who they will exclude as opposed to who they will protect. This results in the continued denial of protection for those seeking asylum in the Southeast Asian region and the legitimisation of that denial.

As my study on the Indochinese refugee crisis will demonstrate, Southeast Asian states came to use terms such as 'asylum seeker', 'genuine refugee' and 'non-genuine refugee', which are given meaning by the legal framework provided by international refugee law. Their insistence on using such terms as 'illegal migrant', 'economic migrant' or 'non-genuine refugee' was not so much about resisting the legal instruments, as using the framework they provide to delegitimise the migrant population. For there to be a category of 'non-genuine' refugees, there must logically be 'genuine refugees' as laid out in the 1951 Convention. As Koskenniemi points out, this is all about engaging in the political struggle through legal words.[83]

How do these processes work? Rosalyn Higgins, of the New Haven school, describes the relationship between international law and the state as a *process* as opposed to the enforcement of rules by a particular party and the handing down of authoritative judgments by institutions.[84] States justify their actions by reference to the law and others decide whether those justifications were plausible or not. The key question is whether there is a limit to what constitutes as a plausible argument.

---

81 Kennedy, D., 'Theses about International Law Discourse', *German Yearbook of International Law*, Volume 23 (1980), pp. 353–391; Koskenniemi, M., 'The Politics of International Law', *European Journal of International Law*, Volume 1 (1990), pp. 4–32; Purvis, N., 'Critical Legal Studies in Public International Law', *Harvard International Law Journal*, Vol. 32, No. 1 (1991), pp. 81–127 ; Byers, M. *Custom, Power and the Power of Rules: International Relations and Customary International Law* (Cambridge: Cambridge University Press, 1999), pp. 45–46; Rajagopal, *International Law from Below: Development, Social Movements and Third World Resistance*, 2003.

82 Cutler, A. Claire, 'Critical historical materialism and international law: imagining international law as praxis', in Hobden, S. and John M Hobson (eds.), *Historical Sociology of International Relations* (Cambridge: Cambridge University Press, 2002), p. 182.

83 Koskenniemi, M. *From Apology to Utopia: The Structure of International Legal Argument* (Helsinki: Lakimiesliiton Kustannus, 1989); Koskenniemi, M., 'International Law in Europe: Between Tradition and Renewal', *The European Journal of International Law*, Vol. 16, No. 1 (2005), pp. 113–124.

84 Higgins, R. *Problems and Process: International Law and How We Use It* (Oxford: Oxford University Press, 1994).

Critical legal scholars argue that legal interpretation is infinitely malleable when the political context is sympathetic.[85] The New Haven School, however, posits that there are important limits.[86] Questioning whether there are such limits, where they lie and how they change, is pivotal to this study and is a theme I return to in the conclusion. Is the critical legal interpretation of laws as being indefinite and politically malleable correct, or is the New Haven school correct in identifying limits to legal argumentation?

How rejection has been legitimised

I argue that the majority of Southeast Asian states have refused to accede to the primary international refugee law instruments because they have never felt obliged to do so. This lack of a sense of obligation derives from two sources. First, they have been able to plausibly argue that both the 1951 Convention and 1967 Protocol were formulated in a Eurocentric environment; thus these international instruments were regarded as largely irrelevant to the irregular migrant problem confronted in Southeast Asia. Second, during the Indochinese refugee crisis (1975–1996), the international community was willing to provide material assistance to Southeast Asian states and to provide resettlement places for those officially recognised as refugees. Southeast Asian states learnt to manipulate the refugee problem in order to secure this aid. The refusal to accede to the international instruments was a key tenet of the manipulation strategy.

It is important to recognise at the outset, however, that the region's relationship with international refugee law was not one of a simple and straightforward

85 Kennedy, D., 'Theses about International Law Discourse', *German Yearbook of International Law*, Volume 23 (1980), pp. 353–391; Koskenniemi, *From Apology to Utopia: The Structure of International Legal Argument*, 1989; Koskenniemi, M., 'The Politics of International Law', *European Journal of International Law*, Volume 1 (1990), pp. 4–32; Purvis, N., 'Critical Legal Studies in Public International Law', *Harvard International Law Journal*, Vol. 32, No. 1 (1991), pp. 81–127; Kratochwil, F. V., 'How do Norms Matter?', in Byers, M. (ed.), *The Role of Law in International Politics* (Oxford: Oxford University Press, 2000); Koskenniemi, M., 'Comments on Chapter 1 and 2', in Byers, M. and George Nolte (eds.), *United States Hegemony and the Foundations of International Law*, 2003; Koskenniemi, M., 'International Law and Hegemony: A Reconfiguration', *Cambridge Review of International Affairs*, Vol. 17, No. 3 (2004), pp. 197–218; Koskenniemi, M., 'International Law in Europe: Between Tradition and Renewal', *The European Journal of International Law*, Vol. 16, No. 1 (2005), pp. 113–124.

86 McDougal, M., 'Some Basic Theoretical Concepts about International Law: A Policy Oriented Framework of Inquiry' in Falk, R and Saul Mendlovitz (eds.), *The Strategy of World Order*, vol. II, *International Law* (New York: World Law Fund, 1966); McDougal, M. and Harold Lasswell, 'The Identification and Appraisal of Diverse Systems of Public Order' in Falk, R. and Saul Mendlovitz (eds.), *The Strategy of World Order*, vol. II, *International Law* (New York: World Law Fund, 1966); McDougal, M. and W. M. Reisman, *International Law in Contemporary Perspective* (New Haven: Yale University Press, 1980); Higgins, *Problems and Processes: International Law and How We Use It*, 1994; Byers, *Custom, Power and the Power of Rules: International Relations and Customary International Law*, 1999; Reus-Smit, C., The Politics of International Law', in Reus-Smit, C. (ed.), *The Politics of International Law* (Cambridge: Cambridge University Press, 2004).

rejection. The majority of Southeast Asian states which refuse to accede to the 1951 Convention and 1967 Protocol have nevertheless sought to legitimate their position *within the framework of international refugee law*. These states repeatedly justify their response to asylum seekers by explaining that these groups are 'non-genuine' refugees. The idea of a 'non-genuine' refugee only makes sense within a discursive framework that acknowledges the theoretical possibility of 'genuine' refugees. This framework derives from the definition of a refugee found in the 1951 Convention.

Despite invoking the Convention's language, as my case study of the Indochinese refugee crisis demonstrates (Chapters 3–6), Southeast Asian states were largely unchallenged in their argument that the instruments did not apply to them. Nor were these states compelled to change their behavior towards asylum seekers. They consistently argued that the legal instruments were not applicable to the type of displaced persons they were encountering and, on the rare occasion that they agreed to permit the UNHCR to conduct refugee status determinations, such decisions were always taken on the condition that the refugees were resettled *elsewhere*.

In chapters 1 and 2, I provide an account of the drafting of the 1951 Convention and the 1967 Protocol. I argue that this process produced what many saw as a Eurocentric legal framework for identifying and managing refugees. The fact that the Convention and Protocol were widely seen as Eurocentric permitted many Southeast Asian states to claim that the legal instruments did not bind them and that they were irrelevant. Most of Chapter 1 will be concerned with the post World War II period in which the provision of legal protection and material assistance to refugees was discussed in the United Nations. However, in this chapter I also evaluate the origins of international refugee instruments during the time of the League of Nations highlighting the Eurocentric influence on international approaches to refugees from the outset. This chapter argues that this Eurocentrism was continued in the 1951 Convention. While concerns about this were raised at the time, the issue was generally dismissed.

In Chapter 2, I analyse the on-going legal and political debates about how best to identify and respond to refugees between the signing of the 1951 Convention and the conclusion of the 1967 Protocol. The aim of this chapter is to outline the position held by Asian states during this process and to evaluate the type of knowledge and experience that was prioritised as the legal framework was amended. Overall, I argue that non-Western understandings of the refugee problem were largely ignored during the drafting process, resulting in a systematic exclusion of Asian states from the construction of international refugee law. This seriously undermined the perceived legitimacy of international refugee law in Southeast Asia. Given this, it was hardly surprising that most of the region's states chose not to formally accede to the treaties, claiming instead a sovereign right to determine for themselves the status of different types of migrants, including refugees. The question for the second part of the book is whether this position changed when the region's states confronted with a refugee crisis of monumental proportions: the Indochinese refugee crisis of 1975–1996.

In Chapters 3–6, I focus in detail on the Indochinese refugee crisis. The number of people estimated to have sought asylum within Southeast Asia during this crisis was between 2.5 and 3 million, though the exact number may never be precisely determined.[87] The responses of Southeast Asian states during this period went though a number of changes shaped by changes in the UNHCR's policies, the willingness of Western states to provide material assistance, and Southeast Asian states' perception of their own interests. However, the majority of states in the region continued to refuse various overtures for them to accede to international refugee law.

In Chapter 3, I look at the early stages of the Indochinese crisis in the period 1975–1979. There was a rapid increase of asylum seekers fleeing Indochina in this period and Southeast Asian states started to argue that the lack of international assistance left them with no option but to refuse entry to any who attempted to gain access to their state by boat or foot. The UN called an international conference in 1979 to address these problems. The conference primarily aimed to persuade Southeast Asian states to take their 'humanitarian responsibilities' more seriously and to provide assistance to the Indochinese migrants. As this chapter demonstrates, however, Southeast Asian states were able to secure greater international support by refusing to adhere to basic customs, such as *non-refoulement*, and by continuing to refuse to accede to the 1951 Convention and 1967 Protocol. Essentially, Southeast Asian states manipulated the crisis by arguing that they would provide temporary assistance for Indochinese seeking asylum, as long as the rest of the world provided material assistance and resettlement places.

Chapter 4 investigates the UNHCR's attempts during the early 1980s to persuade Southeast Asian states to sign the international refugee law instruments. It also examines the effects of the 1979 Conference on Southeast Asian states response to the Indochinese refugee crisis. In 1978 the UNHCR granted *prima facie*[88] refugee status to Indochinese asylum seekers and this had a significant impact on the approaches adopted by Southeast Asia towards the Indochinese. Southeast Asian states continued to insist on remaining outside the international refugee law framework, but agreed to afford temporary asylum on the expectation of continued financial assistance and resettlement places.

Chapter 5 considers the period of the mid 1980s, just before the 1989 International Conference on Indochinese Refugees. The 1979 Conference enabled Southeast Asian states to avoid responsibility for refugee populations by placing the burden of responsibility on the international community. This strategy was partly the result of the West's reluctance to insist Southeast Asian states cease

[87] Robinson, *Terms of Refuge: The Indochinese Exodus and the International Response*, 1998.

[88] *Prima facie* refugees is a term used to identify a large number of people fleeing events in which they may not have actively participated, but fear the consequences for themselves and those around them if they do not flee, it also takes into account those that have been personally threatened or persecuted. In contrast to individual refugee status granted under the 1951 Convention, *prima facie* refugee status is used in situations where individual screening is not possible, though this does not preclude eventual individual screening for refugee status.

practising *refoulement*. However, by the early 1980s many Western states were becoming increasingly reluctant to provide resettlement places for the seemingly endless flow of Indochinese refugees. The result was that the period between the 1979 conference and 1989 conference was one of political contest between the UNHCR, Southeast Asian states and Western states over who would bear primary responsibility for responding to the Indochinese asylum seekers. I demonstrate in this chapter that by the mid 1980s, Southeast Asian states had begun to secure agreement from Western states and the UNHCR about the need for a change of direction in relation to the treatment of Indochinese refugees.

Chapter 6 focuses on how a new consensus was developed about the treatment of Indochinese refugees in the late 1980s. P*rima facie* refugee status for Indochinese asylum seekers ended and a refugee screening process enshrined in the 1989 Comprehensive Plan of Action (CPA) was adopted by Southeast Asian states and Western states, with UNHCR assistance at the 1989 Conference. The main problem with the CPA was that it called for the repatriation of 'non-genuine' asylum seekers. This was not an easy task as many refused to go back to their respective countries (Cambodia, Laos and Vietnam) and eventually had to be forced to return—a practice that clearly amounted to *refoulement*.[89] This practice was carried out with UNHCR assistance. Thus, Southeast Asian states successfully argued that the Indochinese seeking asylum since the early 1980s were not 'genuine' refugees, an argument that had greater resonance as Western states grew more reluctant to provide resettlement places. In other words, Southeast Asian states justified their action by reference to the legal framework of international refugee law. Whilst these arguments were initially shunned by key Western states such as the US, they gained greater legitimacy as the political preferences of outside states began to shift.

[89] Most legal scholars now agree that *refoulement* can be applied to those not yet given refugee status because they are, according to the UNHCR Handbook on Refugee Status Determination, to be seen as *prima facie* refugees until proven otherwise; and thus the rule of *non-refoulement* should apply. Lauterpacht, Sir E. and Daniel Bethlehem, 'The Scope and Content of the principle of *non-refoulement*: Opinion', in Feller, E., Volker Turk and Frances Nicholson (eds.), *Refugee Protection in International Law: UNHCR's Global Consultations on International Protection* (Cambridge: Cambridge University Press, 2003). See also n. 21.

Chapter 1

The Eurocentric 1951 Convention

The First and Second World Wars left large numbers of people displaced throughout Europe, and indeed, throughout the world. Prior to the creation of the Office of the United Nations High Commissioner for Refugees (UNHCR) in 1951, there had been several attempts to create refugee organizations at the international level. These organizations did not work with a formal generally-agreed upon definition for the refugee, and they only dealt with specific groups such as Russians, Armenians and European Jews. As a result, they did not assist all refugees in general. The UNHCR's 1951 Convention Relating to the Status of Refugees (hereafter referred to as the 1951 Convention) was meant to provide an inclusive and representative definition of the 'refugee', and set standards that would guide states' response to refugees. James Read described it as the 'magna carta'[1] of international refugee law.

However, the 1951 Convention and the UNHCR has also been described as right from the beginning being 'enmeshed in the international politics of the East-West conflict and refugees were perceived as elements of power in the bipolar rivalry'.[2] James Hathaway argues that refugee law was a direct product of powerful states' interests dominating the drafting process. The 'universalization' of international refugee law was 'designed and administered by European states for European refugees [and was] accompanied by a substantive and procedural narrowing of

---

1 Read, J. M. Magna Carta for Refugees (New York: United Nations Department of Public Information, 1953).

2 Loescher, G. *The UNHCR and World Politics: A Perilous Path* (New York: Oxford University Press, 2001), p. 6.

the underlying commitment to protection'.[3] Sharing this view, this chapter will demonstrate that both the 1951 Convention and the UNHCR were formulated to serve mainly European interests and the political purposes of Western states. I argue throughout this book that the Eurocentric environment in which international refugee law was created has enabled Southeast Asian states to successfully argue that these laws were not applicable to their irregular migrant problems. In this chapter I will demonstrate how Western states' political and domestic interests inhibited the potential for a broader understanding of the refugee problem. This enabled Southeast Asian states to claim that they could not identify with the purpose and practice of the refugee law instruments. First, Southeast Asian states denied any knowledge of the instruments and once this claim became unfeasible, maintained that the instruments did not apply to the specific refugee situations that they faced.

In this chapter I develop the Eurocentric argument in four parts. The first part focuses on the refugee protection organizations that existed prior to the establishment of the UNHCR and consider why these failed, necessitating the creation of the UNHCR. The second part of the chapter examines the establishment of the UNHCR after the Second World War, and the purposes it was meant to fulfill. The overwhelming concern about the burden of refugees in Western European states and increasing Cold War hostilities dominated decisions about who the UNHCR was to assist. The third part of this chapter will then look at how political and region-centric concerns affected the drafting of the 1951 Convention. I show that suggestions by states such as India and Pakistan about the definition of a refugee and the scope of the Convention's applicability were not included in the final draft. The process of drafting the 1951 Convention provides the focus for the fourth and final part of this chapter. I will identify how the marginalisation of non-Western approaches to refugees during the drafting process affected the newly emerging Southeast Asian states' perception of the instrument, its purpose and applicability to their specific refugee situations.

1.1 *Evolution of international refugee protection*

On 20 February 1921, the President of the International Committee of the Red Cross, Gustav Ador addressed the Council of the League of Nations on the Russian refugee problem.[4] Ador requested that the appointment of a High Commissioner be made, so that he could define the status of Russian refugees and coordinate

[3] Hathaway, J., 'Reconceiving Refugee Law as Human Rights Protection', *Journal of Refugee Studies*, Volume 4, Number 2, 1991, p. 114.

[4] Over one million Russian refugees, who had fled due to the upheaval of World War One and the 1918 Communist Revolution, were scattered across twenty-one European countries which all differed in their treatment of these people. Stoessinger, J. G. *The Refugee and the World Community* (Minneapolis: The University of Minnesota Press, 1956), p. 16.

relief for them.[5] The Council of the League agreed, and on the 27 June 1921 the first High Commissioner for Refugees was set up by the League of Nations.[6] The responsibilities of the High Commissioner, defined by the League Assembly, was 'to coordinate the action of governments and private organizations for the relief of Russian refugees, to regulate the legal status of a large class of persons who had been rendered stateless, and to assist them to find permanent homes and work'.[7] The first High Commissioner, Fridtjof Nansen, maintained that the 'legal rehabilitation of the refugees'[8] was the essential first step to resolving the refugee crisis. In cooperation with the International Labour Organization (ILO), Nansen sought to create a basic identity document for refugees that all states would recognize, and thus prevent *refoulement*—the forced expulsion of refugees—a fate that had befallen the Russian refugees. Initially, most League members did not want to financially support such a scheme.[9] Nansen called an intergovernmental conference in July 1922, in Geneva and here states agreed to adopt the identity document. It would become known as the 'Nansen Passport' and was the first 'measure of uniformity in the legal status of the refugees'.[10] Individual governments issued the Nansen Passport and each government could change the length of its validity. Initially, the passport was only extended to Russians.[11]

In a few short years, Nansen was able to extend the refugee protection mandate to the Armenian refugee population fleeing Turkish genocide in 1924, secure contributions from governments and private donors, and even create a profit for the High Commissioner's Office through the creation and sale of Nansen stamps.[12] By 1926, the High Commission had also become responsible for Assyrian, Assyro-Chaldean and Turk refugee populations.[13] However, in 1926 the protection and assistance services of the High Commissioner came under ILO auspices, and in 1929 the High Commissioner's

[5] Stoessinger, *The Refugee and the World Community*, 1956, p. 14; Jackson, I. C. *The Refugee Concept in Group Situations* (The Hague: Martinus Nijhoff Publishers, 1999), p. 11.

[6] Vernant, J. *The Refugee in the Post-War World* (London: George Allen & Unwin Ltd., 1953), p. 24; for a detailed account of how the High Commissioner for Refugees came to exist under the League of Nations, see Holborn, L. *The League of Nations and the Problem of Refugees: A Study of the Development of International Government and Administration in Post-War Europe* (Radcliffe College: Thesis, 1937).

[7] Stoessinger, *The Refugee and the World Community*, 1956, pp. 15–16.

[8] Stoessinger, *The Refugee and the World Community*, 1956, p. 16.

[9] Stoessinger, *The Refugee and the World Community*, 1956, p. 17.

[10] Stoessinger, *The Refugee and the World Community*, 1956, p. 18.

[11] For more on this see Holborn, L. W., 'The Legal Status of Political Refugees 1920–1938, *American Journal of International Law*, Volume 32, Issue 4 (Oct. 1938), pp. 680–703; Marrus, M. R. *The Unwanted: European Refugees in the Twentieth Century* (New York: Oxford University Press, 1985); Gallagher, D. *The Era of Refugees: The Evolution of the International Refugee System* (Washington: Refugee Policy Group, 1989).

[12] Vernant, *The Refugee in the Post-War World*, 1953, p. 24.

[13] Holborn, L. W., 'The Legal Status of Political Refugees 1920–1938, *American Journal of International Law*, Volume 32, Issue 4 (Oct. 1938), p. 686; Vernant, *The Refugee in the Post-War World*, 1953, p. 24.

Office was moved again to come under the authority of the Secretary-General of the League of Nations.[14]

There were a number of attempts to 'supplement and consolidate the measures of legal protection',[15] such as the 1933 Convention Relating to the International Status of Refugees, the 1936 Provisional Arrangement Concerning the Status of Refugees Coming from Germany and the 1938 Convention Concerning the Status of Refugees from Germany. However, with the death of the greatly respected Nansen in 1930, these instruments struggled to gain enough state support to meet new refugee crises caused by events first in Russia, Armenia and Turkey, then in Germany and Austria. In 1935, James MacDonald resigned from the position of High Commissioner after only two years in the job, citing his reason as feeling 'virtually powerless without more definite authority in his negotiations with governments, and that the problem had to be tackled at its source'.[16] Stoessinger explains the source of the problem being due to the League's failure to adequately fund and protect refugees:

> The League was an organization of nation-states aiming for universality, and thus protection of refugees from a given state was bound to arouse the hostility of an actual or potential member of the League of Nations. Refugees were *ipso facto* enemies of some nation-state which was already a member of the League or which, it was hoped, would become a member. Hence, all political refugees were a source of political embarrassment to the League and the organization, in its work on behalf of the uprooted, was actually divided against itself.[17]

The flight of Jews from Germany had begun in 1933, which also marked the first year of Nazi rule. This was then followed by the elimination of civil rights for Jews in 1935. In spite of the early flight of Jews from Germany, Jewish and European observers at the time thought this was a 'temporary, disorganized violence that would cease and that Nazism would not last'.[18] At the same time, Germany's economy appeared to be surviving the financial crisis of 1931 which had led to large scale depression and mass unemployment throughout the rest of Europe and the United States.[19] As a result, Western European states and the United States were more

---

14 Holborn, L. W., 'The Legal Status of Political Refugees 1920–1938, *American Journal of International Law*, Volume 32, Issue 4 (Oct. 1938).

15 Vernant, *The Refugee in the Post-War World*, 1953, p. 24. For a more in depth analysis of the inter-war refugee protection period see Skran, C. *Refugees in Inter-War Europe: The Emergence of a Regime* (Oxford: Clarendon Press, 1995). Claudia Skran argues that the inter-war period is crucial to understanding how our contemporary responses to refugees have not far evolved from this period and sheds light on how the UNHCR mandate of protection came to exist.

16 Vernant, *The Refugee in the Post-War World*, 1953, p. 25; Also see Holborn, L. W., 'The Legal Status of Political Refugees 1920–1938, *American Journal of International Law*, Volume 32, Issue 4 (Oct. 1938), pp. 691–694; Skran, *Refugees in Inter-War Europe: The Emergence of a Regime*, 1995, p. 255. Holborn and Skran credit McDonald's resignation as a key move in highlighting greater public awareness of Nazi's actions, even though it did not at the time spur greater refugee protection.

17 Stoessinger, *The Refugee and the World Community*, 1956, p. 32.

18 Sassen, S. *Guest and Aliens* (New York: The New Press, 1999), p. 91.

19 Sassen, *Guest and Aliens*, 1999, pp. 91–92; Stoessinger, *The Refugee and the World Community*, 1956, p. 30.

concerned with domestic opposition to an influx of Jewish refugees than to the Jews' plight. As anti-semitism spread across Eastern Europe, Jewish groups found few havens in the West. During the domestic crises sparked by the 1929 Wall Street crash, no state wanted to take Jewish refugees fleeing a fear of persecution that was widely believed to be non-existent.[20]

In the meantime, three separate refugee organizations were attempting to deal with refugees in the 1930s all in a relatively *ad hoc* fashion. The Nansen Office cared for Russian, Saar and Armenian refugees; the High Commissioner for Refugees from Germany obviously cared for this group, but without any funds or authority to adequately do its job; and the International Labour Office studied refugees' entry into the European labor market.[21] In 1938, the work of these three organizations was collapsed under a single High Commissioner's Office, set up within the League to be responsible for refugees. The Office was to provide legal protection and material aid for all refugees who fell under the mandate of the three predecessor organizations (approximately 600,000 people).[22] However, the High Commissioner was not mandated to provide direct assistance to refugees, but had to rely upon governments and non-governmental agencies to accomplish this goal.[23] Vernant describes the High Commissioner's work up until 1946 as accomplishing a 'valuable service in many areas in matters of protection'.[24] Contrary to this, Sassen argues that 'there was... no particular will it seems either in the League of Nations or in individual states, to address this refugee crisis [in the 1930s] effectively. Less was done than in the World War I aftermath'.[25] Stoessinger also disagrees with Vernant, describing the League's attempts as 'impotent' for the 'complete repudiation of the pleas repeatedly voiced to the German government by the new High Commissioner and a continuing reluctance on the part of the democracies to lower their immigration barriers made the new amalgamation of refugee organs little more than a gesture'.[26]

Shortly before the Second World War began, thirty-states met in Evian, France to discuss the 'growing exodus of refugees from Germany and Austria'.[27] The President of the United States, Franklin Roosevelt, called the conference to secure an international commitment to provide immigration places for those fleeing persecution in Europe. The states that gathered in Evian formed the Intergovernmental Committee on Refugees (IGCR) with the purpose of assisting persons who had not yet left their country of origin (mainly Austria or Germany), but who needed to

---

20 Sassen, *Guest and Aliens*, 1999, p. 93.

21 Stoessinger, *The Refugee and the World Community*, 1956, p. 37.

22 Vernant, *The Refugee in the Post-War World*, 1953, p. 25; Simpson, J. H. *Refuges: A Review of the Situation Since September 1938* (London: The Royal Institute of International Affairs, 1939).

23 Vernant, *The Refugee in the Post-War World*, 1953, p. 26.

24 Vernant, *The Refugee in the Post-War World*, 1953, p. 26.

25 Sassen, *Guest and Aliens*, 1999, p. 92.

26 Stoessinger, *The Refugee and the World Community*, 1956, p. 42.

27 Vernant, *The Refugee in the Post-War World*, 1953, p. 26; Skran, *Refugees in Inter-War Europe: The Emergence of a Regime*, 1995, see Chapter 6 in particular.

'emigrate on account of their political opinions, religious beliefs or racial origin'.[28] A further purpose was to assist those who had already left their country of origin, but did not yet have a place of permanent residence. However, the IGCR did not play any role in developing emigration arrangements for refugees, or any funds for such a purpose. Thus, the IGCR, like the High Commissioner, was severely handicapped by the attitudes of countries before and during the early days of the Second World War. Thus the IGCR was 'mainly confined to diplomatic representations in an effort to find opportunities for the permanent settlement overseas of refugees receiving temporary asylum in European countries'.[29]

By the end of 1943, over fifteen million people throughout Europe had fled the advancing German armies; another eight million Europeans had been deported to Germany as forced laborers; and six million Jews were sent to concentration camps in Poland.[30] Large numbers of the first two groups survived the war, but very few of the third group.[31] In addition, refugees fleeing totalitarianism started to flee the eastern areas of Europe to escape the coming of communism. Over a million Russians, Ukrainians, Byelorussians, Poles, Latvians, Lithuanians and Estonians joined the Nazis who had been fleeing from the Soviet advance.[32] At the same time in Asia, millions had been displaced by the Japanese imperialist invasion into Asia, to then be followed by millions of Chinese fleeing the Communist Party that seized power in China in 1948.[33] The estimated figure of people displaced due to the Second World War was between thirty to sixty million people.[34]

Two factors at the end of World War Two helped to radically transform international attempts at refugee protection. The first was a sense of guilt by the Western states for their failure to respond to reports of Jewish persecution, and the second was the emerging Cold War. As late as 1942, the Allied Powers had been 'long skeptical and cautious in their attitude to the reports flowing in from informed Jewish quarters'.[35] But by the end of 1942 the reports of persecution had been verified. In April 1943, the Allied Powers held a conference in Bermuda to discuss 'what international action might be possible both then and after the war to solve the whole refugee problem'.[36] When the Executive Committee of the IGCR met on the 4 April 1943, the mandate of the group was expanded to include 'all persons, wherever they may be, who, as a result of events in Europe, have had to leave, or

---

[28] Skran, *Refugees in Inter-War Europe: The Emergence of a Regime*, 1995, Chapter 6.

[29] Vernant, *The Refuge in the Post-War World*, 1953, p. 2; see also Skran, *Refugees in Inter-War Europe: The Emergence of a Regime*, 1995, in particular Chapter 6.

[30] Stoessinger, *The Refugee and the World Community*, 1956, p. 47; see also the work of Proudfoot, M. J. *European Refugees: 1939–1952 A Study in Forced Population Movement* (London: Faber and Faber, 1957) for a comprehensive analysis of refugee movements during 1939–1952.

[31] Proudfoot, *European Refugees: 1939–1952 A Study in Forced Population Movement*, 1957.

[32] Stoessinger, *The Refugee and the World Community*, 1956, p. 48.

[33] Stoessinger, *The Refugee and the World Community*, 1956, p. 48.

[34] The figure of 30 million comes from Vernant, *The Refuge in the Post-War World*, 1953, p. 30; the figure of 60 million comes from Proudfoot, *European Refugees: 1939–1952 A Study in Forced Population Movement*, 1957, p. 21.

[35] Stoessinger, *The Refugee and the World Community*, 1956, p. 48.

[36] Stoessinger, *The Refugee and the World Community*, 1956, p. 48.

may have to leave, their countries of residence because of the danger to their lives or liberties on account of their race, religion or political beliefs'.[37] By July 1946, this mandate included Spanish Republican refugees and displaced persons unwilling to return to their country of origin. The organization that took over the IGCR's mandate on the 9 November 1943 was the United Nations Rehabilitation and Relief Administration (UNRRA).[38] The UNRRA was to provide assistance to three groups of people that were products of events up to and including Second World War: refugees who had escaped persecution or war; displaced persons such as the Reich's forced laborers and the few Jews that survived; and unrepatriable refugees, those who refused to return to their country of origin.[39]

The UNRRA's mandate was limited in that they could only work under Allied military command and assist these three groups if they were within Allied nations or had been liberated by Allied armies; the UNRRA could not branch out on its own to assist people.[40] However, the UNRRA expended a large budget between November 1943 and June 1947, with $3.6 billion spent on repatriation assistance as well as agricultural and industrial post-war production and the rebuilding of social infrastructure such as public health and education.[41] Germany, Austria and Italy had the highest numbers of 'displaced persons' and were the most anxious that repatriation of these people was quickly achieved.[42] However, the efforts to repatriate people proved to be very slow. There were a number of reasons for this, such as transport difficulties in the post-war period and famine in war-devastated countries. Most importantly, though, many people did not want to be repatriated either because of their experience of past persecution in their country of origin or because their country of return no longer existed due to annexation or redrawn state boundaries.[43]

By the beginning of 1946, the UNRRA had repatriated three-quarters of the displaced persons in Europe, but they were still struggling to find solutions for 1,676,000 'unrepatriables'.[44] The 'unrepatriables' were mainly from territories annexed by the Soviet Union—Poles, Baltics and Ukrainians. The majority of these people could not claim an individual fear of persecution, nor had they been displaced due to war—both key conditions for avoiding repatriation.[45] The Soviet

[37] UNGA, *Agenda of the Sub-Committee Annex 1, Proposal concerning Refugees submitted by the Delegation of the United Kingdom*, Meetings of the Joint Sub-Committee of the Second and Third Committees, Official Records of the 1st Session, Part 1, A/C.2/7 and A/C.3/3, 22 January 1946, p. 41.

[38] For a more thorough appraisal of the UNRRA see Woodbridge, G. *The History of UNRRA* (New York: Columbia University Press, 1950).

[39] Stoessinger, *The Refugee and the World Community*, 1956, pp. 49–51.

[40] Loescher, *The UNHCR and World Politics: A Perilous Path*, 2001, p. 35.

[41] Loescher, *The UNHCR and World Politics: A Perilous Path*, 2001, p. 35.

[42] Loescher, *The UNHCR and World Politics: A Perilous Path*, 2001, p. 35.

[43] Vernant, *The Refuge in the Post-War World*, 1953, pp. 30–31.

[44] Vernant, *The Refuge in the Post-War World*, 1953, p. 31.

[45] Vernant, *The Refuge in the Post-War World*, 1953, pp. 30–31; Loescher, *The UNHCR and World Politics: A Perilous Path*, 2001, p. 36. The Netherlands delegate actually stressed the need for the term 'refugee' not to be 'misused' and applied to 'non-repatriables'. The Netherlands suggested

Union was initially able to convince the Allied powers to return a large majority of Eastern Europeans to the Soviet Union (many of whom were then be sent to forced labour camps),[46] but large numbers of the Jewish population were spared repatriation.[47]

In December 1945, the UNRRA decided that for 'humanitarian reasons', the principle of 'internal displacement' could be adopted. Therefore, a person 'displaced' in their own country or sent to a camp as a result of war, under the UNRRA mandate, could be provided with assistance. The first group that was classified as *a priori* eligible for assistance was the Jewish population. This response was largely driven by the widespread sense of 'guilt' because between 1932 and 1942, the Western world denied the rising level of persecution facing Jews in Germany and Eastern Europe. Both Stoessinger and Loescher have noted a correlation between the creation of 'extermination camps' by the Nazis and the West's continual refusal to expand their immigration numbers to the Jews.[48] There were political consequences for the decision to prioritize Jewish refugees. In order to restrict numbers, other mainly Eastern European displaced populations were forced to 'produce "concrete evidence" of persecution' in order to receive assistance from the UNRRA.[49] Given the emerging ideological clash between communism and capitalism, this decision prompted the United States to begin limiting its support for the UNRRA; the US wanted those fleeing communist East Europe to be readily accepted as refugees.[50] At the same time, the Soviet Union argued that the Western powers were encouraging Soviet nationals to resist repatriation so as to undermine the Soviet Bloc.[51]

The US, a major financial contributor to the UNRRA,[52] increasingly criticized the UNRRA for repatriating sometimes unwilling persons to Eastern Europe.[53] The US argued that the UNRRA and the IGCR had done 'good work within its terms of reference and with the resources at its disposal, but it is quite evident, as the United Kingdom delegation has pointed out, that this Committee has not sufficient resources nor a sufficiently large and authoritative organization to handle the entire problem'.[54] The key problem being, what to do when people did

that 'non-repatriables' instead be called 'uprooted people'. UNGA, *Agenda of the Sub-Committee Annex 3a, Problem of Refugees: Speech delivered by the Representative of the Netherlands at the Fourth Meeting of the Third Committee*, Meetings of the Joint Sub-Committee of the Second and Third Committees, Official Records of the 1st Session, Part 1, A/C.3/10, 22 January 1946, p. 52.

46 Loescher, *The UNHCR and World Politics: A Perilous Path*, 2001, p. 36.

47 Vernant, *The Refuge in the Post-War World*, 1953, p. 31.

48 Stoessinger, *The Refugee and the World Community*, 1956, p. 42; Loescher, *The UNHCR and World Politics: A Perilous Path*, 2001, p. 33.

49 Vernant, *The Refuge in the Post-War World*, 1953, p. 31.

50 Holborn, L. *The International Refugee Organization: A Specialized Agency of the United Nations Its History and Work 1946–1952* (London: Oxford University Press, 1956). See Holborn also for a detailed account of how the IRO came to replace the UNRRA.

51 Loescher, *The UNHCR and World Politics: A Perilous Path*, 2001, pp. 37–38.

52 Loescher, *The UNHCR and World Politics: A Perilous Path*, 2001, p. 38.

53 Holborn, *The International Refugee Organization: A Specialized Agency of the United Nations Its History and Work 1946–1952*, 1956, Chapter One.

54 UNGA, *Agenda of the Sub-Committee Annex 5a, Problem of Refugees: Speech delivered by the Representative of the United states of America at the Fourth Meeting at the Third Committee*, Meetings

not want to return to their country of origin—especially when that country was a communist dictatorship. In 1947, the US announced that it intended to stop funding the UNRRA. This led to the end of that organization.[55]

In January 1946, France's view was quite different to the United States. France argued that it was in a better position than the US to know what should be done because the US 'had not been called upon to deal with it [refugee influxes] on their own territory'.[56] France argued that 'statutory refugees' needed to be distinguished from 'displaced persons'.[57] 'Statutory refugees' were those forced to flee due to belonging to a particular group facing persecution in their state of origin; they could not be returned to their country of origin and therefore host countries received greater assistance and there was a higher chance of resettlement for such people. 'Displaced persons' on the other hand were the product of war and thus, in spite of what the US was arguing, their need for refuge was temporary. This distinction would lead to a more appropriate division of international aid and 'avoid a reversion to the chaotic pre-war position where, through force of circumstances, the nearest frontiers were forcibly overrun by streams of unfortunate people'.[58] For instance, France wanted the 400,000 Spanish refugees they were sheltering to be declared as 'statutory refugees' because their cause for refuge belonged to the pre-war definition of a refugee under the Nansen Office.[59] Ultimately, France argued, decisions about refugee status had to fall within the purview of governments directly affected by the refugee populations. Even if the decision was placed in the hands of an Executive Committee of the UNRRA, that body still needed direction from those states most affected.[60] In essence, France was arguing that the US had no role

of the Joint Sub-Committee of the Second and Third Committees, Official Records of the 1st Session, Part 1, A/C.3/13, 22 January 1946, p. 57.

55 UNGA, *Agenda of the Sub-Committee Annex 5, Proposal concerning Refugees submitted by the Delegation of the United States of America*, Meetings of the Joint Sub-Committee of the Second and Third Committees, Official Records of the 1st Session, Part 1, A/C.3/20, 22 January 1946, p. 56.

56 UNGA, *Agenda of the Sub-Committee Annex 6, 'Statutory Refugees' and 'Displaced Persons': Memorandum Submitted by the Delegation of France*, Meetings of the Joint Sub-Committee of the Second and Third Committees, Official Records of the 1st Session, Part 1, A/C.3/16, 22 January 1946, pp. 57–58.

57 UNGA, *Agenda of the Sub-Committee Annex 6, 'Statutory Refugees' and 'Displaced Persons': Memorandum Submitted by the Delegation of France*, Meetings of the Joint Sub-Committee of the Second and Third Committees, Official Records of the 1st Session, Part 1, A/C.3/16, 22 January 1946, p. 58.

58 UNGA, *Agenda of the Sub-Committee Annex 6, 'Statutory Refugees' and 'Displaced Persons': Memorandum Submitted by the Delegation of France*, Meetings of the Joint Sub-Committee of the Second and Third Committees, Official Records of the 1st Session, Part 1, A/C.3/16, 22 January 1946, p. 58.

59 UNGA, *Agenda of the Sub-Committee Annex 6, 'Statutory Refugees' and 'Displaced Persons': Memorandum Submitted by the Delegation of France*, Meetings of the Joint Sub-Committee of the Second and Third Committees, Official Records of the 1st Session, Part 1, A/C.3/16, 22 January 1946, p. 58.

60 UNGA, *Agenda of the Sub-Committee Annex 6, 'Statutory Refugees' and 'Displaced Persons': Memorandum Submitted by the Delegation of France*, Meetings of the Joint Sub-Committee of the Second and Third Committees, Official Records of the 1st Session, Part 1, A/C.3/16, 22 January 1946, p. 60.

in directing actions towards refugees in other states. What France was calling for in practical terms was that 'groups' of refugees such as Jews, were an identifiable group that could be given refugee status and resettled. Displaced persons, such as those fleeing Eastern Europe post-World War II, needed to prove a genuine individual fear of persecution, as they were not an identifiable group targeted for persecution. Displaced persons were encouraged to return to their country of origin, and their return was to be of a 'lasting nature' in order to prevent continual streams of these 'unfortunate people'.[61]

One thing that France and the United States did agree on in late January 1946 was that refugee assistance should be offered at an international level, and a new organization needed to be created to deal with both categories of people. The International Refugee Organization (IRO) was established in 1946. The US primarily supported and funded the IRO, insisting that both refugees and displaced persons be treated the same.

The IRO was introduced on 12 February 1946, when the General Assembly adopted resolution 8(I) stating that 'the problem of refugees and displaced persons of all categories is one of immediate urgency'[62] and recommended that a special committee be formed to examine the problem that was 'international in scope and nature'.[63] Twenty states[64] formed this committee and met in London between April and June 1946. The outcome of this was a draft constitution for a non-permanent specialized agency which, in cooperation with the United Nations and through the Economic and Social Council, was to conduct 'repatriation, assistance, protection, and re-settlement of re-establishment of the refugees and displaced persons coming within its mandate'.[65] The IRO's proposed mandate was adopted by the General Assembly on 15 December 1946.

An important development within the IRO was that all Western states agreed that individuals could be recognized as refugees; this was in contrast to the earlier refugee conventions that identified refugees only on a group basis.[66] Member states of the IRO also agreed that Eastern Europeans should not be forcibly repatriated. However, Eastern European governments strongly disagreed with this approach, and insisted that forced repatriation of their 'dissident nationals' was legitimate.

---

61 UNGA, *Agenda of the Sub-Committee Annex 6, 'Statutory Refugees' and 'Displaced Persons': Memorandum Submitted by the Delegation of France*, Meetings of the Joint Sub-Committee of the Second and Third Committees, Official Records of the 1st Session, Part 1, A/C.3/16, 22 January 1946, p. 61.

62 UN Department of Social Affairs, *A Study of Statelessness* (New York: UN, August 1949), p. 39.

63 UN Department of Social Affairs, *A Study of Statelessness* (New York: UN, August 1949), p. 39.

64 Australia, Belgium, Brazil, Byelorussian Soviet Socialist Republic, Canada, China (prior to 1971 the Chinese delegation was represented by Taiwan), Colombia, Czechoslovakia, Dominican Republic, France, Lebanon, Netherlands, New Zealand, Peru, Poland, Ukrainian Soviet Socialist Republic, Union of Soviet Socialist Republics, United Kingdom, United States of America, Yugoslavia.

65 Vernant, *The Refugee in the Post-War World*, 1953, p. 33.

66 Prior to this, as mentioned above, refugees were recognised as fleeing persecution based on membership to a particular nationality, as opposed to individual persecution. Stoessinger, *The Refugee and the World Community*, 1956, pp. 62–63; Loescher, *The UNHCR and World Politics: A Perilous Path*, 2001, p. 38.

Why, the Eastern European bloc asked, would Western countries wish to support 'traitors, quislings, and war criminals'[67] who were refusing to return to their 'liberated' countries of origin? In response, the Belgian delegate argued that 'a refugee, for very legitimate political reasons, might not wish to return home'[68] and that treason did not always enter such a decision.

Western governments and the United States in particular, clearly wanted to support Eastern European refugees because they were of 'symbolic and instrumental use in the Cold War'.[69] How better to undermine the legitimacy of a growing enemy than to demonstrate that its alternative ideology was so bad that its own people did not want to return? This overtly political motivation of the IRO affected its ability to conduct its operations. When the IRO began operations in 1947 there were 712,000 refugees under its mandate but by the end of 1951, when the IRO was coming to a close (to be replaced by the UNHCR), the number had grown to 1,449,000 refugees.[70] During the whole course of the IRO operations, 1,619,000 refugees were registered by the IRO; 73,000 were repatriated, 97,000 died or disappeared and 643,000 were resettled in the United States, Australia and Israel alone.[71]

In keeping with the United Nations General Assembly discussions in early 1946, it was decided that two types of 'uprooted people' would be eligible for official IRO aid. The first were 'displaced persons' forcibly uprooted by the German and Japanese occupations during the war.[72] This meant that forced laborers or those deported because of racial, religious or political reasons were all eligible refugees. The second category eligible for aid were 'traditional refugees'—individuals who voluntarily fled the Nazi and Fascist regimes, 'as well as others who were unable or unwilling to avail themselves of the protection of their home governments'.[73] This category comprised the largest number of refugees and included White Russians and Armenians, who had initially fled their home due to events during and after World War One, Spanish republicans and those who had already fled or were fleeing communist regimes in Eastern Europe. Overall, the IRO mandate 'was unprecedented in its inclusiveness though exhibiting a markedly European emphasis'.[74] Applicants' pleas for refugee status were considered liberally more often than not. The IRO was entrusted with the political and legal protection of recognized refugees. To do

[67] Stoessinger, *The Refugee and the World Community*, 1956, p. 66.
[68] Stoessinger, *The Refugee and the World Community*, 1956, p. 67.
[69] Loescher, *The UNHCR and World Politics: A Perilous Path*, 2001, p. 39. However, it needs to be acknowledged that there were, indeed, a huge war criminal population amongst the East Europeans seeking refugee status. The Refugee Convention sought to deal with this population by introducing exclusion clause 1F(a) (see Appendix 1). Thank you to an anonymous reviewer for this point.
[70] Vernant, *The Refugee in the Post-War World*, 1953, pp. 36–37.
[71] Vernant, *The Refugee in the Post-War World*, 1953, p. 37.
[72] Stoessinger, *The Refugee and the World Community*, 1956, p. 86.
[73] Stoessinger, *The Refugee and the World Community*, 1956, p. 86.
[74] Stoessinger, *The Refugee and the World Community*, 1956, p. 88.

this, it was given the right to conduct negotiations and conclude agreements with governments to improve the status of these refugees.[75]

As Stoessinger notes, however, the IRO's refugee eligibility criteria focused on the 'motive of flight', thus excluding those who migrated for more general, non-political reasons. To receive assistance, the motive for flight had to be 'primarily political, that is, persecution or fear of persecution by the person's home government'.[76] This continued the focus of the League of Nations High Commission for Refugees, where political reasons had dominated the eligibility criteria for being a refugee. The Russians and Armenians first recognized as refugees were identified as fleeing brutal communist regimes. Those who fled due to economic reasons, such as to improve their standard of living, had never been granted refugee status on these grounds regardless of the severity of their economic plight; and as the Jewish experience showed in the 1930s, asylum seekers could also be rejected on political grounds. However, determining the distinction between the economic and political motives that caused an individual to flee was complicated.[77] As the Indochinese refugee case study will demonstrate (see Chapter 3–6), there is no easy way of making this distinction. Indeed, the judgment is often based more on the political characterization of the state that a person is fleeing, than the person's individual reason for fleeing.[78] Thus, in the 1940s individuals may have fled communist Russia for economic reasons, yet were granted refugee status because they were fleeing a regime widely considered as politically illegitimate.

In 1949 member states decided to terminate the IRO, largely because the financial pressure on the major contributor, the United States, grew too great.[79] Upon reflection, the IRO made three very important contributions that had a significant effect on the development of the UNHCR and the 1951 Convention. The first was that a person's refugee status needed to be *individually* assessed. In 1946, East European states successfully argued that their displaced populations were not to be considered as refugees *prima facie*. Moreover, it was recognized that permitting entire groups to claim refugee status risked unleashing huge waves of refugees, something

---

[75] UN Department of Social Affairs, *A Study of Statelessness* (New York: UN, August 1949), p. 49.

[76] Stoessinger, *The Refugee and the World Community*, 1956, p. 86.

[77] Stoessinger, *The Refugee and the World Community*, 1956, p. 86; Velikonja, J., 'Postwar Population Movements in Europe', *Annals of the Association of American Geographers*, Vol. 48, No. 4 (Dec., 1958), pp. 458–472.

[78] See Antonio Fortin for a further discussion of this in, A. Fortin, 'The Meaning of "Protection" in the Refugee Definition', *International Journal of Refugee Law*, 12 (4), 2001, pp. 548–576.

[79] See Stoessinger, J. G. *The Refugee and the World Community* (Minneapolis: The University of Minnesota Press, 1956), Chapter 7 to Chapter 9 for a detailed study of the IRO and its end; Loescher, *The UNHCR and World Politics: A Perilous Path*, 2001, Chapter 2, which provides a brief, but detailed analysis of the international refugee protection agencies up to the UNHCR. For more thorough accounts of each refugee protection agency up until the UNHCR see for the League of Nations: Holborn, *The League of Nations and the Problem of Refugees: A Study of the Development of International Government and Administration in Post-War Europe*, 1937; for the UNRRA: Woodbridge, *The History of UNRRA*, 1950; and for the IRO: Holborn, *The International Refugee Organization: A Specialized Agency of the United Nations Its History and Work 1946–1952*, 1956. Skran, *Refugees in Inter-War Europe: The Emergence of a Regime*, 1995, provides an excellent inter-World War period account of these organizations.

that deeply troubled Western states. Second, the UNHCR inherited from the IRO the idea that genuine refugees had a *political* motivation for leaving their country of origin. Third, the geographical context in which the political struggle between communism and capitalism was occurring meant that the process of identifying a refugee became rooted in the European context and experience.

1.2 *The creation of the UNHCR*

During 1949, a large number of resolutions and amended resolutions concerning refugees were placed on the General Assembly agenda for discussion by member states including Asian states (India, Pakistan and China mainly). The position that ultimately prevailed was one held by the Western Europeans and the US. For the Western Europeans, the most important objective of the new refugee protection agency was that it provide material assistance to those still in camps and resettlement continued to be the preferred solution. Therefore, the new agency would require the legal authority to bestow refugee status, and a budget to enable this. On the other hand, the US wanted an end to the exorbitant financial contributions that it had been making since the UNRRA's creation, and one way of achieving this was to have a temporary refugee agency with narrower authority and limited functions. In particular, the US wanted any new agency to have no independent funding authority. This section of the chapter will trace the arguments made by states in the General Assembly on the matter of refugees and stateless persons. It will demonstrate how European states and the US dominated the discussions regarding the creation of the UNHCR and the 1951 Convention. It was in these discussions, I argue, that the 1951 Convention and UNHCR operations came to be seen as Eurocentric by developing states. This in turn marginalized those who did not share or ally with the Eurocentric approach to the refugee problem.

At the time that the UNHCR Statute and 1951 Convention was being drafted, the world's refugee crisis was dire and worsening. The partition of Pakistan from India in 1947 prompted many Muslims to leave India for Pakistan, and Hindus to make the trip in the opposite direction. The estimated number displaced in these two countries was over fourteen million, and their difficulties were described as a 'terrible plight'.[80] In 1948, the Arab population in Palestine was in a struggle against the creation of a Zionist state. After a lengthy struggle, the state of Israel was formed. The Arab Israeli conflict lead to the mass exodus of Palestinian refugees into neighbouring states, while Jewish refugees from Arab countries fled to Israel: both groups were fleeing in fear of reprisals.[81] The outbreak of the Korean War in

[80] Vernant, *The Refugee in the Post-War World*, 1953, p. 738.

[81] Stoessinger, *The Refugee and the World*, 1956; Barakat, H. I., 'The Palestinian Refugees: An Uprooted Community Seeking Repatriation', *International Migration Review*, Vol. 7, No. 2 (Summer 1973), pp. 147–161; Gallagher, *The Era of Refugees: The Evolution of the International Refugee System*, 1989; Morris, B. *The Birth of the Palestinian Refugee Problem Revisited* (Cambridge: Cambridge University Press, 2003).

late 1950 also caused the movement of seven million North Korean refugees seeking asylum in South Korea.[82] Under the IRO however, these populations were not technically considered to be refugees. Nor would these populations be embraced under the new refugee definition in spite of the fact that these refugee crises were occurring at the same time of the drafting process for the UNHCR mandate and 1951 Convention.

In 1949, the Third Special Session of the IRO's General Council prepared a recommendation to the Economic and Social Council of the United Nations.[83] Their two main proposals were that an international body to protect refugees and stateless persons be set up after the termination of the IRO's services on 30 June 1950; and that a convention on the international status of refugees and stateless persons be prepared.[84] In addition, the Council requested that the agency be equipped with funds to enable it to take responsibility for the care and maintenance of difficult refugee cases.[85]

During a Council session, France strongly argued that assistance (funding) should be given equal weight to protection (through the provision of refugee status), and that both needed to be a priority when discussing the work of a future international refugee protection organization.[86] In response, the United States argued that 'there had been insufficient discussion on the wisdom or the necessity of setting up an international fund'.[87] However, the remaining European countries, including the United Kingdom, insisted that a UN office with no means of securing its own funding would render useless any of its other work in protection.[88] At the same time, Norway argued against the Secretary-General's recommendation that a general convention simply *renew* the existing ones, and suggested that a new convention be drafted to *replace* earlier ones 'many of which had been ratified only by a small number of states'.[89] Here, we observe two powerful arguments being placed on the future UNHCR's agenda. First, that protection and assistance should be equally fundamental to the UNHCR's mandate. Second, that the UNHCR should preside over a new refugee protection regime, with a new convention and with the

[82] Vernant, *The Refugee in the Post-War World*, 1953; Stoessinger, *The Refugee and the World Community*, 1956; Gallagher, *The Era of Refugees: The Evolution of the International Refugee System*, 1989; Stueck, W. *The Korean War: An International History* (Princeton: Princeton University Press, 1995).

[83] IRO, *Future International Action concerning Refugees Document GC/81*, General Council, Third Special Session, GC/SR/42, 4 July 1949.

[84] UNGA, *Report of the Economic and Social Council 1948–1949*, Fourth Session, Volume 5, p. 56.

[85] IRO, *Summary Record of the Forty-First Meeting*, General Council, Third Special Session, GC/SR/41, 4 July 1949, p. 6.

[86] IRO, *Summary Record of the Forty-First Meeting*, General Council, Third Special Session, GC/SR/41, 4 July 1949, p. 8.

[87] IRO, *Summary Record of the Forty-Second Meeting*, General Council, Third Special Session, GC/SR/42, 4 July 1949, p. 9.

[88] IRO, *Summary Record of the Forty-First Meeting*, General Council, Third Special Session, GC/SR/41, 4 July 1949; IRO *Summary Record of the Forty-Second Meeting*, General Council, Third Special Session, GC/SR/42, 4 July 1949.

[89] IRO *Summary Record of the Forty-Second Meeting*, General Council, Third Special Session, GC/SR/42, 4 July 1949, p. 9.

expectation that the UNHCR could and would 'encourage new ratifications of such conventions, making recommendations and so on'.[90]

Also noticeable in the IRO discussions regarding the new refugee agency was the emphasis on European refugees. As shown above, the refugee population around the world was growing. Yet the delegates in the IRO thought 'it was in the interests of the Western European countries that the pressure of a large mass of displaced persons on their frontiers be reduced as much as possible'.[91] The Italian delegate requested that 'preferential treatment should be accorded, out of the surplus funds above mentioned, to the refugees still remaining at 30 June 1950 in those European countries which had been most heavily burdened with large numbers of refugees'.[92] The Italian delegate then went on to say that if this was not agreed to by the IRO, the Italian government would 'remove completely from Italian territory during the year 1949–1950 all the refugees under the mandate of the IRO'.[93] As we will discuss later, this manipulative strategy was also employed by several Southeast Asian states during the Indochinese refugee crisis.

For their part, Belgium and France were concerned that the draft resolution on the UNHCR would commit European states to accept responsibility for all refugees on their soil and the 'European governments were in danger of falling victims of an optimism regarding the future which they themselves did not share'.[94] A Committee was thus created, composed of Australia, Belgium, Denmark, Netherlands, France, Italy, Luxembourg, Switzerland, the United Kingdom and United States to discuss the effects each proposal within the draft resolution would have upon Western European countries. Consequently, on the 7th July 1949, the Resolution on the Completion of the Programme of the Organization (GC/89/Rev.1) was adopted, with date line restrictions for the care and maintenance of refugees. The aim was to lessen the load on European states during the IRO to UNHCR transfer.[95] The IRO mandate was extended to 31 December 1951, to coincide with the beginning of the UNHCR's mandate at the beginning of 1952. In addition, the Draft Resolution on Future International Action Concerning Refugees was passed and contributed significantly to Belgium and France's Draft Resolution for a Study on the Position of Stateless Persons.[96] Belgium and France presented this resolution

---

90 Statement by France. IRO, *Summary Record of the Forty-First Meeting*, General Council, Third Special Session, GC/SR/41, 4 July 1949, p. 8.

91 Statement by Netherlands. IRO, *Summary Record of the Forty-First Meeting*, General Council, Third Special Session, GC/SR/41, 4 July 1949, p. 4.

92 IRO, *Summary Record of the Forty-Third Meeting*, General Council, Third Special Session, GC/SR/43, 6 July 1949, p. 4.

93 IRO, *Summary Record of the Forty-Third Meeting*, General Council, Third Special Session, GC/SR/43, 6 July 1949, p. 4.

94 IRO, *Summary Record of the Forty-Third Meeting*, General Council, Third Special Session, GC/SR/43, 6 July 1949, p. 6.

95 IRO, *Summary Record of the Forty-Eighth Meeting*, General Council, Third Special Session, GC/SR/48, 4 July 1949, p. 3.

96 IRO, *Summary Record of the Forty-Eighth Meeting*, General Council, Third Special Session, GC/SR/48, 4 July 1949, pp. 4, 8; IRO, *Summary Record of the Fiftieth Meeting*, General Council, Third Special Session, GC/SR/50, 7 July 1949.

in the Economic and Social Council in 1949 and included a proposal for the establishment of a High Commissioner's Office. They argued that such an office was needed to 'keep in touch with the question of refugees throughout the world', to promote international conventions defining the status of refugees, administer assistance funds and report to the Economic and Social Council on the 'effectiveness of existing international measures for the legal protection of refugees'.[97]

In 1949 at the fourth session of the United Nations General Assembly, Resolution 428 (V) was passed, creating the Office of the United Nations High Commissioner for Refugees. In the build up to the creation of the UNHCR the decision about who would be recognized and assisted as a refugee was a fundamental part of the process. It was widely considered to be essential for the new organization to have a clear idea of who it was meant to assist and under what circumstances. From the beginning, France presented itself as the experienced participant in these meetings due to its history in approaching 'the problem of refugees' and thus was well versed in presenting solutions about 'how the problem should be solved on the international plane'.[98] In particular, France argued that it was necessary 'to decide on some form of international action calculated to solve the far wider problem of the existence and protection of refugees in general'.[99] The IRO, continued France, had been too narrow and this was why the refugee problem remained.[100]

Sweden and Belgium agreed with France that the new refugee agency needed to protect and assist refugees, arguing that the High Commissioner's powers 'should not be confined to legal protection as the question of refugees also raised problems of a material and social nature'.[101] The United Kingdom agreed with all of this, but pointed out that the High Commission should always 'act as an adviser to various Governments. His task would be to supervise the application of international conventions on refugees by their signatory States'.[102] However, the UK argued that this was where the High Commissioner's authority should stop, for the High Commissioner should not 'assume functions in certain countries which should properly be carried out by the Governments themselves'.[103]

In reply to this view of the UNHCR, there were statements of concern expressed about how quickly the UNHCR's mandate was being decided, and how much of its operations were designated in Europe. In particular, many non-European states

97 United Nations Social and Economic Council, *Study on the Position of Stateless Persons*, Belgium and France: Draft Resolution, 4 August 1949, E/1447/Rev.1, pp. 1–2.

98 UNGA, *Official Records of the Third Committee*, Fourth Session, 250th Meeting, 4 November 1949, p. 105.

99 UNGA, *Official Records of the Third Committee*, Fourth Session, 250th Meeting, 4 November 1949, p. 105.

100 UNGA, *Official Records of the Third Committee*, Fourth Session, 250th Meeting, 4 November 1949, p. 105.

101 UNGA, *Official Records of the Third Committee*, Fourth Session, 250th Meeting, 4 November 1949, p. 106.

102 UNGA, *Official Records of the Third Committee*, Fourth Session, 250th Meeting, 4 November 1949, p. 111.

103 UNGA, *Official Records of the Third Committee*, Fourth Session, 250th Meeting, 4 November 1949, p. 111.

feared that the new organization would impose a heavy financial burden on them without doing much to alleviate refugee crises outside Europe. In the remainder of this chapter I will demonstrate how these concerns directly counter the allegation that 'non-Western European countries' opposition to the 1951 Convention was 'meek and hardly noticeable' during discussions of the draft.[104] Non-Western states did articulate a desire for the 1951 Convention and the UNHCR to broadly encompass refugee experiences outside of Europe.

Brazil, for example, expressed concern about the potential costs the United Nations could face if the new organization was to 'provide legal protection for refugees, to resettle them and, in the meantime, provide for their livelihood'.[105] Brazil was concerned with the potential financial implications faced by the UNHCR and member states if deciding on such a proposal was based on a 'decision of principle the consequence of which might be to increase four times the budget of the United Nations'.[106] Mexico also was concerned with the potential cost of such an organization, stating that 'many countries, including his own, found that their economic position made it impossible for them to participate in the activities of the IRO...The Mexican Government for its part, would refuse to undertake an obligation if it was not sure that it could fulfill it'.[107]

Like Mexico and Brazil, Lebanon argued the case for a small protection office that had the opportunity to raise funds, but would not be funded by statutory grants 'because the protection of refugees might well involve bitter political controversies in which the United Nations Secretariat should not become implicated'.[108] Pakistan also pointedly questioned why it should finance 'the legal protection of an undefined number of refugees in Europe, while obtaining no benefits for the millions of refugees in its own country'?[109] Already here a vocal dissent was building against the idea that the international community as a whole should have to support European states in financially dealing with their refugee problem.

For its part, the United States strenuously argued that states should not to have to bear the burden of a large UNHCR fund, stating that the new international refugee agency was not a relief agency. The UNHCR, it insisted, only needed to 'establish a protection service which would require only a comparatively small staff'[110] and a small budget. The United States position was based on its experience

---

[104] Bem, K., 'The Coming of a "Blank Cheque"—Europe, the 1951 Convention, and the 1967 Protocol', *International Journal of Refugee Law*, Vo. 16, No. 4, 2004, p. 618.

[105] UNGA, *Official Records of the Third Committee*, Fourth Session, 250th Meeting, 4 November 1949, p. 107.

[106] UNGA, *Official Records of the Third Committee*, Fourth Session, 250th Meeting, 4 November 1949, p. 107.

[107] UNGA, *Official Records of the Third Committee*, Fourth Session, 250th Meeting, 4 November 1949, p. 112.

[108] UNGA, *Official Records of the Third Committee*, Fourth Session, 260th Meeting, 11 November 1949, p. 128.

[109] UNGA, *Official Records of the Third Committee*, Fourth Session, 260th Meeting, 11 November 1949, p. 128.

[110] UNGA, *Official Records of the Third Committee*, Fourth Session, 257th Meeting, 8 November 1949, p. 114.

of providing the majority of the IRO budget, which continually rose as more refugees required assistance.[111] However, France, supported by other Western European countries, argued that 'large-scale operational funds' for the refugees in their countries was necessary.[112] The outcome of this funding debate was that the United States and United Kingdom (which was also concerned about bearing a large financial commitment to the new refugee organization) were successful in persuading the other states to make General Assembly approval a precondition for all voluntary contributions.[113] Therefore, the UNHCR was to have a small annual budget for administration costs and a small emergency fund, but the bulk of its funding would come from voluntary donations.

It is important to note that developing states' concern with the UNHCR's financial expenditure were coming from a different direction to the concerns expressed by the US and UK. Their growing dissent was directed at the fact that they felt they were being expected to stretch their limited financial means to assist only European refugees. Even Greece for instance, wanted to know what happened when legal protection did not arise in the case of those who had left because of the Greek civil war. Greece argued that the displacement of its civilians did not necessitate international protection, but that their humanitarian situation was just as distressing as those cases where protection was seen as warranted.[114] The Pakistani delegate expressed confusion in general with the whole discussion, saying that according to the US delegate,

> IRO had already successfully fulfilled three of those tasks; the majority of displaced persons had been repatriated or resettled and only the question of legal protection remained to be solved. If that were so, why could IRO not complete that last task, which was relatively simple? Why should it be entrusted at that time to the United Nations? Such a change in procedure might entail supplementary expenses for the Members of the United Nations which did not belong to IRO and the Committee should decide whether or not that was justified.[115]

Importantly, Pakistan demanded a revision of the term 'refugee' which was being discussed in relation to the potential scope of UNHCR operations, saying that it currently,

> (O)nly applied to victims of events which had occurred during the Second World War in Europe. After the end of hostilities, however, other events had taken place in other parts of the world. If the United Nations was to be entrusted with that problem, it should consider it on a world-wide basis. For example, a year and a half

111 Loescher, *UNHCR and World Politics: A Perilous Path*, 2001, p. 43.
112 Loescher, *UNHCR and World Politics: A Perilous Path*, 2001, p. 44.
113 Loescher, *UNHCR and World Politics: A Perilous Path*, 2001, pp. 43–44.
114 UNGA, *Official Records of the Third Committee*, Fourth Session, 250th Meeting, 4 November 1949, p. 110.
115 UNGA, *Official Records of the Third Committee*, Fourth Session, 258th Meeting, 9 November 1949, p. 115.

> earlier, Pakistan had been compelled to receive from 6 to 7 million refugees coming from various parts of India.[116]

The Indian delegation shared Pakistan's concerns, arguing that as they were looking after six million refugees they 'hoped that the United Nations would acknowledge that India was performing an international as well as a national duty by helping those people, and that it would not be asked to shoulder any further responsibility regarding European refugees'.[117] The Indian delegate said that he agreed with Pakistan's proposal that it should be up to the IRO to finish what it had started in relation to the European refugees, and then develop a convention for the legal protection of all refugees.[118]

Lebanon also endorsed this position, arguing that 'there were new categories of refugees who did not come under the protection of the IRO; for example those in Greece, Pakistan, India and China…any resolution the Committee adopted should establish the High Commissioner as the protector of *all* refugees'.[119] Brazil argued that Pakistan's position for new categories of refugees to be recognized was correct and timely, insisting that the:

> IRO, having been created to take care of a specific category of refugees and displaced persons, had had the right, even the duty, to discriminate between various categories; the United Nations, however, could hardly exercise such a right if it employed funds derived from its regular budget, to which all Members were contributors.[120]

Thus, developing states seemed to agree that the definition of a refugee, which determined who the UNHCR would assist, should be broad in order to encompass a wider range of people.

Western states had three different responses to these arguments. The UK, Belgium and Scandinavian countries agreed in some respects with the developing states; they also originally wanted a broad, general definition to cover present and future refugee flows.[121] The UK led this group arguing that 'any other than a broad definition would seriously impede the High Commissioner's freedom to advise on general refugee protection'.[122] The United States, now backed by France, wanted a narrow definition which clearly demarcated categories of refugees that needed protection. However, right up to the penultimate meeting for the Third Committee

---

116 UNGA, *Official Records of the Third Committee*, Fourth Session, 258th Meeting, 9 November 1949, p. 115.

117 UNGA, *Official Records of the Third Committee*, Fourth Session, 259th Meeting, 10 November 1949, p. 123.

118 UNGA, *Official Records of the Third Committee*, Fourth Session, 259th Meeting, 10 November 1949, p. 123.

119 UNGA, *Official Records of the Third Committee*, Fourth Session, 260th Meeting, 11 November 1949, p. 128. Emphasis added.

120 UNGA, *Official Records of the Third Committee*, Fourth Session, 262nd Meeting, 14 November 1949, p. 137.

121 Loescher, *The UNHCR and World Politics: A Perilous Path*, 2001, p. 45.

122 UNGA, *Official Records of the Third Committee*, Fourth Session, 262nd Meeting, 14 November 1949, p. 139.

of the General Assembly in 1949,[123] the French and United States delegations disagreed with each other also on the wording of the refugee definition. France preferred a definition of a refugee that emphasized an individual determination by the receiving state, as opposed to the United States, which wanted to keep to the pre-war 'categories' of refugees. France argued that if preferred 'categories' of refugees were introduced it would lead to the endless introduction of new ones.[124] France stressed that a general use of the word refugees would in fact allow the Assembly to add to the definition and:

> (A) clause defining the circumstances in which they should be applied. Moreover, a problem concerning refugees would not automatically become a matter for the High Commissioner, nor would he be empowered to submit it to Governments. He could act only within the limits of his functions, which were not very broad.[125]

Here we see the central concerns behind the US and French arguments. Both states were keen to argue that the UNHCR not have a large number of refugees to assist because neither wanted the new organization's funding and protection function to become too large. France did not want an enlarged UNHCR because that would reduce its ability to concentrate its financial and protection work in Europe. The US simply had little interest in financially supporting such an organization. Furthermore, a generous refugee definition could possibly detract from the political statement to be made from declaring Eastern European escapees as refugees, if those fleeing India, Pakistan or Greece also received refugee status. As these two states saw it, an enlarged UNHCR would not satisfy their interests as effectively as an organization with a narrower focus.

The outcome of this discussion was that Belgium, Netherlands, Norway, the UK and Australia all agreed to support the French and United States joint resolution. Therefore, the extent of UNHCR operations would be to identify and assist refugees within Europe, who were fleeing due to political persecution before and just after the Second World War.[126] Canada for one was grateful that the French delegate had removed the phrase 'the powers of the High Commissioner shall extend to *all* refugees' because 'it would be unrealistic to extend the responsibility of the high commissioner to cover every possible category or refugee'.[127] However, in spite of the success of the joint resolution, the US remained unhappy with the European states' insistence on the UNHCR being able to secure large-scale funding. The US argued that this made the UNHCR more a relief agency than a legal protection agency for refugees, and that it should be more limited in size and programmes

123 Also referred to as the Economic and Social Committee.

124 UNGA, *Official Records of the Third Committee*, Fourth Session, 263rd Meeting, 15 November 1949, p. 140.

125 UNGA, *Official Records of the Third Committee*, Fourth Session, 263rd Meeting, 15 November 1949, p. 140.

126 The date ended up being determined as 1 January 1951. UNGA, *Official Records of the Third Committee*, Fourth Session, 263rd Meeting, 15 November 1949.

127 UNGA, *Official Records of the Third Committee*, Fourth Session, 261st Meeting, 12 November 1949, p. 131.

than what the European states wanted.[128] In essence, the US wanted a cheaper continuation of the IRO, but European states did not. As a result, the US did not vote in favor of the resolution which formed the UNHCR.[129]

India and Pakistan expressed concern with the final resolution too, though for very different reasons. India lamented that 'it would be difficult for India to contribute to a budget to be used only for the legal protection of certain refugees when there were millions of refugees in dire need on its own territory'.[130] Furthermore, said India,

> The Indian Government did not want to shirk any of its international responsibilities, and it wished to take part in any humanitarian work undertaken by the United Nations. In spite of its own difficulties, it would have voted for the establishment of a High Commissioner's Office if it had been convinced that the need for it was imperative. It did not think, however—and the discussion had confirmed that opinion—that there was any great need to set up an elaborate international organization whose sole responsibility would be to give refugees legal protection. At a time when its own refugees were dying of starvation, it would be obliged to vote against all the resolutions submitted, and hoped that the stand it had taken would not be misinterpreted.[131]

Pakistan agreed, suggesting that they had 'gathered the unfortunate impression that some delegations entertained serious doubts as to the purely humanitarian aspect of the problem of refugees and also that politics had perhaps made an unwelcome intrusion into the question'.[132] Pakistan further argued that 'they, India, Mexico and Brazil had all expressed grave misgivings about its [draft resolution] ultimate implications' and 'no definite answer had been received and the situation was extremely confused'.[133] The Pakistani delegate maintained that he did not understand why there would be a 'continuous flow of refugees' in Europe, now that the war was over.[134] Pakistan opined that 'the only other refugees in the world were the Asian refugees. Yet it was not proposed to bring them under the competence of the High Commissioner'.[135] Pakistan announced that it would also vote against the joint draft resolution because,

---

128 Loescher, *The UNHCR and World Politics: A Perilous Path*, 2001, pp. 43–44.

129 Loescher, G. *Beyond Charity: International Cooperation and the Global Refugee Crisis* (New York: Oxford University Press, 1993), pp. 53–54, 55–58; Loescher, *The UNHCR and World Politics: A Perilous Path*, 2001, p. 43.

130 UNGA, *Official Records of the Third Committee*, Fourth Session, 263rd Meeting, 15 November 1949, p. 144.

131 UNGA, *Official Records of the Third Committee*, Fourth Session, 263rd Meeting, 15 November 1949, p. 144.

132 UNGA, *Official Records of the Third Committee*, Fourth Session, 264th Meeting, 15 November 1949, p. 145.

133 UNGA, *Official Records of the Third Committee*, Fourth Session, 264th Meeting, 15 November 1949, p. 145.

134 UNGA, *Official Records of the Third Committee*, Fourth Session, 264th Meeting, 15 November 1949, p. 146.

135 UNGA, *Official Records of the Third Committee*, Fourth Session, 264th Meeting, 15 November 1949, p. 146.

> (W)hen he asked that IRO should continue looking after its own refugees and not burden the whole of the United Nations with that task, he was doing no more than the member States of IRO themselves when they told Pakistan to look after its own refugees without any help from the Untied Nations in the guise of a High Commissioner.[136]

Finally, it is worth noting that despite Brazil and Mexico's earlier arguments against a UNHCR with independent financial means, their responses were mixed on the question of whether to retain a narrow refugee definition. Loescher accounts for this by suggesting that the 'Americans exerted considerable pressure on the Latin Americans'.[137] Thus, the majority of Latin American states present at the time voted in favor of the resolution. The US, by then determined not to support the resolution passing the creation of the UNHCR, was joined by Brazil, Argentina, India, Pakistan and Iraq in voting *against* the resolution. The Philippines, Thailand, Afghanistan, Burma and Iran abstained. Consequently, the Joint Resolution was adopted by 24 votes to 12, with 10 abstentions.[138] The Office of the United Nations High Commissioner for Refugees was established, albeit without a resounding endorsement from the international community, and now needed a Statute and Convention to detail the High Commissioner's role in protecting refugees.

1.3 *Drafting the 1951 Convention and the UNHCR Statute*

The passing of the Joint Resolution in 1949 led to the creation of the Office of the UNHCR. The United Nations General Assembly then had to decide the precise nature the Office's Statute and 1951 Convention. The purpose of the Statute was to provide the High Commissioner with a legal mandate for responding to refugee problems and to define the extent of her/his response to states involved in and affected by refugee problems. The objective of the 1951 Convention was to ensure that people would be protected when fleeing 'oppressive, totalitarian, and especially Communist regimes'.[139] This resulted, of course, in a Eurocentric interpretation of the refugee experience which led to a very narrow interpretation

136 UNGA, *Official Records of the Third Committee*, Fourth Session, 264th Meeting, 15 November 1949, p. 146; Loescher supports Pakistan's statement here in noting that not only did the IRO refuse to help, but 'unlike the refugee situation in Europe which attracted huge sums of money, the governments of India and Pakistan received almost no international assistance and had to rely on their own meagre resources and that of a few NGOs', Loescher, *The UNHCR and World Politics: A Perilous Path*, 2001, n. 59, pp. 48–49.

137 Loescher, *The UNHCR and World Politics: A Perilous Path*, 2001, p. 45.

138 Those who voted in favour were: Lebanon, Liberia, Mexico, Netherlands, New Zealand, Norway, Sweden, United Kingdom of Great Britain and Northern Ireland, Uruguay, Venezuela, Australia, Belgium, Canada, Chile, China, Colombia, Cuba, Denmark, Dominican Republic, Ecuador, France, Greece, Guatemala, Israel. Against: Pakistan, Poland, Ukrainian Soviet Socialist Republics, United States of America, Yugoslavia, Argentina, Brazil, Byelorussian Soviet Socialist Republic, Czechoslovakia, India, Iraq. Abstaining: Philippines, Saudi Arabia, Syria, Thailand, Yemen, Afghanistan, Burma, Egypt, Ethiopia, Iran. UNGA, *Official Records of the Third Committee*, Fourth Session, 265th Meeting, 18 November 1949, p. 150.

139 Loescher, *The UNHCR and World Politics: A Perilous Path*, 2001, p. 44.

of the 'refugee'.[140] The drafting process for both the Statute of the UNHCR and the 1951 Convention took place in 1950. In the Third Committee of the General Assembly, the UNHCR Statute was concluded in 1950. However, the final draft of the 1951 Convention was not passed until it was presented at the Conference of Plenipotentiaries in July 1951.

The Convention and the UNHCR Statute came to differ widely on the definition of a refugee. Originally, the Statute was to have the same definition of a refugee as the Convention. However, in 1950 when the UK started to demand a broader refugee definition, the outcome was a compromise between France, the United States and the UK. The Convention's definition was to remain constrained to those recognized as refugees due to events in Europe prior to 1 January 1951. However, the UNHCR Statute would extend the High Commissioner's mandate, with General Assembly approval, to recognize *any other people* outside Europe and after 1951 who feared for their life due to the persecution conditions laid out in Article 1 of the 1951 Convention.

At the time of the drafting debate over the Convention and the Statute, France argued that the refugee definition needed to be the same in both because 'it would be difficult to separate the text concerning the High Commissioner's office and the convention'.[141] The United States agreed with France, and also approved the definition of the term 'refugee' in Article 1 of the draft Convention (which would become the 1951 Convention). The United States believed that the refugee definition in the draft convention was appropriate because it

> (E)numerated each of the categories of refugees who had been clearly identified and stood in need of international protection. There were other categories of refugees, such as those created by transfers of population, but most of them were entitled to the rights afforded by their countries of residence and were not in need of international protection. In determining the persons to whom the United Nations should grant its protection, it should be noted that the main purpose of such protection was to prevent the person from becoming a liability to the international community.[142]

However, the United Kingdom wanted the UNHCR's Statute and Convention to be broader, as the UNHCR was created on the premise that 'the problem of refugees is international in scope and nature'.[143] Keeping this statement in mind, the UK argued that the High Commissioner's competence 'should extend throughout the world and to all refugees'.[144] Unfortunately the text proposed by the Economic and Social Council arbitrarily restricted the High Commissioner's role, '*making it*

140 Hathaway, *The Law of Refugee Status*, 1991, p. 6.
141 UNGA, *Official Records of the Third Committee*, Fifth Session, 324th Meeting, 22 November 1950, p. 329.
142 UNGA, *Official Records of the Third Committee*, Fifth Session, 324th Meeting, 22 November 1950, p. 331.
143 UNGA, *Official Records of the Third Committee*, Fifth Session, 324th Meeting, 22 November 1950, p. 330.
144 UNGA, *Official Records of the Third Committee*, Fifth Session, 324th Meeting, 22 November 1950, p. 330.

applicable only to certain refugees'.[145] Furthermore, said the UK, the 'draft Convention referred to the status of refugees as only applying to Europeans…in addition to these geographical restrictions, which were contrary to the international nature of refugee problem, the text proposed by the Council introduced restrictions in time'.[146] The UK condemned such principles on humanitarian grounds and insisted that more restrictions would 'complicate the application of the Convention'.[147] The UK insisted that the only criterion for refugee status should be whether the potential refugee had no government to which 'he could turn for protection and therefore needed that of the High Commissioner'.[148] Both Belgium and the Netherlands agreed with the UK.[149] The Netherlands delegate remarked on 'the need for a broad and general definition of the term "refugee" and was opposed to any attempt to limit such a definition artificially'.[150]

The United States replied to the UK proposal by arguing that 'it was impossible to define in a simple sentence the persons who should benefit from the proposed protection. The adoption of too simple a formula would give rise to varying interpretations and would help to cause great confusion…on the contrary, it was essential to be most precise'.[151] Poland and the Byelorussian Soviet Socialist Republic both argued that either of the definitions being called for by the Western states was 'proof of the desire of certain parties to use refugees for political purposes contrary to the principles of peaceful co-operation among peoples, for it was designed to enable certain countries to continue to use refugees as agents to provoke political disorder in their country of origin'.[152] Byelorussia insisted that 'the fact that the problem of refugees and displaced persons still existed was clearly the fault of the United States, the United Kingdom and France, of their occupation authorities in Germany and Austria, and of the International Refugee Organization, which, under the influence of those countries, had been transformed from an organ of repatriation into a slave labour agency'.[153]

145 UNGA, *Official Records of the Third Committee*, Fifth Session, 324th Meeting, 22 November 1950, p. 330. Emphasis added.
146 UNGA, *Official Records of the Third Committee*, Fifth Session, 324th Meeting, 22 November 1950, p. 331.
147 UNGA, *Official Records of the Third Committee*, Fifth Session, 324th Meeting, 22 November 1950, p. 331.
148 UNGA, *Official Records of the Third Committee*, Fifth Session, 324th Meeting, 22 November 1950, p. 331.
149 UNGA, *Official Records of the Third Committee*, Fifth Session, 324th Meeting, 22 November 1950, p. 333; UNGA, *Official Records of the Third Committee*, Fifth Session, 325th Meeting, 24 November 1950, p. 337.
150 UNGA, *Official Records of the Third Committee*, Fifth Session, 325th Meeting, 24 November 1950, p. 337.
151 UNGA, *Official Records of the Third Committee*, Fifth Session, 324th Meeting, 22 November 1950, p. 331.
152 UNGA, *Official Records of the Third Committee*, Fifth Session, 324th Meeting, 22 November 1950, p. 332.
153 UNGA, *Official Records of the Third Committee*, Fifth Session, 325th Meeting, 24 November 1950, p. 335.

The argument over the refugee definition intensified when growing support for the UK's broader definition of a refugee started to challenge the Franco-US draft resolution calling for the more narrow definition. Chile and Venezuela declared their support for the UK proposal, with Chile arguing that 'the proposed definition of the term 'refugee' [by US and France] was a complete negation of the essence of that draft covenant [the Office's function]...Such a definition would set up a privileged caste of refugees and would amount to bestowing that title only upon a limited group'.[154] It was 'short-sighted' continued Chile, to set up an organization in the belief that history would never repeat itself 'at a time when additional millions of human beings had become refugees as a result of the aggression against the Republic of Korea'.[155]

However, the Venezuelan and Australian delegates, while supportive of the UK draft resolution for a broader refugee definition, did not object to the refugee definition being different in the Statute and Convention.[156] The South African delegate actually argued that the decision regarding the definition of a refugee in the Convention should be postponed until the Conference of Plenipotentiaries. South Africa argued that this would ensure that the Convention was voted on not just by member states of the United Nations, but also by 'a number of nations which were not represented in the United Nations and which might well be able to make a valuable contribution'.[157]

France responded vigorously to this decline in support for its resolution. First, France reminded the Committee that it had already been 'urged' by the delegations in the 1948 Committee to reconcile its own point of view regarding the issue of refugees with the United States. In 1948, France had originally asked for the refugee definition to go beyond the IRO categories, but the narrow definition was all that the United States had been willing to provide for at the time. Furthermore, said France, it was

> (E)asy to adopt a generous attitude and accuse those who had done the most work but it was very clear that without them no body would have been set up and consequently there would be no need to improve it. It would be unjust, by a skilful use of general formulas and generous declarations, to bring accusations of selfish motives against the delegations thanks to whose efforts the question had not been buried.[158]

154 UNGA, *Official Records of the Third Committee*, Fifth Session, 325th Meeting, 24 November 1950, p. 338.

155 UNGA, *Official Records of the Third Committee*, Fifth Session, 325th Meeting, 24 November 1950, p. 338.

156 UNGA, *Official Records of the Third Committee*, Fifth Session, 325th Meeting, 24 November 1950, p. 338; UNGA, *Official Records of the Third Committee*, Fifth Session, 326th Meeting, 24 November 1950, p. 341.

157 UNGA, *Official Records of the Third Committee*, Fifth Session, 326th Meeting, 24 November 1950, p. 342.

158 UNGA, *Official Records of the Third Committee*, Fifth Session, 326th Meeting, 24 November 1950, p. 344.

France argued that what really mattered at this stage was that a text be developed that the majority of states were willing to sign. All France wanted was 'the High Commissioner to know exactly which refugees would be placed under his protection ... There was some doubt [anyway] whether the definition proposed by the United Kingdom declaration, supported by the Belgian delegation, would include the 8 million refugees from Pakistan and Kashmir, the 6 or 8 million *Voksdeutsche*, whose nationality was not always clearly determined, and the 700,000 Arab refugees'.[159] Regardless of this doubt, France felt that,

> (T)he definition proposed by the United Kingdom and Belgium in fact obliged the High Commissioner, if he carried out his task conscientiously, to ask the advice of the General Assembly and, if he was imprudent, to take decisions which might subsequently be repudiated. According to the Economic and Social Council proposal [the original France and US joint resolution brought forward from 1949]...the High Commissioner would have a specific task to perform from the moment that he entered upon his duties.[160]

The United Kingdom replied that it failed to understand why France, a government with such a history of refugees, 'decided to uphold an argument which did not do justice to the magnitude of the problem'.[161] Unlike France, the UK did not believe that it was idealistic to attempt a broad refugee definition and 'doubted whether a compromise could be reached when an ideal was at stake'.[162] However, the UK was prepared to compromise as evidenced by its 'wish to reiterate that it was not essential to adopt the same definition in the High Commissioner's terms of reference *and* in the convention'.[163] France was less prepared to compromise, questioning 'what was the real point of view of the United Kingdom representative, who claimed it was strictly a matter of legal protection. Legal protection would not constitute an adequate or sustaining diet for the refugees'.[164] For France 'believed in the advantages of realist idealism over idealist realism, or a formula which would be idealistic and reasonable at the same time'.[165] The French delegate suggested that the UK's position might 'represent a façade for less generous motives than those which had inspired the more bourgeois formula made with a full knowledge of the

159 UNGA, *Official Records of the Third Committee*, Fifth Session, 326th Meeting, 24 November 1950, p. 345.
160 UNGA, *Official Records of the Third Committee*, Fifth Session, 326th Meeting, 24 November 1950, p. 345.
161 UNGA, *Official Records of the Third Committee*, Fifth Session, 326th Meeting, 24 November 1950, p. 345.
162 UNGA, *Official Records of the Third Committee*, Fifth Session, 326th Meeting, 24 November 1950, p. 345.
163 UNGA, *Official Records of the Third Committee*, Fifth Session, 326th Meeting, 24 November 1950, p. 345. Italics added.
164 UNGA, *Official Records of the Third Committee*, Fifth Session, 326th Meeting, 24 November 1950, p. 346.
165 UNGA, *Official Records of the Third Committee*, Fifth Session, 326th Meeting, 24 November 1950, p. 346.

facts'.[166] It has been suggested that the UK's insistence on a broader refugee definition was motivated by the possibility that it would be facing a large population of people with British passports fleeing developing countries after the decolonization process.[167]

During this debate, the delegations of Egypt, Lebanon and Saudi Arabia issued a joint resolution on behalf of the Palestinian refugees. First of all they found the 'definition of the term "refugee" adopted by the Economic and Social Council to be unduly restrictive, because it was limited in time and space and omitted certain categories of refugees'.[168] On the other hand, they did not like the United Kingdom resolution either, which now was a joint amendment with Belgium, Canada and Turkey. This definition, the Arab states argued, would 'submerge in the general mass of refugees certain groups which were the particular concern of the General Assembly and the right of which to repatriation had been recognized by General Assembly resolutions'.[169] The certain group they were referring to was of course, the Palestinian population, who fled or was forced to flee, after the creation of the state of Israel. The Arab states' resolution demanded that the joint amendment include a section stating that 'the mandate of the High Commissioner's Office shall not extend to categories of refugees at present placed under the competence of other organs or agencies of the United Nations'.[170] The Palestinian refugees then, and to this day, remained under the mandate of the United Nations Relief and Work Agency for Palestinian Refugees and not the UNHCR.[171]

Turkey and China also favored a more general definition of the refugee than what the French were offering. Turkey argued that 'in the convention the status of refugees a general definition should be adopted. Otherwise the scope of the convention would be limited to the liquidation of the question of European war refugees'.[172] Legal protection was also important, Turkey argued, because if refugees could not receive material assistance, 'at least legal protection would give them the

---

166 UNGA, *Official Records of the Third Committee*, Fifth Session, 326th Meeting, 24 November 1950, p. 346.

167 Loescher also suggests that the relative geographic isolation of the UK also meant that it could afford to be generous to refugees. Loescher, *The UNHCR and World Politics: A Perilous Path*, 2001, p. 44.

168 UNGA, *Official Records of the Third Committee*, Fifth Session, 328th Meeting, 27 November 1950, p. 358.

169 UNGA, *Official Records of the Third Committee*, Fifth Session, 328th Meeting, 27 November 1950, p. 358.

170 UNGA, *Official Records of the Third Committee*, Fifth Session, 328th Meeting, 27 November 1950, p. 358.

171 Forsythe, D. P., 'UNRWA, the Palestine Refugees, and World Politics: 1949–1969', *International Organization*, Vol. 25, No. 1 (Winter 1971), pp. 26–45; Radley, K. R., 'The Palestinian Refugees: The Right to Return in International Law', *The American Journal of International Law*, Vo. 72, No. 3 (July 1978), pp. 586–614; Shiblak, A., 'Residency Status and Civil Rights of Palestinian Refugees in Arab Countries', *Journal of Palestine Studies*, Vol. 25, No. 3 (Spring 1995), pp. 36–45; Morris, *The Birth of the Palestinian Refugee Problem Revisited*, 2003.

172 UNGA, *Official Records of the Third Committee*, Fifth Session, 329th Meeting, 29 November 1950, p. 362.

opportunity of re-making their lives in another country'.[173] China, then represented by the nationalists in Taiwan, argued that 'the definition proposed by the Economic and Social Council was too limited, both in space and time. It related mainly to certain categories of persons in Europe or regions bordering on Europe…those restrictions were entirely arbitrary'.[174]

To counter these arguments, the United States reminded states that a broad refugee definition would have financial implications for all states—be it in the Statute or the Convention.[175] Furthermore, the definition sponsored by the UK, Turkey, Belgium and Canada would provide protection for populations from Germany, India, Pakistan and Turkey, 'categories of refugees who did not require international protection but raised substantial questions of assistance'.[176] As far as the United States was concerned 'it had not been shown in the debate that any specific refugees requiring international protection had been excluded from that definition'.[177]

France agreed that regardless of the debate about the definition, a 'convention which only included unlimited pledges would never see the light'.[178] Loescher also suggests that France's support for the US on the definition was due to its growing belief that a broader refugee definition would mean less financial assistance for the organization from the US.[179] As for the Statute, France argued that the question was not really about the definition of a refugee, but who the 'delegation of powers'[180] should be afforded to. Should the High Commissioner have the power to confer refugee status, which is what would have happened if the broad definition was decided on? Alternatively, should states within the General Assembly have the power to decide who deserved refugee status, which is what would have happened if it was decided that the definition should be narrow? France argued that either way, a reasonable and prudent High Commissioner would wait for the General Assembly decision on a refugee group before making any moves, so in this respect a broad definition would be superfluous.[181]

The breakthrough came with a compromise proposed by New Zealand, which suggested that the two groups of countries with draft amendments meet to

173 UNGA, *Official Records of the Third Committee*, Fifth Session, 329th Meeting, 29 November 1950, p. 362.
174 UNGA, *Official Records of the Third Committee*, Fifth Session, 329th Meeting, 29 November 1950, p. 362.
175 UNGA, *Official Records of the Third Committee*, Fifth Session, 329th Meeting, 29 November 1950, p. 362.
176 UNGA, *Official Records of the Third Committee*, Fifth Session, 329th Meeting, 29 November 1950, p. 363.
177 UNGA, *Official Records of the Third Committee*, Fifth Session, 329th Meeting, 29 November 1950, p. 364.
178 UNGA, *Official Records of the Third Committee*, Fifth Session, 329th Meeting, 29 November 1950, p. 364.
179 Loescher, *The UNHCR and World Politics: A Perilous Path*, 2001, n. 61, p. 49.
180 Loescher, *The UNHCR and World Politics: A Perilous Path*, 2001, n. 61, p. 49.
181 UNGA, *Official Records of the Third Committee*, Fifth Session, 329th Meeting, 29 November 1950, p. 365.

exchange views and develop a joint text.[182] It was at this meeting where the final creation of the 1951 Convention and Statute would take place and the outcome was to be disappointing for those whose hopes rested on the UK and its partners supporting the broad definition of a refugee. The result was the creation of an Office with a narrow mandate and a Convention widely perceived as Eurocentric by postcolonial states.

1.4 *The outcome of the 1951 Convention and the UNHCR Statute*

The UNHCR was to be an organization that provided international protection for refugees, but only those who fled due to circumstances prior to 1 January 1951 in Europe. International protection was to entail repatriation, economic and social integration and assistance—all funded through voluntary contributions by member states of the General Assembly. The High Commissioner would also be allowed to appeal for voluntary contributions from governments and individuals to set up a fund for emergency assistance. According to the UNHCR Statute, the extent of the High Commissioner's role was to assist those in flight, but not 'address those factors and forces likely to produce large-scale movements of people across international borders'.[183] Finally, the UNHCR was to oversee the accession to and implementation of an international refugee protection instrument, the 1951 Convention Relating to the Status of Refugees. This section of the chapter will look at how the 1951 Convention came to reflect a Eurocentric appreciation of the refugee problem; and why the UNHCR's Statute was meant to fill this 'gap' by maintaining a more universal mandate, despite having little actual power to *universally* protect refugees.

A working party of Belgium, Canada, France, Israel, Turkey, the United Kingdom, the United States of America and Venezuela reached a 'compromise text of the definitions of the term "refugee"'[184] both for the Convention and the Statute. Importantly, none of the states who called for either a more permissive regime than the UK option or who raised serious doubts about a refugee regime that clearly prioritized European needs, were included in the working party. However, the working party stated that 'unsuccessful efforts had been made to include interested delegations'[185] other than those already in the working party, but no reasons were provided for their refusal. The delegation in attendance was able to reach agreement in that the Statute would allow the High Commissioner to assist a greater number of refugees than those defined in the 1951 Convention, subject to prior General

[182] UNGA, *Official Records of the Third Committee*, Fifth Session, 329th Meeting, 29 November 1950, p. 364.
[183] Loescher, *The UNHCR and World Politics: A Perilous Path*, 2001, 46.
[184] UNGA, *Official Records of the Third Committee*, 330th Meeting, 30 November 1950, p. 367.
[185] UNGA, *Official Records of the Third Committee*, 330th Meeting, 30 November 1950, p. 367.

Assembly approval. The text stated that the High Commissioner's competence extended not only to refugees as defined in the 1951 Convention, but also to:

> *Any other person* [outside of the 1951 Convention definition] who is outside the country of his nationality, or if he has no nationality, the country of his formed habitual residence, because he had or had well-founded persecution by reason of his race, religion, nationality or political opinion and is unable, or because of such fear, is unwilling to avail himself of the probation of the government of his nationality, or if he has no nationality, to return to the country of his formed habitual residence.[186]

The 1951 Convention however, had a more specific sub-set of refugee categories; the result was in Article 1:

> A. For the purposes of the present Convention, the term refugee shall apply to any person who:
> (1) Has been considered a refugee under the Arrangements of 12 May 1926 and 30 June 1928 or under the Conventions 28 October 1933 and 10 February 1938, the Protocol of 14 September 1939 or the Constitution of the Refugee Organization;
>
> Decisions of non-eligibility taken by the International Refugee Organization during the period of its activities shall not prevent the status of refugee being accorded to persons who fulfil the conditions of paragraph 2 of this section;
>
> (2) As a result of events occurring before 1 January 1951 and owing to well-founded fear of persecution for reasons of race, religion, nationality, membership of a particular social group or political opinion, is outside the country of his nationality and is unable or, owing to such fear, is unwilling to avail himself of the protection of that country; or who, not having a nationality and being outside the country of his former habitual residence as a result of such events, is unable or, owing to such fear, is unwilling to return to it.
>
> In the case of a person who has more than one nationality, the term 'the country of his nationality' shall mean each of the countries of which he is a national, and a persons shall not be deemed to be lacking the protection of the country of his nationality if, without any valid reason based on well-founded fear, he has not availed himself of the protection of one of the countries of which he is a national.
>
> B. (1) For the purposes of this Convention, the words 'events occurring before 1 January 1951' in Article 1, Section A, shall be understood to mean either
> (a) 'events in Europe before 1 January'; or
> (b) 'events occurring in Europe or elsewhere before 1 January 1951';
> and each Contracting State shall make a declaration at the time of signature, ratification or accession, specifying which of these meanings it applies for the purpose of its obligations under this Convention.[187]

At France's suggestion, the recommendation for the refugee definition in the UNHCR Statute to be separate from the 1951 Convention was discussed and

---

186 UNGA, *Resolution 428 (V) Statue of the High Commissioner's Office*, 14 December 1950.

187 Weis, P. *The Refugee Convention 1951: The Travaux Preparatoires Analysed, with a Commentary by the late Dr Paul Weis* (Cambridge: University of Cambridge, 1995), pp. xiii–xiv.

amended at the Conference of Plenipotentiaries in Geneva on 2–25 July 1951. The following states were represented by delegations at this Conference: Australia, Austria, Belgium, Brazil, Canada, Colombia, Denmark, Egypt, France, Federal Republic of Germany, Greece, Holy See, Iraq, Israel, Italy, Luxembourg, Monaco, Netherlands, Norway, Sweden, Switzerland, Turkey, United Kingdom of Great Britain and Northern Ireland, United States of America, Venezuela and Yugoslavia. Cuba and Iran were represented by observers. The Conference unanimously adopted the Convention Relating to the Status of Refugees on 25 July 1951 (see Appendix 1). However, before concluding this section, it is significant to note *who did not attend:* Afghanistan, Brazil, China, India, Lebanon, Mexico, Pakistan, Philippines and Thailand. In earlier meetings, many of these states had spoken out against aspects of the Convention and Statute. Some states were also directly critical of the Conference of Plenipotentiaries at the end of 1950 (in the 330th meeting of the Third Committee). China argued against the Conference in the first place stating that 'holding the conference at headquarters [in New York] would avoid extra expenditure' for those countries perhaps not able to afford delegations tripping to Geneva for the conference; Brazil gave the same reason for why it would be absent from the Conference.[188] Lebanon opposed the Plenipotentiaries Conference itself; it argued that the General Assembly should adopt the text of the Convention which would then only be subject to modification by the Conference of Plenipotentiaries; Afghanistan and the Philippines agreed with Lebanon's position.[189]

India had 'previously abstained from participation in the debate on the question of refugees'[190] because of the little concern that the UNHCR would have with refugee issues outside of Europe. However, in one of the last sessions of the Third Committee in 1950, India presented a final statement on how they viewed the varying treatment of refugee issues across the world:

> It had been possible to resettle many refugees and displaced persons because they had been Europeans, and countries such as Australia had opened their doors to them. International aid had not been requested for the millions of refugees in India and Pakistan: she [Indian delegate] wished to ask the Australian representative whether those people would be permitted to settle in his country, which had invited emigrants from the British Commonwealth. One reason why the problem of the Palestine refugees could not be solved was that the possibilities of emigration were limited to Asia. The United Nations should try to help not only special sections of the world's population, but all afflicted people everywhere. Suffering knew no racial or political boundaries: it was the same for all... The whole problem of refugees could never be solved, however, until it became evident that the humanitarian sentiments expressed by the representatives were an accurate reflection of

[188] UNGA, *Official Records of the Third Committee*, 330th Meeting, 30 November 1950, p. 370; UNGA, *Official Records of the Third Committee*, 337th Meeting, 6 December 1950, p. 413.

[189] UNGA, *Official Records of the Third Committee*, 330th Meeting, 30 November 1950, p. 371; UNGA, *Official Records of the Third Committee*, 332nd Meeting, 1 December 1950, p. 378, 380.

[190] UNGA, *Official Records of the Third Committee*, 332nd Meeting, 1 December 1950, p. 377.

> their governments' intentions and that the United Nations had the same concern for all peoples, regardless of race.[191]

Thus, India also decided not to attend the Geneva conference, because of the strict terms of reference in defining a refugee. The voluntary absence of two of the three most populous countries in the world raises a significant question mark about the agreement of UN members and thus of the fairness of the 1951 Convention.

The draft resolution regarding the Convention (A/C.3/L.142) and the draft statute (A/C.3/L.151) compiled by the Third Committee of the General Assembly, was passed by 26 votes to 5 with 12 abstentions.[192] It was then forwarded to the General Assembly where they became Resolutions 428 (V) (Statute) and 429 (V) (Convention). These were then sent to the Conference of the Plenipotentiaries where they were voted on and passed unanimously.[193]

In conclusion, the most important point to note about the difference between the Statute and the Convention was that the UNHCR Statute provided the High Commissioner with the mandate to recognize persons who became refugees as a result of events after 1951 and outside of Europe, but only with General Assembly approval (see Appendix 2).[194] The Statute then divided refugees into two 'categories' which affected the level of protection and assistance provided to them. Those who met the Convention definition of a refugee were also defined in the Statute as 'Convention' refugees or legitimate refugees, and states could be called upon to provide financial assistance and legal protection for this group. However, those considered to be refugees due to events after 1951 and living outside Europe were 'mandate' refugees, and thus the UNHCR could not expect states to provide legal protection or assistance for this group.[195] The High Commissioner would have to go 'cap in hand' for assistance for mandate refugees and it was unlikely that a state would allow the resettlement or local integration of such refugees.[196] In addition, the Statute specified whether its mandate was to recognize these refugees on a group or individual basis—further complicating any attempt by the UNHCR to address refugees fleeing as groups in Africa and Asia, not to mention post-war Europe.[197] The conferment of refugee status under the Convention was limited to events prior to 1951 and in Europe, remaining the most important factor in terms of determining who received legal protection and material assistance.

---

191 UNGA, *Official Records of the Third Committee*, 332nd Meeting, 1 December 1950, p. 377.

192 UNGA, *Official Records of the Third Committee*, 344th Meeting, 11 December 1950, p. 454.

193 In the *Travaux Preparatoires* by Dr Weis all the articles referred to in the Conference were adopted unanimously. Weis, *The Refugee Convention 1951: The Travaux Preparatoires Analysed, with a Commentary by the late Dr Paul Weis*, 1995.

194 Grahl-Madsen, A. *The Land Beyond: Collected Essays on Refugee Law and Policy*, edited by P. Macalister-Smith and Gundmundur Alfredsson (The Hague: Martinus Nijhoff Publishers, 2001), pp. 84–91.

195 Holborn, *Refugees: A Problem of Our Time. The Work of the United Nations High Commissioner for Refugees, 1951–1972*, Volume 1, 1975, pp. 93–94.

196 Loescher discusses the problems with the Statute in relation to those recognized not to be 'statutory refugees'. Loescher, *The UNHCR and World Politics: A Perilous Path*, 2001, pp. 81–95.

197 Hathaway, *The Law of Refugee Status*, 1991, p. 12.

1.5 *Conclusion*

The UNHCR did not arise out of a purely humanitarian concern with refugees across the world. Rather, it was a product of power politics,[198] where states attempted to garner for themselves the best possible solutions for the problems they were facing. The developing states were no different from developed states in that they also wanted a refugee agency that would suit their domestic needs. The difference was that developed states overwhelmed the process with their collective political interests dominating the outcome. However, this victory came at a cost. Many developing states, particularly Brazil, India, Mexico and Pakistan were not silent in their concerns with the shape that the UNHCR and its Convention was taking.

Thus, there are three points worth noting at this stage. First, the Convention limited UNHCR assistance and legal protection to Europe and to refugees fleeing events prior to 1 January 1951. This marginalized other regions from such specialized assistance. Second, the UNHCR Statute failed to meet this gap in protection for refugees outside of Europe because of the limited means by which it could seek assistance for 'mandate' refugees. Third, and this is the most important repercussion of the drafting process of the 1951 Convention and UNHCR Statute, neither instruments had anything contained in it that represented non-European views. As a result, it was not surprising that the inability of the Statute, let alone the Convention, to universally protect and assist refugees made the UNHCR largely despondent and weak outside of Europe through the 1950s. In Chapter 2, I examine how the UNHCR attempted to address its Eurocentric image by trying to 'universalize' the 1951 Convention.

[198] Koskenniemi, *Apology to Utopia: the Structure of International Legal Argument*, 1989, p. xxi.

Chapter 2

1967 Protocol—an Addendum to the 1951 Convention

The need for a supplement to the 1951 Convention was identified in the late 1950s. By the mid-1960s the UNHCR had grown increasingly frustrated with its limited mandate, growing refugee problems in Europe and Africa that were beyond the technical reach of the Convention, and a lower than expected number of accessions to the Convention, particularly amongst recently decolonized states. In Europe, the 1960s saw an end to the legacy of refugees from the Second World War, but a continuation of refugee flows from communist Eastern Europe. At the same time, the number of refugees in Africa was growing rapidly as a result of violent struggles for decolonization and accompanying civil wars post-independence.[1] Asia was also experiencing a higher number of refugees caused in particular by the communist regime in China and the breakup of French Indochina. Here, the UNHCR was able to provide material assistance but it was not mandated to provide legal or protective assistance because the region's states had not acceded to the Convention and because the region's refugees did not meet the Convention's definitional requirements.[2]

In contrast to those seeking refuge in Europe, refugees deemed to fall outside the Convention's refugee definition were assisted as 'mandate refugees' under the

[1] Jackson, The Refugee in Group Situations, 1999, pp. 143–175.

[2] Holborn, *Refugees: A Problem of Our Time*, 1975, pp. 657–659; Loescher, *The UNHCR and World Politics: A Perilous Path*, 2001, p. 188.

UNHCR's 'good offices'.[3] However, the problem the UNHCR faced with 'mandate refugees' was that legal protection and durable solutions such as resettlement or repatriation were difficult to achieve because this kind of assistance required cooperation with other, often unwilling, states. This meant extending the UNHCR's efforts and the responsibilities of states towards refugees beyond the scope of the Convention.

The second problem that faced the UNHCR links to the first, in that the growing number of refugees in Africa outside of UNHCR's mandate was causing an added worry as African states started to consider developing their own regional refugee instruments and even an Office for Refugees to deal with their refugee problem. The rationale behind these African initiatives was that they could set up a Convention and Office that would be more in keeping with their particular problems, which at the time were not within the realm of the 1951 Convention. The UNHCR feared that if newly decolonized states saw more benefits from forming their own regional instruments, the Office would fall into irrelevance as the bulk of refugee work was becoming increasingly focused on the postcolonial world.[4] Furthermore, the creation of such regional groupings threatened to replace the idea of a common global standard for dealing with refugees as different regional mechanisms would have granted refugees different rights and levels of assistance.[5]

For the UNHCR, the 1967 Protocol was seen as a tool that might remedy these problems.[6] The Protocol was formulated as an Addendum to the 1951 Convention, yet was a separate legal instrument developed with the intention of permitting states to adopt the 1967 Protocol and still be bound by the 1951 Convention (eliminating the need for separate accession to the latter). The key difference between the 1951 Convention and 1967 Protocol was the removal of the Convention's time and geographic constraints. Therefore, the 1967 Protocol contains the same definition of a refugee as the 1951 Convention—but without the defining limits of 'events occurring before 1 January 1951' or 'events in Europe before 1 January 1951'.[7]

---

3 An 'umbrella idea' which brought refugees who did not come within the competence of the UN. Goodwin-Gill, *The Refugee in International Law*, 1996, p. 10.

4 Soguk, *States and Strangers: Refugees and Displacements of Statecraft*, 1999, p. 175; Loescher, G. *The UNHCR and World Politics: A Perilous Path*, 2001, pp. 124–125.

5 UNGA, *Report on the Fourteenth Session of the Executive Committee of the High Commissioner's Programme*, Official Records, Twentieth Session, 25 October–2 November 1965, p. 23; UNHCR, *Visit of Dr Urrutia to Legal Division on 13 April 1966*, 18 April 1966; Folio 1602, 16/1/3 GEN, Series 1, Fonds 11, p. 2; Soguk, *States and Strangers: Refugees and Displacements of Statecraft*, 1999, p. 174; Loescher, *The UNHCR and World Politics: A Perilous Path*, 2001, p. 125.

6 UNHCR, *Explanatory Note*, Handed to Mr Goormaghtigh of the Carnegie Endowment on 24 September 1964; Folio 24, 16/1/3 AMEND, Series 1, Fonds 11; Soguk, *States and Strangers: Refugees and Displacements of Statecraft*, 1999, p. 173.

7 Article 1B specifies that the application of the definition of the 'refugee' in Article 1A of the 1951 Convention is either (a) 'events occurring in Europe before 1 January 1951'; or (b) 'events occurring in Europe *or elsewhere* before 1 January 1951' (italics added). Weis, P. *The Refugee Convention 1951: The Travaux Preparatoires Analysed, with a Commentary by the late Dr Paul Weis* (Cambridge: University of Cambridge, 1995), xiii–xiv.

The removal of these limitations aimed at making the Convention *universal.* Thus enabling the UNHCR to expand its Offices in a legitimate and effective way, and prevent its weakening.

According to Jackson and Bem, amongst others, the 1967 Protocol was not necessary because states were permitted to accede to the 1951 Convention but derogate from the time and geographic constraints in Article 1B.[8] In a similar vein, Goodwin-Gill insists that the Protocol was legally unnecessary because the argument that the Convention was undermined by its Eurocentism was 'superficial' owing to the fact that all UN member states were invited to send representatives to the Conference of Plenipotentiaries charged with drafting the Convention.[9] However, as this chapter will demonstrate, there was certainly a strong perception within the UNHCR and amongst many states, particularly in Africa and Asia, that the 1951 Convention was Eurocentric.[10] The domination of Eurocentrism had, in turn, led to significant limitations on the UNHCR. Furthermore, the number of UN member states had increased significantly between 1951 and 1967, shifting the balance of votes in the General Assembly away from Europe and Latin America towards Africa and Asia enough for the presence of these new states to argue for a stronger contribution to the formulation of new international legal instruments. By the mid 1960s, there was a clear consensus amongst most states and within the UNHCR that an addendum to the Convention was indeed necessary.[11] The question that will concern this chapter is whether the 1967 Protocol addressed developing states concerns about the Eurocentrism of international refugee law institutions and instruments. The answer to this question offers further insight into why Southeast Asian states continued to reject these instruments, which in turn shaped their response to the Indochinese refugee crisis (see Chapters 3–6).

In this chapter, I will argue that the 1967 Protocol failed to resolve developing states' claim of Eurocentrism within the 1951 Convention. This was because the removal of the time and geographic limitations only dealt with half of the problem with the 1951 Convention. On the one hand, the 1967 Protocol assisted the universalization of the legal regime by removing the time and geographic barriers which had constrained the UNHCR's work in developing regions. However, on the other hand, the Protocol did not expand the definition of a refugee to include, for example, the variety of causes that compel refugees to flee and the scope of possible responses to refugees was still rooted in particular political circumstances confronting Europe in the immediate aftermath of the Second World War. Essentially, the

[8] Jackson, *The Refugee In Group Situations*, 1999; Bem, K., 'The Coming of the "Blank Cheque"—Europe, the 1951 Convention, and the 1967 Protocol', *International Journal of Refugee Law*, Vol. 16, No. 4 (2004), pp. 609–627.

[9] Goodwin-Gill, *The Refugee in International Law*, 1996, p. 297, n. 3.

[10] UNHCR, High Commissioner Schnyder to Mr Stavropoulos, *Memorandum by the United Nations High Commissioner for Refugees on the Report of the Colloquium on Legal Aspects of Refugee Problems held in April 1965 in Bellagio (Como), Italy*, 6 August 1965; Folio 136, 16/1/3 AMEND, Series 1, Fonds 11.

[11] Holborn, *Refugees: A Problem of Our Time*, 1975, p. 180.

Protocol was about making as few changes as necessary in order to bring a higher number of refugees under the UNHCR's ambit. The Protocol was certainly not the product of a wide-ranging reconsideration of the global refugee problem based on the world's vastly different experiences of refugees. As a result, the Protocol made little headway in changing Southeast Asian attitudes towards international refugee law, as I will demonstrate in detail in the following chapters.

In this chapter, I explore the creation of the 1967 Protocol in four sections. First, I look at the difficulty that the UNHCR was having reconciling the 1951 Convention's refugee definition with the broader definition of a refugee contained in its mandate (see Chapter 1) and the growing number of 'mandate' refugees as opposed to 'Convention' refugees. The second section of the chapter will look at the UNHCR's attempts to develop a relationship with the newly decolonized states. Creating the new Protocol played a significant part in the UNHCR's attempts to persuade African states in particular to remain within its ambit. The third section of the chapter will focus on the debate about what amendment to the 1951 Convention was required by analyzing the discussions on the issue at Bellagio, Italy in 1965. Once the process of negotiating an addition to the Convention began, the UNHCR had an urgent need to respond to growing 'non-Convention' refugee problems. For the UNHCR, the Protocol was therefore primarily concerned with quelling African and other developing states' anxiety about the narrowness of the Convention; preventing the proliferation of an already developing regional instrument in Africa; and thwarting a call in the General Assembly for a complete revision of the 1951 Convention by its new members. In the final section of the chapter, I reflect on Southeast Asian responses to the 1967 Protocol, and consider the UNHCR's overtures to the region's states to encourage them to partake in the universalization of international refugee law.

2.1 *UNHCR and the concept of 'old' and 'new' refugees*

According to Bem, the Protocol was created by 'generous' European states acting for humanitarian reasons in order to extend 'international legal protection to other refugees',[12] having sorted out the European refugee problems caused by the Second World War and the spread of communism. However, this argument is somewhat contradictory as Bem, as well as Jackson and Goodwin-Gill, argue that the 1967 Protocol was an unnecessary piece of legislation, insisting that the Convention already afforded protection to all refugees being assisted by the UNHCR.[13] Both claims are overly simplistic, and there is a critical need to examine the 1967 Protocol

[12] Bem, K., 'The Coming of a "Blank Cheque"—Europe, the 1951 Convention, and the 1967 Protocol', *International Journal of Refugee Law*, Vol. 16, No. 4 (2004), p. 627.

[13] Bem, K., 'The Coming of a "Blank Cheque"—Europe, the 1951 Convention, and the 1967 Protocol', *International Journal of Refugee Law*, Vol. 16, No. 4 (2004), pp. 609–627; Jackson, I. C., *The Refugee In Group Situations* (The Hague: Martinus Nijhoff, 1999); Goodwin-Gill, G. *The Refugee in International Law* (Oxford: Clarendon Press, 1996), 297, n. 3.

in order to uncover its rationale to a greater extent than has been done so far in the literature.[14] I demonstrate in this chapter that even after the 1967 Protocol, the central point of contention remained the narrow definition of a refugee and the failure to recognize that developing states did not have the same bureaucratic and financial capacity as developed states to determine refugee status, let alone assist and protect them.

The UNHCR's first aim in lobbying for a Protocol was the universalization of international refugee law and, in turn, the universalization of the UNHCR's mandate. The Protocol removed the temporal and geographic constraints that had prevented the UNHCR from taking a greater role in refugee protection. But the Protocol did not address what would become the greatest difficulty in relation to the Indochinese refugee crisis, namely how to provide protection for *groups* of refugees comprising individuals who could not prove that they faced individual persecution (the problem of determining individual persecution amongst large groups of asylum seekers remains a more prevalent problem in developing countries) and those who fled due to more generalized violence/persecution.[15] The Protocol did not address what High Commissioner Schnyder saw as the tension between refugee protection for those who fled *en masse*, often amidst armed conflicts (the norm for refugee movements in the developing world)[16] and protection for those that had individual reasons for flight (the norm which was more articulated in

[14] With the exception of Louise Holborn, there has been little discussion of the 1967 Protocol and upon what premise it was created and what response it received. Holborn, *Refugees: A Problem of Our Time The Woks of the United Nations High Commissioner for Refugees 1951–1972*, 1975. Works that critically evaluate the 1951 Convention, but not the 1967 Protocol include, *inter alia*: Hathaway, *The Law of Refugee*, 1991; Goodwin-Gill, *The Refugees in International Law*, 1996; Jackson, *The Refugee in Group Situations*, 1999; Loescher, *A Perilous Path: The UNHCR and World Politics*, 2001.

[15] See Zolberg, A., et al. *Escape From Violence: Conflict and the Refugee Crisis in the Developing World*, 1989; Hathaway, J., 'Reconceiving Refugee Law as Human Rights Protection', *Journal of Refugee Studies*, Vol. 4, No. 2 (1991), pp. 113–131.

[16] The High Commissioner wrote in 1966 that he had 'given further consideration to a further legal problem, which arises in connection with the substantive definition of the term "refugee" in the 1951 Convention. Experience, and more especially recent experience of new refugee situations in Africa, has shown that certain States, for various reasons, may not be able to resort to individual eligibility determination… Having regard to this experience, it might be of advantage if the existing definition was supplemented by certain criteria for the prima facie determination of such group eligibility'. UNHCR, High Commissioner Schnyder to Mr Stavropoulos, *Memorandum by the United Nations High Commissioner for Refugees on the Report of the Colloquium on Legal Aspects of Refugee Problems held in April 1965 in Bellagio (Como), Italy*, 6 August 1965; Folio 136, 16/1/3 AMEND, Series 1, Fonds 11, pp. 6–7. The need for individual status determination still exists today for those in fear of refoulement, as demonstrated by Michael Alexander and Michael Kagan. Alexander, M., 'Refugee Status Determination Conducted by UNHCR', *International Journal of Refugee Law*, Vol. 11, No. 2 (1999), pp. 251–289; Kagan, M., 'The Beleaguered Gatekeeper: Protection Challenges Posed by UNHCR Refugee Status Determination', *International Journal of Refugee Law*, Vol. 18, No. 1 (2006), 1–29. See also Zolberg, A., et al. *Escape From Violence: Conflict and the Refugee Crisis in the Developing World*, 1989; Hathaway, *The Law of Refugee Status*, 1991, pp. 10–11; Schmeidl, S., 'Conflict and Forced Migration: A Quantitative Review', in Zolberg, A. R. and Peter M. Benda (eds.), *Global Migrants, Global Refugees: Problems and Solutions*', 2001.

the 1951 Convention).[17] Nor did the Protocol directly address the fact that the 1951 Convention contained bureaucratized standards and procedures for host states in relation to the determination and treatment of refugees. Arguably, this problem was exacerbated by the way states chose to implement the 1951 Convention, which does not necessarily insist upon such a bureaucratized approach to refugee status determination. In developing states, such capacity is often lacking. Moreover, refugees often come under the domain of the state's most organized bureaucratic structure, the military, which tend to see refugees as a security rather than humanitarian problem.[18]

The outcome was that the 1967 Protocol overlooked an inherent tension that the UNHCR had been attempting to deal with since the 1950s. This tension of how to deal with the type of refugee influx commonly confronting states in Africa and Asia as opposed to the types of influx that confronted developed states in Europe and North America created an important division. The division was between those states that wanted the UNHCR to develop a role in protecting mass influx refugees and those that insisted the onus remain on the individual to prove that he or she were targeted for persecution. The direction of the Protocol itself was the result of a choice made by the UNHCR to avoid the creation of a larger, more nuanced, Convention that might have tackled this fundamental question and instead lobby for a Protocol that simply removed the Convention's time and geographic constraints that were preventing its universal application. Therefore, although the question of mass influx response was certainly raised by the UNHCR prior to the drafting of the Protocol, in the end the Protocol did not address the issue.

As the UNHCR had grown in organizational strength, the potential for it to provide more widespread protection also increased. By 1954, the UNHCR was emerging from a financial crisis that almost saw it close down. The organization was saved by a Ford Foundation grant in 1952 of approximately $2.9 million.[19] In

17 UNHCR, High Commissioner Schnyder to Mr Stavropoulos, *Memorandum by the United Nations High Commissioner for Refugees on the Report of the Colloquium on Legal Aspects of Refugee Problems held in April 1965 in Bellagio (Como), Italy*, 6 August 1965; Folio 136, 16/1/3 AMEND, Series 1, Fonds 11; UNGA, *Official Records of the Third Committee*, Twenty-First Session, 1447th Meeting, 5 December 1966, 416; McGuiness, M., 'Legal and Normative Dimensions of the Manipulation of Refugees', in Stedman, S. J. and Fred Tanner (eds.), *Refugee Manipulation: War, Politics, and the Abuse of Human Suffering*, 2003.

18 For more on this point see Chatelard, G. 'Jordan as a transit country: semi-protectionist immigration policies and their effects on Iraqi forced migrants', *New Issues in Refugee Research*, Working Paper No. 61, (Geneva: UNHCR Research Unit, 2002).

19 Donor states opposed the UNHCR being able to raise its own funds for a variety of operational purposes. European states wanted to put all of their funds, including foreign aid, into the local integration of their refugees. France in particular made every effort to create problems for the UNHCR as their French UN Representative Robert Rochefort had aspired to be the Deputy High Commissioner, with a US representative as High Commissioner. Meanwhile, the United States had set up the Intergovernmental Committee for European Migration (ICEM, now the International Organization for Migration [IOM]) which managed the migration of refugees *and* labour migrants; was fully funded and operated by the United States outside of the UN and only democratic nations friendly to the US were on the board. ICEM was directly concerned with those fleeing communist East Europe. As a result, the US would not fund the UNHCR. See

the early 1950s, High Commissioner Gerrit Jan van Heuven Goedhart presented a number of speeches to the General Assembly insisting that protection without material assistance—the image of the UNHCR set out in the Convention—was an incomplete mechanism for addressing the problem of refugees. Goedhart pointed out that there were 400,000 refugees who remained in camps throughout Europe because they had been rejected for resettlement on account of age, illness or disability.[20] He stressed the need to integrate these refugees and, on 2 February 1952, the General Assembly agreed to allow Goedhart to raise funds through member state donations to provide the UNHCR with the capacity to provide material assistance to these refugees. The General Assembly permitted Goedhart to raise $3 million for this purpose but by March 1954, he had secured only $1 million in donations.[21] Meanwhile the US had donated $45 million to the Intergovernmental Committee for European Migrants (see note 19).[22]

When the UNHCR obtained $2.9 million in a grant from the Ford Foundation in 1952, the Office was able to involve itself for the first time in providing administrative assistance to refugees in Western Europe and play a role in coordinating the activities of NGOs in this region.[23] The Ford donation encouraged other donations—including donations from governments—marking an important shift in the UNHCR's operations from a preoccupation with legal protection towards a greater interest in assistance.[24] The UNHCR's widely perceived success in directing material assistance to refugee groups during the Berlin crisis in 1953 helped to further this shift.[25] The Berlin experience encouraged the General Assembly to approve an expanded financial budget for the UNHCR in 1954, which included a significant allocation for assistance. Member states were to be part of a United Nations Refugee Emergency Fund (UNREF) Executive Committee[26] (now the UNHCR Executive Committee). The UNREF Executive Committee would then, as it does now, advise the High Commissioner on protection and assistance programmes and play a 'direct over-sight role over the Office's finances'.[27] The Executive Committee could directly control the UNHCR's activities and, as a result, the UNHCR

Holborn, *Refugees: A Problem of Our Time*, 1975, p. 387; Loescher, *Beyond Charity: International Cooperation and the Global Refugee Crisis*, 1993, pp. 62–63; Soguk, *States and Strangers: Refugees and Displacements of Statecraft*, 1999, p. 172; Loescher, *The UNHCR and World Politics: A Perilous Path*, 2001, pp. 61–62, 67.

20 Loescher, *The UNHCR and World Politics: A Perilous Path*, 2001, p. 63.

21 Loescher, *The UNHCR and World Politics: A Perilous Path*, 2001, p. 63.

22 Loescher, *The UNHCR and World Politics: A Perilous Path*, 2001, p. 64.

23 See Soguk, *States and Strangers: Refugees and Displacements of Statecraft*, 1999, p. 172; Loescher, *The UNHCR and World Politics: A Perilous Path*, 2001, p. 67.

24 Holborn, *Refugees: A Problem of Our Time*, 1975, p. 324.

25 In 1953 the number of East Germans fleeing went from 15 000 in December 1952 to 48 000 in March 1953, due to fear of increasing Sovietisation of East Germany. Goedhart used his Ford funding to assist with temporary housing, assistance and organizations voluntary agencies to deliver assistance. Read, J. *The United Nations and Refugees—Changing Concepts* (Geneva: Carnegie Endowment for Peace, 1962).

26 General Assembly Resolution 5388 (VI) and 832 (IX) respectively.

27 Loescher, *The UNHCR and World Politics: A Perilous Path*, 2001, p. 70.

began to secure a much higher proportion of its funding from member states as opposed to private institutions.

The improving financial situation and increased state support prompted the UNHCR to attempt to expand its mandate. China (then Taiwan) requested assistance for those fleeing the communists as early as 1952. In Europe, Austria and Yugoslavia asked for UNHCR assistance with Hungarian refugees in 1956, following their foiled revolt against communism. Tunisia and Morocco sought assistance from the UNHCR with a large number of Algerians fleeing the civil war. However, the limits of both the UNHCR's mandate and the Convention were revealed by the variable treatment these cases received (see below). As explained at the end of Chapter 1, a 'Convention' refugee was one recognized as fleeing events in Europe prior to 1 January 1951 due to an individual fear of political persecution. A 'mandate' refugee was one generally recognized to need the assistance of the High Commissioner's 'good offices' because they were fleeing political persecution. But a 'mandate' refugee did not fall under the time and geographic conditions in the 1951 Convention (or in most cases, as individuals who could prove their direct fear of political persecution).[28] Therefore, these groups also received different levels of assistance. It is significant that in the late 1950s, out of the three major groups to seek UNHCR refugee assistance through the Executive Committee (excluding the post-WWII population), the Hungarians were given 'Convention' refugee status, while the two classified as 'mandate' refugees were in developing regions (Chinese and Algerian refugees). This outcome prompted the third High Commissioner, Felix Schnyder, to stress in 1961 the need to abandon the notions 'old' (traditional European/'Convention' refugees) and 'new' (other/'mandate' refugees) refugees. Schnyder argued that both groups should be treated similarly by the UNHCR and offered access to equal levels of legal protection and material assistance.[29] I will briefly consider these three cases in turn.

2.1.1 *China*

This prompts the question of how the separation between 'Convention' and 'mandate' refugees was understood in the 1950s and 1960s, and most importantly, how this distinction impacted upon the formation of the 1967 Protocol. At the UN General Assembly in 1952, China (Taiwan) requested that the hundreds of thousands of Chinese fleeing communism since 1945 be considered refugees and their plight brought to the attention of the UNHCR.[30] From the High Commissioner's

[28] For more on this see: UNHCR, *Memorandum by the United Nations High Commissioner for Refugees on the Report of the Colloquium on Legal Aspects of Refugee Problems held in April 1965 in Bellagio (Como), Italy*, 23 September 1965; HCR/RS/31, Series 1, Fonds 11, 16/1/3 GEN, 5; Goodwin-Gill, *The Refugee in International Law*, 1996; Hathaway, *The Law of Refugee Status*, 1991; Kourula, P. *Broadening the Edges: Refugee Definition and International Protection Revisited* (The Hague: Martinus Nijhoff Publishers, 1997).

[29] Jackson, *The Refugee Concept in Group Situations*, 1999, pp. 102–106.

[30] UNGA, *Colloquium on the Legal Aspects of Refugee Problems*, Note by the High Commissioner,

perspective, however, this request was problematic.[31] There were several reasons for this. First, the existence of two Chinas meant that Taiwanese China, which was the then internationally recognized China, presented a national territory in which people were safe to reside and thus the refugees could not be identified as such under the 1951 Convention.[32] However, the sheer scale and cost of the Chinese refugee problem meant that they could not all live in Taiwan, thus further complicating the situation if this was regarded as the sole solution.[33]

The second problem was related to British administered Hong Kong, where most of the Chinese had sought asylum. The UK opposed the provision of UNHCR assistance for Chinese refugees primarily because it believed such assistance would encourage further flight. Britain had not signed Hong Kong to the 1951 Convention and thus the territory had no obligation to the Convention or to any refugee arrivals. Britain argued that the People's Republic of China (PRC) should be recognized as a legitimate state and therefore Chinese refugees *did* have a legitimate state of origin to return to and doing so would not pose a threat to their personal security.[34] A third problem was caused by the fact that the Chinese refugees had fled *en masse* and the UNHCR lacked both the funds and the administrative capability to screen each individual. Moreover, it was far from apparent what would happen to these individuals even if they were screened and found to be refugees, with Taiwan unable to accept them and Britain not wanting them.[35]

Within this context, High Commissioner Goedhart wanted to determine whether the UNHCR could potentially assist the Chinese as refugees and he commissioned a study on the Chinese who had managed to enter Hong Kong and the nature of their situation. The study was duly approved by the Advisory Committee of the High Commissioner's Programme (now Executive Committee).[36] It found that 'it seemed safe to assume that fear of persecution in a country in the throes of a revolution was seldom without foundation' and therefore 'objectively speaking it could be accepted that a well-founded fear of persecution was not excluded'.[37] Despite these findings, the problem of the 'two Chinas' and the British refusal to accept that the UNHCR's mandate covered the Chinese refugees in Hong Kong, meant that the refugees did not fall under the High Commissioner's mandate and were not eligible for assistance. When the so-called Hambro report was released

Executive Committee of the High Commissioner's Programme, Thirteenth Session, 5 May 1965, A/AC.96/INFO.40, Annex 1, 1. Rockefeller Foundation Archives, Record Group 1.2, Series 200, Box 484, Folder 4143.

31 Holborn, *Refugees: A Problem of Our Time*, 1975, pp. 657–658, 676–677.

32 Jackson, *The Refugee Concept in Group Situations*, 1999, p. 92.

33 Loescher, *The UNHCR and World Politics: A Perilous Path*, 2001, p. 93.

34 Loescher, *The UNHCR and World Politics: A Perilous Path*, 2001, pp. 93–94; Holborn, *Refugees: A Problem of Our Time*, 1975, p. 376. PRC was formally recognized as the legitimate state of China by the UN in 1974.

35 Jackson, *The Refugee Concept in Group Situations*, 1999, p. 91.

36 The study was carried out by Dr Edvard Hambro, *The Problem of Chinese Refugees in Hong Kong* (Leiden: A. W. Sijthoff, 1955). Jackson, *The Refugee Concept in Group Situations*, 1999, pp. 90–91; Loescher, *The UNHCR and World Politics: A Perilous Path*, 2001, p. 93.

37 Jackson, *The Refugee Concept in Group Situations*, 1999, p. 91.

in 1955, the Executive Committee placed 'considerable emphasis on the need to address the humanitarian problems of this group without regard to purely legal considerations'.[38] In 1957, the new High Commissioner Auguste Lindt,[39] placed the issue of the Hong Kong refugees on the Executive Committee's agenda again; it was decided that although this population did not fall under the mandate of the UNHCR the problem was of 'concern to the international community'.[40] As a result, the High Commissioner was authorized by the General Assembly to 'use his good offices to encourage arrangements for contributions'.[41] The Chinese refugees were therefore included in this new UNHCR fundraising arrangement. However, it should be noted in passing that the UNHCR did not have much success in raising contributions to assist the Chinese refugees. For instance, there is evidence to suggest that even had these refugees fallen under the remit of the 1951 Convention, Western states would not have provided resettlement places for them.[42] What this case illustrates is that the UNHCR Statute could assist refugees who for one reason or another fell outside the Convention's definition of a refugee. However, the British refusal to allow the UNHCR to address this situation fully incapacitated the UNHCR's protection work. In addition, despite the findings of the Hambro report documenting that fear of political persecution was the reason for people fleeing mainland China, the fact that flight had taken place in such large numbers meant that the political and practical repercussions overrode humanitarian concerns.

2.1.2 *Hungary*

The failed Hungarian revolt followed by the Soviet invasion and occupation in November 1956, led to the exodus of some 200,000 Hungarians to Austria and Yugoslavia.[43] These were relatively well-educated and/or prosperous refugees fleeing communist oppression and there was little opposition amongst Western states to these refugees receiving UNHCR assistance and legal protection.[44] Unsurprisingly then, refugee advocates had little difficulty persuading member states that these refugees fell under the UNHCR Statute. This refugee population was also immediately granted *prima facie* refugee recognition under the 1951 Convention. After individual screening in a state that had acceded to the 1951 Convention, all were eligible for resettlement.[45] Western European states, plus the US, Australia, Canada, Israel and Latin American states agreed with the UNHCR's conclusion

---

38 Jackson, *The Refugee Concept in Group Situations*, 1999, p. 92.
39 High Commissioner Goedhart died of a heart attack suddenly in mid-1956.
40 Jackson, *The Refugee Concept in Group Situations*, 1999, p. 93.
41 Jackson, *The Refugee Concept in Group Situations*, 1999, p. 93.
42 Holborn, *Refugees: A Problem of Our Time*, 1975, p. 679; Loescher, *The UNHCR and World Politics: A Perilous Path*, 2001, p. 95.
43 Holborn, *Refugees: A Problem of Our Time*, 1975, p. 391.
44 Loescher, *The UNHCR and World Politics: A Perilous Path*, 2001, p. 87.
45 Jackson, *The Refugee in Group Situations*, 1999, p. 119.

and provided resettlement places for the Hungarians.[46] That the Hungarians could be declared 'Convention refugees' despite the revolt taking place in 1956 was a product of legal gymnastics. It was argued that the Hungarian exodus was indeed a result of 'events prior to 1951' because the Communist Party had established a People's Republic in Hungary in 1947–48.[47]

According to Loescher, the Hungarian situation gave rise to a realization that the UNHCR had a similar duty to grant *prima facie* recognition, where applicable to the Statute, in other situations of political upheaval—regardless of where and when this occurred.[48] In practice, however, there remained a sharp distinction between the treatment of refugees in Europe and those in the rest of the world; and between what events could be construed as having occurred before 1 January 1951. This is evident in the different international responses to the Chinese refugees and the Hungarian refugees. However, during debates about how best to respond to Algerian refugees, the UNHCR made significant headway towards balancing this tension.

2.1.3 *Algeria*

A war was fought between the Algerian nationalist movement and colonial France from 1954 to 1962. In 1957, it reached new levels of brutality, prompting the exodus of thousands of refugees into neighboring Tunisia and Morocco. Both of these states requested UNHCR assistance, becoming the first developing states to do so (in itself a fact worth noting). Both countries had recently become independent of France and were supporters of the Algerian independence movement.[49] In sharp contrast with the response to the Hungarian refugee crisis, the UNHCR was more circumspect in the Algerian case. It ensured that although the Algerians were referred to as 'refugees' in internal discussions, and although in his private communications with governments the High Commissioner confirmed that the refugees were *prima facie* refugees according to the 1951 Convention, there were no public statements confirming this.[50] As a result, the Algerians were not publicly recognized as 'Convention' refugees. Clearly, this was partly a result of the political tensions surrounding the Algerian War. The movement of refugees had also occurred *en masse*, making individual status determination practically impossible. Despite this, by the end of 1958, the UNHCR was officially providing material assistance to help Tunisia and Morocco with the Algerian refugee population.[51]

---

46 Loescher, *The UNHCR and World Politics: A Perilous Path*, 2001, p. 86.

47 Holborn, *Refugees: A Problem of Our Time*, 1975, p. 394; Loescher, *The UNHCR and World Politics: A Perilous Path*, 2001, p. 86.

48 Loescher, *The UNHCR and World Politics: A Perilous Path*, 2001, p. 98.

49 Loescher, *The UNHCR and World Politics: A Perilous Path*, 2001, pp. 97–99.

50 See Jackson, *The Refugee in Group Situations*, 1999, pp. 120–142 for a more in-depth appraisal of the Algerian refugee status debate. Also, Ruthstrom-Ruin, C. *Beyond Europe: The Globalization of Refugee Aid* (Lund: Lund University Press, 1993).

51 The resolution put forward by Tunisia and Morocco for UNHCR assistance due to the urgency of the Algerian refugee problem was, interestingly, supported by Libya, Pakistan, Sudan, Cambodia, Turkey, Japan, United Arab Republic, USSR, Albania, Liberia, Ethiopia, Haiti and Indonesia. Jackson, *The Refugee in Group Situations*, 1999, pp. 126–127.

The conduct of the war by the French was notoriously brutal. In addition to ransacking villages, the French forcibly resettled peasants in guarded encampments and made systematic use of torture. This brutality persuaded High Commissioner Lindt to argue that there was a strong humanitarian imperative to respond to Tunisia and Morocco's requests for help.[52] However, the level of assistance that Lindt could offer was tempered by the political context. In short, it was politically unfeasible to declare that France, a permanent member of the UN Security Council, was conducting political persecution in Algeria to the extent that those fleeing could be considered *prima facie* refugees.

Lindt continued to insist, though, that the UNHCR had to respond to the requests for assistance by Tunisia after the first arrival of 85,000 Algerians. Lindt questioned how the UNHCR could provide *prima facie* recognition to Hungarians and not to Algerians simply because of the wider political context?[53] Furthermore, he feared that if the UNHCR did not respond, the Office would forever be seen by developing countries as 'the High Commissioner for European refugees only'.[54] Importantly, the US, by now a major donor to the UNHCR, supported UNHCR assistance to the Algerian refugees as long as it was done discretely. The US calculated that assistance delivered through the UNHCR would represent a show of good will to African states and would help prevent the spread of communism in North Africa.[55] As a result, and despite the potential consequences, the UNHCR decided to provide *prima facie* refugee status to the Algerian refugees under the 'good offices' section of UNHCR Statute. This was an important precedent and highlighted the UNHCR's sensitivity to developing states perception of it as a 'European institution' and the need to change that image.[56] However, the Algerian case also demonstrates some of the powerful constraints that were placed on the UNHCR in this endeavor.

In the early to mid 1960s, there was a rising number of refugees in developing states, in particular Africa and Asia. This was largely due to wars caused by armed struggles for decolonization, border disputes, and civil conflicts. As a result, refugee problems in Europe started to pale in comparison with the mass influx of refugees occurring in developing regions. Loescher credits Lindt's successor as High Commissioner, Felix Schnyder, who was elected by the General Assembly in 1960, as being the key player in expanding the UNHCR's presence outside Europe and in utilizing 'good offices' authority of the UNHCR to assist refugee groups not previously addressed by the Statute or Convention.[57] The need to constantly stretch

52 Loescher, *The UNHCR and World Politics: A Perilous Path*, 2001, pp. 97–98.
53 Loescher, *The UNHCR and World Politics: A Perilous Path*, 2001, p. 98.
54 Loescher, *The UNHCR and World Politics: A Perilous Path*, 2001, p. 98.
55 Loescher, *The UNHCR and World Politics: A Perilous Path*, 2001, p. 99.
56 Jackson, *The Refugee in Group Situations*, 1999, pp. 120–142; Soguk, *States and Strangers: Refugees and Displacements of Statecraft*, 1999, p. 173; Loescher, *The UNHCR and World Politics: A Perilous Path*, 2001, pp. 98–101, 105–110.
57 Loescher, *The UNHCR and World Politics: A Perilous Path*, 2001, p. 106.

the 'good offices' function in this way provided part of the rationale for eventually abandoning the time and geographic constraints within the 1951 Convention.[58]

2.2 *UNHCR and refugee crises in the developing world*

Another aim of the UNHCR in fostering the Protocol had been to attract more accessions to the 1951 Convention. This was closely linked to the organization's third aim with the 1967 Protocol: preventing or forestalling the proliferation of regional refugee instruments, such as the Organization of African Unity (OAU) 1969 Refugee Convention, which could take precedence over the UNHCR and create a system of differential regional refugee protection. Through the 1960s the UNHCR was called upon to assist hundreds of thousands of refugees in Africa under General Assembly Resolution 1673 (XVI) of 1961, which allowed the High Commissioner to extend the mandate function of 'good offices' to 'groups of refugees'.[59] The High Commissioner's argument (see above) for the need for the international community to assist 'new' groups of refugees, and not restrict its activities to so-called 'old' refugees (located in Europe), finally paid dividends in terms of who the UNHCR could now assist.[60] The crises in Africa that the UNHCR became involved in during the 1960s involved Angolan refugees in the Congo, Ghanaian refugees in Togo, and Rwandan refugees in Tanganyika, Uganda, Burundi and Congo. By the mid 1960s, the UNHCR assistance programme in Africa had expanded to include refugees from Portuguese Guinea in Senegal, refugees from Mozambique in Tanzania, Zambia, Kenya and Swaziland; refugees from Sudan in Uganda, Ethiopia, Central African Republic and Congo; refugees from the Democratic Republic of Congo in Zambia and the Central African Republic; refugees from Burundi into Rwanda in 1966 and refugees from Ethiopia in Sudan in 1967. By the late 1960s there were further movements of refugees from Chad, Southern Africa and Namibia.[61]

During this period, the UNHCR was criticized for providing a large amount of material assistance without concomitant levels of legal protection. The emphasis on material assistance as the sole solution to the problems in Africa was widely considered flawed.[62] It certainly served to strengthen the idea that there was a

[58] Soguk, *States and Strangers: Refugees and Displacements of Statecraft*, 1999, p. 173; Loescher, *The UNHCR and World Politics: A Perilous Path*, 2001, p. 106.

[59] Jackson, *The Refugee in Group Situations*, 1999, p. 104. It needs to be noted that this was assistance only—not protection.

[60] See Jackson, *The Refugee in Group Situations*, 1999, pp. 99–104.

[61] For an in-depth appraisal of the legal status and assistance provided to these entire refugee groups see Holborn, *Refugees: A Problem of Our Time*, 1975, pp. 957–1386; Jackson, *The Refugee in Group Situations*, 1999, pp. 143–177.

[62] High Commissioner Schynder started emphasizing the 'new refugees' needed material assistance as opposed to the 'old refugees' almost immediately. As a result, legal protection for refugees in Africa was obviously, not considered by Schynder as the solution to the 'new refugees'. See

fundamental difference between European and non-European refugees; the former were seen to primarily need legal protection (plus assistance) while the latter were only provided with material assistance. This characterization clearly had its roots in the fact that the UNHCR was initially formed to respond to refugee problems in Europe alone.[63] Even though Europe underwent massive social, economic and border upheavals after both world wars, there was a familiar sense of laws, administration and pre-existing norms about where people 'fitted' and about where those who did not 'fit' should go. Europe's main refugee concern after the Second World War was to resettle refugees within a post-war context of relative peace. Africa, especially, confronted an entirely different situation. There, refugees were fleeing war and being settled in a context of ongoing violence, often in places where the state either was not yet fully formed or was also involved in conflict. The 1951 Convention simply did not provide a realistic mechanism for dealing with refugees in this context. High Commissioner Schnyder attempted to address this problem by expanding the 'good offices' concept, making it applicable to the large groups of refugees in Africa and focusing on material assistance; but this was all the 'good offices' concept could provide. The result was neglect of legal protection and a failure to address the insecurity and settlement problems faced by refugees in host countries.

The UNHCR's practice in Asia prior to the 1967 Protocol was similar in certain respects to the consideration it gave to African refugee needs. The emphasis here was also on the notion that the High Commissioner 'was compelled to create responses different from those developed in his work in Europe'.[64] Therefore, the UNHCR focused on the provision of material assistance and relief measures through the "good offices" function. Assistance was provided through the provision of medical, food, clothing, cooking and consumable goods, often in conjunction with NGOs who would carry out the actual assistance programmes. But this assistance did not provide UNHCR protection to these groups or offer refugees any durable solutions. Assistance was provided to the Chinese in Hong Kong and Macao, the Tibetans in India and Nepal and Indochinese refugees fleeing colonial France due to independence struggles. However, these groups were not given *prima facie* refugee recognition. Instead, they were assisted under the 'good offices' provisions because 'eligibility for the status of refugee could not be specifically determined'.[65] However, as mentioned earlier, Schnyder was concerned with the increasing gap between 'old'

UNGA, *Colloquium on the Legal Aspects of Refugee Problems,* Note by the High Commissioner, Executive Committee of the High Commissioner's Programme, Thirteenth Session, 5 May 1965, A/AC.96/INFO.40, Annex 1; Jackson, *The Refugee in Group Situations*, 1999, 103–104.

63 This has been repeatedly argued by Zolberg, A., et al. *Escape From Violence: Conflict and the Refugee Crisis in the Developing World*, 1989; Hathaway, J., 'Reconceiving Refugee Law as Human Rights Protection', *Journal of Refugee Studies*, Vol. 4, No. 2 (1991), pp. 113–131; Chimni, B. S. 'The Geopolitcs of Refugee Studies: A View from the South', *Journal of Refugee Studies*, Vol. 11, No. 4 (1998), pp. 350–374; Soguk, *States and Strangers: Refugees and Displacements of Statecraft*, 1999; Loescher, *The UNHCR and World Politics: A Perilous Path*, 2001.

64 Holborn, *Refugees: A Problem of Our Time*, 1975, p. 657.

65 Holborn, *Refugees: A Problem of Our Time*, 1975, p. 658.

or Convention refugees and the increasing number of 'new' or Statute refugees. Such a gap, he felt, was untenable particularly as the majority of the UNHCR's work was being conducted in developing countries.[66] Unlike the majority of African states though, Asian states had not signed onto the 1951 Convention or developed regional refugee mechanisms. Although they could have opted out of the time and geographic constraints in their accession to the 1951 Convention, Asian states still resisted overtures by the UNHCR during this period.[67]

This then brings us to the third key issue underlying the UNHCR's advocacy of a Protocol, the potential emergence of regional refugee mechanisms. The growing refugee problem in Africa led to the emergence of a regional refugee instrument, the Organization of African Unity (OAU) Refugee Convention. This contained a broader refugee definition that took into account the possibility of mass influx and generalized fears of violence. However, Deputy High Commissioner Sadruddin Aga Khan spoke with relief when the OAU decided that African states, though members of the OAU Refugee Convention, still needed to accede to the 1951 Convention. He declared that this demonstrated that the Convention had become 'more universally recognized'[68]—implying of course that it was not before. However, Algeria and Nigeria both quickly pointed out that the OAU Convention did not mitigate the limitations that existed in the 1951 Convention, its lack of applicability to Africa, and the need for it to be reformed or replaced with a new instrument.[69] So although the UNHCR was quick to applaud African states for taking the initiative in developing a regional instrument, it was also determined to ensure that the region continued to acknowledge the UNHCR Statute and the 1951 Convention as the primary global instruments; regional instrument would be secondary.[70] However, the hostility of many African states to the 1951 Convention also confirmed the need for the UNHCR to start considering the views of developing states more seriously and recognize the different needs of these new states.[71] Likewise, the lack of accessions in Asia demonstrated a need for the UNHCR to make the refugee instrument relevant to Asian states.

---

66 UNHCR, *Explanatory Note*, Handed to Mr Goormaghtigh of the Carnegie Endownment on 24 September 1964; Folio 24, 16/1/3 AMEND, Series 1, Fonds 11; see also 'Chapter Five: Expansion into Africa under Schnyder', Loescher, *The UNHCR and World Politics: A Perilous Path*, 2001.

67 UNHCR, Deputy High Commissioner to J Asscher, *Interoffice Memorandum: 1951 Convention*, 21 March 1956; Folio 535, 16/1/3 GEN, Series 1, Fonds 11. Overtures to individual Asian states were also made for them to accede so as to encourage other Asian states: UNHCR, Deputy High Commissioner to Minister for Foreign Affairs of Afghanistan, *Correspondence*, 3 November 1959; Folio 849, 16/1/3 GEN, Series 1, Fonds 11, p. 2; UNHCR, Deputy High Commissioner to Primer Minister and Minister for Foreign Affairs of Federation of Malaya, *Correspondence*, 4 November 1959; Folio 852, 16/1/3 GEN, Series 1, Fonds 11, p. 2.

68 UNGA, *Report on the Fourteenth Session of the Executive Committee of the High Commissioner's Programme*, Official Records, Twentieth Session, 25 October–2 November 1965, p. 23.

69 UNGA, *Report on the Fourteenth Session of the Executive Committee of the High Commissioner's Programme*, Official Records, Twentieth Session, 25 October–2 November 1965, p. 24.

70 UNHCR, *Visit of Dr Urrutia to Legal Division on 13 April 1966*, 18 April 1966; Folio 1602, 16/1/3 GEN, Series 1, Fonds 11, p. 2; Soguk, *States and Strangers: Refugees and Displacements of Statecraft*,1999, p. 174; Loescher, *The UNHCR and World Politics: A Perilous Path*, 2001, p. 125.

71 Loescher, *The UNHCR and World Politics: A Perilous Path*, 2001, pp. 124–26.

While Africa's political leaders were 'eager to raise their status and improve their image in the international political system' through belonging to a global refugee regime, the UNHCR was happy to 'socialize new states to accept the promotion of refugees' norms as part of becoming law-abiding members of the international community'.[72] Asian states did not adopt the same position, and this was reflected in the lack of Asian accessions to the instruments in the 1960s.[73] However, Asian states were not alone in their reluctance to sign the 1951 Convention because the 'new refugee situations are, of course, no more covered by that dateline'.[74] In 1965, several Latin American states also expressed a lack of interest in the Convention as they felt it had 'no application to their problems because of the dateline'.[75] This general level of discontent with international refugee law was more clearly articulated once discussions about developing a new refugee instrument began in earnest in 1965.

2.3 *The Bellagio Colloquium—creating the 1967 Protocol*

In 1964, the High Commissioner, supported by the Belgian delegate in the Executive Committee,[76] proposed an initiative to resolve the situation where the 'High Commissioner deals with the "old" groups of refugees on the basis of the Statue and assists new groups of refugees by virtue of his good offices function . . . without necessarily having to examine their eligibility under the Statute'.[77] For under the Convention, 'hardly any of the new groups of refugees can be considered as falling within its scope owing to the dateline of 1 January 1951'.[78] The key question, however, was how the UNHCR and Executive Committee could go about removing the dateline? The Belgian delegate, who first raised the issue, suggested a

[72] Loescher, *The UNHCR and World Politics: A Perilous Path*, 2001, pp. 105–6.

[73] UNHCR, I. C. Jackson to The Representative, UNHCR Branch Office for Nepal, *Accession by Nepal to the 1951 Convention and the Protocol*, 16 September 1967; Folio 4741, 16/1/3 GEN, Series 1, Fonds 11; UNHCR, W. K. McCoy to UNHCR Geneva, *Memorandum: Malaysia—Attitude to Convention*, 15 March 1969; Folio 1829, 16/1/3 GEN, Series 1, Fonds 11; UNHCR, W. K. McCoy to UNHCR Geneva, *Memorandum: Singapore—Attitude to Convention*, 24 March 1969; Folio 1831, 16/1/3 GEN, Series 1, Fonds 11; UNHCR, W. K. McCoy to UNHCR Geneva, *Memorandum: Indonesia—Attitude to Convention*, 6 May 169; Folio 1839, 16/1/3 GEN, Series 1, Fonds 11; UNHCR, E. Jahn to Mr Goundian, *Asian-African Committee*, 6 February 1970; Folio 1879, 16/1/3 GEN, Series 1, Fonds 11, p. 2.

[74] UNHCR, High Commissioner Schnyder to Mr John Goormaghtigh, *Correspondence*, 20 July 1964; Folio 16, 16/1/3 GEN, Series 1, Fonds 11, p. 1.

[75] UNHCR, *Visit of Dr Urrutia to Legal Division on 13 April 1966*, 18 April 1966; Folio 1602, 16/1/3 GEN, Series 1, Fonds 11.

[76] UNHCR, High Commissioner Schnyder to Mr John Goormaghtigh, *Correspondence*, 20 July 1964; Folio 16, 16/1/3 GEN, Series 1, Fonds 11, p. 2.

[77] UNHCR, *Explanatory Note*, Handed to Mr Goormaghtigh of the Carnegie Endowment on 24 September 1964; Folio 24, 16/1/3 AMEND, Series 1, Fonds 11, p. 2.

[78] UNHCR, *Explanatory Note*, Handed to Mr Goormaghtigh of the Carnegie Endowment on 24 September 1964; Folio 24, 16/1/3 AMEND, Series 1, Fonds 11, p. 2.

supplement to the Convention such as a Protocol.[79] However, High Commissioner Schnyder argued that a number of states had expressed a reluctance to 'assume legal obligations with regard to new refugee situations the nature and scope of which they cannot yet foresee'.[80] This was not very different to the arguments leveled in 1951 (see Chapter 1) where an overriding concern about signing a binding obligation for a future number of unknown refugee groups produced a legal definition of the refugee that owed more to prudential calculations of national interest than humanitarian sentiment.[81] The UNHCR therefore proposed a colloquium in which a number of legal experts representing their respective states and regions would discuss the removal of the dateline and how such a change would be attached to the 1951 Convention.

Thirteen legal experts attended the Colloquium on Legal Aspects of Refugee Problems in Bellagio, Italy from 21 to 28 April 1965. The countries from which the participants originated was Algeria, Colombia, France, Ghana, Hungary, India, Italy, Norway, Switzerland, United Kingdom, United States and Yugoslavia (the thirteenth delegate was from the World Council of Churches).[82] What was notable about this colloquium at the outset though was its members' insistence that there would be no revision of the Convention *itself*,[83] although it was:

> (I)ncreasingly recognized that the refugee problem was universal in nature and of indefinite duration and that, in this respect, the Convention was therefore no longer adequate. An increasing number of refugees were not covered by its terms, particular as it was limited to persons who had become refugees as a result of events occurring before 1 January 1951.[84]

By late 1966, the new High Commissioner Sadruddin Aga Khan went so far as to declare a Protocol as necessary because:

> The Convention had led to *an unfortunate discrimination* among the different groups of refugees, in particular with regard to the African refugees. Such discrimination

[79] UNHCR, High Commissioner Schnyder to Mr John Goormaghtigh, *Correspondence*, 20 July 1964; Folio 16, 16/1/3 GEN, Series 1, Fonds 11, p. 2.

[80] UNHCR, High Commissioner Schnyder to Mr John Goormaghtigh, *Correspondence*, 20 July 1964; Folio 16, 16/1/3 GEN, Series 1, Fonds 11, p. 2.

[81] Mr Lawrence Finkelstein to Mr Boyd Compton, *Memorandum: Proposed Colloquium on Legal Status of Refugees*, 21 October 1964; Rockefeller Foundation Archives, Record Group 1.2, Series 200, Box 484, Folder 4143, p. 2.

[82] UNGA, *Colloquium on the Legal Aspects of Refugee Problems*, Note by the High Commissioner, Executive Committee of the High Commissioner's Programme, Thirteenth Session, 5 May 1965, A/AC.96/INFO.40, Annex 1, p. 1. Rockefeller Foundation Archives, Record Group 1.2, Series 200, Box 484, Folder 4143, p. 2.

[83] UNGA, *Colloquium on the Legal Aspects of Refugee Problems*, Note by the High Commissioner, Executive Committee of the High Commissioner's Programme, Thirteenth Session, 5 May 1965, A/AC.96/INFO.40, Annex 1, p. 1. Rockefeller Foundation Archives, Record Group 1.2, Series 200, Box 484, Folder 4143, pp. 2–4.

[84] UNHCR, High Commissioner Schnyder to Mr Stavropoulos, *Memorandum by the United Nations High Commissioner for Refugees on the Report of the Colloquium on Legal Aspects of Refugee Problems held in April 1965 in Bellagio (Como), Italy*, 6 August 1965; Folio 136, 16/1/3 AMEND, Series 1, Fonds 11, p. 2.

conflicted with the Statute of his Office and was contrary to the universal spirit of the Convention itself.[85]

Regardless of the Convention's noted limitations, the result of the Colloquium was an agreement that a Protocol be attached to the 1951 Convention, removing the time and geographic constraints and accession to the Protocol would bring automatic accession to all the other articles in the 1951 Convention (therefore separate accession to both instruments was not required). This proposal was passed by the Executive Committee of the High Commissioner's Programme in November 1966.[86] The draft Protocol was then submitted to the General Assembly after consideration by the Economic and Social Council. To all intents and purposes, it appeared that developing states were finally receiving the independent universal refugee instrument they had long called for. In principle, it appeared that the Protocol would have the effect of universalizing the Convention and it was to be recognized as a separate legal document to the 1951 Convention.[87]

On closer inspection, however, the Protocol did not fully address these concerns and it ultimately failed to rectify the 1951 Convention's inherent limitations noted by Khan in 1966.[88] This judgment is based on two principal factors. The first was the choice of a Protocol rather than a revised Convention to replace the anachronistic 1951 Convention. Considering the force and regularity with which states such as Nigeria, Algeria, Asian and Latin American states (see above) objected to the 1951 Convention, it is not at all clear why a complete review of the 1951 Convention did not take place. Second, the Protocol essentially universalized the European definition of a refugee and attendant support mechanisms rather than developing a system based on the type of refugee crises confronting Africa, Asia and elsewhere. The Protocol had failed to progress according to the needs that High Commissioner Schnyder had identified when first broaching the topic in 1964. As a result, the Protocol did not persuade the majority of Southeast Asian states that international refugee law was relevant to solving the irregular migrant problems they confronted. The next three sections of this chapter will address this failure. First, I will look at the problems with selecting a 'Protocol' as opposed to

85 UNGA, *Official Records of the Third Committee*, Twenty-First Session, 1447th Meeting, 5 December 1966, p. 416.

86 UNGA, *Summary Records of the 141st to the 152nd Meetings held from 31 October to 8 November 1966*, Executive Committee of the High Commissioner's Programme, Sixteenth Session, A/AC.96/SR.141–152, p. 71.

87 Though Hathaway argues that the 1967 Protocol's universalization of the 1951 Convention was only 'substantive' in that it did not review the content of the definition itself. Hathaway, *The Law of Refugee Status*, 1991, pp. 10–11. Arguments supporting the 1967 Protocol as being the hallmark of the 1951 Convention's universalization are: Holborn, *Refugees: A Problem of Our Time*, 1975, p. 179; Soguk, *States and Strangers: Refugees and Displacements of Statecraft*, 1999, pp. 173–174; Loescher, *The UNHCR and World Politics: A Perilous Path*, 2001, pp. 124–125. Goodwin-Gill expresses doubt in general about the necessity of the separate instrument: Goodwin-Gill, *The Law of Refugee Status*, 1996, p. 297.

88 UNGA, *Official Records of the Third Committee*, Twenty-First Session, 1447th Meeting, 5 December 1966, p. 416; Hathaway, *The Law of Refugee Status*, 1991, pp. 10–11.

alternative routes for broadening the 1951 Convention. Second, I will look at the failure of the Protocol to broaden the refugee definition. I will then conclude with an examination of Southeast Asian's states continued resistance to the international refugee law instruments after the 1967 Protocol.

2.4 *Why a Protocol?*

The Protocol has been described as an 'innovation in international law'[89] in contrast to the 1951 Convention; it was quickly developed and passed in order to resolve growing complaints from developing states about the UNHCR and the 1951 Convention. Within two years of the Colloquium's draft Protocol being presented to the UNHCR's Executive Committee, the Protocol had come into force by 4 October 1967 (see Appendix 3).[90] The question remains however, *why* was a Protocol decided upon and what benefits/losses came from this 'exclusionary' approach?

It was agreed by the Bellagio Colloquium and the UNHCR that a Protocol was the most effective way to remove the Convention's time constraints for a number of reasons. First, the time constraints needed to be removed as swiftly as possible so that refugee groups currently not covered would be 'granted similar benefits by means of an international instrument'.[91] A legally binding instrument was necessary, but a new Convention would 'be too lengthy and cumbersome to beat the need for urgency'.[92] The Protocol would be the most effective means of avoiding:

> (T)he traditional amendment process which would have required calling an international conference of representatives of every government that was a party to the Convention. Such a conference would have consumed a great deal of time, would have opened up the entire Convention to possible amendments, and would have meant that any amendment proposed had to be accepted by every contracting party before it took effect.[93]

Second, a Protocol was seen as the way to go rather than an even quicker approach (for example a resolution or recommendation) because these more expedient alternatives would have no force and would 'lose the support of the African states'.[94] As noted earlier, African support was considered essential in the face of the emerging

89 Holborn, *Refugees: A Problem of Our Time*, 1975, p. 181.
90 Holborn, *Refugees: A Problem of Our Time*, 1975, p. 180.
91 UNGA, *Colloquium on the Legal Aspects of Refugee Problems*, Note by the High Commissioner, Executive Committee of the High Commissioner's Programme, Thirteenth Session, 5 May 1965, A/AC.96/INFO.40, Annex 1, p. 1. Rockefeller Foundation Archives, Record Group 1.2, Series 200, Box 484, Folder 4143, p. 2.
92 UNHCR, *Memorandum by the United Nations High Commissioner for Refugees on the Report of the Colloquium on Legal Aspects of Refugee Problems held in April 1965 in Bellagio (Como), Italy*, 23 September 1965; HCR/RS/31, Series 1, Fonds 11, 16/1/3 GEN, p. 2.
93 Holborn, *Refugees: A Problem of Our Time*, 1975, p. 181.
94 UNHCR, *Visit of Dr Urrutia to Legal Division on 13 April 1966*, 18 April 1966; Folio 1602, 16/1/3 GEN, Series 1, Fonds 11, p. 2.

regional approaches.[95] The UNHCR also feared that a resolution would open a Pandora's Box and prompt the General Assembly discussing the 'whole substance of the Convention'.[96] To avoid this, the UNHCR suggested that only 'a limited number of states'[97] should discuss an amendment to the Convention. The Pandora's Box fear was grounded in the fact that there remained a large number of governments resistant to the idea of accepting increased legal obligations, as they saw it, to an unforeseen number of potential refugees. Moreover, the High Commissioner wanted to limit the discussion to a small number of legal experts representing Europe, Africa, Asia, Latin America and the United States to permit the development of the core principles on this matter which would 'stimulate a concerted state practice'.[98] Third, the Protocol could effectively remove the time constraints from the Convention, while creating a new legal instrument that would be open to states not yet party of the Convention.[99] Fourth, the Protocol, as a legal instrument applying to 'new refugee situations should take the existing legal structure fully into account and should therefore be built upon the 1951 Convention'.[100] In the words of the High Commissioner—the 1951 Convention was still the 'most comprehensive instrument so far adopted in this field'.[101] Moreover, the 1951 Convention was already seen to contain 'a definition of the term "refugee" which is capable of universal application'.[102] However, the same memorandum raises a concern about the 1951 Convention's refugee definition,

> (E)xperience, and more especially recent experience of new refugee situations in Africa, has shown that certain States may not, for various reasons, be able to resort to individual eligibility determination…[and] it might be of advantage if the existing definition were supplemented by certain criteria for the prima facie determination of such group eligibility.[103]

95 Loescher, *The UNHCR and World Politics: A Perilous Path*, 2001, pp. 124–25.

96 UNHCR, *Visit of Dr Urrutia to Legal Division on 13 April 1966*, 18 April 1966; Folio 1602, 16/1/3 GEN, Series 1, Fonds 11, p. 2.

97 UNHCR, High Commissioner Schnyder to Mr John Goormaghtigh, *Correspondence*, 20 July 1964; Folio 16, 16/1/3 GEN, Series 1, Fonds 11, p. 2.

98 UNHCR, High Commissioner Schnyder to Mr John Goormaghtigh, *Correspondence*, 20 July 1964; Folio 16, 16/1/3 GEN, Series 1, Fonds 11, p. 2.

99 UNHCR, *Memorandum by the United Nations High Commissioner for Refugees on the Report of the Colloquium on Legal Aspects of Refugee Problems held in April 1965 in Bellagio (Como), Italy*, 23 September 1965; HCR/RS/31, Series 1, Fonds 11, 16/1/3 GEN, p. 2; UNHCR, *Visit of Dr Urrutia to Legal Division on 13 April 1966*, 18 April 1966; Folio 1602, 16/1/3 GEN, Series 1, Fonds 11, p. 2.

100 UNHCR, *Memorandum by the United Nations High Commissioner for Refugees on the Report of the Colloquium on Legal Aspects of Refugee Problems held in April 1965 in Bellagio (Como), Italy*, 23 September 1965; HCR/RS/31, Series 1, Fonds 11, 16/1/3 GEN, p. 3.

101 UNHCR, *Memorandum by the United Nations High Commissioner for Refugees on the Report of the Colloquium on Legal Aspects of Refugee Problems held in April 1965 in Bellagio (Como), Italy*, 23 September 1965; HCR/RS/31, Series 1, Fonds 11, 16/1/3 GEN, p. 3.

102 UNHCR, *Memorandum by the United Nations High Commissioner for Refugees on the Report of the Colloquium on Legal Aspects of Refugee Problems held in April 1965 in Bellagio (Como), Italy*, 23 September 1965; HCR/RS/31, Series 1, Fonds 11, 16/1/3 GEN, p. 3.

103 UNHCR, *Memorandum by the United Nations High Commissioner for Refugees on the Report of the Colloquium on Legal Aspects of Refugee Problems held in April 1965 in Bellagio (Como), Italy*, 23 September 1965; HCR/RS/31, Series 1, Fonds 11, 16/1/3 GEN, p. 5.

Nevertheless, the UNHCR rationalized that this 'legal problem' could not be considered in the Protocol debate because it was more important that 'the new international instrument should be both simple and *generally acceptable*'.[104] I will discuss the consequences of this decision in following sections on the outcome of the 1967 Protocol. For now it is important to note that further issues pertaining to the 1951 Convention *were* raised but were dismissed mainly out of concern that this would lead to the failure of the Protocol or an unending and unproductive discussion about the Convention.[105] Ultimately, prudential considerations took precedence over wider questions about the continued relevance of the Convention.

The Protocol achieved its prudential aim in that there was little debate in the Executive Committee or the General Assembly about the need for such an instrument. Many developing states in particular had been pushing for a long time for the UNHCR instrument to become universal, and Western states were not perturbed by the decolonized regions having to deal with their own refugee problems, now that it was not the concern of the former colonizers.[106] The desire for an instrument more responsive to global refugee problems was reflected in the speed with which the 1967 Protocol came into force: it was passed by the General Assembly on 16 December and came into force on 4 October 1967. The 1967 Protocol gained twenty-seven ratifications in the following two years; by 1972 fifty-two states were party to it. This was in contrast to the 1951 Convention which took ten years to achieve just twenty-seven ratifications.[107] However, did the 1967 Protocol meet the expectations of the states that it was mainly intended for—developing states dealing with large refugee groups? In the next section, I will this address question.

2.5 *The inadequacy of the 1967 Protocol*

At the Executive Committee session in 1966, the Protocol was placed on the agenda for discussion and was then to be submitted to the UN General Assembly through the Economic and Social Council so that 'the Secretary-General might be authorized to open the Protocol for accession by Governments within the shortest possible time'.[108] The UNHCR was confident of accessions because it had already

---

[104] UNHCR, *Memorandum by the United Nations High Commissioner for Refugees on the Report of the Colloquium on Legal Aspects of Refugee Problems held in April 1965 in Bellagio (Como), Italy*, 23 September 1965; HCR/RS/31, Series 1, Fonds 11, 16/1/3 GEN, p. 5. Emphasis added.

[105] UNHCR, *Visit of Dr Urrutia to Legal Division on 13 April 1966*, 18 April 1966; Folio 1602, 16/1/3 GEN, Series 1, Fonds 11, p. 2; Holborn, L. *Refugees: A Problem of Our Time* (New Jersey: Scarecrow Press, 1975), p. 181.

[106] Holborn, *Refugees: A Problem of Our Time*, 1975, pp. 180–186; Loescher, *The UNHCR and World Politics: A Perilous Path*, 2001, pp. 122–26.

[107] Holborn, *Refugees: A Problem of Our Time*, 1975, p. 182.

[108] UNGA, *Report of the United Nations High Commissioner for Refugees Part Two: Report on the Sixteenth Session of the Executive Committee of the High Commissioner's Programme from 31 October–8 November 1966*, Official Records of Twenty-First Session, Supplement No. 11 (A/6311/Rev.1), p. 19.

confirmed a number of states' support for widening the Convention.[109] In addition, the only states questioned about the introduction of the Protocol were those already members of the 1951 Convention and the state members of the Executive Committee at that time. Therefore, the total number of governments consulted was fifty-eight.[110] Membership of the Executive Committee at the Sixteenth Session comprised twenty-nine member states: five from Africa (Algeria, Madagascar, Nigeria, Tunisia and the United Republic of Tanzania); three from Latin America (Brazil, Colombia and Venezuela); four from the Middle East (Iran, Israel, Lebanon and Turkey). The remainder included fourteen states from Europe (Austria, Belgium, Denmark, Federal Republic of Germany, France, Greece, Holy See, Italy, Netherlands, Norway, Sweden, Switzerland, United Kingdom of Great Britain and Northern Ireland, and Yugoslavia), Australia, Canada, and United States of America. Only one state—China—was from Asia. There were no representatives from Southeast Asia.

The general consensus within the Executive Committee, which had the authority to decide on whether the Protocol would progress to the Economic and Social Council, was that the 1951 Convention be made 'universally applicable to refugees'.[111] Therefore, the Committee agreed to the High Commissioner submitting the draft Protocol to the General Assembly with the proviso that some governments intended to make 'further comments or submit amendments when the draft Protocol was examined by the Economic and Social Council and by the General Assembly'.[112]

There were some dissenting voices but these were limited in the General Assembly. The main criticism of the Protocol did not come to a head until it was passed at the General Assembly. During the discussions on the draft Protocol, two African states expressed discontent. Nigeria argued that the Protocol did not 'go far enough to solve the problems'.[113] First, the assistance provided to African refugees 'did not even represent one tenth of the already very small subsistence allowance given to refugees elsewhere than in Africa'.[114] Second, many African countries with 'still under-developed' economies were shouldering a 'crushing burden when the *problem*

109 Holborn, *Refugees: A Problem of Our Time*, 1975, p. 180.

110 UNGA, *Report of the United Nations High Commissioner for Refugees Part Two: Report on the Sixteenth Session of the Executive Committee of the High Commissioner's Programme from 31 October–8 November 1966*, Official Records of Twenty-First Session, Supplement No. 11 (A/6311/Rev.1), p. 18.

111 UNGA, *Report of the United Nations High Commissioner for Refugees Part Two: Report on the Sixteenth Session of the Executive Committee of the High Commissioner's Programme from 31 October–8 November 1966*, Official Records of Twenty-First Session, Supplement No. 11 (A/6311/Rev.1), p. 18.

112 UNGA, *Report of the United Nations High Commissioner for Refugees Part Two: Report on the Sixteenth Session of the Executive Committee of the High Commissioner's Programme from 31 October–8 November 1966*, Official Records of Twenty-First Session, Supplement No. 11 (A/6311/Rev.1), p. 18.

113 UNGA, *Official Records of the Third Committee*, Twenty-First Session, 1449th Meeting, 6 December 1966, p. 436.

114 UNGA, *Official Records of the Third Committee*, Twenty-First Session, 1449th Meeting, 6 December 1966, p. 437.

had not been of their making'.[115] Nigeria argued that African refugee problems had been caused by colonialism, and in particular, by the countries that had colonized Africa. They had a duty, Nigeria argued, to contribute to the UNHCR programme and 'acknowledge that they had a moral obligation to alleviate as much as possible the hardships for which they were responsible'.[116] Uganda said it would support the Protocol, but like Nigeria, felt that 'the text of the draft too general in nature and felt that it did not place the emphasis where it belonged'.[117] In particular, the economic burden caused by rising refugee populations in Africa required more specific resolutions to deal with problems and the 1951 Convention could not facilitate this.[118]

Other concerns about the 1967 Protocol expressed by developing states in the General Assembly largely focused on the need to provide more development assistance for refugee populated areas in developing states. There were also calls for more legal assistance and protection and it was hoped that the Protocol would fulfill this need. This emphasis on the need for the Protocol to deliver assistance benefits drove its swift passage and led to little dissent. However, a number of states expressed concern about the rapidity with which the 1967 Protocol was passed and with the lack of wide participation in the drafting and development of the Protocol.

At the end of the debate in the General Assembly—and after the vote had been finalized—delegates from the United Arab Republic (today Egypt and Syria), Afghanistan and Jamaica all expressed concerns about the Protocol because 'as an important United Nations treaty, it should have been discussed and adopted in its entirety before states were asked to accede to it'.[119] Madagascar also 'would have preferred the General Assembly to consider the articles of the draft protocol in the light of comments by States ... but had voted in favor of the draft resolution as a whole because if felt that the extension of the High Commissioner's mandate should not be delayed'.[120] The Philippines delegate had also voted in favor of the Protocol because 'it felt that there should be no discrimination between persons who had become refugees before 1 January 1951 and those who had become refugees after that date'[121] and because of the urgency of the High Commissioner's work. Contrary to the 1967 Protocol representing an 'innovation' for international law, the Philippine delegate expressed the opposite view. He said the Philippines,

115 UNGA, *Official Records of the Third Committee*, Twenty-First Session, 1449th Meeting, 6 December 1966, p. 437.

116 UNGA, *Official Records of the Third Committee*, Twenty-First Session, 1449th Meeting, 6 December 1966, p. 437.

117 UNGA, *Official Records of the Third Committee*, Twenty-First Session, 1449th Meeting, 6 December 1966, p. 440.

118 UNGA, *Official Records of the Third Committee*, Twenty-First Session, 1449th Meeting, 6 December 1966, p. 440.

119 UNGA, *Official Records of the Third Committee*, Twenty-First Session, 1450th Meeting, 7 December 1966, p. 446.

120 UNGA, *Official Records of the Third Committee*, Twenty-First Session, 1450th Meeting, 7 December 1966, p. 447.

121 UNGA, *Official Records of the Third Committee*, Twenty-First Session, 1450th Meeting, 7 December 1966, p. 446.

> (W)ould have preferred the Committee to discuss in detail every article of the Protocol…in the future, his delegation would insist that the articles of important international instruments should be considered in detail and would not consider the present case as a precedent.[122]

As discussed above, a UNHCR internal memo on the Bellagio Colloquium noted the need for the Protocol to be an 'independent instrument'[123] from the 1951 Convention. It needed to address the global nature of the refugee problem while embodying the principles of the 1951 Convention. To some extent, the 1967 Protocol refuted this need. However, it did not address the severe conditions which refugees and their hosts in developing countries endured, particularly when compared to conditions in developed states. The Protocol was unable to address the problems confronting many developing countries faced with mass influxes of refugees because the Convention's insistence upon individual refugee status determination was carried into the Protocol. Such individual determinations were simply not possible in cases of mass influx or other emergencies in developing countries. There are a number of reasons for this. First, there is often a lack of bureaucratized structures to handle such crises, and second, the military traditionally handle border breaches as security threats, preventing access to refugee determination procedures (even if they did exist).[124] Finally, in developing countries many refugees are forced to flee due to a general fear of violence caused by armed conflicts, as opposed to the specific fear of political persecution required by the 1951 Convention.[125] The 1967 Protocol did not change this situation; there was no 'certain criteria for the *prima facie* determination of such group eligibility'[126] within either of the refugee legal instruments. This perpetuated a problem for developing states forced to deal with mass refugee influxes, without the bureaucratic capacity to make individual status determination.

---

122 UNGA, *Official Records of the Third Committee*, Twenty-First Session, 1450th Meeting, 7 December 1966, p. 446.

123 UNHCR, *Memorandum by the United Nations High Commissioner for Refugees on the Report of the Colloquium on Legal Aspects of Refugee Problems held in April 1965 in Bellagio (Como), Italy*, 23 September 1965; HCR/RS/31, Series 1, Fonds 11, 16/1/3 GEN, pp. 2–4.

124 Chatelard, G. 'Jordan as a transit country: semi-protectionist immigration policies and their effects on Iraqi forced migrants', *New Issues in Refugee Research*, Working Paper No. 61 (Geneva: UNHCR Research Unit, 2002).

125 Schmeidl, 'Conflict and Forced Migration: A Quantitative Review', in Zolberg, A. R. and Peter M. Benda (eds.), *Global Migrants, Global Refugees: Problems and Solutions*', 2001; McGuiness, 'Legal and Normative Dimensions of the Manipulation of Refugees', in Stedman, S. J. and Fred Tanner (eds.), *Refugee Manipulation: War, Politics, and the Abuse of Human Suffering*, 2003.

126 UNHCR, *Memorandum by the United Nations High Commissioner for Refugees on the Report of the Colloquium on Legal Aspects of Refugee Problems held in April 1965 in Bellagio (Como), Italy*, 23 September 1965; HCR/RS/31, Series 1, Fonds 11, 16/1/3 GEN, p. 5.

2.6 *Asian responses to the 1967 Protocol*

The principle problem with the 1967 Protocol was that several key aspects—the definition of a refugee, the provision of assistance, and the expectations placed on states' bureaucratic capacity to respond to refugees—remained identical to the 1951 Convention. This represented a problem for many Southeast Asian states who wanted the instruments to reflect something of their knowledge and experience of refugees. However, as demonstrated above, the UNHCR feared that developed states would object to such demands and refuse to provide financial support.

After the 1967 Protocol was passed by the General Assembly, the UNHCR invested a lot of time attempting to garner Southeast Asian support for the instruments. The UNHCR frequently expressed frustration with the region's general refusal to accede to these instruments.[127] For their part, several Southeast Asian states claimed in the 1960s and 1970s that they had 'no knowledge' of the instruments because they were not involved in the drafting process. This was despite the fact that they had delegations at the General Assembly vote on the 1967 Protocol (and in a very small number of cases at the debate about the 1951 Convention).[128] Furthermore, they argued that such an instrument might curtail their sovereign right to decide who entered their territory. Finally, Southeast Asian states claimed that there would be times when they would choose not to adhere to the Convention on instrumental grounds, so accession would do little to alter current practice (further details provided in Chapter 4).

In the 1980s, the UNHCR attempted to redress this situation and persuade Southeast Asian states to accede. One way it did this was by lobbying Southeast Asian legal experts rather than governments—largely due to the long history of the latter's resistance to such overtures.[129] For example, in 1981 the UNHCR organized a Working Group on Current Problems in the International Protection of Refugees and Displaced Persons in Asia. The Southeast Asian participants were legal practitioners and the meeting was held in San Remo, Italy—somewhat

[127] UNHCR, W. K. McCoy to UNHCR Geneva, *Attitude to the Convention etc. in Indonesia*, 6 April 1969; Folio 1839A, 16/1/3 GEN, Series 1, Fonds 11, p. 2; UNHCR, V. Tedesco to Mr Tanner, *Correspondence*,17 April 1969; Folio 1837, 16/1/3 GEN, Series 1, Fonds 11; UNHCR, Mr O. Goundian to E. Jahn, *Report on the Asian-African Committee*, 6 February 1970; 16/1/3 GEN, Series 1, Fonds 11 ;UNHCR, UNHCR Legal Adviser in Asia to General Legal Section, *Explanatory Questions and Answers on the 1951 Convention and the 1967 Protocol*, 4 May 1982; Folio 245, 671.1 GEN, Series 2, Fonds 11.

[128] In 1967 at the General Assembly vote India, Malaysia, Philippines, Singapore and Thailand were all present. India was present at the 1951 Convention vote also in the General Assembly. UNHCR, W. K. McCoy to UNHCR Geneva, *Malaysia—Attitude to the Convention*, 15 March 1969; Folio 1829, 16/1/3 GEN, Series 1, Fonds 11; UNHCR, W. K. McCoy to UNHCR Geneva, *Singapore—Attitude to the Convention*, 24 March 1969; Folio 1831, 16/1/3 GEN, Series 1, Fonds 11; UNHCR, W. K. McCoy to UNHCR Geneva, *Attitude to the Convention etc. in Indonesia*, 6 April 1969; Folio 1839A, 16/1/3 GEN, Series 1, Fonds 11; UNHCR, Note for the File, *Meeting with Mr Dhar, the Indian Representative to the Executive Committee on 22 October 1969*, 27 October 1969; 16/1/3 GEN, Series 1, Fonds 11.

[129] UNHCR, D. McNamara to UNHCR Headquarters, *ASEAN Law Association—1980 General Assembly*, 19 January 1981; Folio 111, 383 ASEAN Protection, pp. 2–3.

removed from the situation at hand in Southeast Asia. The Working Group noted the exceptional political, social and economic problems that large-scale influxes of refugees could pose for developing countries.[130] It 'believed' that the 'development of international refugee law should be a priority task for the States of Asia. In particular, a *balanced and realistic development of that law* would be a valuable contribution to peace and stability in the Asian region'.[131] This statement seems to suggest two things. First, that Southeast Asian states were facing the problems they were in part because they were not all members of the 1951 Convention and 1967 Protocol. Second, either the current practice by Asian states in relation to refugees was not balanced or realistic, or Asian states were concerned that accession to international refugee law would not enable them to create balanced and realistic responses to large-scale refugee influxes.

However, the Working Group report emphasized international law's utility and condemned Asian states for not accepting international refuge law. It also referred to Asian states' 'special problems' created by large-scale influxes and how Asia, as a region, was more a 'geographical expression than a homogenous continent',[132] and thus more difficult to persuade about the benefits of international refugee law. Asia's diversity also needed recognition, as did the fact that a legal system developed in Western Europe would not work for Asia. Because,

> (I)n the development of a global legal system…it was essential, if the system were to be universally realistic and effective, that there be an adequate Asian contribution. The absence of such a contribution could only be to the detriment of the entire international community'.[133]

The report of the Working Group said:

> Believed that in the domain of the law the heart of the challenge was to *proceed* from the point of national sovereignty to international principles for the solution of refugee problems, whether at the regional or universal level….the Group believed that recent events had shown that to rest on national sovereignty was no longer adequate, since refugee problems, particularly those arising from large-scale influx, were international, even global in nature, and in many situations satisfactory solutions could only be obtained through international solidarity and co-operation.[134]

---

130 UNHCR, *Report of the Working Group on Current Problems in the International Protection of Refugees and Displaced Persons in Asia*, Under the Auspices of the UNHCR, International Institute of Humanitarian Law, San Remo, 19–22 January 1981 (Geneva: UNHCR, March 1981), pp. 2–3.

131 UNHCR, *Report of the Working Group on Current Problems in the International Protection of Refugees and Displaced Persons in Asia*, Under the Auspices of the UNHCR, International Institute of Humanitarian Law, San Remo, 19–22 January 1981 (Geneva: UNHCR, March 1981), p. 5.

132 UNHCR, *Report of the Working Group on Current Problems in the International Protection of Refugees and Displaced Persons in Asia*, Under the Auspices of the UNHCR, International Institute of Humanitarian Law, San Remo, 19–22 January 1981 (Geneva: UNHCR, March 1981), p. 5.

133 UNHCR, *Report of the Working Group on Current Problems in the International Protection of Refugees and Displaced Persons in Asia*, Under the Auspices of the UNHCR, International Institute of Humanitarian Law, San Remo, 19–22 January 1981 (Geneva: UNHCR, March 1981), p. 5.

134 UNHCR, *Report of the Working Group on Current Problems in the International Protection of Refugees*

However, this approach represented a problem for Southeast Asian states. For if acting through international solidarity was the only way to solve refugee problems, how could international law also protect state sovereignty? Furthermore, refugees were arriving in specific states, not in some great international sphere. In addition, it was not clear *which* law needed to proceed from national sovereignty to international principles for the solution of refugee problems. Whilst the argument being made by the Working Group was that states can only be fully sovereign when they comply with the rules of international law, Southeast Asian states argued that states, particularly developing ones, were only truly sovereign when they also play a role in the drafting of international law. This theme emerges repeatedly throughout the following four chapters and links with the book's overall argument that Southeast Asian states rejected international refugee law because they did not feel obliged to accede.

2.7 *Conclusion*

Was the adoption of the 1967 Protocol the moment where the 1951 Convention and UNHCR itself became truly universal? In a small and superficial sense it was, but in a larger more practical sense it was not. The abandonment of the time and geographical limitations on the definition of refugee status marked an important step forward. However, this was the sum of the Protocol's contribution. A problem remains with the refugee definition as its focus on political persecution has been at the cost of assisting and protecting larger numbers of people fleeing generalized situations of violence and abuse.

States expressed discontent with the speed that the 1967 Protocol was passed and its failure to address these issues at the voting session of the Protocol. Yet these same states expressed a reluctance to voice such concerns before the Protocol for fear of it not being passed and the Convention then not becoming *universalized* by the removal of the time and geographic constraints.[135] As a result, the 1967 Protocol was a compromise between the short-term humanitarian needs of refugees and the interests of states in Europe, Africa and Asia, which effectively sidelined serious discussion about many of the key sources of tension.

By 1981, when the UNHCR sponsored Working Group for discussion of refugees and displaced persons in Asia was held, the UNHCR had in fact capitulated to the fact that the Convention and Protocol were still rooted in the 'legal system in Western Europe'[136] and this was why their contribution of refugee knowledge

---

and Displaced Persons in Asia, Under the Auspices of the UNHCR, International Institute of Humanitarian Law, San Remo, 19–22 January 1981 (Geneva: UNHCR, March 1981), p. 5.

135 UNGA, *Official Records of the Third Committee*, Twenty-First Session, 1450th Meeting, 7 December 1966, pp. 446–447.

136 UNHCR, *Report of the Working Group on Current Problems in the International Protection of Refugees and Displaced Persons in Asia*, Under the Auspices of the UNHCR, International Institute of Humanitarian Law, San Remo, 19–22 January 1981 (Geneva: UNHCR, March 1981), p. 5

for that system was essential. However, in order to understand the development of Southeast Asian states' response to refugees and their understanding of international legal instruments pertaining to refugees, we need to examine their response to a refugee crisis. The Indochinese refugee population from 1975 to 1996 offers an excellent case. In this chapter, as in Chapter 1, I have demonstrated that international refugee law developed in the 1950s and 1960s while rooted in Western values and interests. The result was that these instruments did not constitute a serious attempt to develop a genuinely inclusive global understanding of, and response to, refugees. The cost of this was that Southeast Asian states had no sense of ownership of the law and thus felt no obligation to accede to the 1951 Convention and 1967 Protocol.

The 1951 Convention and 1967 Protocol's primary concerns were founded in a Eurocentric, Cold War environment that dominated the identity of a refugee and the procedures that responded to individuals fleeing their homelands. As such, they excluded alternative ways of understanding refugees by ruling out a broader, more generalized, refugee definition that incorporated groups or bureaucratic weakness in receiving states. By doing so, however, the legal framework inadvertently enabled some states to challenge its legitimacy on the grounds of Eurocentrism, which in turn weakened it and reduced the costs associated with refusing to abide by such 'legal obligations'. As will be discussed in Chapters 3–6, Southeast Asian states' refusal to sign the 1951 Convention and 1967 Protocol during the Indochinese refugee crisis from 1975 onwards was enabled by their ability to plausibly point to the Eurocentric nature of these texts as a legitimate reason for them not to accede. As such, they were able to demonstrate that the instruments were not relevant to their situation. However, the Indochinese refugee crisis also demonstrates that the relationship between Southeast Asian states and international refugee law was more than a zero-sum relationship of rejection. Southeast Asian states sought to legitimise their treatment of Indochinese asylum seekers by arguing their case *within* the legal framework provided by international refugee law. Southeast Asian states became adept at explaining why, within the parameters of the legal framework, their irregular migrant populations were 'non-genuine' refugees—thus legitimising their description of Indochinese asylum seekers as 'illegal migrants' or 'economic migrants'—in contrast to the 'genuine' refugee as expressed in the 1951 Convention and 1967 Protocol.

Chapter 3

The Beginning of the Indochinese Refugee Crisis: 1975–1979

Between 1975 and 1996, approximately three million people from Cambodia, Laos and Vietnam sought refuge in Southeast Asia and were either returned to their country of origin or resettled in third countries.[1] Of all the Southeast Asian states where the Indochinese sought first asylum, only the Philippines became a signatory to international refugee law during this period.[2] This chapter begins the exploration of why the largest refugee crisis to confront Southeast Asia since the Second World War did not prompt states in the region to accede to international refugee law. It looks at the initial stages of the Indochinese refugee crisis—between 1975 and 1979.

The chapter will proceed in three parts. The first part provides a brief historical overview of the myriad conflicts that inspired the Indochinese refugee crisis. The second part traces the development of Southeast Asian responses to the outbreak of the crisis. In particular, I focus on communications between Southeast Asian states and the UNHCR about the potential role of international refugee law in dealing with this crisis, and the key role that Western states played in enabling

---

[1] Robinson, *Terms of Refuge: The Indochinese Exodus and the International Response*, 1998, p. 2; UNHCR. *The Status of Refugees*, 2000, p. 102; Loescher, *The UNHCR and World Politics: A Perilous Path*, 2001. However, Robinson (1998), UNHCR (2000) and Loescher (2001) all note that the precise number of Indochinese who sought asylum may never be known as thousands perished in Southeast Asian waters at the hands of pirates. In addition, there were many who were able to seek refuge in the region—but did so covertly and thus their numbers are unknown.

[2] Philippines acceded on the 22 July 1981.

Southeast Asian states to manipulate the crisis to serve their perceived short-term interests. In 1978 and early 1979, the dramatic increase of asylum seekers in the region prompted Southeast Asian states to adopt brutal rejection practices against these populations. Southeast Asian states *refouled*[3] people seeking asylum in unseaworthy boats and refused to process those that managed to reach the shoreline. These actions prompted some Western states and the UNHCR to take a greater role in the crisis. This was negotiated through the 1979 Conference on Refugees and Displaced Persons in Southeast Asia. In the third and final section of this chapter, I discuss the outcome of the 1979 Conference and focus in particular, on the absence of demands for Southeast Asian states to adopt greater responsibility for the Indochinese refugee populations, other than providing temporary asylum. I argue that this outcome can be directly attributed to Southeast Asian states ability to manipulate the political and legal uncertainty surrounding the Indochinese refugee crisis in the period 1975–1979.

3.1 *A background to the Indochinese refugee crisis*

Indochina was highly unstable after World War II and the French remained determined to cling to what remained of their empire in the face of numerous concerted nationalist movements. The ensuing violence and instability prompted several refugee movements. Thailand had already received a significant number of Vietnamese and Laotian refugees who had fled the repression of pro-independence movements by the French in the 1940s and 1950s.[4] At the time, Thailand supported these independence movements and the refugees' arrival was not unwelcome, as Thailand hoped to gain more regional influence with the defeat of French imperialism. The majority of refugees were ethnic Vietnamese from Cambodia, Laos and Vietnam, and members of the Viet Minh (Vietnam communist party) or Lao Issara (Free Laotians). The Thai government at the time was largely unconcerned about having pro-communist Viet Minh migrants seek refuge in their thousands along their border regions. Indeed, Thai citizenship was offered to asylum seekers as they crossed the border and many were resettled in Thai provinces.[5]

---

[3] To *refoule* an asylum seeker to their country of origin, without first determining their claim to refugee status, is a breach of Article 33 in the 1951 Convention. However, the rule of *non-refoulement* has become so important that it is now considered to have customary status in international law. This means that even states not party to the 1951 Convention are expected to obey this law. See Lauterpacht, Sir E. and Daniel Bethlehem, 'The Scope and Content of the Principle of *non-refoulement*: Opinion', in Feller, E., Volker Turk and Frances Nicholson (ed.), *Refugee Protection in International Law: UNHCR's Global Consultations on International Protection* (Cambridge: Cambridge University Press, 2003). For a dissenting view see Hailbronner, K., 'Non-refoulement and "Humanitarian" Refugees: Customary International Law or Wishful Legal Thinking?', *Virginia Journal of International Law*, Vol. 26, No. 4 (1986).

[4] Poole, P. A. *The Vietnamese in Thailand: A Historical Perspective* (London: Cornell University Press, 1970).

[5] Poole, *The Vietnamese in Thailand: A Historical Perspective*, 1970, p. 41.

As the war between the Viet Minh and French forces continued (often called the First Indochinese War), Thailand's attitude towards refugees began to change. The Thai government became increasingly concerned about communist sympathy amongst its ethnic Chinese and Vietnamese communities and was fearful that its large recently victorious communist neighbor, China, would start to view these communities as a vehicle for introducing a communist opposition in Thailand. These fears were heightened when it became clear that the Viet Minh community in Thailand was receiving Chinese military aid to continue their struggle against the French.[6] Restrictions were then placed on the refugees by the Thai government. They could only live and work in the thirteen provinces along the Eastern and Northern borders of Thailand; the Viet Minh were asked to close their office in Bangkok; and in 1950 Thailand formally recognized the French-sponsored Bao Dai government in Vietnam. Thailand also acquiesced with France's request to restrict Viet Minh activities on the Thai-Lao border. Travel within the region was then limited for refugees, as they were assigned to one of five regions and had to seek permission from the Thai Ministry of the Interior before being allowed to travel to a neighboring province. The Viet Minh victory at Dien Bien Phu in 1954 led to the signing of the Geneva Accords. It was agreed that Cambodia and Laos would be declared 'neutral' states and that Vietnam would be temporarily divided into Northern and Southern halves pending elections.[7] The US assisted Thailand by meeting South Vietnamese officials to discuss the repatriation of refugees. At the same time, China's promise of peaceful coexistence seemed to have relaxed regional tensions enough for the ethnic Chinese population to start receiving more conciliatory treatment from the Thai government. However, the political involvement of Thailand's ethnic Vietnamese in the political wrangling between North and South in Vietnam meant that the Thai government remained determined to secure the return of these refugees to Vietnam over the following few years. In 1959, this was partially achieved when the Rangoon Accord on the repatriation of Vietnamese refugees was concluded by Thailand and North Vietnam. Between 1960 and 1964 approximately 35,000 refugees were repatriated. However, an estimated 50,000 refugees had fled to Thailand during the First Indochinese War (1946–1954).[8] The UNHCR believed that Thailand continued to shelter approximately 40,000 North Vietnamese after the end of the war.[9]

---

6 Poole, *The Vietnamese in Thailand: A Historical Perspective*, 1970, pp. 44–45; See also Chanda, N. *Brother Enemy: The War after the War* (New York: Collier, 1986); Weisner, L. *Victims and Survivors: Displaced Persons and Other War Victims in Vietnam, 1964–1975* (New York: Greenwood Press, 1988); Evans, G. and K. Rowley, *Red Brotherhood at War: Vietnam, Cambodia and Laos since 1975*, 2nd edn. (London: Verso, 1990).

7 Robinson, *Terms of Refuge: The Indochinese Exodus and the International Response*, 1998, p. 12.

8 Poole, *The Vietnamese in Thailand: A Historical Perspective*, 1970, p. 63; Robinson, *Terms of Refuge: The Indochinese Exodus and the International Response*, 1998, p. 15.

9 UNHCR, Asian Regional Section to UNHCR Geneva, *Outgoing Cable*, 2 September 1975; Folio 11, 671.1 GEN; Series 1, Fonds UNHCR 11, p. 4.

The Second Indochinese War began in 1964, when North Vietnamese forces allied with Viet Cong guerillas in the south launched attacks against the South Vietnamese government. With the Soviet Union assisting the North Vietnamese, it did not take long for the United States to become involved in what it perceived as a defensive attack against the encroaching threat of communism in the region. Over time, the United States played a significant role in the Vietnam conflict as well as in civil wars in Cambodia and Laos.[10] However, the superpower was unable to prevail. At the end of the Second Indochinese War in 1975 the United States withdrew all its forces from various locations in the Indochinese region, evacuating 65,000 Vietnamese and leaving hundreds of thousands of US supporters in Cambodia, Laos and Vietnam to their fate.[11] In April 1975, Saigon fell to the Vietnamese People's Army and the United States' immediate withdrawal left behind many who had assisted the South Vietnamese and US forces. In the same month, the Khmer Rouge captured Phnom Penh, and renamed Cambodia 'Democratic Kampuchea'. The Khmer Rouge ruled for three years which were characterized by genocidal brutality, and only came to an end with Vietnam's invasion of Cambodia in 1978. Cambodia's troubles continued after its liberation by Vietnam as the Khmer Rouge—indirectly supported by Thailand, the US, and UK—continued to wage an insurgency against the new regime installed by Hanoi. At the same time, the Laotian civil war, waged by the CIA-assisted Vientiane government and communist Pathet Lao forces was concluded by a communist victory, prompting an exodus of anti-communists. The CIA orchestrated the withdrawal of all foreign personnel from Laos, but left thousands of desperate Hmong (Lao hilltribe peoples who had supported government forces) stranded. During the following four years, Laos and Vietnam entered a turbulent period of communist reform. China and Vietnam also waged a brief border war in early 1979. Taken together, these crises prompted a wave of population movements as people fled the region by boat or land to seek asylum elsewhere in Southeast Asia.

3.2 *Southeast Asian responses at the beginning of the Indochinese refugee crisis: 1975–1977*

By 31 July 1975, approximately 184,000–200,000 Indochinese had already left their country of origin.[12] The UNHCR estimated that this figure comprised

[10] Daum, Andreas W., Lloyd C. Gardner and Wilfried Mausbach (eds.), *America, the Vietnam War, and the World: Comparative and International Perspectives* (Washington, D.C.; German Historical Institute New York: Cambridge University Press, 2003).

[11] Robinson, *Terms of Refuge: The Indochinese Exodus and the International Response*, 1998, p. 13, 17–19; Loescher, *The UNHCR and World Politics: A Perilous Path*, 2001, p. 190.

[12] UNHCR, E Soeprapto to Director of Protection Division, 'Mid-Annual Review of the Implementation of Programme of Work for 1975', 17 September 1975; 671.1 GEN; Series 2, Fonds UNHCR 11.

approximately 9,000 Cambodians, 32,000 Laotians and 143,000 Vietnamese.[13] The majority of Cambodian and Lao asylum seekers fled to Thailand, whereas the majority of Vietnamese had either been evacuated with US support or left by boat and were granted temporary asylum wherever they reached shore—mainly in Hong Kong, Japan, Malaysia, the Philippines, the Republic of Korea, Singapore and Thailand.

During this time there were mixed reports from the UNHCR about the level of cooperation being offered by Southeast Asian states. A UNHCR Executive Committee report in 1975 stated that right from the beginning, the UNHCR had difficulty ensuring that Indochinese people seeking asylum by boat would be rescued at sea or provided with asylum upon arrival in Southeast Asian states.[14] Ships that rescued asylum seekers from sinking boats were not always allowed to disembark those they had rescued.[15] On the other hand, E. Soeprapto, a UNHCR officer in the Asian Regional Section, reported in September 1975 that where the asylum seekers had resettlement offers, Asian states accepted these populations for temporary asylum with relatively few difficulties.[16] Indeed, by November 1975 the Asian Regional Section of the UNHCR requested that Headquarters create a Protection Officer position in Bangkok, because of the thousands of Indochinese asylum seekers who needed to have their refugee status determined as a precursor to resettlement in third countries.[17] The crucial point in all this, however, is that in 1975 the UNHCR's public position remained ambiguous. The UNHCR had not formally recognized the Indochinese as *prima facie* refugees, nor had it been asked by any Southeast Asian state to investigate the status of these asylum seekers.[18]

At the end of the Second Indochinese War, Southeast Asian states insisted that permanent resettlement of refugee within their borders was neither possible nor desirable. Consequently, the UNHCR did not ask governments in the region to

---

13 UNGA, *Report on UNHCR Assistance Activities in 1974–1975 and Proposed Voluntary Funds Programme and Budget for 1976, Addendum 1 Special Operations*, Submitted by the High Commissioner, Executive Committee of the High Commissioner's Programme, Twenty-Sixth Session, A/AC.96/516/Add.1, 15 September 1975, p. 17.

14 UNGA, *Report on UNHCR Assistance Activities in 1974–1975 and Proposed Voluntary Funds Programme and Budget for 1976, Addendum 1 Special Operations*, Submitted by the High Commissioner, Executive Committee of the High Commissioner's Programme, Twenty-Sixth Session, A/AC.96/516/Add.1, 15 September 1975, p. 17.

15 UNGA, *Report on UNHCR Assistance Activities in 1974–1975 and Proposed Voluntary Funds Programme and Budget for 1976, Addendum 1 Special Operations*, Submitted by the High Commissioner, Executive Committee of the High Commissioner's Programme, Twenty-Sixth Session, A/AC.96/516/Add.1, 15 September 1975, p. 19.

16 UNHCR, E Soeprapto to Director of Protection Division, 'Mid-Annual Review of the Implementation of Programme of Work for 1975', 17 September 1975; 671.1 GEN; Series 2, Fonds UNHCR 11, p. 2.

17 UNHCR, N Bwakira to Director of Protection Division, *Mid-Annual Review of the Implementation of Programme of Work for 1975: ASIA*, 13 November 1975; Folio 17, 602.3 ASIA; Series 2, Fonds UNHCR 11.

18 UNHCR, N Bwakira to Director of Protection Division, *Mid-Annual Review of the Implementation of Programme of Work for 1975: ASIA*, 13 November 1975; Folio 17, 602.3 ASIA; Series 2, Fonds UNHCR 11.

make a commitment to provide asylum, protection or local settlement for Indochinese asylum seekers. In fact, 'there was no mention of refugees at all' in the earliest communications between the UNHCR and Southeast Asian states in the immediate aftermath of the Vietnam war.[19] This created the space for Southeast Asian states to argue that they would only provide temporary asylum for refugees if the international community agreed to provide permanent resettlement places. This policy first took shape as an *ad hoc* response to the early stages of the refugee crisis, but by 1979 it had become the cornerstone of Southeast Asia's declared policy on the matter. The UNHCR's attempts to persuade Southeast Asian states to consider locally integrating some of the refugee arrivals were promptly refused. As suggested above, prior to the Indochinese refugee crisis, Southeast Asian states had resisted the UNHCR's attempts to persuade them to accede to the 1951 Convention and 1967 Protocol. Exclusion from the drafting process had enabled Southeast Asian states to claim they knew nothing of the instruments, that accession would threaten local legal systems and would even damage ASEAN's policy of 'non-interference'.[20]

There is some evidence that the UNHCR may have initially supported Southeast Asian states in this position. In 1975, Soeprapto recommended that the UNHCR should not push for accessions to the 1951 Convention or 1967 Protocol. Getting Southeast Asian states to provide temporary asylum to Indochinese was seen at the time as an important part of keeping the refugee crisis from escalating. Southeast Asian states had agreed to provide temporary asylum on the proviso that UNHCR would seek resettlement places. Any pressure on these states to permanently integrate asylum seekers may, Soeprapto warned, jeopardize the availability of temporary asylum.[21] Soeprapto argued that the specific context confronting Southeast Asian states needed to be taken into account when considering their lack of commitment to the international instruments. He listed the region's already high population and birth rate, the fact that Southeast Asian states were developing and needed all possible resources for their present population, their need for political stability, the centrality of security considerations in the handling of any problems and that persuading these states to voluntarily provide temporary asylum had been

[19] Robinson, *Terms of Refuge: The Indochinese Exodus and the International Response*, 1998, p. 20.

[20] ASEAN policy of 'non-interference' is a cornerstone of the ASEAN relationship in that states do not interfere in the affairs of other states. The 'non-interference' principle relates to ASEAN's primary goal of state consolidation and legitimisation. Acknowledging a neighbor's citizen as being a 'refugee' would threaten this ASEAN principle, as to declare a person to be a legitimate refuge requires at the same time, a declaration that the state of origin treats its people illegitimately; see Acharya, *Constructing a Security Community in Southeast Asia: ASEAN and the Problem of Regional Order*, 2001; Haacke, J. *ASEAN's Diplomatic and Security Culture: Origins, Development and Prospects* (London: RoutledgeCurzon, 2003) and Fortin, A., 'The Meaning of "Protection" in the Refugee Definition', *International Journal of Refugee Law*, Vol. 12, No. 4, 2001, pp. 548–576. UNHCR, The UNHCR Representative for Southeast Asia, *Promotion of International Protection in Southeast and East Asia*, 28 June 1974; Folio 97A, 671.1 GEN; Series 2, Fonds UNHCR 11.

[21] UNHCR, E Soeprapto to Director of Protection Division, *Mid-Annual Review of the Implementation of Programme of Work for 1975*, 17 September 1975; Folio 48, 671.1 GEN; Series 2, Fonds UNHCR 11, p. 2.

difficult enough. Rather strangely perhaps for a UNHCR official, he concluded that, 'becoming a party to the international instruments would only add unnecessary burdens' to Southeast Asian states.[22] The UNHCR Asian Regional Section concluded that the UNHCR should be grateful for the cooperation that Southeast Asian states were providing and any further attempts to persuade them to sign international instruments, or commit more than what they believed they could, should be avoided for an indefinite period.[23]

A further explanation for Soeprapto's recommendation was that the UNHCR at the time was reluctant to categorize the people fleeing Cambodia, Laos and Vietnam as *prima facie* refugees.[24] This was evident in the UNHCR's programmes during this period, which refer to the Indochinese as 'displaced persons'—not refugees. Recall that under the 1951 Convention a refugee was a person who sought refugee status 'owing to well-founded fear of persecution for reasons of race, religion, nationality, membership of a particular social group or political opinion, is outside the country of his nationality and is unable or, owing to such fear, is unwilling to avail himself of the protection of that country'.[25] *Prima facie* refugee status was granted to refugees in situations where it is unfeasible for them all to be individually assessed according to the 1951 Convention. Therefore, *prima facie* refugee status was sometimes granted to refugees fleeing *en masse.* UNHCR officials suggested that the majority of people fleeing Cambodia, Laos and Vietnam, were displaced due to a change of regime and a general fear of the new regime, and that none of them could claim membership of a particular group that was being persecuted.[26] The dilemma, however, was that whatever one called them, these populations were displaced, were increasing in numbers, and did not wish to return to their country of origin.[27]

---

22 UNHCR, E Soeprapto to Director of Protection Division, *Mid-Annual Review of the Implementation of Programme of Work for 1975*, 17 September 1975; Folio 48, 671.1 GEN; Series 2, Fonds UNHCR 11, p. 2.

23 UNHCR, E Soeprapto to Director of Protection Division, *Mid-Annual Review of the Implementation of Programme of Work for 1975*, 17 September 1975; Folio 48, 671.1 GEN; Series 2, Fonds UNHCR 11, p. 2.

24 Robinson, *Terms of Refuge: The Indochinese Exodus and the International Response*, 1998; Jackson, *The Refugee Concept in Group Situations*, 1999, p. 316, 319; Loescher, *The UNHCR and World Politics: A Perilous Path*, 2001.

25 UNHCR, *1951 Convention Relating to the Status of Refugees* (Geneva: UNHCR, 1951).

26 In all UNHCR documents up until the beginning of 1977, UNHCR refers to the Indochinese as 'displaced persons', for example, A/AC.96/516/Add.1, 15 September 1975, described the Indochinese situation as: Assistance to *Displaced Persons* and *Uprooted Persons* in Indochina (emphasis added). There is no reference to the Indochinese as refugees in these documents, and in fact the UNHCR says that its primary duty was to respond to all parties only on "purely humanitarian grounds" (9). UNGA, *Report on UNHCR Assistance Activities in 1974–1975 and Proposed Voluntary Funds Programme and Budget for 1976, Addendum 1 Special Operations*, Submitted by the High Commissioner, Executive Committee of the High Commissioner's Programme, Twenty-Sixth Session, A/AC.96/516/Add.1, 15 September 1975; Gill Loescher also makes this point about UNHCR's reluctance to acknowledge the Indochinese as *bona fide* refugees. Loescher, *The UNHCR and World Politics: A Perilous Path*, 2001, p. 190–191.

27 Robinson, *Terms of Refuge: The Indochinese Exodus and the International*, 1998, p. 24.

By the end of 1975 the crisis was clearly complicated. As more people fled Indochina, the UNHCR, the US and Southeast Asian states all began to recognize the sheer scale of the potential problem. The UNHCR had to respond to a growing number of asylum seekers arriving in states which would only provide temporary asylum on the proviso that the population would be resettled elsewhere without delay.[28] The US was growing weary of being seen as the only state that should take responsibility for resettling all those seeking asylum, while Southeast Asian states were determined to ensure that the US and UNHCR maintained responsibility for resettling these populations.[29] At the same time, as argued above, the UNHCR's efforts to persuade Southeast Asian states to sign the 1951 Convention and 1967 Protocol had taken a back seat.

In October 1975, over 55,000 'displaced persons' were in Thailand (15,000 Cambodians, 1, 500 Vietnamese and 39,000 Laotians)[30] and the need for financial support was increasing. The UNHCR continued to maintain that its sole function was to provide humanitarian assistance to the displaced persons and to assist with voluntary repatriation or resettlement in states that offered places.[31] The UNHCR chose not to argue that these groups were *prima facie* refugees or insist that other states provide resettlement offers. Noting that Thailand's response to the crisis had become increasingly *ad hoc*, the UNHCR signed a bilateral agreement with Thailand on 30 July 1975.[32] This stated that the UNHCR would provide Thailand with material assistance in return for the government's agreement to temporarily hold asylum seekers while the UNHCR sought 'lasting solutions to their problem, including assistance with voluntary repatriation and resettlement in other countries'.[33]

However, the US remained dissatisfied with the level of assistance being offered by the UNHCR. At the Third Committee of the United Nations General Assembly in November 1975, the US argued what was really needed was a discussion of how the UNHCR was going to protect these refugees and ensure that the international

---

28 Robinson, *Terms of Refuge: The Indochinese Exodus and the International*, 1998, p. 24.

29 UNGA, *Report on UNHCR Assistance Activities in 1974–1975 and Proposed Voluntary Funds Programme and Budget for 1976, Addendum 1 Special Operations*, Submitted by the High Commissioner, Executive Committee of the High Commissioner's Programme, Twenty-Sixth Session, A/AC.96/516/Add.1, 15 September 1975, p. 17.

30 UNGA, *Report on UNHCR Assistance Activities in 1974–1975 and Proposed Voluntary Funds Programme and Budget for 1976, Addendum 2 Assistance to Displaced Persons from Indochina in Thailand*, Submitted by the High Commissioner, Executive Committee of the High Commissioner's Programme, Twenty-Sixth Session, A/AC.96/516/Add.2, 2 October 1975, p. 2.

31 Jackson, *The Refugee Concept in Group Situations*, 1999, p. 324.

32 UNGA, *Report on UNHCR Assistance Activities in 1974–1975 and Proposed Voluntary Funds Programme and Budget for 1976, Addendum 2 Assistance to Displaced Persons from Indochina in Thailand*, Submitted by the High Commissioner, Executive Committee of the High Commissioner's Programme, Twenty-Sixth Session, A/AC.96/516/Add.2, 2 October 1975, p. 2.

33 UNGA, *Report on UNHCR Assistance Activities in 1974–1975 and Proposed Voluntary Funds Programme and Budget for 1976, Addendum 2 Assistance to Displaced Persons from Indochina in Thailand*, Submitted by the High Commissioner, Executive Committee of the High Commissioner's Programme, Twenty-Sixth Session, A/AC.96/516/Add.2, 2 October 1975, p. 2.

community shared this refugee burden.[34] The US did not believe that the problem should rest on its shoulders alone and frequently requested that other Western states recognize that people fleeing communism deserved a 'non-Communist alternative'.[35] The United States did not place diplomatic pressure on Southeast Asian states during this time because 'a large refugee presence in the ASEAN countries could create domestic unrest and jeopardize current friendly relations between the United States and the ASEAN countries'.[36] Thus, because of the imperative to maintain good economic and diplomatic relations with Southeast Asian states, it appears that the United States did not expect Southeast Asian states to bear the burden of dealing with the Indochinese refugees alone. However, the UNHCR was aware that most Western, particularly European, states were reluctant to take responsibility for the potentially large number of refugees flowing out of Indochina, and so the UNHCR continued to favor voluntary repatriation as the best solution. In the UNHCR's view, local integration in Southeast Asian states was politically impossible and, as these populations were not refugees, it argued that resettlement should only be considered in exceptional cases.[37]

Over the next two years, Thailand and other Southeast Asian states started to increase their resistance to the disembarkation of asylum seekers even on a temporary basis.[38] Thailand, the Philippines and Indonesia all argued that allowing so-called 'boat people' to land would only lead to a greater influx; they said the problem was a global one and that the Southeast Asian states should not have to deal with it alone.[39] At the same time, the United States increasingly pressured the UNHCR to appeal for international resettlement places.[40] Twenty, mainly Western, states responded to this appeal between 1975 and 1977. The key reasons for their response were the United States' influence on its allies and a collective concern for the growing dangers that the Indochinese asylum seekers were facing in the

---

[34] Robinson, *Terms of Refuge: The Indochinese Exodus and the International Response*, 1998, p. 22.

[35] Suhrke, A., 'Indochinese Refugees: The Impact on First Asylum Countries and Implications for American Policy', *A Study Prepared for the Use of the Joint Economic Committee Congress of the United States* (Washington: US Government Printing Office, 1980), p. 3.

[36] Suhrke, A., 'Indochinese Refugees: The Impact on First Asylum Countries and Implications for American Policy', *A Study Prepared for the Use of the Joint Economic Committee Congress of the United States* (Washington: US Government Printing Office, 1980), p. 3.

[37] UNGA, *Report on UNHCR Assistance Activities in 1974–1975 and Proposed Voluntary Funds Programme and Budget for 1976, Addendum 2 Assistance to Displaced Persons from Indochina in Thailand*, Submitted by the High Commissioner, Executive Committee of the High Commissioner's Programme, Twenty-Sixth Session, A/AC.96/516/Add.2, 2 October 1975.

[38] Summary reports by UNHCR on the 'boat people' for each week through this period shows the increasing denial by Southeast Asian states to boat people arrivals unless the UNHCR guaranteed that the asylum seekers' asylum would be temporary only. UNHCR, *Weekly Notes*; File 602.3; Series 2, Fonds UNHCR 11.

[39] Loescher, *The UNHCR and World Politics: A Perilous Path*, 2001, p. 192; Thailand, the Philippines and Indonesia all emphasise this in UNGA, *Summary Record of the 285th Meeting held on 5 October 1977*, Executive Committee of the High Commissioner's Programme, Twenty-Eighth Session, A/AC.96/SR.285, 10 October 1977; and UNGA, *Summary Record of the 287th Meeting held on 6 October 1977*, Executive Committee of the High Commissioner's Programme, Twenty-Eighth Session, A/AC.96/SR.287, 17 October 1977.

[40] Loescher, *The UNHCR and World Politics: A Perilous Path*, 2001, pp. 191–192.

region. Loescher and Robinson both note how the United States at this time was more than willing to recognize the Indochinese as refugees because their flight served as a justification for the US decision to wage war in Indochina—the many refugees leaving communist regimes was seen as proof of the justified fight against communism in this region.[41]

3.3 *The deepening crisis: 1977–1978*

The UNHCR's position started to change in 1977. Gradually, it adopted the view that regardless of the protestations of Southeast Asian states, Indochinese asylum seekers were at least *prima facie* refugees (until proven otherwise) deserving the protection afforded by the 1951 Convention and 1967 Protocol. In his 1977 annual report, Prince Sadruddin Aga Khan, the High Commissioner for Refugees clarified the UNHCR's position on refugees and displaced persons. He stated that a person who does not cross an internationally recognized border should be treated as a displaced person; a refugee is someone who fits the definition of a refugee under Article 1, of the 1951 Convention, or when the General Assembly through a resolution, calls upon the UNHCR to protect and assist a particular group of people.[42] However, Ivor Jackson argues that the term 'displaced persons', which was the UNHCR's preferred label for the Indochinese between 1975–77, was introduced by the UNHCR to identify groups of people who could mount a *prima facie* case for refugee status.[43] By labeling them 'displaced persons', Jackson argues, the UNHCR accepted Southeast Asian claims that Indochinese asylum seekers were not necessarily refugees although the possibility was left open that they could become so.[44] In other words, the UNHCR had tacitly awarded itself the role of determining who was, and who was not, a *bona fide* refugee.[45] In 1977, the UNHCR's Executive Committee formed the 'Sub-Committees of the Whole on International Protection' and released 'Note(s) on Asylum and Non-Refoulement'. At these meetings, member states from the Executive Committee discussed matters of refugee protection. In the Notes, states were reminded of the fact that asylum seekers should never be refused asylum because an asylum seeker could be a legitimate refugee. In the Note on Asylum, it was said that Indochinese leaving

41 Robinson, *Terms of Refuge: The Indochinese Exodus and the International Response*, 1998; Loescher, *The UNHCR and World Politics: A Perilous Path*, 2001.

42 UNGA, *Report on the Twenty-Eighth Session of the Executive Committee of the High Commissioner's Programme, High Commissioner's Opening Statement*, Executive Committee of the High Commissioner's Programme, Twenty-Eighth Session, A/AC.96/549 Annex 1, 4 October 1977, p. 4.

43 Jackson, *The Refugee Concept in Group Situations*, 1999, p. 323.

44 A legal positivist position though, would claim that a person is a refugee if they meet the Convention definition and this is *regardless* of whether they are determined as such. This implies that the Convention's rules are exogenous to the determination process and depends on a rigid separation of the written law from its political, social and normative context. See Higgins, *Problems and Processes: International Law and How We Use It*, 1994.

45 Jackson, *The Refugee Concept in Group Situations*, 1999, p. 323.

in small boats for other countries in the region were being refused permission to land and that people were losing their lives as a result. The Note succinctly advised that this practice should not continue.[46] By noting these *refoulement* practices the UNHCR had begun to implicitly identify the Indochinese asylum seekers as *prima facie* refugees.[47]

Unsurprisingly, many Southeast Asian states rejected this view. Several used the October 1977 UNHCR Executive Committee to insist that the Indochinese *displaced persons* were not their responsibility. Rather, it was one of 'international dimensions and only concerted and substantial international action could resolve it'.[48] Japan, the Philippines and Indonesia all agreed with Thailand's insistence on international assistance in return for the continuing availability of temporary asylum.[49] This view was by now, the cornerstone of Southeast Asian policy towards Indochinese asylum seekers and would continue as such well into the 1990s.

By the end of 1977, the Indochinese refugee population had further worsened. In Malaysia, the number of boat people had risen from 1,157 at the beginning of the year to 6,974 by December. Within the first six months of 1978, 13,219 boat people sought refuge in Malaysia. Malaysia also had approximately 90,000 Filipinos seeking refuge from the conflict in the Mindanao islands at the same time. The UNHCR, in its Assistance Activities report for 1977–78, stated that as the refugee population kept increasing, the cost of resettlement and the urgent need for places also increased.[50] The UNHCR also argued that the rising number of boat people in transit was caused by countries of first asylum providing only 'limited opportunities for local integration'.[51] In Thailand, for example, the refugee population had risen from 25,000 at the beginning of 1977, to 97,600 by 1 January 1978, and 113,300 on 30 June 1978. The ethnic breakdown in June 1978 was 96,000 from Laos, 14,000 from Cambodia and 3,200 from Vietnam.[52] In the two years

---

46 United Nations Social and Economic Council, *Note on Asylum*, Submitted by the High Commissioner, Executive Committee of the High Commissioners' Programme, Economic and Social Committee, Twenty-Eighth Session, EC/SCP/4, 24 August 1977, p. 3.

47 To *refoule* an asylum seeker to their country of origin, without first determining their claim to refugee status, is a breach of Article 33 in the 1951 Convention.

48 UNGA, *Summary Record of the 285th Meeting held on 5 October 1977*, Executive Committee of the High Commissioner's Programme, Twenty-Eighth Session, A/AC.96/SR.285, 10 October 1977, p. 9.

49 UNGA, *Summary Record of the 285th Meeting held on 5 October 1977*, Executive Committee of the High Commissioner's Programme, Twenty-Eighth Session, A/AC.96/SR.285, 10 October 1977, p. 9.

50 UNGA, *Report on UNHCR Assistance Activities in 1977–1978 and Proposed Voluntary Funds Programmes and Budget for 1979*, Submitted by the High Commissioner, Executive Committee of the High Commissioner's Programme, Twenty-Ninth Session, A/AC.96/553, 9 August 1978, p. xiv.

51 UNGA, *Report on UNHCR Assistance Activities in 1977–1978 and Proposed Voluntary Funds Programmes and Budget for 1979*, Submitted by the High Commissioner, Executive Committee of the High Commissioner's Programme, Twenty-Ninth Session, A/AC.96/553, 9 August 1978, p. xiv.

52 UNGA, *Report on UNHCR Assistance Activities in 1977–1978 and Proposed Voluntary Funds Programmes and Budget for 1979*, Submitted by the High Commissioner, Executive Committee of the High Commissioner's Programme, Twenty-Ninth Session, A/AC.96/553, 9 August 1978, p. xiv.

since 1975, the UNHCR had been able to resettle only 63,300 asylum seekers in Thailand to third countries.

By October 1978, the number of asylum seekers had dramatically risen once again. Arrivals into Southeast Asian states had risen from 5,800 in 1 January 1978 to over 13,000 by 31 August 1978, with only 3,500 being resettled. Therefore, the rate of arrivals was now far outstripping the rate of departures to resettlement locations in third countries.[53] Given that most of the region's states tied continuing acceptance of asylum seekers to their rapid departure to third states for resettlement, the increasing disparity between incomings and outgoings was a major cause of concern.

In the last few months of 1978, three factors served to further strain the relationship between Southeast Asian states and the UNHCR. The first factor, indicated above, was the dramatically rising numbers of Indochinese seeking asylum in Southeast Asian states in the later half of 1978. The second factor was the beginning of organized people trafficking/smuggling[54] with Southeast Asian individuals commissioning boats in order to transport mainly ethnic Chinese from Vietnam to various destinations in Southeast Asia. This often took place with the cooperation of the Vietnamese authorities, who were not displeased that potential Chinese fifth columnists were leaving. Most of these boats attempted to disembark their 'people cargo' in Southeast Asian states, creating a situation where *bona fide* refugees became intermingled with people who had fled with the consent and assistance of the Vietnamese government (although it should be noted that people who paid for their flight might also have been refugees).

The third factor that further strained the relationship between Southeast Asian states and UNHCR was the increasing instability of Indochina itself, with the invasion by Vietnam into Cambodia, the brief skirmish war between China and Vietnam in early 1979 and the further increase in the regional asylum seeker population that these two armed conflicts provoked. Not only did these conflicts have tangible negative consequences, measured in terms of victims and increased numbers of asylum seekers, they also had an important negative impact on the potential for regional cooperation. This third factor in particular made Southeast Asian states increasingly determined, in the face of regional instability, to maintain their domestic stability by stemming the flow of asylum seekers and guarantee international assistance.

---

53 UNGA, *Report on Report on UNHCR Assistance Activities in 1977–1978 and Proposed Voluntary Funds Programmes and Budget for 1979 Addendum 1*, Submitted by the High Commissioner, Executive Committee of the High Commissioner's Programme, Twenty-Eighth Session, A/AC.96/553/Add.1, 3 October 1978, p. 5.

54 The UNHCR documents at the time, referred to the 'trafficking' of Indochinese refugees. Since then, I am aware that there has been a more precise delineation between the term 'trafficking' and 'smuggling' as enclosed in Protocol against the Smuggling of Migrants by Land, Sea and Air, supplementing the United Nations Convention against Transnational Organised Crime, 15 November 2002 and Protocol to Prevent, Suppress and Punish Trafficking in Persons, especially Women and Children, supplementing the United Nations Convention against Transnational Organised Crime, 15 November 2000.

3.4 *Rising gap between incoming asylum seekers and resettlement places: 1978–1979*

In 1978, the UNHCR admitted that the ever increasing number of asylum seekers was not being matched by a requisite growth in resettlement places.[55] It was at this point that Southeast Asian states started to doubt the UNHCR's ability to deliver what had been promised and Southeast Asian states began to take a harder line towards asylum seekers, including the *refoulement* of boat people and people that reached borders by land. The prevalent explanation for Southeast Asian states' hardened stance against the refugees in the late 1970s has been that it was a racist reaction against the predominantly ethnic Chinese asylum seekers.[56] However, in Thailand the ethnic Chinese population were the smallest contingent of refugees; Laotian and Cambodians formed the bulk of the refugees. In general, the 'racism' explanation does not match the situation that was developing at the time in Southeast Asia.

First of all, 'racist' states rarely offer temporary asylum to those they are prejudiced against and as mentioned earlier, the majority of Southeast Asian states were commended by the UNHCR in 1975 for their willingness to provide temporary asylum for populations not even yet processed as *bona fide* refugees. Second, while it is true that the position of Southeast Asian states towards Indochinese refugees hardened in 1978, this was less a response to the refugees themselves and more a response to the lack of international assistance and the increasing gap between resettlement places being offered and the number of refugees arriving. It is thus important to note what the region's states actually argued when they complained about the increasing number of Indochinese asylum seekers. Mr. Adlan, the observer for Malaysia at the 1978 UNHCR Executive Committee meeting, raised concerns about the increasing burden Southeast Asian states were experiencing with the Indochinese asylum seekers. He claimed it was a problem that not one Southeast Asian state was a member of the Executive Committee, in spite of the fact that UNHCR had declared Southeast Asia as an 'area giving cause for great concern'.[57] Adlan identified a pressing need for permanent Southeast Asian representation on

---

55 UNGA, *Report on Report on UNHCR Assistance Activities in 1977–1978 and Proposed Voluntary Funds Programmes and Budget for 1979 Addendum 1*, Submitted by the High Commissioner, Executive Committee of the High Commissioner's Programme, Twenty-Eighth Session, A/AC.96/553/Add.1, 3 October 1978, p. 4.

56 O'Connor Sutter, V. *The Indochinese Refugee Dilemma* (Baton Rouge: Louisiana State University Press, 1990); Muntarbhorn, *The Status of Refugees in Asia*, 1992; Suhrke, 'The "High Politics" of Populations Movements: Migration, State and Civil Society in Southeast Asia', in Weiner, M. (ed.), *International Migration and Security*, 1993; Robinson, *Terms of Refuge: The Indochinese Exodus and the International Response*, 1998; Castles, 'International Migration and the Nation-State in Asia', in M. A. B. Siddique (ed.), *International Migration into the 21st Century: Essays in Honour of Reginald Appleyard*, 2001.

57 UNGA, *Summary Record of the 295th Meeting held on 10 October 1978*, Executive Committee of the High Commissioner's Programme, Twenty-Ninth Session, A/AC.96/SR.295, 12 October 1978, p. 10.

the Executive Committee in order for the Committee to understand and make decisions based on the experiences of states involved. In line with this, Adlan also stressed 'an urgent need for the international community to make a greater effort to find resettlement opportunities for those refugees now in Malaysia in particular, and South-East Asia in general'.[58]

Malaysia, Thailand and other Southeast Asian states expressed similar concerns to visiting UNHCR officials and in the Executive Committee about the level of resettlement places being offered by other states. They complained that third states were making their selection criteria too stringent in order to reduce the number of Indochinese refugees they resettled.[59] Most Southeast Asian states felt that the number of resettlement places being offered by third states was not keeping pace with refugee arrivals and that the processing of asylum seekers was too slow. Even the United States admitted that the assistance being provided by third states to the Indochinese refugees 'left much to be desired'.[60] Thus, the rising number of asylum seekers and failure of higher resettlement offers caused a great deal of concern among Southeast Asian states who were deeply worried that they would be called upon to bear the full burden of assisting the asylum seekers.

3.5 *The role of people smugglers*

Prior to 1978, many refugees found asylum by crossing the land border into Thailand, where some would then be sent on to Malaysia for processing, or stay in Thailand for processing and resettlement. Others found their way in small boats to the territorial waters of countries in Southeast Asia. Many of these boats were unseaworthy and had to be rescued by larger vessels whilst still in international waters. However, with the increase of anti-Chinese sentiment in Viet Nam, many ethnic Chinese became increasingly desperate to leave and were willing to pay people smugglers to guarantee their departure. Therefore, trafficking asylum seekers loomed as a potentially lucrative business for those with boats and government contacts. A vessel called the *Southern Cross* was one of the first organized people trafficking movements where an ethnic Chinese businessman negotiated with the Vietnamese government to collect a number of asylum seekers willing to pay to

58 UNGA, *Summary Record of the 295th Meeting held on 10 October 1978*, Executive Committee of the High Commissioner's Programme, Twenty-Ninth Session, A/AC.96/SR.295, 12 October 1978, p. 10.

59 UNHCR, High Commissioner to Assistant Secretary for Human Rights and Humanitarian Affairs, US Office of the Assistant Secretary of States, *Correspondence*, 4 October 1978; Folio 6, 100.THA.GEN—Thailand—General; Series 2, Fonds UNHCR 11; UNGA, *Summary Record of the 295th Meeting held on 10 October 1978*, Executive Committee of the High Commissioner's Programme, Twenty-Ninth Session, A/AC.96/SR.295, 12 October 1978, p. 10.

60 UNGA, *Summary Record of the 295th Meeting held on 10 October 1978*, Executive Committee of the High Commissioner's Programme, Twenty-Ninth Session, A/AC.96/SR.295, 12 October 1978, p. 3.

leave. A vessel was purchased, which was commanded by a Finish sea captain and a Singaporean businessman, who controlled the 'financial arrangements'.[61]

The *Southern Cross* collected hundreds of asylum seekers waiting at the mouth of Saigon River. Vietnamese officials were paid for gathering the asylum seekers there, and then after stowing the asylum seekers and their payment in gold on board, the ship radioed for help in international waters saying that it had been swamped by hundreds of asylum seekers from four large fishing junks. The *Southern Cross* then proceeded to attempt to disembark its passengers in Malaysia but was prevented by the Malaysian government, which was starting to adopt a hard-line in accepting more asylum seekers. The Malaysian authorities would only take the critically ill off the ship and then the Malaysian Navy escorted the *Southern Cross* back into international waters. Singapore would not accept the ship either. The *Southern Cross* then sailed into Indonesian waters and deliberately drifted onto the rocky outcrop that was Pengibu Island. The Indonesian authorities were suspicious of the ship grounding itself, but did not seem to suspect that the ship was trafficking refugees. The UNHCR requested that the Indonesian authorities grant the Vietnamese temporary asylum while third country resettlement places were found.

However, the same group that dispatched the *Southern Cross* were now making bigger plans. The plan was to purchase another vessel, the *Hai Hong*, and take the 'people cargo' to Hong Kong. However, upon arrival, the Vietnamese government expected the *Hai Hong* to take the 1,200 paying passengers *and* a further 1,300 passengers for free. The Vietnamese officials insisted that if the *Hai Hong* did not comply, all crewmen and the Captain on board the *Hai Hong* would be arrested and the ship's exit would be blocked. The *Hai Hong* organizers then complied with the Vietnamese authorities and the extra 1,300 were taken on board. Thus, there were some 2,450 passengers when the vessel set sail for refuge on the 24 October 1978. Unsurprisingly, the conditions on board were cramped and very unsafe. After a typhoon made the passage to Hong Kong impossible, the ship started to have engine trouble and with food and water running low the Captain decided to head for Indonesian waters. But upon arrival on a remote island at the top of the Indonesian archipelago, the *Hai Hong* did not radio Indonesian officials for assistance. Instead, it contacted the office of the UNHCR in Malaysia.

This time around there was immediate suspicion about the *Hai Hong*'s story. Why had the Captain not immediately notified authorities when refugees had forcibly boarded the boat in international waters? How had 2,450 asylum seekers survived the typhoon in small boats to then swamp the *Hai Hong*? The *Hai Hong* Captain told Indonesian officials that the ship had been swamped a day earlier, 21 October, than what he had told UNHCR. The Captain also claimed that the asylum seekers had forced the *Hai Hong* to head for Australia. None of these reported events added up. The dates that the *Hai Hong* gave did not match the distance it covered;

[61] Wain, B. *The Refused: The Agony of the Indochina Refugees* (Hong Kong: Dow Jones [Asia] Company Ltd., 1981), p. 26.

there was also doubt that asylum seekers would have demanded for Australia when Thailand and Malaysia were the main destinations boat people requested for disembarkation when rescued by ships until then. The Indonesians, doubtful of the *Hai Hong's* story and not wanting to further increase their asylum load, decided to expel the ship from its waters and escorted it back into international waters.[62] At the same time, the UNHCR and Western governments investigated the *Hai Hong* and discovered that not only had the vessel been registered for a trip it did not make, but that a ship fitting the description of the *Hai Hong* had been seen in Vietnam on 24 October collecting refugees, with Vietnamese authorities present. It was already known Vietnamese asylum seekers often had to bribe security officials to get past the borders, but now it was becoming apparent that the Vietnamese authorities were actually complicit in shipping their own citizens abroad. This *Hai Hong* case contributed to the Southeast Asian states view that a hard line against asylum seekers was necessary to discourage further trafficking.[63]

The Australian government told the UNHCR that this voyage had to fail and stand as a deterrent to future attempts. Barry Wain claims the UNHCR office in Kuala Lumpur reached the same conclusion; it communicated with its Geneva head office about the possibility of labeling the people on board the *Hai Hong* as 'illegal immigrants'. However, when the Kuala Lumpur office made a public announcement on 3 November, it concentrated on how the 'activities of unscrupulous elements'[64] were jeopardizing the UNHCR's attempts to find durable solutions for genuine refugees. Meanwhile the *Hai Hong* was traveling between Southeast Asian states, not being allowed to disembark anywhere. The situation on board became desperate with the death of one woman, the birth of two babies and passengers on board becoming increasingly uneasy with their situation. On 8 November, the Captain of the *Hai Hong* spoke to the UNHCR office in Kuala Lumpur, giving its course, which was towards to Malaysian waters in the Straits of Malacca, but he refused to provide information about the destination of the ship or the conditions on board. On 9 November, the *Hai Hong* anchored just off Port Klang, 25 miles west of Kuala Lumpur. The Royal Malaysian Navy and marine police vessels blocked the *Hai Hong* from entering the port and refused to allow anyone to disembark. When the police did board the ship to investigate, they found large numbers of people were dehydrated and ill from lack of adequate water and food, children with open sores and an extreme lack of sanitation on the ship. The Malaysian government delivered water, food and medical supplies, but insisted that the *Hai Hong* leave Malaysian waters. The chief police officer explained that the ship had to leave because the claims made by the Captain were not believable. It was inconceivable that 2,500 people had gathered at one place in the South China Sea to board the ship successfully.[65] The view of Malaysia, other Southeast Asian states and several

[62] Wain, *The Refused: The Agony of the Indochina Refugees*, 1981, p. 28.
[63] Wain, *The Refused: The Agony of the Indochina Refugees*, 1981, p. 28.
[64] Wain, *The Refused: The Agony of the Indochina Refugees*, 1981, p. 27.
[65] Wain, *The Refused: The Agony of the Indochina Refugees*, 1981, p. 30.

Western states was that the *Southern Cross* and now the *Hai Hong* had illegally trafficked people with the assistance of the Vietnamese authorities.[66]

Malaysia, like Indonesia and Australia, refused to recognize the *Hai Hong's* passengers as refugees deserving asylum. The UNHCR at this stage also seemed convinced that the people who had paid for their passage would *not* meet the 1951 Convention's definition of a refugee. However, attempts by UNHCR officials to board the *Hai Hong* were blocked by the Malaysian authorities due, they claimed, to choppy seas and the possibility that the officials would be taken hostage. Wain doubted these reasons, given that two foreign journalists had been allowed to board only the day before.[67] When, a few days later, the UNHCR's Kuala Lumpur office again attempted to arrange for food and medical supplies to be taken on board, the government informed the UNHCR that the ship was to be taken out to international waters and no one was to board with supplies or otherwise.

The UNHCR stepped up its efforts to assist the passengers on the *Hai Hong* on 15 November when its Kuala Lumpur office declared that they be considered *prima facie* refugees. The UNHCR considered these passengers to be refugees and their status justified the granting of immediate asylum by the Malaysian government. However, the Malaysian government refused to recognize the *Hai Hong* passengers as refugees. At the time, a New York Times article describing the Malaysian stand-off said that

> (T)he issue for Malaysia, according to the Cabinet minister, is not the publicly stated one that the *Hai Hong* passengers were not genuine refugees but a fear that, if they were admitted to Malaysia's over-crowded refugee camps, other ships carrying thousands of passengers would follow. As long as Malaysian authorities continue to be human in dealing with refugees the Western countries . . . are pushing Western responsibilities off on Malaysia's shoulders.[68]

Wain argues it was at this moment that distrust between UNHCR and Southeast Asian countries intensified, and this lack of trust would continue on both sides for the remainder of the crisis.[69] Before this point, the relationship between Southeast Asian states and the UNHCR had been cordial at best. Now though, the Southeast Asian authorities perceived the UNHCR to be apparently supporting 'illegal migrants' in a situation where the region's governments had given a clear indication of their views about the matter. This only helped to exacerbate the idea that the UNHCR was unwilling as well as unable to properly assist the region's states. In response, the UNHCR claimed that payment for passage did not eliminate the possible validity of a refugee claim, nor could the conditions on board the *Hai Hong* continue indefinitely. Moreover, it insisted that these peoples' claims needed processing. In the end, the UNHCR was able to secure enough resettlement offers

---

66 Wain, *The Refused: The Agony of the Indochina Refugees*, 1981, p. 31.

67 Wain, *The Refused: The Agony of the Indochina Refugees*, 1981, p. 32.

68 Kamm, H., 'While Refugees Wait Off Malaysian Coast, Talks Remain at Impasse', *The New York Times*, 18 November 1978.

69 Wain, *The Refused: The Agony of the Indochina Refugees*, 1981, p. 33.

by Western states to persuade the Malaysian authorities to allow the *Hai Hong* passengers to disembark and be processed for resettlement. Nonetheless, the stand-off over the *Hai Hong* was the trigger for a prolonged disagreement between the UNHCR and Southeast Asian states over the conditions that invalidated a claim for refugee status.

3.6 *Conflict in Indochina*

The third factor to shape the increasingly harsh response of Southeast Asian states, which made them reluctant to recognize even the most basic rights of refugees was the increasing political instability in Indochina by the end of 1978. The Vietnamese invasion of Cambodia, on 25 December 1978, not only increased the flow of refugees from Cambodia into Thailand in particular, but it also led to even higher numbers of Vietnamese seeking refuge from the fighting on the two borders. Vietnam justified the attack by arguing that the Khmer Rouge's constant attacks on villages on the Vietnamese side of their shared border legitimated the use of force in self-defence. Vietnam also argued that the Khmer Rouge had planned to invade Vietnam and even argued that it had actually invaded on the request of the new Cambodian government that had overthrown the Khmer Rouge.[70] These arguments were not widely accepted by states in the region and China retaliated to what it saw as an acceptable demonstration of Vietnamese regional hegemony by launching an offensive against Vietnam in February 1979.

In the second half of 1978, Thailand, Malaysia, Indonesia, the Philippines and Singapore had become increasingly resistant to providing further temporary asylum and were refusing permission to disembark ships laden with Indochinese asylum seekers. This practice was also extended to unseaworthy vessels containing asylum seekers. The crisis came to a peak in November 1978 when Thailand proclaimed that it would accept no more asylum seekers.[71] Then, four hundred asylum seekers died in the space of just eleven days when six boats capsized off the Thai and Malaysian coastline. At this time, there were already 61,729 boat refugees in camps throughout Malaysia, Hong Kong, Thailand, Indonesia, Philippines, Singapore, Macau, South Korea and Japan. Thailand alone had a total 140,000 refugees when the refugees who had sought asylum by land from Laos, Cambodia and Vietnam were included.[72] By the end of 1978, China also had 200, 000 Vietnamese refugees. Even after its borders were closed in July 1978, approximately 8,000 refugees were still entering China each month.[73]

---

70 Nicholas Wheeler discusses the Vietnam's intervention in Cambodia in more depth in his book, *Saving Strangers: Humanitarian Intervention in International Society* (Oxford: Oxford University Press, 2000). What Wheeler says is interesting about Vietnam's justification for their actions is that though they could have stressed humanitarian arguments very easily in light of the fact that the Khmer Rouge committed genocide atrocities—they did not.

71 Loescher, *The UNHCR and World Politics: A Perilous Path*, 2001, p. 205.

72 Robinson, *Terms of Refuge: The Indochinese Exodus and the International Response*, 1998, p. 32.

73 Robinson, *Terms of Refuge: The Indochinese Exodus and the International Response*, 1998, p. 39.

With the onset of a rising crisis in the region in late 1978, the UNHCR called a meeting amongst 'concerned states' to discuss the 'rapidly deteriorating' situation in Southeast Asia.[74] The Meeting on the Displaced Persons and Refugee Situation in South East Asia was held in December 1978, and it concluded that, 'there could be no humane or durable solutions unless Governments grant at least temporary asylum in accordance with internationally accepted humanitarian principles'.[75] However, it was also noted that resources and infrastructure in first asylum countries were being stretched to their limit, and that their continued provision of temporary asylum 'depended on commitments for resettlement in third countries and the avoidance of residual problems in the area'.[76] The meeting concluded that the region's dependence on international relief should not escalate because of the potential 'adverse consequences',[77] instead, self-sufficiency projects should be intensified and promoted. We can draw two important conclusions from the resolutions that came out of this meeting. First, the meeting's emphasis on the need for Southeast Asian states to provide asylum, based on internationally accepted humanitarian principles, demonstrates that these states were not responding to appeals for them to treat asylum seekers according to the principles set out in international refugee law, in particular the principle of *non-refoulement*. The proposed strategy, of making the provision of international relief conditional on Southeast Asian states taking a greater role in providing temporary and longer term asylum places, clearly backfired. The international community agreed to provide $US12 million and only 5,000 more resettlement places; this was described by the Malaysian representative as a mere 'drop in the ocean'.[78] Second, just before the 1978 meeting, the term 'self-sufficiency projects' was used for the first time by the UN High Commissioner for Refugees Poul Hartling in a private letter on the situation in Thailand to the US Secretary of State. His intention was for the term 'self-sufficiency projects' to replace 'local settlement' or 'resettlement' which, according to Hartling, only caused 'confusion and misunderstandings' for the Thai government.[79] So-called 'self-sufficiency projects' he said, would be more acceptable

[74] UNGA, *Report on UNHCR Assistance Activities in 1978–1979 and Proposed Voluntary Funds Programmes and Budget for 1980*, Submitted by the High Commissioner, Executive Committee of the High Commissioner's Programme, Thirtieth Session, A/AC.96/564, 14 August 1979, p. xv.

[75] UNGA, *Background Note Dated 9 July 1979 prepared by the United Nations High Commissioner for Refugees for the Meeting on Refugees and Displaced Persons in South-East Asia*, Convened by the Secretary-General of the United Nations as Geneva 20–21 July 1979, Annex 1, A/34/627, 7 November 1979, p. 11.

[76] UNGA, *Background Note Dated 9 July 1979 prepared by the United Nations High Commissioner for Refugees for the Meeting on Refugees and Displaced Persons in South-East Asia*, Convened by the Secretary-General of the United Nations as Geneva 20–21 July 1979, Annex 1, A/34/627, 7 November 1979, p. 11.

[77] The meaning implied in the report was that Southeast Asian states would rely on international support to the point where they would not take on any responsibility to develop assistance projects themselves—which is precisely what occurred.

[78] Loescher, *The UNHCR and World Politics: A Perilous Path*, 2001, p. 206; Kamm, H., 'Geneva Meeting Yields Few Pledges of Aid for Indochinese Refugees', *The New York Times*, 17 December 1978.

[79] UNHCR, High Commissioner to Assistant Secretary for Human Rights and Humanitarian

to Southeast Asian states because refugees would be involved in development programmes with local Thai populations and would eventually be assimilated. The wider Thai economy would also benefit from the investment attached to this programme. Hartling argued that this would obviate the need to grant refugee status to asylum seekers and would encourage other Southeast Asian states to take more of the burden.[80] Of course, 'self-sufficiency projects' were quite clearly aimed at shifting the burden from the West onto Southeast Asian states and presented a rationale to justify reducing the number of resettlement places offered by third states. The UNHCR's association with this plan was particularly damaging. It deepened Southeast Asian distrust of the UNHCR and taught Southeast Asian states that compliance with the UNHCR's demands would in all likelihood lessen their chances of receiving financial and humanitarian assistance (as will be further suggested in Chapter 4 and 5). It was these two lessons, learnt at the December 1978 meeting, which contributed to a hardening of Southeast Asian responses to the escalation of refugees in the beginning of 1979.

In every Southeast Asian state, and in the region's peripheral states, the number of Indochinese refugee arrivals dramatically increased in the first half of 1979.[81] China estimated that it had 250,000 Indochinese refugees in total, but were willing to settle most of these refugees if they wanted this. Hong Kong's total rose from 10,900 at the end of 1978 to over 53,000 by June 1979, with a resettlement rate of only 5,000 in this six month period. In Indonesia, the number of arrivals rose from 700 in 1977, to 3,000 in 1978 and then 43,000 in the first six months of 1979. Once again, the resettlement rate remained low: just 2,000 in the first six months of 1979. Malaysia's Indochinese refugee population rose from 6,000 in 1977 to 63,000 in 1978; then in the first six months of 1979 more than 50,000 people arrived. The total number of people resettled was approximately 42,000 in all of 1978 and the first six months of 1979. Therefore, by June 1979 Malaysia had 75,000 'boat people' still in need of a durable solution. In the Philippines, refugee numbers had never been as high as in other ASEAN states because of its relative distance from Indochina. However, by 1979 the Philippines had also experienced a notable increase in refugee numbers. In 1977, the Philippines' boat arrival population was 1,200, but by June 1979 it was 5,200. Japan's numbers actually declined, with 722 arrivals and 596 departures in 1978, and in the first six months of 1979, 269 people arrived and 305 departed, leaving Japan with a total caseload of 561 refugees in June 1979. Singapore set a 'ceiling limit' whereby

Affairs, US Office of the Assistant Secretary of States, 4 October 1978; Folio 6, 100.THA. GEN—Thailand—General; Series 2, Fonds UNHCR 11, p. 2.

80 UNHCR, High Commissioner to Assistant Secretary for Human Rights and Humanitarian Affairs, US Office of the Assistant Secretary of States, 4 October 1978; Folio 6, 100.THA. GEN—Thailand—General; Series 2, Fonds UNHCR 11, p. 2.

81 The following numbers for each country comes from: UNGA, *Report on UNHCR Assistance Activities in 1978–1979 and Proposed Voluntary Funds Programmes and Budget for 1980*, Submitted by the High Commissioner, Executive Committee of the High Commissioner's Programme, Thirtieth Session, A/AC.96/564, 14 August 1979, pp. 141–179.

it would accept no more than 1,000 refugees in its territory seeking permanent asylum at any one time, and their stay had a 120 day limit. Therefore, Singapore would not allow anyone to enter its territory unless resettlement places in third countries could be guaranteed for every person permitted to seek asylum. In 1978, 1,865 refugees arrived in Singapore with the swift departure for resettlement of 1,182. By June 1979, Singapore had only 445 Indochinese refugees. During this tumultuous period, Thailand's position was particularly difficult.[82] By June 1979, the total number of refugees in Thailand's camps stood at over 173,000. Out of this number, 50,000 had arrived in the first six months of 1979. However, the total number of resettlement places offered in that period was just 17,000. Laotians, who still represented the highest number of refugees in Thailand, were arriving at the rate of 4,700 a month since 1978.[83] On top of this, there were 85,000 Cambodians on the Thai border who had been attempting to enter camps since Vietnam's invasion of Cambodia. The Thai government refused UNHCR requests to provide assistance to these refugees and, unlike the other refugee populations, these people were placed under the authority of the military as opposed to the Ministry of the Interior. Furthermore, the UNHCR weekly notes from the Asian Regional Section in May 1979, estimated that there had been attempts by at least 150,000 Cambodians in mid-April to enter or pass through Thailand.[84] Most of this population had been forcibly or voluntarily returned to Cambodia. Then, '42,000 were returned to Democratic Kampuchea at the beginning of June 1979' by the Thai military authorities.[85]

Archival evidence suggests that the situation in Thailand was actually far worse than the UNHCR's reports were admitting. A UNHCR memo in July 1979 stated that UNHCR had not been able to trace the majority of the population forcibly returned to Cambodia.[86] The majority were now under the control of Vietnamese forces and their status was unknown.[87] Another 7,000 ethnic Chinese had been

[82] UNGA, *Report on UNHCR Assistance Activities in 1978–1979 and Proposed Voluntary Funds Programmes and Budget for 1980,* Submitted by the High Commissioner, Executive Committee of the High Commissioner's Programme, Thirtieth Session, A/AC.96/564 (14 August 1979), p. 165.

[83] Robinson, *Terms of Refuge: The Indochinese Exodus and the International Response,* 1998, p. 50.

[84] UNHCR, S Bari to Director of Protection, *Weekly Notes for 24 to the 31 May 1979,* 31 May 1979; Folio 101, 602.3 ASIA; Series 2, Fonds UNHCR 11, p. 2.

[85] UNGA, *Report on UNHCR Assistance Activities in 1978–1979 and Proposed Voluntary Funds Programmes and Budget for 1980,* Submitted by the High Commissioner, Executive Committee of the High Commissioner's Programme, Thirtieth Session, A/AC.96/564 (14 August 1979), p. 165.

[86] UNHCR, S Bari to Director of Protection, *Weekly Notes for 29 June to the 5 July 1979,* 5 July 1979; Folio 106, 602.3 ASIA; Series 2, Fonds UNHCR 11, p. 2.

[87] The UNHCR never publicly condemned the Thai government for their action. Daniel Unger says that it was because the United States requested that UNHCR did not due to the fact that Thailand was still being relied upon as the first state of asylum for most Indochinese arrivals. Also, as Robinson accounts, because the ICRC head delegation in Bangkok was ordered to leave Thailand upon condemning the Thai government and military for such action. High Commissioner Poul Hartling expressed concern in a letter to Prime Minister Kriangsak, and through the US, France, Australian and Canadian embassies present were able to secure asylum for 1,500 before

abandoned in the border area and 2,800 had attempted to remain as close to the Thai-Cambodia border as possible. However, 800 of these on the border were stranded in the middle of a minefield without food and dying from exploding mines, illness and starvation.[88] W. Courtland Robinson says that in fact out of the 154,925 Cambodia who attempted to enter Thailand in this period, 108,719 had been forcibly pushed back into Cambodia by the end of June 1979.[89] Robinson also points out that the number that died from being forcibly returned into Cambodian territory at gun point by the Thai military will never be really known due to the dense forest and the unknown number killed by Vietnamese and Khmer Rouge forces. The Thai military reportedly also opened fire on asylum seekers when they refused to cross areas known to be strewn with mines.[90]

Therefore, by the end of 1978 and the beginning of 1979 there were a number of interacting factors affecting Southeast Asian states' response to the unfolding refugee crisis. However, Southeast Asian states responded by adopting a hardline position towards asylum seekers; to prevent the escalation of this population and compel the international community to 'share the burden'. Southeast Asian states were frustrated with the UNHCR's refusal to declare that asylum seekers on board ships like the *Hai Hong* were illegal migrants. This, combined with the decreasing number of resettlement offers, was causing Southeast Asian states to distrust the UNHCR's ability to assist with the refugee problem. Southeast Asian states had agreed to provide temporary asylum in the early stages of the refugee crisis, but as refugee numbers increased, as resettlement offers decreased and as the Indochinese region became more unstable, they decided at the beginning of 1979 to attempt to renegotiate their response to the crisis.

3.7 *1979 Conference on Refugees and Displaced Persons in Southeast Asia*

As indicated above, by June 1979, Southeast Asian states were beginning to refuse to allow any ship carrying 'boat people' or rescued asylum seekers to disembark on their shores.[91] Thailand also employed this policy for land arrivals (discussed

they were also to be forcibly removed. Unger, "Ain't Enough Blanket: International Humanitarian Assistance and Cambodian Political Resistance", in Stedman, S. J. and Fred Tanner (eds.), *Refugee Manipulation: War, Politics and the Abuse of Human Suffering*, 2003; Robinson, *Terms of Refuge: The Indochinese Exodus and the International Response*, 1998, p. 49.

88 UNHCR, S Bari to Director of Protection, *Weekly Notes for 29 June to the 5 July 1979*, 5 July 1979; Folio 106, 602.3 ASIA; Series 2, Fonds UNHCR 11, p. 2.

89 Robinson, *Terms of Refuge: The Indochinese Exodus and the International Response*, 1998, p. 50.

90 Robinson, *Terms of Refuge: The Indochinese Exodus and the International Response*, 1998, pp. 45–49.

91 From the 15 March to 5 July 1979, each UNHCR Memo *Weekly Notes* reports the chronological increase of Southeast Asian states refusal to accept any more Indochinese asylum seekers, and their attempts to prevent the asylum seekers from arriving on shore or crossing land borders. First Indonesia, then Malaysia, Philippines and Thailand, all declare there were to be no more admission of asylum seekers into their territory. Then throughout May, each of these countries started to

above). On 30 June 1979, ASEAN issued a joint communiqué stating that its member states would not accept new arrivals.[92] They also declared their right to 'return all refugees—including those held in transit camps—to their countries of origin, unless they were accepted for resettlement "within a reasonable time"'.[93] In June 1979 the UN Secretary General Kurt Waldheim invited the ASEAN countries and sixty-six other states to attend a Meeting on Refugees and Displaced Persons in Southeast Asia to be held in Geneva on 20–21 July 1979. ASEAN gave its support to the conference and agreed to discuss potential refugee processing centre sites in Indonesia and the Philippines, which, it hoped, would lessen the first asylum load borne by other Southeast Asian states.[94]

The UN placed three key objectives on the agenda at the 1979 Indochinese conference. The first objective was to persuade Southeast Asian states to resume the provision of temporary asylum to Indochinese refugees. It was acknowledged that this could not happen until the second objective was met, which was to persuade the international community, particularly the West, to provide more resettlement places and liberalize its procedures for processing Indochinese refugees so that more could be accepted. In addition, it was hoped that these states (many of whom were also major UNHCR donor states) would increase their contributions for the care and maintenance of refugees awaiting resettlement in asylum camps. The third objective was to persuade Vietnam to cooperate with the refugee effort and this meant that the Vietnamese authorities needed to stop encouraging mass departures.

Secretary-General Waldheim opened the conference by stressing the severity of the Indochinese refugee problem. Over 350,000 people were being provided with temporary asylum in ASEAN countries and Hong Kong and in the preceding four years over a million from Indochina had sought asylum.[95] The Secretary-General stressed that, in light of these figures and the dire situation, it was essential that the 'rest of the world should act in a decisive way to ease this tremendous burden

tow unseaworthy boats back into international waters. No ship was allowed to disembark rescued asylum seekers unless UNHCR gave direct resettlement guarantees for each person. All appeals from the UNHCR High Commissioner and the UN Secretary-General for Southeast Asian states to respect the principles of asylum, non-refoulement and duty to rescue those in distress at sea was ignored. By early July, the UNHCR was unable to account for missing boat people in Malaysian and Indonesian waters. UNHCR, *Weekly Notes 29 June to 5 July 1979*; File 602.3; Series 2, Fonds UNHCR 11, pp. 1–2.

92 ASEAN, *Joint Communiqué of the Twelfth ASEAN Ministerial Meeting*, Bali, Indonesia, 30th June 1979 (Jakarta: Terbatas, ASEAN Sekretariat Nasional, 1979).

93 UNHCR, *Weekly Notes 29 June to 5 July 1979*; File 602.3; Series 2, Fonds UNHCR 11, p. 1.

94 UNGA, *Background Note Dated 9 July 1979 prepared by the United Nations High Commissioner for Refugees for the Meeting on Refugees and Displaced Persons in South-East Asia*, Convened by the Secretary-General of the United Nations as Geneva 20–21 July 1979, Annex 1, *Report of the Secretary-General*, A/34/627, 7 November 1979, p. 4.

95 UNGA, *Background Note Dated 9 July 1979 prepared by the United Nations High Commissioner for Refugees for the Meeting on Refugees and Displaced Persons in South-East Asia*, Convened by the Secretary-General of the United Nations as Geneva 20–21 July 1979, Annex 1, A/34/627, 7 November 1979, p. 5.

imposed upon those countries'.[96] If the rest of the world did this it would '*enable those States* [Southeast Asian] *to adhere to the principle of first asylum* and to contribute within the limit of their possibilities to an over-all action that would lead to desirable solutions for the refugees'.[97] This statement helped to reaffirm Southeast Asian states' belief that they were owed assistance, and not obliged to act. In essence, it was being said that Southeast Asian responses to the crisis could be conditional, as Southeast Asian states could only be expected to provide first asylum if other states provided resettlement places; Waldheim allowed Southeast Asian states to strengthen their strategy of using the UNHCR to further their own interests, despite the UNHCR's mandated obligations which suggested otherwise.

Furthermore, the perception that Southeast Asian states were different from states in other regions in terms of their capacity to respond to a refugee crisis, was vindicated when the Secretary-General argued that the first asylum states were still developing countries 'confronted with serious economic and social constraints, [and] it was essential then that countries outside the area assumed the *principal responsibility* for resettlement'.[98] Western states responded to Waldheim's call by pledging 260,000 resettlement places at this conference. This was a significant jump from the 125,000 places that had been offered just a few months earlier in May 1979.[99] The financial contribution totaled $US160 million, with an extra US$25 million dedicated solely to what were described as durable solutions.[100] It should be noted that both the resettlement numbers and financial contribution were significantly larger than those offered to African states in 1979, despite the fact that Africa had the world's highest refugee population at the time. Africa received US$68,501,700 for 1979, and only a few hundred resettlement places that year.[101] The UNHCR tended more towards local integration for refugees in Africa as the

---

[96] UNGA, *Background Note Dated 9 July 1979 prepared by the United Nations High Commissioner for Refugees for the Meeting on Refugees and Displaced Persons in South-East Asia*, Convened by the Secretary-General of the United Nations as Geneva 20–21 July 1979, Annex 1, A/34/627, 7 November 1979, p. 5.

[97] UNGA, *Background Note Dated 9 July 1979 prepared by the United Nations High Commissioner for Refugees for the Meeting on Refugees and Displaced Persons in South-East Asia*, Convened by the Secretary-General of the United Nations as Geneva 20–21 July 1979, Annex 1, A/34/627, 7 November 1979, p. 5. Emphasis added.

[98] UNGA, *Background Note Dated 9 July 1979 prepared by the United Nations High Commissioner for Refugees for the Meeting on Refugees and Displaced Persons in South-East Asia*, Convened by the Secretary-General of the United Nations as Geneva 20–21 July 1979, Annex 1, A/34/627, 7 November 1979, p. 5. Emphasis added.

[99] UNGA, *Background Note Dated 9 July 1979 prepared by the United Nations High Commissioner for Refugees for the Meeting on Refugees and Displaced Persons in South-East Asia*, Convened by the Secretary-General of the United Nations as Geneva 20–21 July 1979, Annex 1, *Initiatives Taken Since the Meeting*, A/34/627, 7 November 1979, p. 7.

[100] UNGA, *Background Note Dated 9 July 1979 prepared by the United Nations High Commissioner for Refugees for the Meeting on Refugees and Displaced Persons in South-East Asia*, Convened by the Secretary-General of the United Nations as Geneva 20–21 July 1979, Annex 1, A/34/627, 7 November 1979, p. 7.

[101] UNGA, *Report on the Resettlement of Refugees*, Submitted by the High Commissioner, Executive Committee of the High Commissioner's Programme, Thirtieth Session,, A/AC.96/568, 28 August 1979, pp. 2–3.

best solution, on the basis that it was better for African refugees to 'remain within their own cultural region'.[102] Therefore, African states continued to make do with local integration solutions and comparatively small amounts of financial support for refugees often seeking asylum in a neighboring war torn country.[103]

In contrast, the financial and resettlement offers to Southeast Asian states underlined the fact that more cooperation was forthcoming from Western countries when protection measures were breached as opposed to when they were followed. Consequently, the Philippines government agreed to the creation of a refugee processing centre as did Indonesia. The plan was that refugees already processed and awaiting resettlement would be sent to these countries, in order to free up the first asylum camps mainly in Malaysia and Thailand. All costs for these centres were to be fully funded by donor states through the UNHCR. Although the Secretary-General remarked that assistance to first asylum states came with the expectation that the principle of asylum for refugees arriving by land or sea would be respected, there was also acknowledgement that first asylum states had the right to expect there would be 'no residual problems',[104] meaning that the refugees would not be permitted to stay in the long term.

A quick comparison between the July 1979 Conference and the December 1978 Conference demonstrates that Southeast Asian states had learnt that non-cooperation reaped higher dividends than cooperation. Recall that in December 1978 most Southeast Asian states were still cooperating by providing temporary refuge to asylum seekers. Yet the first asylum states were bitterly disappointed with the offers of support and assistance made in December 1978 (see above). In 1979, however, after first asylum states had started practicing *refoulement* more assistance was forthcoming from Western states. Therefore, the lesson learned for Southeast Asian states was that the 'squeaky wheel gets the grease'. Crucially, it was not until Southeast Asian states insisted the situation was beyond their control and that they no longer felt compelled to adhere to provide first asylum because resettlement states were not keeping their end of the deal, that the West began to offer significant levels of assistance.

One of the most significant points of contention at the 1979 Conference was the question of Vietnam's responsibility for the refugee crisis. Since Vietnam's

---

102 UNGA, *Report on the Resettlement of Refugees*, Submitted by the High Commissioner, Executive Committee of the High Commissioner's Programme, Thirtieth Session, A/AC.96/568, 28 August 1979, pp. 2–3.

103 UNGA, *Report on the Resettlement of Refugees*, Submitted by the High Commissioner, Executive Committee of the High Commissioner's Programme, Thirtieth Session, A/AC.96/568, 28 August 1979, pp. 2–3; UNGA, *Report on the UNHCR Assistance Activities in 1978–1979 and Proposed Voluntary Funds Programme and Budget for 1980, Observations of the Advisory Committee on Administrative and Budgetary Questions*, Submitted by the High Commissioner, Executive Committee of the High Commissioner's Programme, Thirtieth Session, A/AC.96/570, 27 September 1979.

104 UNGA, *Background Note Dated 9 July 1979 prepared by the United Nations High Commissioner for Refugees for the Meeting on Refugees and Displaced Persons in South-East Asia*, Convened by the Secretary-General of the United Nations as Geneva 20–21 July 1979, Annex 1, A/34/627, 7 November 1979, p. 6.

invasion of Cambodia, Southeast Asian states had repeatedly insisted that the UNHCR and UN had a duty to ensure that the refugee problem was addressed at its 'root cause'. Southeast Asian states argued that it was unfair that countries such as Vietnam could cause and encourage refugee problems and not be expected to contribute to the solution. While ASEAN states wished for a more permanent solution by forcing Vietnam to withdraw its forces from Cambodia (thus stemming at least one large cause of the refugee influx), they also attempted to put pressure on Vietnam by refusing diplomatic recognition until it stopped encouraging the trafficking of people.[105] However, ASEAN failed to persuade enough other states to follow its lead. In particular, it failed to persuade the UNHCR. UNHCR officials insisted that their mandate was non-political; this caused increasing frustration in Southeast Asia as the refugee agency refused to condemn Vietnam's policy of encouraging flight.

Instead of condemning Vietnam, UNHCR began negotiations with the Vietnam government at the beginning of 1979. In February 1979, Deputy High Commissioner for Refugees, Dale de Haan, convened an informal meeting in Geneva to discuss a potential 'orderly movement' of people from Vietnam. Prior to the meeting, Vietnam confirmed that it was willing to accelerate family reunion cases, but not all Vietnamese would be allowed to leave. The groups not allowed to leave included those with military obligations, those in possession of state secrets or irreplaceable skills, and those on trial.[106] There were mixed feelings about this initiative. Canada wondered how an outflow would be conducted and what would happen if Vietnam objected to some people leaving; Japan supported the initiative; France opposed it (France would be first in line for having to accept the majority of the family reunion cases); Thailand was concerned that the initiative would see the redirection of international funds away from its refugees; and the United States, in public at least, did not offer an opinion.[107]

However, the UNHCR persisted in its attempts to begin this 'orderly departure' process. In February a UNHCR delegate went to Hanoi to discuss the details and it was agreed that family reunion cases and special humanitarian cases would be the first group of persons allowed to leave. Lists were prepared by the Vietnamese government and by the receiving countries. Then the lists were compared and those who appeared on both lists were the first to exit.[108] By the July 1979 Conference and with the rapid increase of boat arrivals throughout the region, there was significant support within the region and amongst Western states for the refugee problem to be addressed at its 'root cause', meaning an acceleration of the orderly departure process. The Memorandum of Understanding, which led to the Orderly Departure Programme (ODP), was signed between Vietnam and UNHCR in

---

105 ASEAN, *Joint Communiqué of the Twelfth ASEAN Ministerial Meeting*, Bali, Indonesia, 30th June 1979 (Jakarta: Terbatas, ASEAN Sekretariat Nasional, 1979).
106 Robinson, *Terms of Refuge: The Indochinese Exodus and the International Response*, 1998, p. 56.
107 Robinson, *Terms of Refuge: The Indochinese Exodus and the International Response*, 1998, p. 56.
108 Robinson, *Terms of Refuge: The Indochinese Exodus and the International Response*, 1998, p. 57.

May 1979, and included a seven-point plan which Vietnam pledged to follow at the July conference. However, the departure rate was slow at first—just 2,000 by December 1979 but by 1984, there were more ODP departures than people leaving 'illegally' by boat.[109]

At the 1979 Conference, the Vietnamese government was also encouraged to prevent illegal departures and this remains one of the most controversial activities UNHCR was part of during the Indochinese refugee crisis.[110] At the Conference, the Vietnamese government signed a moratorium, stating that it would cooperate with the ODP and stop 'illegal departures'. Stein argues that the moratorium was significant because it acknowledged, albeit tacitly, that Vietnam had the ability to control its citizens' departure. It also potentially allowed the Vietnamese government to 'apply draconian measures to citizens forced into life-periling flight by other draconian measures and to curtail fundamental UN recognized rights to travel freely and to choose one's place of residence'.[111] However, it is not obvious that the UNHCR was a 'part' of this plan.[112] UNHCR's concerns about the moratorium were proved justified; within a month, the Vietnamese brutally cracked down on people attempting to flee. Thousands were arrested, some were executed and countless numbers were forced to remain in Vietnam with their right to seek asylum denied.[113]

The Conference did not make any headway towards a peaceful resolution of the Vietnamese occupation of Cambodia, which had caused the exodus of Cambodians to the Thai-Cambodian border and into Thailand.[114] However, it was successful in the sense that three objectives were met: the resumption of temporary asylum provision by Southeast Asian states; a commitment by Western states to provide more resettlement places; and Vietnam's cooperation in orderly departures. Yet it was the less positive outcomes that would come to shape Southeast Asian responses for the remainder of the Indochinese refugee crisis. The first was that Southeast

---

109 UNGA, *Report on the Resettlement of Refugees*, Submitted by the High Commissioner, Executive Committee of the High Commissioner's Programme, Thirty-Sixth Session, A/AC.96/661, 26 July 1985, p. 4; Robinson, *Terms of Refuge: The Indochinese Exodus and the International Response*, 1998, p. 57.

110 Stein, B., 'The Geneva Conferences and the Indochinese Refugee Crisis', *International Migration Review*, Vol. 13, No. 4, (Winter 1979), p. 722.

111 Stein, B., 'The Geneva Conferences and the Indochinese Refugee Crisis', *International Migration Review*, Vol. 13, No. 4, (Winter 1979), p. 722. According to Article 14 in the 1948 Universal Declaration of Human Rights 'everyone has the right to seek and to enjoy in other countries asylum from persecution'. UNGA, *1948 Universal Declaration of Human Rights*, Resolution 217 A(III), 10 December 1948.

112 Robinson, *Terms of Refuge: The Indochinese Exodus and the International Response*, 1998, p. 58; Stein, B., 'The Geneva Conferences and the Indochinese Refugee Crisis', *International Migration Review*, Vol. 13, No. 4, (Winter 1979), pp. 722–723.

113 Stein, B., 'The Geneva Conferences and the Indochinese Refugee Crisis', *International Migration Review*, Vol. 13, No. 4, (Winter 1979), pp. 722, 723.

114 UNGA, *Background Note Dated 9 July 1979 prepared by the United Nations High Commissioner for Refugees for the Meeting on Refugees and Displaced Persons in South-East Asia*, Convened by the Secretary-General of the United Nations as Geneva 20–21 July 1979, Annex 1, *Initiatives Taken Since the Meeting*, A/34/627, 7 November 1979, p. 14.

Asian states were successful in arguing that this refugee crisis was different and required different solutions; therefore, they would not take part in 'old' solutions, such as the 1951 Convention and 1967 Protocol. This point was made regularly by all Southeast Asian states present at the 1979 Conference.[115] Ultimately, Southeast Asian states succeeded in persuading the UNHCR and international community of their case. This is indicated by the fact that very little pressure was applied on Southeast Asian states to provide permanent resettlement places. In turn, though, their rejection of the durable solutions most practiced in developing states (such as local settlement) was *further* indication of their belief that international refugee law lacked relevance to their situation and was not universal in application (see Chapters 1 and 2).[116]

A second outcome of the 1979 Conference was evidence that Southeast Asian states were concerned that any sign of capitulation to the refugee influx would be seen as weakness and encourage others to flee. As shown earlier, the most common refrain by Southeast Asian states when refusing further boat arrivals was that this was a necessary deterrent measure. Furthermore, these states did not want to cede their autonomy or authority on refugee entry and status to organizations such as UNHCR. The ASEAN communiqué in June 1979 was a statement of Southeast Asian states' sovereign right to declare who could and could not enter their territory.[117]

Therefore, Southeast Asian states learned that 'hard hearts could drive hard bargains'.[118] By breaching international law and delivering an ultimatum to the international community in the first six months of 1979, Southeast Asian states were able to achieve the highest offering of resettlement places, receive the highest financial contribution and were expected to do no more than offer temporary asylum. In essence, breaching international refugee law had delivered the outcomes these states wanted. As Robinson points out, what UNHCR and Western countries learnt was that 'temporary haven for the boat people would have to be purchased, on a one-to-one ratio if necessary, with resettlement offers'.[119] At the time, this was not a particular problem for states such as the US; it was geographically removed from boat arrivals yet able to offer an alternative political environment for those fleeing communism. It was important for the United States to acknowledge all

115 UNGA, *Background Note Dated 9 July 1979 prepared by the United Nations High Commissioner for Refugees for the Meeting on Refugees and Displaced Persons in South-East Asia*, Convened by the Secretary-General of the United Nations as Geneva 20–21 July 1979, Annex 1, A/34/627, 7 November 1979.

116 In 1980, the UNHCR held a review of international refugee protection in Asia up to 1980 and invited Asian legal expert opinion. The most frequent statement made by the lawyers and Ministers from Asian states present was that the 1951 Convention and 1967 Protocol was not applicable to their experience or developing needs. UNHCR. *Round Table of Asian Experts on Current Problems in the International Protection of Refugees and Displaced Persons*, April 1980. Publication Box 4, Section One.

117 ASEAN, *Joint Communiqué of the Twelfth ASEAN Ministerial Meeting*, Bali, Indonesia, 30th June 1979 (Jakarta: Terbatas, ASEAN Sekretariat Nasional, 1979).

118 Robinson, *Terms of Refuge: The Indochinese Exodus and the International Response*, 1998, p. 31.

119 Robinson, *Terms of Refuge: The Indochinese Exodus and the International Response*, 1998, p. 31.

fleeing Vietnamese as refugees because this highlighted that, despite the outcome of the Vietnam War, not everyone living in Vietnam was happy with the outcome.[120] This was to change in the 1980s (see next chapter). Another outcome of the 1979 Conference was that Southeast Asian states were confirmed in their view that international refugee law instruments were irrelevant. When they did the opposite of what they were expected to do in regard to refugees, they still received UNHCR assistance and resettlement places for refugees. If they did cooperate, the Southeast Asian states were expected to bear the burden independently.

3.8 *Conclusion*

Between 1975 and 1979 therefore, over one million Indochinese refugees sought asylum in Southeast Asian states. But not one state in the region felt compelled to sign onto the international refugee law instruments in this period. Indeed, Southeast Asian states decreased their level of 'burden sharing' in the sense that the UNHCR and Western states were forced to take a higher level of responsibility in finding solutions for the asylum seekers. In 1978, Southeast Asian states started to expel asylum seekers or refuse asylum to them when the number of resettlement places were no longer keeping pace with the number of arrivals. Southeast Asian states claimed to know little of the international refugee instruments. Furthermore, despite widespread evidence that Southeast Asian states were not fully cooperating, their manipulation of the situation at the 1979 Conference placed the onus on Western states and Vietnam to take primary responsibility for dealing with the problem.

Whether or not there is agreement with the way in which Southeast Asian states, the UNHCR or Western states acted during the early stages of the Indochinese refugee crisis, there can be no doubt that by 1979 Southeast Asian states had become adept at manipulating the situation to suit their particular needs. The primary ambition of the region's states was to shift the responsibility to protect Indochinese refugees from themselves and place it on others. This was proving to be a successful response to the crisis. As a result, the 1979 Conference and Western states response to the Indochinese refugee crisis only served to further entrench Southeast Asian states desire to continue their policy of refugee manipulation. The consequences this would have for the remainder of the Indochinese crisis is explored in the next chapter.

---

[120] Loescher, *The UNHCR and World Politics: A Perilous Path*, 2001, p. 208.

Chapter 4

After the 1979 Conference: the Early 1980s

Immediately after the 1979 Conference, there was a collective sigh of relief from all the actors involved. To the first asylum countries, resettlement countries and UNHCR, it seemed that a solution to the problem had been found. However, the sense of relief did not last long. In August and September 1979, boat people were again being refused entry by Malaysian and Thai authorities; Thailand was also denying entry to refugees from Laos and an increasing number from Cambodia.[1] Though these actions indicated a rapid failure of the 1979 Conference, on closer inspection it is not surprising that Southeast Asian states continued to act in this manner or that they continued to do so for the remainder of the Indochinese refugee crisis.

This chapter will assess the on-going response to the refugee crisis immediately after the 1979 Conference. The aim is to explore why, after the 1979 Conference, the majority of Southeast Asian states continued to reject international refugee law and refused to comply with even the most basic requirement - to provide temporary asylum to all Indochinese asylum seekers.[2] This continued refusal to abide by even the most rudimentary practices of refugee protection stemmed from a determination

[1] UNHCR, O. Bayer. Protection Officer, Asia Regional Section to P. M. Moussalli, Director of Protection, *Weekly Notes 3 to 9 August 1979*, 9 August 1979; Folio 110, 602.3; UNHCR, S. Bari, Protection Office, Asia Section to E. Jahn, Acting Director of Protection, *Weekly Notes 31 August to 5 September 1979*, 5 September 1979; Folio 113, 602.3.

[2] The Philippines did sign in 1981, however, to this day, they have not implemented any of the laws required to ratify the Convention and Protocol.

by Southeast Asian states that they not bear the burden of the Indochinese refugee crisis alone. This determination developed in two specific responses which this chapter explores. The first response was to deny asylum to the Indochinese at times when Southeast Asian states felt that international assistance was not forthcoming. The experience of the mass arrivals in late 1978 and early 1979, followed by a perceived failure of Western states to provide adequate assistance was still fresh in the memory of Southeast Asian states. The level of international assistance only increased when Southeast Asian states refused to accept asylum seekers at their borders. As a result, Southeast Asian states shaped their response to asylum seekers according to the level of international assistance they required. The majority of Southeast Asian states continued to believe that accession to the 1951 Convention and 1967 Protocol would have reduced their bargaining power. Thus, they continued to claim the instruments were not applicable to their situation.

The second response explored in this chapter is that during this stage of the Indochinese crisis Southeast Asian states continued to reject the refugee law instruments, enabling them to argue that they had a 'right to reject' asylum seekers. During the early 1980s, the UNHCR attempted to introduce a refugee protection regime in Southeast Asia but failed in its endeavors. In this chapter I propose that there were three main reasons that account for this failure. First, Southeast Asian states argued that they had 'no knowledge of the instruments'. The lack of Southeast Asian state involvement in the drafting of the international refugee instruments enabled them to deny knowledge of them. Second, they had 'no desire to sign'. Southeast Asian states claimed to derive more benefits from not implementing these laws. The third and arguably most important point is that the majority of Southeast Asian states had 'no need to sign'. At this stage of the crisis, Western states and the UNHCR remained committed to providing resettlement and assistance for the Indochinese asylum seekers. This allowed Southeast Asian states to secure adequate assistance for the Indochinese with little commitment on their part.

The chapter is divided into three parts. In the first part, I explore the immediate aftermath of the 1979 Conference and demonstrate that Southeast Asian states remained determined to ensure that the international community maintained their promise of resettlement and assistance. During this period, the pushbacks and *refoulement* by Southeast Asian states (discussed in Chapter 3) continued for at least two reasons: to deter future asylum seekers and 'warn' resettlement states and the UNHCR that Southeast Asian states would carry out their threat to refuse temporary asylum if international assistance did not continue. At the same time, the UNHCR attempted to introduce refugee protection principles at a regional level. This is the focus of the second and third parts of the chapter. The second part of the chapter investigates the UNHCR's attempts to encourage the region to create its own refugee protection regime. However, Southeast Asian states resisted this move and declared that what they were already doing was more than enough. The third and final part of the chapter then examines the UNHCR's abandonment of the idea of a regional protection regime and reversion back to its traditional practice of encouraging individual states to accede to the 1951 Convention and 1967 Protocol. I explore the UNHCR's discussions with each Southeast Asian state during this stage of the Indochinese refugee crisis. In particular, I focus on the reasons why the UNHCR only convinced one state, the Philippines, to sign the legal instruments. Malaysia is used as a case study to delve more deeply into why Southeast Asian states did not accede to the international refugee instruments during this period. I focus especially on Malaysia because in the literature it is often argued that Malaysia's racist practices against its non-Malay citizens played a key role in determining why it did not accede to the 1951 Convention. However, I suggest that the racism argument is an inadequate explanation. Rather, Malaysia's response to the international refugee law can be attributed to more general regional sentiments and in particular the strategy of manipulation identified in the previous chapter. The UNHCR's failure to convince more than one state to accede to the instruments during the Indochinese refugee crisis therefore tells us a great deal more about Southeast Asian states' perception of the instruments, their sense of little obligation to them and their use.

4.1 *The immediate aftermath of the 1979 Conference*

The first outcome of the 1979 Conference, which affected attitudes for the remainder of the crisis, was that Southeast Asian states felt justified in maintaining the threat of non-cooperation if resettlement states did not maintain their quotas and if the UNHCR did not maintain its assistance programmes. As a result, even though the 1979 Conference was widely viewed as making a positive contribution, Southeast Asian states were keen to ensure that the international community remained aware of the fact that the Indochinese refugee crisis was a shared international burden—not just a Southeast Asian problem. Consequently, during the early 1980s, Southeast Asian states did not hesitate in using *refoulement* and pushback measures to 'remind' the international community of its obligations. Western states, in particular the US, Australia and Japan, were quick to excuse Southeast Asian actions and comply with its demands.

Most Southeast Asian states recognized that the 1979 Conference had delivered favorable outcomes. In Malaysia, for example, the rate of resettlement departures had risen to 8,000 per month, in comparison to the period of January to June 1979, where the departures had been just over 4,000 a month. The number of new arrivals in Malaysia also dropped, from 75,000 at the end of June to 55,000 by mid-September.[3] For the region in general, land and boat arrivals of asylum seekers dropped from 25,750 in July to 14,282 in September.[4] Resettlement offers also

[3] UNGA, *Report on the UNHCR Assistance Activities in 1978–1979 and Proposed Voluntary Funds Programmes and Budget for 1980*, Executive Committee of the High Commissioner's Programme, Thirtieth Session, A/AC.96/564, 14 August 1979, p. 157; UNGA, *Report on the UNHCR Assistance Activities in 1978–1979 and Proposed Voluntary Funds Programmes and Budget for 1980, Addendum*, Executive Committee of the High Commissioner's Programme, Thirtieth Session, A/AC.96/564/Add.1, 28 September 1979, p. 10.

[4] Despite an increase of boat arrivals in the Philippines and Singapore (6,500 and 1,260 respectively). UNGA, *Report on the UNHCR Assistance Activities in 1978–1979 and Proposed Voluntary Funds*

rose from the 260,000 places provided by Western states in the 1979 Conference, to 273,500 places for the period of July 1979 to June 1980. The UNHCR was aiming for 25,000 departures for resettlement per month from the region, and the current resettlement rate had risen from 18,161 in July to 25,495 refugees leaving for resettlement from the region in September 1979.[5] It is clear from this that the (mainly Western) resettlement states had taken greater responsibility for Indochinese refugees. The financial assistance that had been provided for the Indochinese crisis was also significant, standing at $US155, 435,494 in September 1979, with the largest contributors being Japan and the United States.[6]

There was evidence too of greater UNHCR activism after the 1979 Conference. The UNHCR became more involved with governments in the region to ensure that boat people were rescued from sinking boats or isolated islands. In August 1979 it convened a Meeting of Experts on Rescue Operations for Refugees and Displaced Persons in Distress in the South China Sea. This meeting decided that special resettlement arrangements needed to be in place for occasions where the flag state (the country where a ship was registered) was not prepared to provide resettlement guarantees, in order to ensure that the boat people were still allowed to disembark in the country of first asylum.[7] This initiative was aimed at overcoming two problems. First, to ensure that boat people in distress would not be overlooked by passing ships because of the difficulty of procuring disembarkation at a country of first asylum, when no resettlement offers had been made. Second, it aimed to reduce boat people's vulnerability to pirate attacks. Pirates frequently rammed, robbed, murdered and/or raped boat people stranded on remote islands. These practices sometimes occurred with the tacit approval of first asylum states (see Section 5.4, Chapter 5).[8]

Programmes and Budget for 1980, Addendum, Executive Committee of the High Commissioner's Programme, Thirtieth Session, A/AC.96/564/Add.1, 28 September 1979, p. 13, 15. The total number of Indochinese refugees in ASEAN countries and Hong Kong at this time was 342,998. 181,184 of these were 'boat people' and 161,814 people had entered by land into Thailand. UNGA, *Office of the United Nations High Commissioner for Refugees Meeting on Refugees and Displaced Persons in South-East Asia*, Convened by the Secretary-General of the United Nations at Geneva on 20 and 21 July 1979 and Subsequent Developments, Initiatives Taken Since the Meeting, Thirty-Fourth Session, Agenda Item 83, A/34/627, 7 November 1979, p. 8.

5 UNGA, *Office of the United Nations High Commissioner for Refugees Meeting on Refugees and Displaced Persons in South-East Asia*, Convened by the Secretary-General of the United Nations at Geneva on 20 and 21 July 1979 and Subsequent Developments, Initiatives Taken Since the Meeting, Thirty-Fourth Session, Agenda Item 83, A/34/627, 7 November 1979, p. 8.

6 Japan ended up contributing half of the total amount spent by the UNHCR on the Indochinese refugee crisis from 1975–1995. UNGA, *Office of the United Nations High Commissioner for Refugees Meeting on Refugees and Displaced Persons in South-East Asia*, Convened by the Secretary-General of the United Nations at Geneva on 20 and 21 July 1979 and Subsequent Developments, Annex 2, Thirty-Fourth Session, Agenda Item 83, A/34/627/Annex 2, 7 November 1979, pp. 1–2.

7 UNGA, *Office of the United Nations High Commissioner for Refugees Meeting on Refugees and Displaced Persons in South-East Asia*, Convened by the Secretary-General of the United Nations at Geneva on 20 and 21 July 1979 and Subsequent Developments, Initiatives Taken Since the Meeting, Thirty-Fourth Session, Agenda Item 83, A/34/627, 7 November 1979, p. 11.

8 UNHCR, Michel Moussalli to Sq Ldr Prasong Soonsiri, *Correspondence*, 17 January 1984, 010.

A further activity undertaken by UNHCR in the immediate aftermath of the 1979 Conference was to organize material assistance for refugees, as the majority of Southeast Asian states refused to provide for refugees' basic needs. Indonesia and the Philippines also insisted that their Refugee Processing Centres (RPC) be entirely funded and administered by the UNHCR.[9] Therefore, the UNHCR needed to organize local volunteer organizations such as the Malay Red Crescent and international agencies such as the UNDP, WFP, ILO, WHO and many more, to provide education, vocational training, medicine, sanitation, nutrition, engineering, social welfare, food, blankets and clothing.[10]

The assistance provided by Southeast Asian states was strictly limited to the provision of temporary asylum while resettlement places were organized for the refugees. This was exemplified in an internal UNHCR discussion about the purposes of the July 1979 meeting. In this discussion the UNHCR identified two critical aims. The first was to gain Vietnam's assistance in organizing the orderly departure of refugees, 'which could stop or at least reduce to manageable proportions the influx into first asylum countries'.[11] The second was to persuade third states to provide more offers of resettlement places, which would also serve to reduce the backlog in camps in the first asylum countries in Southeast Asia.[12] Importantly, there was no discussion of what obligations Southeast Asian states were expected to take responsibility for. There were two main reasons for this. First, states such as the United States remained willing at this time to take responsibility for the Indochinese refugees, because their departure still served to demonstrate the political instability that communist regimes created.[13] Second, UNHCR staff remained painfully aware that they could not pressure Southeast Asian states to comply with international legal instruments that they were not party to. This fact imposed a powerful restriction on the extent

THA, Folio 500; UNHCR, Bayandor, D., *Report on Situation of the VNBP*, Annual Review Meeting of Vietnamese Boatpeople, 30 January 1984, Kuala Lumpur; 010.MLS, 12–14.

[9] The provision of funding and technical expertise by Japan and Switzerland was very important for getting these RPCs started also. UNGA, *Office of the United Nations High Commissioner for Refugees Meeting on Refugees and Displaced Persons in South-East Asia,* Convened by the Secretary-General of the United Nations at Geneva on 20 and 21 July 1979 and Subsequent Developments, Initiatives Taken Since the Meeting, Thirty-Fourth Session, Agenda Item 83, A/34/627, 7 November 1979, p. 9.

[10] UNGA, *Office of the United Nations High Commissioner for Refugees Meeting on Refugees and Displaced Persons in South-East Asia,* Convened by the Secretary-General of the United Nations at Geneva on 20 and 21 July 1979 and Subsequent Developments, Initiatives Taken Since the Meeting, Thirty-Fourth Session, Agenda Item 83, A/34/627, 7 November 1979, pp. 11–12.

[11] UNGA, *Office of the United Nations High Commissioner for Refugees Meeting on Refugees and Displaced Persons in South-East Asia,* Convened by the Secretary-General of the United Nations at Geneva on 20 and 21 July 1979 and Subsequent Developments, Initiatives Taken Since the Meeting, Thirty-Fourth Session, Agenda Item 83, A/34/627, 7 November 1979, p. 13.

[12] UNGA, *Office of the United Nations High Commissioner for Refugees Meeting on Refugees and Displaced Persons in South-East Asia,* Convened by the Secretary-General of the United Nations at Geneva on 20 and 21 July 1979 and Subsequent Developments, Initiatives Taken Since the Meeting, Thirty-Fourth Session, Agenda Item 83, A/34/627, 7 November 1979, p. 13.

[13] Robinson, *Terms of Refuge: The Indochinese Exodus and the International Response*, 1998, pp. 161–162.

to which the UNHCR could speak out against the actions of the Southeast Asian states and thus what they could reasonably expect of these states.

Southeast Asian practices in relation to the provision of asylum and respect for non-refoulement was only briefly discussed by the political organs of the UNHCR. Immediately after the 1979 Conference, there was no concerted effort to persuade Southeast Asian states to fulfill their humanitarian responsibilities to the Indochinese, nor were they even criticized for their widespread practice of *refoulement.* Instead, the UNHCR referred to the 'serious political, economic and social problems in South-East Asian countries' that made adherence to first asylum difficult, implicitly accepting the central claims being put forward by Southeast Asian states.[14] This response stood in sharp contrast to the UNHCR's policy towards Africa at the time, which placed emphasis on African states' responsibility to allow the local integration of refugees. In the African case, the need for resettlement places was considered less important because 'it is to be expected that the vast majority of refugees would wish to avail themselves of solutions which would enable them to maintain their roots or, at the very least, to preserve their regional or cultural identities'.[15] The differences between the UNHCR's attitude towards Africa and Southeast Asia could not have been more striking. One of the central differences between the two continents, as indicated in Chapter 3, was that African states had tended to sign onto international refugee law, whilst Southeast Asian states had not. In addition, the United States in particular was willing to support its Southeast Asian allies because of perceived vital strategic interests in the region. Sadly for much of Africa, the US had no such interests there.

For the remaining six months of 1979, the UNHCR's reports show that Indonesia, Malaysia and Thailand in particular, all pushed boat people back out to international waters. Though the number of pushbacks was quite small overall, and minimal in Malaysia, it was still a disturbing trend considering the 1979 Conference's efforts to prevent pushbacks. During general debate at the UNHCR's Executive Committee meeting, African states collectively expressed discontent with the unbalanced way the world's refugee situation was being addressed. They argued that the 'media attention being paid to the Indochinese refugees should not divert attention away from other needy area',[16] and that in light of their very large refugee situation, assistance to Africa should be increased.

---

14 UNGA, *Office of the United Nations High Commissioner for Refugees Meeting on Refugees and Displaced Persons in South-East Asia*, Convened by the Secretary-General of the United Nations at Geneva on 20 and 21 July 1979 and Subsequent Developments, Conclusion, Thirty-Fourth Session, Agenda Item 83, A/34/627, 7 November 1979, p. 13.

15 UNGA, *Report on the Resettlement of Refugees, Submitted by the High Commissioner*, Executive Committee of the High Commissioner's Programme, Thirty-First Session, A/AC.96/580, 15 August 1980, p. 1.

16 UNGA, *Report of the Executive Committee of the Programme of the United Nations High Commissioner for Refugees on the Work of its Thirtieth Session,* Executive Committee of the High Commissioner's Programme, Thirtieth Session, A/AC.96/572, 8–16 October 1979, p. 7.

However, Southeast Asian states' refusal to cooperate on any terms other than linking continued assistance to the provision of temporary asylum did not go unnoticed. For instance, the Dutch delegate expressed concern with the lengths to which the UNHCR was going to accommodate the Indochinese refugee problem. He noted that in constructing the ODP (Orderly Departure Programme) in Vietnam, the UNHCR was assisting people who had not yet left their country of origin—a condition for refugee status. The Netherlands argued that the UNHCR's mandate was being stretched to accommodate its activities in Southeast Asia.[17] The French delegate agreed with the need for an expanded UNHCR mandate, but implicitly supported African states' concerns by referring to how African states had been able to resolve the majority of their displacement problems through regional solutions. In contrast, France lamented that the international community was accommodating 'vast areas of the world afflicted by refugee problems where no regional convention had yet been concluded and no States had even acceded to the 1951 Convention and 1967 Protocol'.[18] Given the context of the meeting, it was obvious that France was referring to Southeast Asia.

However, when concern was expressed about how much support was being provided to the Indochinese refugee crisis, states such as the US, Australia, China and Japan defended Southeast Asia's demands for significant financial and resettlement assistance. The Australian delegate insisted that

> Responses to the refugee problem must extend beyond the granting of asylum or temporary refuge to include international co-operation in immediate assistance to refugees and assistance for their eventual resettlement. When a State found it difficult to grant or continue to grant asylum, *other States, in a spirit of international co-operation, should take appropriate measures to lighten the burden of that States individually, jointly or through UNHCR.*[19]

The US delegate agreed, arguing that

> (I)t must be borne in mind that that *burden of coping with the refugee problem generally fell on the developing countries, which could least afford to provide assistance.* Moreover, refugee problems often exacerbated existing political, economic and social problems in developing countries of first asylum.[20]

Therefore, he concluded, the United States did not have any problems with the UNHCR extending its mandate to refugees in Southeast Asia.

---

[17] UNGA, *Summary Record of the 305th Meeting on 9th October 1979*, Executive Committee of the High Commissioner's Programme, Thirtieth Session, A/AC.96/SR.305, 11 October 1979, p. 5.

[18] UNGA, *Summary Record of the 305th Meeting on 9th October 1979*, Executive Committee of the High Commissioner's Programme, Thirtieth Session, A/AC.96/SR.305, 11 October 1979, p. 13.

[19] UNGA, *Summary Record of the 305th Meeting on 9th October 1979*, Executive Committee of the High Commissioner's Programme, Thirtieth Session, A/AC.96/SR.305, 11 October 1979, p. 3. Emphasis added.

[20] UNGA, *Summary Record of the 305th Meeting on 9th October 1979*, Executive Committee of the High Commissioner's Programme, Thirtieth Session, A/AC.96/SR.305, 11 October 1979, p. 8. Emphasis added.

The Chinese delegation also argued that the international community's assistance was essential, particularly as they did not believe that the refugee numbers were decreasing. In particular, China raised the on-going conflict in Cambodia as creating the conditions for a future refugee influx of between one and three million people.[21] Thus, the Chinese delegate warned other states against assuming that the situation was improving because UNHCR reports indicated a drop in the number of Indochinese refugees. China insisted that conditions could rapidly deteriorate and that the level of assistance should not be reduced.

Finally, Japan,[22] one of the two largest financial providers to the Indochinese assistance fund, argued that the 'problem of Indo-Chinese refugees had a direct bearing on the peace and security of South-East Asia as a whole'.[23] Furthermore, 'sympathetic consideration should be given to the special situation faced by ASEAN countries as a result of the large-scale influx of refugees. While temporary refuge should be granted on humanitarian grounds, *it was equally important to create the necessary conditions to ensure that those countries would feel no apprehension in granting refuge*'.[24] When considered with the statements made by the US and Australia, Japan's position indicates an important defence of the ASEAN position.

The Japanese insisted that Southeast Asian policy towards the refugees was justifiable because they were developing states and needed to pay particular attention to their political, social and economic fragility. Thus in light of how precarious the situation in these countries could potentially become, Japan argued that they could not respond to the asylum population like Western countries could unless international assistance was provided. Although France's point about Africa's difficulties was accurate, this became redundant when financially prominent countries such as United States and Japan were excusing the actions of ASEAN states. Such support was demonstrated in both words and deeds. For instance when Thai coastguards pushed Vietnamese boats out to sea in September 1979, the UNHCR was able to facilitate their disembarkation only after the US had issued an 'unofficial and confidential agreement that the US will accept all the refugees not accepted by other countries'.[25]

Support for Southeast Asian states within the UN clearly emboldened them. In September 1979 Malaysia turned away boats from its shores despite the fact that in the previous month nearly 10,000 refugees were moved from their camps

---

21 UNGA, *Summary Record of the 305th Meeting on 9th October 1979*, Executive Committee of the High Commissioner's Programme, Thirtieth Session, A/AC.96/SR.305, 11 October 1979, p. 9.

22 At the 1980 meeting, Japan and Thailand were the first Asian states to be admitted as 'delegates' to the Executive Committee since China.

23 UNGA, *Summary Record of the 305th Meeting on 9th October 1979*, Executive Committee of the High Commissioner's Programme, Thirtieth Session, A/AC.96/SR.305, 11 October 1979, p. 14.

24 UNGA, *Summary Record of the 305th Meeting on 9th October 1979*, Executive Committee of the High Commissioner's Programme, Thirtieth Session, A/AC.96/SR.305, 11 October 1979, p. 14. Emphasis added.

25 UNHCR, S. Bari, Protection Officer, Asia Section to Dr E. Jahn, Acting Director of Protection, *Weekly Notes 31 August to 5 September 1979*, 5 September 1979; Folio 113, 602.3 GEN, p. 1.

for resettlement in third countries. In addition, Malaysia 'privately and publicly reiterated that its official hard-line policy remains unchanged. According to the RO [UNHCR Regional Office] in Kuala Lumpur, 'there may even be a further hardening of the Government of Malaysia's attitude if there are large scale arrivals in the future'.[26] Thus, when the Malaysian observer spoke at the Executive Committee meeting at the end of 1979, his statement consisted entirely of demands for assistance from the international community. The observer noted that Malaysia still had over 50,000 'Vietnamese emigrants' awaiting resettlement places and that in September the number of refugees reaching its shores had increased. Malaysia thus urged the international community to keep increasing their resettlement numbers.[27] The observer for Malaysia said that it was the support of US, France and the 'understanding shown by Australia and Japan in relation to the situation that ASEAN states were facing' was most reassuring.[28] In other words, the minimal level of protection and assistance being offered by Malaysia was contingent on the continuation of material assistance from the UNHCR and the West.

Unsurprisingly, Indonesia adopted a position very similar to Malaysia's. It argued that:

> The countries members (sic) of ASEAN had endeavored to help those refugees but the burden had become too heavy; that influx had caused local problems and unsettled local conditions on their territory. From that point of view it had to be recognized that the refugee problem was not merely humanitarian but also affected the national security of the States and might constitute a threat to the political and economic stability of the region.[29]

Therefore, Indonesia, like Malaysia and Thailand, requested that more pressure be put on the Vietnamese government to increase the number of ODPs. Second, Indonesia insisted that resettlement countries should quicken the pace of refugee departures for resettlement and increase their intake.[30] The Philippine government went so far as to suggest that developing countries in other regions should take on Indochinese refugees for permanent resettlement with the provision of financial assistance from the international community.[31]

---

26 UNHCR, S. Bari to Mr P. M. Mousalli, *Weekly Notes 12 to 18 October 1979*, 18 October 1979; Folio 121, 602.3 ASIA, pp. 1–2.

27 UNGA, *Summary Record of the 306th Meeting on 9th October 1979*, Executive Committee of the High Commissioner's Programme, Thirtieth Session, A/AC.96/SR.306, 12 October 1979, p. 6.

28 UNGA, *Summary Record of the 306th Meeting on 9th October 1979*, Executive Committee of the High Commissioner's Programme, Thirtieth Session, A/AC.96/SR.306, 12 October 1979, p. 6.

29 UNGA, *Summary Record of the 308th Meeting on 10th October 1979*, Executive Committee of the High Commissioner's Programme, Thirtieth Session, A/AC.96/SR.308, 15 October 1979, p. 9.

30 UNGA, *Summary Record of the 308th Meeting on 10th October 1979*, Executive Committee of the High Commissioner's Programme, Thirtieth Session, A/AC.96/SR.308, 15 October 1979, pp. 9–10.

31 UNGA, *Summary Record of the 308th Meeting on 10th October 1979*, Executive Committee of the High Commissioner's Programme, Thirtieth Session, A/AC.96/SR.308, 15 October 1979, p. 10.

Southeast Asian states' perception of the broader role of the international community and the severity of the crisis was perhaps best summed up by the Thai delegation. The Thai delegate, Mr Angkanarak, argued that

> The critical proportions reached by the influx of refugees in 1979 had caused severe political, socio-economic and security problems in the ASEAN countries and had had a destabilizing effect on the entire region. The Meeting held at Geneva in July to discuss the problem, although encouraging, had *fallen short of providing an over-all and lasting solution, so the ASEAN countries had decided to alleviate the situation in the meantime by establishing processing centres for refugees awaiting resettlement.*[32]

The inference here was that the international community and UNHCR were not providing genuine assistance to ameliorate the problems confronted by ASEAN states, despite the fact that the refugee processing centres in Indonesia and the Philippines were entirely funded by the UNHCR's Special Programme. Instead, Thailand argued—rather disingenuously—that ASEAN states had to rely upon their own collective solutions.

In the immediate aftermath of the 1979 Conference, therefore, Southeast Asian states continued to adhere to their strategy of manipulating the refugee situation and as a result divisions began to appear in the UNHCR's Executive Committee meetings. The level of support offered by states such as the United States and Japan was crucial as it limited UNHCR's criticism of Southeast Asian states. Furthermore, Southeast Asian states generally believed that the strategy of manipulation was producing favorable outcomes. The international situation allowed them to continue responding to the crisis on their terms and there was little pressure on them to sign the 1951 Convention and 1967 Protocol. Even if there had been greater pressure, it would have proven pointless in the face of actors such as the United States, who were willing to excuse and support the Southeast Asian states' actions. However, the UNHCR believed that this situation could not continue indefinitely. Thus, the UNHCR attempted, in a variety of ways, to garner Southeast Asian accessions to these legal instruments. This next section will look at what the UNHCR attempted to do in this regard in the period immediately after the 1979 Conference, and why it had little success.

4.2 *The attempt to create a regional refugee protection regime*

In April 1980, the UNHCR attempted to promote regional refugee protection by establishing a forum to discuss a regional protection regime. It invited Southeast Asian state representatives and the region's legal experts to a 'Round Table of Asian Experts on Current Problems in the International Protection of Refugees

32 UNGA, *Summary Record of the 307th Meeting on 10th October 1979*, Executive Committee of the High Commissioner's Programme, Thirtieth Session, A/AC.96/SR.307, 15 October 1979, p. 6. Emphasis added.

and Displaced Persons' in San Remo, Italy. There were two important points to be drawn from this meeting. The first intimated the adoption of a more robust line by the UNHCR. In an important and overtly critical statement, P. M. Moussalli, Director of International Protection UNHCR, stated that Southeast Asian states saw 'burden-sharing' to mean that asylum would be provided only if there was a guarantee of reciprocal assistance from other states. This expectation, Moussalli argued, was contrary to the basic humanitarian principles which created an international law for refugee protection.[33] The second point was that because of this, Southeast Asian states continued to see international refugee law as inapplicable to the region. I will discuss each of these points in more detail.

In his somewhat remarkable statement, Moussalli argued that international protection for refugees was premised on three fundamental foundations. The first was that the UNHCR could not fulfill its role unless Southeast Asian states understood that refusal of asylum was tantamount to *refoulement*, and recognized that it was essential that the region collectively agreed with this basic principle.[34] Providing asylum was an essential part of the refugee protection process, because if people were immediately turned back to their country of origin without their refugee status being assessed there was a chance that *refoulement* could occur, placing individuals in great danger. Thus, the UNHCR could not condone or ignore the fact that Southeast Asian states had not always respected the first step of protection, the provision of asylum, nor that their actions had led to 'some tens of thousands of similar cases have, unfortunately, been forced back across borders or towed out to sea in dangerous circumstances'.[35]

The second foundation for international protection identified by Moussalli was that all developing countries needed to uphold universal principles of protection by acceding to international refugee law instruments. Even though Southeast Asian states were under strain, Moussalli stressed that all states must preserve 'the lives of persons fleeing their countries' and this was best achieved through accession to the 1951 Convention and 1967 Protocol.[36] Accession to these instruments was

---

[33] UNHCR, *Round Table of Asian Experts on Current Problems in the International Protection of Refugees and Displaced Persons*, April 1980. Publication Box 4, Section One.

[34] To *refoule* an asylum seeker to their country of origin, without first determining their claim to refugee status is a breach of Article 33 in the 1951 Convention. However, the rule of *non-refoulement* has become so important that it is now considered to have customary status in international law. This means that even states not party to the 1951 Convention are expected to obey this law. See Lauterpacht, Sir E. and Daniel Bethlehem, 'The Scope and Content of the Principle of *non-refoulement*: Opinion', in Feller, E., Volker Turk and Frances Nicholson (ed.), *Refugee Protection in International Law: UNHCR's Global Consultations on International Protection*, 2003. For a dissenting view see Hailbronner, K., 'Non-refoulement and 'Humanitarian' Refugees: Customary International Law or Wishful Legal Thinking?', *Virginia Journal of International Law*, Vol. 26, No. 4 (1986).

[35] UNHCR, *Round Table of Asian Experts on Current Problems in the International Protection of Refugees and Displaced Persons*, April 1980. Publication Box 4, Section One, p. 13.

[36] UNHCR, *Round Table of Asian Experts on Current Problems in the International Protection of Refugees and Displaced Persons*, April 1980. Publication Box 4, Section One, p. 13.

an essential part of the 'further development of the international standards for the treatment of refugees'.[37]

Finally, even though states, particularly developing states, were entitled to expect the international community to assist them with large-scale influxes, burden-sharing should not substitute individual state responsibility. Southeast Asian states argued that the Indochinese refugee burden was beyond their ability to respond to and in turn, 'bartered' the provision of temporary asylum for international assistance. However, Moussalli argued that these states had a responsibility, regardless of their economic and political situation, to provide basic conditions for asylum seekers and refugees. This third point on refugee protection was an important one, which Moussalli was at pains to stress:

> The principle of burden-sharing and the arrangements reached for its practical implementation should also not be *regarded as a pre-condition to the observance of basic humanitarian principles*. It is axiomatic that asylum seekers should not be rejected at a frontier or expelled if this would oblige them to return to or remain in a country where their life or freedom would be threatened. Equally, asylum seekers should not be refused temporary asylum if this would involve their returning to the high seas where their very live may be in danger. The observance of *these principles should not vary according to the extent to which the burden-sharing arrangements are at any given moment considered to be adequate*.[38]

Moussalli concluded by arguing that Asia had much work to do in addressing international protection for refugees both as a region and as individual states. However, he also stressed that the UNHCR's role was to assist governments with the promotion of humanitarian principles in relation to refugees.

Unsurprisingly, most of the Southeast Asian representatives at the meeting did not take kindly to Moussalli's robust stance and disagreed with each of his three foundations of refugee protection in one form or another. First, Southeast Asian representatives did not agree with the idea that the provision of asylum was a way of preventing *refoulement*, particularly in the Indochinese refugee case. Ricardo Puno, Minister of Justice for the Philippines, insisted that *non-refoulement* 'only precludes the return of a person already within the territory to a country in which he fears persecution; *it does not necessarily imply recognition of a duty on the part of the State to admit persons seeking asylum*'.[39] Furthermore, Southeast Asian states, who were not parties to the Convention or Protocol, were 'under no treaty obligations to admit the activities intended for the international protection of refugees'.[40]

---

37 UNHCR, *Round Table of Asian Experts on Current Problems in the International Protection of Refugees and Displaced Persons*, April 1980. Publication Box 4, Section One, p. 13.

38 UNHCR, *Round Table of Asian Experts on Current Problems in the International Protection of Refugees and Displaced Persons*, April 1980. Publication Box 4, Section One, p. 14. Emphasis added in italics.

39 UNHCR, *Round Table of Asian Experts on Current Problems in the International Protection of Refugees and Displaced Persons*, April 1980. Publication Box 4, Section One, p. 73. Emphasis added.

40 UNHCR, *Round Table of Asian Experts on Current Problems in the International Protection of Refugees and Displaced Persons*, April 1980. Publication Box 4, Section One, p. 73.

The Indonesian delegate, Rooslan Soeroso agreed. Indonesia, Soeroso argued, had the right to 'repatriate these *displaced persons* to their country of origin, and [furthermore] to categorically refuse entry into Indonesia'.[41] However, he insisted that Indonesia had practiced *non-refoulement* for the 'boat people' in particular, and that their provision of asylum was determined on a case by case basis and 'considered carefully on its merits'.[42] Yet, as Indonesian practice in general indicates, asylum was not something Indonesia felt compelled to provide except in 'worthy' cases. This worthiness was determined by supposedly 'humanitarian' principles but not international refugee law, as Indonesia did not recognize the latter.[43]

The two Thai delegates had rather different perspectives on what obligations their country had in relation to *non-refoulement* and the provision of asylum. Professor Vitit Muntarbhorn, a legal expert from Chulalongkorn University, argued that 'Thailand's non-ratification of these instrument means that *prima facie,* it had complete discretion in determining the legal status of displaced persons on Thai soil, and in the event of treating a displaced persons as an illegal immigrant, in deciding whether to enforce its immigration law'.[44] However, Thailand granted temporary asylum despite its domestic immigration laws (discussed further in Section 5.3, Chapter 5), identified all entrants as 'illegal'. This suggested to Muntarbhorn that Thailand can be 'described as acting in conformity with its "moral" obligation on an international plane'.[45] He argued that Thailand's 'Open Door Policy', which provided temporary refuge and included a policy of not *refouling* refugees except on a voluntary basis (although there was much evidence to the contrary) indicated a recognition and observance of *non-refoulement*, even if within a 'limited sphere'.[46] The second delegate from Thailand, Professor Kosol Sobhak-Vichitr, also from Chulalongkorn University, argued that the people fleeing Indochina must be considered as refugees because of the situation they were fleeing and that Thailand 'has no choice but to accept them for the sake of humanitarianism'.[47] The difference here was while Muntarbhorn acknowledged Thailand's right to deny entry to asylum seekers, Sobhak-Vichitr did not. He argued that Thailand had a humanitarian obligation to acknowledge these people as refugees and argued that it was important that the

[41] UNHCR, *Round Table of Asian Experts on Current Problems in the International Protection of Refugees and Displaced Persons*, April 1980. Publication Box 4, Section One, p. 118.

[42] UNHCR, *Round Table of Asian Experts on Current Problems in the International Protection of Refugees and Displaced Persons*, April 1980. Publication Box 4, Section One, p. 119.

[43] UNHCR, *Round Table of Asian Experts on Current Problems in the International Protection of Refugees and Displaced Persons*, April 1980. Publication Box 4, Section One, p. 118.

[44] UNHCR, *Round Table of Asian Experts on Current Problems in the International Protection of Refugees and Displaced Persons*, April 1980. Publication Box 4, Section One, p. 168.

[45] UNHCR, *Round Table of Asian Experts on Current Problems in the International Protection of Refugees and Displaced Persons*, April 1980. Publication Box 4, Section One, p. 169.

[46] UNHCR, *Round Table of Asian Experts on Current Problems in the International Protection of Refugees and Displaced Persons*, April 1980. Publication Box 4, Section One, p. 169.

[47] UNHCR, *Round Table of Asian Experts on Current Problems in the International Protection of Refugees and Displaced Persons*, April 1980. Publication Box 4, Section One, p. 178.

refugee population not be viewed as a threat to regional security.[48] Sobhak-Vichitr argued that *non-refoulement* was a principle of humanitarianism (or has the status of customary law) that applied to refugees regardless of whether the host state has formally signed international refugee law; all refugees in the country and on the border should 'obtain the same priority of care'.[49]

Therefore, although one Thai delegate thought *non-refoulement* was applicable; the majority of the delegates argued that *non-refoulement* was not applicable because their region had not signed the international refugee law instruments. For most states in the region, the principle of *non-refoulement* was associated with international refugee law instruments; nor was it considered to be a part of their customary law.[50] This was important. It indicated that, as Muntarbhorn suggested, for Southeast Asian states the only reason why states permitted temporary asylum was because of a notion of charitable humanitarianism. The problem with charity is that it can be short-lived.

If genuine obligations arose only from signing international refugee law, the question that remained to be answered was why Southeast Asian states had not signed onto international refugee law? At the UNHCR meeting in April 1980, Southeast Asian states were united in arguing that their status as developing states provided a justification for their reluctance to sign the instruments. Singapore argued that the Indochinese refugee influx was part of Vietnam's plan to destabilize Southeast Asia and thus make it vulnerable to communist domination. According to Singapore, the 'refugee problem cannot only be regarded as an exercise in humanitarianism. It must be recognized that the problem is rapidly acquiring a political dimension which would be unwise to disregard and fatal to ignore'.[51] Singapore therefore rejected the view that according to international law, states should provide assistance to all eligible people that requested it. It was concerned that 'if a country cannot discharge its responsibility towards its citizens then the world community should take over this responsibility. Now, if this precedent is set here [Southeast Asia] then the refugee question can at a certain point become the responsibility not of the country where the refugees originated, but of others who are expected to take it over'.[52] Singapore argued this was a wrong distribution of responsibility between states and a potential disaster when considering the millions of people, mainly in developing countries, who would have to be accepted by unwitting states on those grounds.

48 UNHCR, *Round Table of Asian Experts on Current Problems in the International Protection of Refugees and Displaced Persons*, April 1980. Publication Box 4, Section One, p. 178.

49 UNHCR, *Round Table of Asian Experts on Current Problems in the International Protection of Refugees and Displaced Persons*, April 1980. Publication Box 4, Section One, p. 178.

50 An international law will be considered as 'customary' when it is acknowledged by most states to exist—*opinion juris*—and when the majority of states observe or practice the law. Customary status implies then that states will adapt their practice in order to adhere to the law.

51 UNHCR, *Round Table of Asian Experts on Current Problems in the International Protection of Refugees and Displaced Persons*, April 1980. Publication Box 4, Section One, p. 182.

52 UNHCR, *Round Table of Asian Experts on Current Problems in the International Protection of Refugees and Displaced Persons*, April 1980. Publication Box 4, Section One, p. 182.

The Philippines agreed with Singapore's argument that the international protection of refugees should be based on principles of humanitarianism not law: 'Asians prefer to base the legal protection of refugees, not on treaty obligations, but on elementary considerations of humanity'.[53] The Philippines argued that largely because, the 'rationale of refugee law is the *civitas maxima*, or the community of States.....in this region, developing states—in accordance with the age-old tradition of Asian hospitality—have matched the generosity of the developed States in admitting and caring for refugees'.[54] However, Southeast Asian states were developing states and therefore 'incapable of bearing singly the burden of a sudden mass influx of refugees'.[55] Nor were Southeast Asian states under any legal obligation to bear the burden of refugees, being non-members of the 1951 Convention and 1967 Protocol.

From these statements by Singapore and the Philippines it becomes clear why Southeast Asian states were the reluctant to sign the 1951 Convention and 1967 Protocol.[56] The Philippines, Indonesia and Thailand (discussed below) insisted that as sovereign states they were under no obligation to act unless they voluntarily bound themselves to international refugee law. As the Philippines argued on the issue of protection, 'diplomatic protection is enforceable by all the methods at the disposal of the State under international law. International protection by an agency, while of a legal nature, is enforceable only by moral suasion... *international protection is based merely upon the goodwill of the host country*'.[57]

Indonesia and Thailand also expressed reservations with Moussalli's expectation that developing countries should provide protection according to the principle of universality. Indonesia, like the Philippines and Singapore, was quick to stress that they viewed the matter of refugee protection 'as a humanitarian problem to be faced and solved not only by Indonesia, but also by the world community'.[58] Furthermore, Indonesia argued that the permanent settlement of refugees was impossible for a country already facing the burden of caring for its own people.[59] Indonesia stated that it only agreed to temporary protection because of UNHCR assistance and resettlement offers. The problem with the current legal approach was,

---

[53] UNHCR, *Round Table of Asian Experts on Current Problems in the International Protection of Refugees and Displaced Persons*, April 1980. Publication Box 4, Section One, p. 73.

[54] UNHCR, *Round Table of Asian Experts on Current Problems in the International Protection of Refugees and Displaced Persons*, April 1980. Publication Box 4, Section One, p. 73.

[55] UNHCR, *Round Table of Asian Experts on Current Problems in the International Protection of Refugees and Displaced Persons*, April 1980. Publication Box 4, Section One, p. 73.

[56] I include the Philippines because though they became a member of both instruments in 1981 with the promise of financial reward from the United States, they are yet to implement any of the articles into domestic law. Muntarbhorn, *The Status of Refugees in Asia*, 1992; Robinson, *Terms of Refuge: The Indochinese Exodus and the International Response*, 1998.

[57] UNHCR, *Round Table of Asian Experts on Current Problems in the International Protection of Refugees and Displaced Persons*, April 1980. Publication Box 4, Section One, p. 72.

[58] UNHCR, *Round Table of Asian Experts on Current Problems in the International Protection of Refugees and Displaced Persons*, April 1980. Publication Box 4, Section One, p. 118.

[59] UNHCR, *Round Table of Asian Experts on Current Problems in the International Protection of Refugees and Displaced Persons*, April 1980. Publication Box 4, Section One, p. 118.

in Indonesia's opinion, that it was overly simplistic because it provided no means of solving the problem. Like Singapore, Indonesia concluded that the solution lay in the country of origin assuming primary responsibility, not the host countries forced to take on the problem.[60]

Muntarbhorn argued that Thailand's political, social and economic problems were important constraints on how it could respond to the refugee problem and that those constraints should not be 'underestimated'.[61] Sobhak-Vichitr, of course, disagreed, arguing that these problems should not become barriers to the provision of refugee protection.[62] Where both Muntarbhorn and Sobhak-Vichitr agreed was that Thailand had been relatively generous to refugees from Indochina. Muntarbhorn argued that Thailand's officials did not use the word refugee to describe the Indochinese because of its specific legal meaning within the international community. However, Muntarbhorn continued, except for the fact that Thailand was not a signatory to the 1951 Convention and 1967 Protocol, the use of the word 'displaced person' by Thailand could be compared to the definition of a refugee in the Convention. He was not completely correct here; the word 'displaced person' or 'Pou Opayon' in Thai relates to 'He who escapes from dangers due to an uprising, fighting or war, and enters the Kingdom *in breach* of the Immigration Act'.[63] By this definition, asylum seekers are illegal. The 1951 Convention acknowledges a persons' need to escape a country because of a fear of persecution due to race, religion, nationality or membership of a particular social or political group. Thus, there is no mention of any *breach* of national laws. In fact, the 1951 Convention makes a point of insisting that a person who claims asylum cannot be expelled once found to be a refugee for entering a country without first obtaining official permission.[64]

This was clearly not the case under Thailand's domestic law. Furthermore, in the UNHCR Executive Committee meetings, the Thai government referred to the Cambodians as 'illegal' and as living illegally in Thailand or on the border between Thailand and Cambodia.[65] By not acceding to international refugee law, Thailand ensured that it could have 'complete discretion in determining the legal status of displaced persons on Thai soil, and in the event of treating a displaced person as an illegal immigrant, in deciding whether to enforce its immigration law'.[66] Even

60 UNHCR, *Round Table of Asian Experts on Current Problems in the International Protection of Refugees and Displaced Persons*, April 1980. Publication Box 4, Section One, p. 119.
61 UNHCR, *Round Table of Asian Experts on Current Problems in the International Protection of Refugees and Displaced Persons*, April 1980. Publication Box 4, Section One, p. 165.
62 UNHCR, *Round Table of Asian Experts on Current Problems in the International Protection of Refugees and Displaced Persons*, April 1980. Publication Box 4, Section One, pp. 177–178.
63 UNHCR, *Round Table of Asian Experts on Current Problems in the International Protection of Refugees and Displaced Persons*, April 1980. Publication Box 4, Section One, p. 167. Emphasis added.
64 UNHCR, *1951 Convention Relating to the Status of Refugees*, Article 32.
65 UNGA, *Summary Record of the 317th Meeting on 7th October 1980*, Executive Committee of the High Commissioner's Programme, Thirty-First Session, A/AC.96/SR.317, 7 October 1980, p. 4.
66 UNHCR, *Round Table of Asian Experts on Current Problems in the International Protection of Refugees and Displaced Persons*, April 1980. Publication Box 4, Section One, p. 168.

though Thailand did not obviously treat all incoming refugees as illegal immigrants, what the above evidence suggests is that like the other Southeast Asian states, the *sovereign right* to decide the legal status of entrants, without the *moral interference* of the international community, was very important to Thailand.

The Philippines, Indonesia and Singapore all referred to the fact that they only provided asylum because the UNHCR promised that the provision of resettlement places and assistance would continue. As developing states, they argued, there should be no expectation that they *could* do more than they were already doing.[67] Therefore, the only progress that UNHCR-encouraged regional forums achieved was the promotion of dialogue about international refugee law. The only result of this dialogue was a more coherent and united ASEAN position that viewed refugee protection principles as infringing their sovereign right to determine who could enter their borders. ASEAN states maintained their collective stance on what they considered as the legitimate response to the Indochinese refugee crisis, and continued to see their provision of asylum as being reciprocal for assistance and resettlement.

4.3 *Ongoing attempts to gain individual state accessions*

The Southeast Asian resistance to collectively provide unconditional asylum meant that the UNHCR had to rely upon more traditional way of encouraging state protection of refugees. In early 1982, the regional offices in Southeast Asia (Indonesia, Philippines, Singapore and Thailand in particular) took a variety of steps to persuade these states to adopt the international refugee law instruments. The drop in refugee numbers across the region (only 43,676 boat people in 1982, compared to 74,671 the year before)[68] and the success in the ODP (over 10 000 left in 1982)[69] buoyed the UNHCR's hopes of securing Southeast Asian states' trust in both the organization and its instruments. However, the UNHCR had little success, yet again. This section will first identify the way in which the UNHCR attempted to procure individual state accessions during 1981–1982. Then, via a state-by-state analysis, it will demonstrate why the UNHCR did not succeed. As suggested at the beginning of the chapter this was because of the Southeast Asian states' position that they had 'no knowledge of the instruments', 'no desire to sign' and 'no need to sign'.

67 UNHCR, Regional Office Manila to High Commissioner, *Incoming Cable*, 19 June 1981; Folio 115, 383 Protection, p. 2; UNHCR, Zia Rizvi to Deputy High Commissioner, *Incoming Cable*, 21 June 1982; Folio 118, 383 Protection.

68 Druke, L. *Preventative Action for Refugee Producing Situations* (Frankfurt am Main: Peter Lang. 1993), p. 80; Robinson, *Terms of Refuge: The Indochinese Exodus and the International Response*, 1998, p. 173.

69 Druke, *Preventative Action for Refugee Producing Situations*. 1993) p. 80; Robinson, *Terms of Refuge: The Indochinese Exodus and the International Response*, 1998, p. 173.

In late November 1981, the UNHCR drafted an 'explanatory note' on the 'nature and implications of the Convention and Protocol' for those unfamiliar with the instruments.[70] This draft indicates how desperate the organization was to pressure States to sign, with questions such as 'why should a government sign the Convention—doesn't it only restrict the way a government can act'?[71] The reply was based primarily on reassurance, as opposed to obligation, for states:

> The Convention does require Governments to recognize the basic rights of refugees. However, most Governments are already doing this in practice and are therefore not restricted by the Convention. The Convention does not interfere with the basic sovereignty of governments.[72]

The UNHCR planned to reassure the Southeast Asian governments that were asking these and similar questions by directly responding to their greatest concern—the perceived loss of their sovereign right to decide who enters their territory—by suggesting that the Convention would not remove this right. However, in reply to this draft, the UNHCR's Legal Section pointed out that the Convention was *not* just concerned with the basic human rights of refugees in principle. It argued that the Convention's objective *was* to change the way that states acted and ensure that in practice refugees were treated in accordance with the minimum standards defined within the Convention.[73] The Legal Section insisted the statement that 'most governments are already doing this in practice' was inaccurate because 'governments are not in fact already treating refugees in accordance with the Convention'.[74] It also argued that the 'non-interference with sovereignty' argument was inaccurate, because the Convention does impose 'an obligation on governments, it does limit their sovereignty to that extent'.[75] The Legal Section advised wording the role of the UNHCR more strongly, whilst arguing that words such as 'obligation' should not be used in relation to *non-refoulement*, because states 'determine who is a refugee and whether that person can remain in its territory'.[76] Words such as 'obligation' even if referred to as an indirect one, could have a 'certain deterrent effect'.[77] Therefore, the UNHCR's Legal Section, like the Asian Regional Section,

[70] UNHCR, Denis McNamara to UNHCR Geneva, *Explanatory Questions and Answers on the Convention and Protocol*, 6 November 1981; Folio 238, 671.1 GEN, p. 1.
[71] UNHCR, Denis McNamara to UNHCR Geneva, *Explanatory Questions and Answers on the Convention and Protocol*, 6 November 1981; Folio 238, 671.1 GEN, p. 2.
[72] UNHCR, Denis McNamara to UNHCR Geneva, *Explanatory Questions and Answers on the Convention and Protocol*, 6 November 1981; Folio 238, 671.1 GEN, p. 2.
[73] UNHCR, F. E. Krens to UNHCR Legal Adviser in Asia, *Explanatory Questions and Answers on the 1951 Convention and the 1967 Protocol*, 4 May 1982; Folio 245, 671.1 GEN, p. 1.
[74] UNHCR, F. E. Krens to UNHCR Legal Adviser in Asia, *Explanatory Questions and Answers on the 1951 Convention and the 1967 Protocol*, 4 May 1982; Folio 245, 671.1 GEN, p. 1.
[75] UNHCR, F. E. Krens to UNHCR Legal Adviser in Asia, *Explanatory Questions and Answers on the 1951 Convention and the 1967 Protocol*, 4 May 1982; Folio 245, 671.1 GEN, p. 1.
[76] UNHCR, F. E. Krens to UNHCR Legal Adviser in Asia, *Explanatory Questions and Answers on the 1951 Convention and the 1967 Protocol*, 4 May 1982; Folio 245, 671.1 GEN, p. 1.
[77] UNHCR, F. E. Krens to UNHCR Legal Adviser in Asia, *Explanatory Questions and Answers on the 1951 Convention and the 1967 Protocol*, 4 May 1982; Folio 245, 671.1 GEN, p. 3.

recognized the delicate balance being maintained with states in Asia. On the one hand UNHCR needed to insist on the universality of certain refugee protection concepts but, on the other hand, there was a need to avoid alienating the region's states by insisting too strongly or being too critical.

In 1982, the UNHCR also conducted a number of consultations between the relevant regional offices and Southeast Asian governments aimed at persuading them to sign the international refugee law instruments. The reason for this may partly be found in discussions in April 1982 between Dennis McNamara, Legal Adviser to the UNHCR for Asia and Dr. Sen, the Secretary-General of the Asian-African Legal Consultative Committee. Dr Sen expressed interest in the UNHCR and its attempts to involve the Asian region in refugee protection dialogue.[78] He suggested that if the UNHCR wanted more states to accede to international refugee law, it would be helpful if it encouraged accessions to the 'existing international instruments, with reservations if necessary, rather than to suggest regional or local adaptations'[79] as had been done at previous meetings, for example at the 1980 Experts Meeting (see above). Dr Sen thought this approach would be viewed as more 'neutral', less binding and therefore more appealing to states in Southeast Asia.

One reason for the new sense of urgency in the UNHCR was its concern that first asylum states in the region were starting to consider implementing their own 'humane deterrence' policies.[80] Thailand's 'humane deterrence policy' was widely viewed by states in the region as a 'necessary' response to the refugee crisis that the country faced.[81] The introduction of screening procedures for refugees in Thailand, though accepted by the UNHCR, was still of concern to the UNHCR because the procedures were not done according to provisions in the 1951 Convention. Furthermore, the popularity of Thailand's policy in the region indicated a possible move towards similar policies across the region. Therefore, the UNHCR actively sought to promote accession to international refugee law instruments by states in the region. In the section that follows I explore UNHCR attempts on a country-by-country basis.

---

[78] UNHCR, Dennis McNamara, *Confidential: Discussion with Dr B. Sen, Secretary General of the Asian-African Legal Consultative Committee*, 13 April 1982; 601.AALCC, pp. 1–2.

[79] UNHCR, Dennis McNamara, *Confidential: Discussion with Dr B. Sen, Secretary General of the Asian-African Legal Consultative Committee*, 13 April 1982; 601.AALCC, p. 2.

[80] UNHCR, Dennis McNamara to UNHCR Geneva, *The Refugee Definition in Asia*, 7 June 1982; Folio 3, 671.1 ASIA, p. 1. 'Humane deterrence' was a term first used by the Thai government to justify the refusal of asylum to people attempting to enter their state; in particular, the Thai government refused asylum seekers access to UNHCR camps, where the procedures for resettlement could be accessed. Instead, Thailand forced many to remain on border camps where the conditions were dangerous, unsanitary and there were no opportunities for resettlement; and insisted on screening procedures for those that managed to cross the border.

[81] Japan, China and Malaysia all expressed support for Thailand's policy of deterrence in the 1982 Executive Committee of the High Commissioner's Programme.

4.3.1 *Indonesia*

In March 1982, the UNHCR Representative for Indonesia and Singapore, Philippe Labreveux referred to his efforts to translate the 1951 Convention and 1967 Protocol into Indonesian so that officials from the Ministry of Foreign Affairs would be able to view the instruments in their own language. However, the main success was in distributing this material in universities, rather than the government. The UNHCR had been unable to even discuss the 'programme of dissemination of refugee law' because the UNHCR's contact within the government, Mr Soeprapto, Deputy Director at the Ministry of Foreign Affairs, kept postponing the discussion due to 'prolonged absences in Europe and the United States'.[82] However, from past discussions, Soeprapto had insisted that accession to the instruments by Indonesia depended on the UNHCR convincing a skeptical President, as well as the Minister of Foreign Affairs, the Army, and the State Security Ministry:

> All of whom had to be convinced, not that there were advantages (material or otherwise) in adhering to the refugee instruments, but that it would be an ostentatious act of solidarity with the international community. We therefore needed to promote a political will rather than try and pull off a technocratic stunt.[83]

The chances of Indonesian accession were low, especially as their key ally in the Indonesian government, Mr Soeprapto, was proving unavailable. The feeling in UNHCR headquarters was that this approach seemed 'terribly limited as it is very much tied to the availability of one person—Mr Soeprapto'.[84] Unsurprisingly, then, the UNHCR's efforts to persuade Indonesia to sign the 1951 Convention and 1967 Protocol made little headway.

4.3.2 *Singapore*

There was a similar lack of progress in Singapore. In March 1982, Shashi Tharoor, head of the UNHCR's Sub-Office in Singapore, sent a memo to Michel Moussalli, the UNHCR's Director of International Protection concerning the status of a protection programme in Asia. Tharoor said that with Singapore there were many practical difficulties which needed to be overcome. The first problem was that Singapore was not a signatory to the 1951 Convention or 1967 Protocol. The second was Singapore's refusal to grant refugees entry unless there was an immediate guarantee of resettlement for that person. Third, the 'openly declared practice of towing refugee boats out of Singapore waters, which, though tantamount to

---

[82] UNHCR, Philippe Labreveux to P. M. Moussalli, *Protection Programme for Asia*, 2 March 1982; Folio 283; 602.3 ASIA, p. 1.

[83] UNHCR, F. E. Krenz to P M Moussalli, *Confidential: Accession of Indonesia to the 1951 Convention and the 1967 Protocol Conversation with Mr Soeprapto*, 4 August 1981; Folio 10, 671.1 INS, p. 1.

[84] UNHCR, Comment by S. Bari to Mr Jackson, *UNHCR Action Sheet*, 17 March 1982; Folio 283, 602.3 ASIA.

refoulement, has been *accepted by the* [UNHCR] *office for years*'.[85] Fourth, a strict admissions policy was adopted in 1977 which made it impossible for people to enter Singapore and claim asylum through the UNHCR—except where there was a specific re-settlement offer for that individual. Finally, the fact that the resettlement of refugees must be conducted in no more than three months in Singapore often forced people to seek resettlement in a third-country where they would otherwise not choose to go.[86]

Tharoor informed Moussalli that the main opposition to change in refugee response was the Singaporean government and that any change of attitude would be due more to 'practical and policy considerations than respect for international principles'.[87] The UNHCR, Tharoor argued, had an uncertain mandate in Singapore due to its presence not being formally recognized by the government. Tharoor was occasionally able to persuade government officials to acknowledge their humanitarian obligations based on the view that the 'UNHCR derives it mandate from the General Assembly of which Singapore is a member. *At some point this bluff is likely to be called*'.[88] Therefore, there was little likelihood that the UNHCR would be successful in persuading Singapore to change its position on refugee protection.

The reasons for Singapore's resistance are illuminated to a degree by Tharoor's account of a meeting with the Singapore Minister of State for Home Affairs and Law, Mr. Jayakumar. Jayakumar asked Tharoor, 'what would change in practical terms if Singapore were to accede?'.[89] He continued by pointing out that he had 'some reservations about international conventions in general. According to his experience they were often ignored by governments if international interests were at stake, no matter whether the country was a party to an international agreement or not'.[90] The Minister confirmed his own opinion, by stating that even if Singapore was to accede to the 1951 Convention, it 'would not change Singapore's policy of granting temporary asylum only'.[91]

Southeast Asian states all suggested that it was unlikely that accession to international conventions would change their domestic behavior. This was no doubt largely because they knew that simply acceding to such instruments would not persuade *them* to change their domestic practices. Two points can be drawn from this. First, Southeast Asian states were relatively honest about their motivations.

85 UNHCR, S Tharoor to P. M. Moussalli, *Protection Programme for Asia*, 16 March 1982; Folio 286A, SIN/82/HQ/053, 602.3 ASIA, p. 1. Emphasis added.

86 UNHCR, S. Tharoor to P. M. Moussalli, *Protection Programme for Asia*, 16 March 1982; Folio 286A, SIN/82/HQ/053, 602.3 ASIA, p. 1.

87 UNHCR, S. Tharoor to P. M. Moussalli, *Protection Programme for Asia*, 16 March 1982; Folio 286A, SIN/82/HQ/053, 602.3 ASIA, p. 1.

88 UNHCR, S. Tharoor to P. M. Moussalli, *Protection Programme for Asia*, 16 March 1982; Folio 286A, SIN/82/HQ/053, 602.3 ASIA, p. 2. Emphasis added.

89 UNHCR, Note for File, *Meeting with the Minister of State for Home Affairs and Law, Singapore, Professor S Jayakumar on 7 July 1982*, Folio 50, in Folio 247A, 31 August 1982, p. 1.

90 UNHCR, Note for File, *Meeting with the Minister of State for Home Affairs and Law, Singapore, Professor S Jayakumar on 7 July 1982*, Folio 50, in Folio 247A, 31 August 1982, p. 1.

91 UNHCR, Note for File, *Meeting with the Minister of State for Home Affairs and Law, Singapore, Professor S Jayakumar on 7 July 1982*, Folio 50, in Folio 247A, 31 August 1982, p. 1.

Second, they perhaps took international instruments more seriously than many other states that were happy to subscribe to legal instruments but not change their practice in accord with them. Why could Southeast Asian states not simply sign the instruments and continue to breach elements of it when they wished? Others states had done and do so on a regular basis. One reason is that, as the Minister from Singapore inferred, Southeast Asian states believed that the instruments were binding. The Minister stated that this was why they would not sign, for if Singapore was a member of the 1951 Convention and was faced with a person seeking asylum from a neighboring country, they would still not find in favor of the refugee.[92] This was no different to practices taken by states that *are* members of the 1951 Convention,[93] the only difference was that Singapore was willing to own this decision and not cover it up by signing instruments that it would not always follow. Even the UNHCR's Sub-Office in Singapore questioned whether accession by Singapore would make a difference; Singapore had accepted the UNHCR's determination of refugee status according to the 'benefit of doubt'[94] with most arrivals which enabled them to seek resettlement, and it was 'arguable whether this [accession] would actually help larger number of refugees or not'.[95] Another explanation, of course, is that the success of refugee manipulation identified in the previous chapter was more effective if Southeast Asian states refrained from acceding to the international refugee instruments.

4.3.3 *The Philippines*

The Philippines is a unique case for the region because it did accede to the 1951 Convention and 1967 Protocol in June 1981. The UNHCR had been in discussion with the Philippines government about accession since the 1950s.[96] Throughout this period, the Philippines greatest concern, and the main barrier to it signing, was that its close ally the United States had not done so.[97] However, even after the

92 UNHCR, Note for File, *Meeting with the Minister of State for Home Affairs and Law, Singapore, Professor S Jayakumar on 7 July 1982*, Folio 50, in Folio 247A, 31 August 1982, p. 2.

93 A good example of a member-state flouting the Convention due to the politics surrounding neighbouring state relations is the United States and Haiti. Haiti, while under authoritarian rule, produced a large number of people that fled by boat to US for asylum in 1970s and early 1980s. However, the US, a friend of anti-communist Haitian President, would not recognise these people as deserving of refugee status.

94 'Benefit of doubt' means that most arrivals are not screened as refugees, rather their status is *prima facie* and therefore Singapore just accepts UNHCR's provision of such status without proof.

95 UNHCR, Note for File, *Meeting with the Minister of State for Home Affairs and Law, Singapore, Professor S Jayakumar on 7 July 1982*, Folio 50, in Folio 247A, 31 August 1982, p. 2.

96 UNHCR, James Read, Deputy High Commissioner to Mr Mauro Calingo, Department of Foreign Affairs, Philippines, *Correspondence*, 23 December 1952; 671.1 1951 Convention 1952–1953. Also, the World Council of Churches (WCC), from looking at correspondence between James Read and Mollie Rule from the WCC during 1952 and 1953 indicate that the WCC would present information and correspondence on behalf of the UNHCR during this period.

97 Mollie Rule, Director of Operations for the WCC, in correspondence with James Read, says 'there is one question which I know Calingo [Philippine Foreign Affairs] will ask, 'Why has the United States of America not signed the Convention?'. She goes on to say 'you know the Philippines, they

United States signed the 1967 Protocol, the UNHCR still had a lot of work to do to convince the Philippines government about the advantages of signing the 1951 Convention and 1967 Protocol. In 1976 for instance, when the UNHCR representative in the Philippines talked to the Philippines government about accession, there was discussion about why other Asian states had not signed the instruments.[98] The UNHCR representative explained that the UNHCR had been primarily concerned with refugees in Europe and that only in the last decade had African states become involved. The support of Asian states though, would add 'great moral force' to the instruments.[99] Despite these approaches, the UNHCR tended to think that the Philippines government was not yet prepared to sign the instruments and that 'approaches, which could possibly create the impression that we are pressing the Philippines into accession, should naturally be avoided'.[100] Nevertheless, UNHCR headquarters endorsed the strategy of dialogue about the instruments with the Philippine government, particularly as the Philippines had been a part of the General Assembly which adopted Resolution 428 (V) on 14 December 1950, which had led to the establishment and mandate of the UNHCR. Their accession would not only 'constitute a most valuable contribution to the strengthening of the role and function of the UNHCR', but may serve to encourage ASEAN countries the 'desirability of becoming party to the instruments'.[101]

However, the Philippines government was concerned that signing the instruments would attract Vietnamese 'boat people'. The UNHCR was quick to assure them that this would not happen.[102] Although this assurance was given directly and repeatedly up until the Philippines government signed in 1981, the test of this assurance would not be known until afterward. In 1982, as the Officer-in-Charge in Manila noted, the Philippines government had not (and to this day has not) implemented any domestic legislation which encompasses articles of the 1951 Convention.[103] After 1981, the Philippines government continued to provide only

are always saying they do not want to follow blindly the lead of the USA but wish to formulate their own policy but in actual fact their whole world is bounded by the USA and they lay great store by the policy of that country!'. Mollie Rule, WCC to James Read, UNHCR, *Correspondence*, 16 February 1953; 671.1 1952–1953.

98 UNHCR, A Dhar to UNHCR Headquarters, *Ratification by the Philippines of the Convention and Protocol*, 30 March 1976; HCR/ML/48, Folio 5, 671.1 PHI, p. 1.

99 UNHCR, A Dhar to UNHCR Headquarters, *Ratification by the Philippines of the Convention and Protocol*, 30 March 1976; HCR/ML/48, Folio 5, 671.1 PHI, p. 2.

100 UNHCR, Otto Gobius, Asia Regional Section to UNHCR Branch Office for the Philippines, *The Philippines and the 1951 Convention and 1967 Protocol*, 7 April 1976; HCR/ML/36, Folio 6, 671.1 PHI, p. 1.

101 UNHCR, Otto Gobius, Asia Regional Section to UNHCR Branch Office for the Philippines, *Philippines and the 1951 Convention and 1967 Protocol*, 23 April 1976; HCR/ML/48, Folio 8, 671.1 PHI, p. 2.

102 UNHCR, W. Blatter, UNHCR Representative in Philippines to Protection Division, UNHCR Headquarters, *Philippine accession to the 1951 Convention and 1967 Protocol*, 31 March 1977; HCR/ML/34, Folio 13, 671.1 PHI, p. 1.

103 UNHCR, David Hay-Edie, Officer-in-Charge, UNHCR Manila to UNHCR Headquarters, *Protection Programme in Philippines: Problems and Promotion*, 15 March 1982; HCR/ML/073, Folio 286, 602.3 ASIA, pp. 1–2.

temporary asylum, and insisted on resettlement over local assimilation, contrary to what was normally expected after accession to the Convention.[104] The UNHCR also remained the primary guarantor of refugee protection for asylum seekers in the Philippines. Moreover, the number of asylum seekers in the Philippines *did rise* after it signed the Convention and Protocol. I am not attempting here to draw a correlation between the Philippine government acceding to the international refugee law instruments and the increase in its asylum seeking population. Nonetheless, there was an increase and this affected how the remaining ASEAN states perceived the outcomes of accession. In the Philippines, refugee numbers rose from 2,500 in 1980 to 16,500 in 1982, with refugees arriving by small boats or being rescued at sea.[105] Most of the time, the Philippines government was amenable to accepting these people (the promise of resettlement places and its link with the US is one reason yet again for this).

Three observations can be made about the accession by the Philippines. First, for Southeast Asian states such as Singapore, the Philippine accession demonstrated precisely why they preferred not to sign. Though the Philippines signed, and made a grand declaratory statement about the human rights of refugees, the lack of domestic implementation rendered the Convention practically useless. For Minister Jayakumar of Singapore, this would only have further demonstrated the irrelevance of the 1951 Convention. Second, whether or not accession was the cause, the increase in the number of refugees entering the Philippines immediately after its accession was enough to further demonstrate to Southeast Asian states that the likely consequences of such accession would be entirely negative. The arrival of more Indochinese asylum seekers in the Philippines after 1981 was notable because the Philippines had not traditionally been a popular area for the Indochinese to seek asylum. In addition, the number of refugees had not substantially increased elsewhere in the region at this time.[106] Third, accession led to further international pressure on the Philippines to accept those rescued at sea and provide more generous asylum conditions. As Indonesia and Singapore indicated, this was an imposition that the remaining Southeast Asian states were keen to avoid.

4.3.4 *Thailand*

The UNHCR's efforts to persuade Thailand to sign the 1951 Convention and 1967 Protocol increased steadily throughout the 1970s and early 1980s when the efforts reached their peak. The recurring theme of this diplomatic initiative was

104 Muntarbhorn, *The Status of Refugees in Asia*, 1992, pp. 82–84.

105 UNHCR, David Hay-Edie, Officer-in-Charge, UNHCR Manila to UNHCR Headquarters, *Protection Programme in Philippines: Problems and Promotion*, 15 March 1982; HCR/ML/073, Folio 286, 602.3 ASIA, p. 1.

106 Druke, *Preventative Action for Refugee Producing Situations*, 1993, p. 80; Robinson, *Terms of Refuge: The Indochinese Exodus and the International Response*, 1998, p. 173.

for the UNHCR to 'tread softly' with the Thai government, regardless of who was in government at the time.

In the early 1970s it was openly acknowledged in correspondence between UNHCR headquarters and its regional mission in Bangkok that the chance of accession was negligible. First of all, the UNHCR was not permitted by the Thai government to discuss the Convention and Protocol with a designated representative from the Foreign Ministry. Therefore, the Bangkok mission had great doubts about whether the documentation they sent to the Ministry was even being received and read.[107] Second, the political climate in Thailand and the struggle between military and civilian forces for political power during the 1970s and 1980s, made it an inappropriate time to press for accession. This reinforced the view that accession would be unlikely because 'this will not change much as it seems in the cards that the powers that be will be the same persons with a different title'.[108] Third, even though the Bangkok office eventually succeeded in arranging a meeting with the head of the foreign ministry's legal department and political department, little progress was made. The UNHCR's representative in Thailand reported that he was 'not optimistic of early results'.[109]

Constant approaches to government officials left the UNHCR in no doubt that by 1973 the Thai government knew what the 1951 Convention and 1967 Protocol were all about.[110] As the years progressed the UNHCR had both instruments translated into Thai in order to ensure that legal experts, military officials and the bureaucracy would have a better chance of knowing what practices the international instruments called for in responding to refugees.[111] Despite being confident in its prediction that the Thai government would not sign the legal instruments, the UNHCR Bangkok regional office invited Thailand to donate to the UNHCR. The UNHCR regional office reported back to head office in Geneva that if Thailand did make a financial contribution they were sure it would only be 'a token contribution'.[112] The interesting dynamic here is that while the UNHCR's regional office was assuring the Thai government that the High Commissioner would consider

[107] UNHCR, Otto Gobius, UNHCR Bangkok to The High Commissioner, *Convention/Protocol—Thailand*, 17 November 1972; HCR/BKK/273, Folio 2, 671.THA, p. 1.

[108] UNHCR, Otto Gobius, UNHCR Bangkok to The High Commissioner, *Convention/Protocol—Thailand*, 17 November 1972; HCR/BKK/273, Folio 2, 671.THA, p. 1.

[109] UNHCR, Otto Gobius, UNHCR Bangkok to The High Commissioner, *Convention/Protocol—Thailand*, 17 November 1972; HCR/BKK/273, Folio 2, 671.THA, p. 2.

[110] UNHCR, Otto Gobius, UNHCR Bangkok to The High Commissioner, *Discussion with Director General for International Organizations at the Foreign Ministry*, 26 January 1973; HCR/BKK/031, Folio 3, 671.THA, p. 1.

[111] UNHCR, S Chetty, Legal Section for Regional Representative, Bangkok to J Colombey, Conference and Treaties Section, UNHCR, *Translation of 1951 Convention in Thai Language*, 14 April 1982; HCR/BKK/HQ/0436, 671.1.GEN, p. 1; UNHCR, S Chetty, Legal Section for Regional Representative, Bangkok to D. McNamara, Head Legal Adviser in Asia, Hong Kong, *Promotion of Refugee Law in Thailand*, 15 February 1982; HCR/BKK/MISC/1005, 602.3 ASIA, p. 1.

[112] UNHCR, Otto Gobius, UNHCR Bangkok to The High Commissioner, *Discussion with Director General for International Organizations at the Foreign Ministry*, 26 January 1973; HCR/BKK/031, Folio 3, 671.THA, p. 1.

'any contribution most welcome',[113] the UNHCR regional office did not perceive a contribution by the Thai government to be significant. At this stage, Thailand remained disinclined to enter into dialogue with the UNHCR about accession. Thailand already had a sizable Indochinese refugee population and the UNHCR's suggestions about accession seemed to offer no solutions to this problem.

By 1977, the UNHCR was attempting to stress the benefits of signing. The argument that the UNHCR put forward was that accession would give the government 'a clear legal basis and guidelines for standards of treatment which have already won a wide measure of acceptance amongst the international community'.[114] Furthermore, 'accession has particular significance for the relations of the country of asylum with the country of origin', for the granting of asylum was to be widely perceived in the international community as a 'peaceful and humanitarian act and that as such cannot be regarded as unfriendly by any other State'.[115] Finally, the UNHCR insisted that signing would be advantageous because it would allow Thailand to make a formal 'humanitarian' response to Indochinese refugees through legal instruments. This approach would facilitate 'the promotion of appropriates [sic] measures of international support designed to lighten the burden of affected States'.[116]

The UNHCR's placatory tone and promise of 'good things to come' in its dialogue with Thailand about accession provides further evidence of the way the UNHCR adapted its strategy according to country-specific needs. Nonetheless, Thai perceptions of the 1951 Convention and 1967 Protocol did not change—as evidenced by the lack of progress made in achieving the necessary interest from the higher echelons of the Thai government. As discussed in Chapter 3, this was mainly because by the late 1970s Thailand knew that the international community would assist them with the Indochinese refugee problem whether it acceded or not. The result was that by 1979, the UNHCR was treading cautiously again. When discussing the 1979 round of promoting accessions to the 1951 Convention and 1967 Protocol in Asia, UNHCR's only reference to Thailand was that: 'unfortunately developments in Thailand [massive increase of Indochinese refugees followed by mass refoulement/pushbacks]... have either prevented such visits or made them unnecessary'.[117]

113 UNHCR, Otto Gobius, UNHCR Bangkok to The High Commissioner, *Discussion with Director General for International Organizations at the Foreign Ministry*, 26 January 1973; HCR/BKK/031, Folio 3, 671.THA, p. 1.

114 UNHCR, The High Commissioner Sadraddin Aga Khan to The Minister for Foreign Affairs, Kingdom of Thailand, *Correspondence*, 15 August 1977; Folio 5, 671.THA, p. 1.

115 UNHCR, The High Commissioner Sadraddin Aga Khan to The Minister for Foreign Affairs, Kingdom of Thailand, *Correspondence*, 15 August 1977; Folio 5, 671.THA, p. 1.

116 UNHCR, The High Commissioner Sadraddin Aga Khan to The Minister for Foreign Affairs, Kingdom of Thailand, *Correspondence*, 15 August 1977; Folio 5, 671.THA, p. 1.

117 UNHCR, Leslie Goodyear, Regional Representative for Western South Asia, Bangkok to The High Commissioner, UNHCR Headquarters, Geneva, *Promotion of the Accession of the 1951 Convention and the 1967 Protocol*, 19 June 1979; Folio 8, 671.1THA, 19 June 1979.

In 1981 and 1982, attempts to promote refugee protection in Thailand took a different track, once again demonstrating the 'brick wall' that the UNHCR continually faced in persuading the Thai government to seriously consider acceding to the 1951 Convention and 1967 Protocol. As mentioned earlier, the UNHCR had already taken upon itself to have the two refugee instruments published in Thai language and had started to conduct discussions and meetings with the legal community in Thailand.[118] Invitations were also sent to the Thai government. The UNHCR claimed greater success with the legal community who attended the Lawasia Conference, 8–12 August 1981.[119] The UNHCR stated that the promotion of accession was its first priority,[120] yet this was not even close to being achieved. As G. Coles from the Protection Division at UNHCR headquarters remarked:

> This makes it very difficult for my section to plan any kind of coherent programme for the development of refugee law. The first argument, I suppose, is to consider Bangkok's proposals in the context of an overall programme. It seems important to finalize that overall programme as soon as possible.[121]

In summary, the connection with Thai legal experts and some government officials led to more discussions, yet as Coles indicated, it did not influence the Thai government on issues related to protecting refugees and providing refugee status.

However, there was interest in some quarters of the Thai government. For instance, in 1981 Murrat Bunnag, the Minister of Justice, attended the UNHCR sponsored legal conferences and discussions and expressed an interest in Thailand acceding to the instruments. However, the Bangkok regional office noted that Minister Bunnag's approval was of 'limited value' because meaningful approval had to come from cabinet and parliament.[122] Therefore, success would only come from convincing all these actors that accession was a matter that should overcome their preoccupation with safeguarding their borders.[123] The UNHCR was not able to do this.

There were two main reasons why Thailand refused to accede. First, Thailand did not see the need to sign because it was already 'mindful of its humanitarian responsibility' in granting temporary refuge to Burmese and Vietnamese in addition

118 UNHCR, S. Chetty, Chief of Protection Section, Bangkok to Protection Section, Headquarters, *Promotion of Refugee Protection in Thailand*, 16 July 1981; Folio 10, 671.THA, pp. 1–2.

119 UNHCR, S Chetty, Chief of Protection Section, Bangkok to Protection Section, Headquarters, *Promotion of Refugee Protection in Thailand*, 16 July 1981; Folio 10, 671.THA, pp. 1–2; UNHCR, S. Chetty, Legal Section, Bangkok to Dennis McNamara, Legal Adviser in Asia, Hong Kong, *Promotion of Refugee Law In Thailand*, 15 February 1982; HCR/BKK/MISC/1005, 602.3 ASIA, pp. 1–2.

120 UNHCR, S. Chetty, Legal Section, Bangkok to Dennis McNamara, Legal Adviser in Asia, Hong Kong, *Promotion of Refugee Law In Thailand*, 15 February 1982; HCR/BKK/MISC/1005, 602.3 ASIA, p. 2. Lawasia is the representation of legal experts from ASEAN states.

121 UNHCR, Comment by G. L. Coles, *UNHCR Action Sheet*, 5 March 1982. Folio 281A, 602.3 ASIA.

122 UNHCR, UNHCR Bangkok to UNHCR High Commissioner, Geneva, *Incoming Cable*, 2 December 1981; Folio 13, 671.THA, p. 1.

123 UNHCR, UNHCR Bangkok to UNHCR High Commissioner, Geneva, *Incoming Cable*, 2 December 1981; Folio 13, 671.THA, p. 1.

to the Cambodians.[124] Second, Thailand did not think that the majority of people seeking asylum were refugees. Rather they were 'economic refugees in search of a better life in a third country' and there needed to be 'closer interrogation [to] reveal which individuals were genuine refugees and which were economic refugees'.[125] As a result, 'while the Thai authorities had no objection to countries accepting Vietnamese civilians and army defectors for resettlement, it considered there should be some assurance that once they were allowed into Thailand to await resettlement they would not be left there as an added burden on Thailand'.[126]

4.3.5 *Malaysia*

In the literature, Malaysia's refusal to sign the 1951 Convention and 1967 Protocol is often explained as racist.[127] However, my investigation of Malaysia's response in the 1970s and 1980s demonstrates that their reasons for *not* signing the instruments is, as with most Southeast Asian states, based on a more complicated set of circumstances. The state of Malaysia was created in 1963;[128] and with a minority Malay population since independence, the primary concern of the United Malays National Organization (UMNO), which has held government to this day, has been to assert the 'special rights' of Malays.[129] The remaining ethnic Chinese and Indian populations, most of whom migrated during British colonization of Malaya to work the tin mines and tap the trees in rubber plantations, had citizenship rights. However, the privileges were all directed to the Malays. For instance, all key government posts were reserved specifically for ethnic Malays. The so-called Bumiputra policy also aimed to encourage Malay entrepreneurialism and lessen control of the economy by ethnic Chinese.[130]

Therefore, there is some justification for the argument that Malaysia's response to refugees was reflective of its racist domestic structure. However, there are a number of points that suggest otherwise. First, Malaysia has a strong Islamic tradition and has a history of accepting refugees because of their Islamic faith (regardless of ethnicity).

---

124 UNGA, *Summary Record of the 369th Session on 9 October*, Executive Committee of the High Commissioner's Programme, Thirty-Fifth Session, A/AC.96/SR.369, 12 October 1984, p. 7.

125 UNGA, *Summary Record of the 369th Session on 9 October*, Executive Committee of the High Commissioner's Programme, Thirty-Fifth Session, A/AC.96/SR.369, 12 October 1984, p. 8. The repercussions of identifying Indochinese refugees as 'economic refugees' will be discussed further in Chapter 5.

126 UNGA, *Summary Record of the 369th Session on 9 October*, Executive Committee of the High Commissioner's Programme, Thirty-Fifth Session, A/AC.96/SR.369, 12 October 1984, p. 7.

127 Wain, *The Refused: The Agony of the Indochina Refugees*, 1980; O'Connor Sutter, *The Indochinese Refugee Dilemma*, 1990; Muntarbhorn, *The Status of Refugees in Asia*, 1992; Suhrke, 'The "High Politics" of Population Movements: Migration, State and Civil Society in Southeast Asia', in Weiner, Myron (ed.), *International Migration and Security*, 1993, pp. 179–200; Robinson, *Terms of Refuge: The Indochinese Exodus and the International Response*, 1998.

128 The predominantly ethnic Chinese Singapore was annexed in 1965.

129 Berger, M. T., 'Decolonizing Southeast Asia: Nationalism, Revolution and the Cold War', in Beeson, M. (ed.), *Contemporary Southeast Asia: Regional Dynamics, National Differences* (Hampshire: Palgrave Macmillan, 2004), p. 35.

130 Allen, R. *A Short Introduction to the History and Politics of Southeast Asia* (New York: Oxford University Press, 1970), p. 158.

Second, throughout the Indochinese refugee crisis, Malaysia accepted the highest number of boat people and refugees in total, second only to Thailand.[131] These actions do not reflect a 'racist state'. Indeed, the UNHCR praised Malaysia for 'fully adhering to the letter and the spirit of that agreement [1979 Geneva Conference Agreement] has been exemplary'.[132] Muntarbhorn's appraisal of Malaysia during the Indochinese refugee crisis was that generally, the 'principle of *non-refoulement* was respected'.[133] Robinson suggests that despite its policy of push-backs (Malaysia was hardly alone in this policy), in the decade after the 1979 Conference, Malaysia 'maintained a creditable record of generosity, granting temporary asylum to more than 250 000 Vietnamese'.[134] These responses are in marked contrast to the majority of other Southeast Asian states during the crisis. Moreover, when considering the sheer volume of refugees that Malaysia held temporarily—the majority of whom were ethnic Chinese—it seems necessary to question why a state that was racist would tolerate even the temporary presence of such people.[135]

The primary reason why Malaysia chose not to sign the 1951 Convention or 1967 Protocol was that like its neighbors, it did not see any benefit in signing. Malaysia formulated its own refugee response policy, which was based on religious preference and an insistence on temporary asylum for all others. Thus, it found more benefit in maintaining its own ad-hoc practice than in signing the 1951 Convention and possibly losing control over such decisions. In 1959, the UNHCR requested the then Federation of Malaya to consider accession to the 1951 Convention. The communication said that at the time, Malaysia's accession could provide a 'useful example'[136] to other Asian states. It was reported though that the Federation of Malaya's response was unenthusiastic.[137] In 1969, the UNHCR's representative, William McCoy, reported on his discussion with the Malaysian government and their attitude towards the 1951 Convention and relatively new 1967 Protocol. The first point made by McCoy was that there had been a need to

> *(D)ispel some misconceptions and to clarify some misunderstandings* on the Convention and Protocol and also on the Mandate of the High Commissioner. Most of the misunderstanding arose out of an *admitted ignorance of the subject matter and an unfamiliarity with the instruments* at issue.[138]

131 Robinson, *Terms of Refuge: The Indochinese Exodus and the International Response*, 1998.

132 UNHCR, Darioush Bayandor, UNHCR Representative for Kuala Lumpur, *Report on Situation of the VNBP*, Annual Review Meeting of Vietnamese Boatpeople, 30 January 1984; 010.MLS, p. 2.

133 Muntarbhorn, *The Status of Refugees in Asia*, 1992, p. 119.

134 Robinson, *Terms of Refuge: The Indochinese Exodus and the International Response*, 1998, p. 190.

135 Suhrke, 'The "High Politics" of Population Movements: Migration, State and Civil Society in Southeast Asia', in Weiner, Myron (ed.), *International Migration and Security*, 1993.

136 UNHCR, James Read, Deputy High Commissioner to Prime Minister and Minister for Foreign Affairs, Federation of Malaya, *Correspondence*, 4 November 1959; Folio 852, 16/1/3/GEN, p. 2.

137 UNHCR, *Report on Mr de Kemoularia's visit to Malaya 12/9/59*, Excerpt from File 27/3/5—WRY/MAL; 13 November 1959, p. 1.

138 UNHCR, W K McCoy to UNHCR Geneva, *Malaysia—Attitude to Convention*, Memorandum, 15 March 1969; MAC/SEA/MAL, Folio 1829, 16/1/3/GEN, p. 1. Emphasis added.

McCoy reported that there was interest in the instruments, and that therefore a follow up was most important but accession 'in the near future is not probable but a serious study of the whole question will certainly enlighten people as to the role of the Office and the interest of the HC in refugees matters in this area'.[139]

Throughout the 1970s, there were numerous attempts by the UNHCR to secure Malaysian accession to the 1951 Convention and 1967 Protocol. Communications, such as 'explanatory notes' were sent to Malaysia similar to those sent to other Southeast Asian countries. The notes argued that 'accession has particular significance for the relations of the country of asylum with the country of origin'.[140] The UNHCR argued in 1977 that possible tension between two countries is 'substantially reduced when the country of asylum is seen to be acting in accordance with its obligations under instruments which are already widely accepted by States'.[141] This note followed a question raised by the UNHCR Southeast Asia representative in 1974 as to why Southeast Asian states may be reluctant to sign the 1951 Convention and 1967 Protocol.

However, the principle of non-interference in the domestic affairs of other ASEAN states remained a hallmark of ASEAN's Treaty of Amity and Cooperation (TAC).[142] Despite the UNHCR's protestations to the contrary, claiming that refugees from a neighboring state were legitimate refugees would have been widely understood as a breach of the principle of non-interference. Under TAC, the non-interference norm was tantamount to preventing criticism of a neighboring state, or providing any form of support to any splinter group which may be destabilizing a member state.[143] The 1951 Convention required that a refugee would be identified by a *legitimate* claim of persecution in their state of origin.[144] Such recognition would

[139] UNHCR, W. K. McCoy to UNHCR Geneva, *Malaysia—Attitude to Convention*, Memorandum, 15 March 1969; MAC/SEA/MAL, Folio 1829, 16/1/3/GEN, p. 1.

[140] UNHCR, Explanatory Note, *On Special aspects of the 1951 Convention and 1967 Protocol relating to the Status of Refugees*, July 1977; Folio 1, 672.MLS, p. 1.

[141] UNHCR, Explanatory Note, *On Special aspects of the 1951 Convention and 1967 Protocol relating to the Status of Refugees*, July 1977; Folio 1, 672.MLS, p. 1.

[142] TAC was formed in 1976 and its purpose has been to enshrine 'mutual respect for sovereign independence, territorial integrity, sovereign equality, national identity and the freedom of every state to lead its own national existence'. Ramcharan, P., 'ASEAN and Non-Interference: A Principle Maintained', *Contemporary Southeast Asia*, 22(1) (2000), p. 65.

[143] Acharya, *Constructing a Security Community in Southeast Asia: ASEAN and the Problem of Regional Order*, 2001, p. 58.

[144] Antonio Fortin and Patricia Tuitt both make the point that no matter how much the UNHCR mandate is non-political in character, which in turn encompasses the 1951 Convention and 1967 Protocol, at the end of the day, it is still up to the state that determine that a person fleeing a fellow state is being mistreated by that state. Fortin argues that the term 'fear of political persecution' was known by the drafters to have political implications that, at the time of the Cold War, was not so much a concern—but it is one that has increasingly affected the Convention's application. Tuitt argues that the 1951 Convention has been successfully manipulated by states to reduce a person's claim of persecution to an analysis of the state they fled, as opposed to their individual fear. Both argue that state adherence to the 1951 Convention becomes an inherently political act. Tuitt, P. *False Images: Law's Construction of the Refugee* (London: Pluto Press, 1996). Fortin, A., 'The Meaning of "Protection" in the Refugee Definition', *International Journal of Refugee Law*, 12 (4), (2001), pp. 548–576.

be understood as interfering then with the norms that TAC tried to institute in ASEAN in 1976. Thus, Malaysia's provision of asylum to its neighboring countries' citizens is worth evaluating further in light of the TAC and their refusal to align their provision of refuge with the 1951 Convention and 1967 Protocol.

Since the early 1970s, Malaysia has had a history of allowing predominantly Muslim people to seek refuge. Between 1972 and 1985 the Malaysian state of Sabah gave citizenship to approximately 40,000 to 90,000 Muslim Filipinos[145] who were fleeing an armed conflict between the predominantly Christian Philippine state and the Muslim separatist group, the Moro National Liberation Front, in the Mindanao Islands. Malaysia was in essence sheltering people that were either by religious or direct association part of a separatist group that the Philippine government had declared martial law against.[146] The fact that the West Malaysian state of Sabah accepted this group as refugees was not well received by the Philippine government.[147] However, these people were not given formal refugee status by the Malaysian government (although the UNHCR and Sabah local government did grant them refugee status) and a large proportion was portrayed as simply fulfilling a labor shortage that existed in the state at the time.[148] Malaysia has never had any domestic legislation that provides asylum seeking or refugee status procedures.[149] Therefore, a person that arrived in Malaysia without a permit, pass or on 'special compassionate grounds' was considered an illegal migrant.[150]

These laws eventually caught up with the Filipinos in 1985 when the Sabah government changed hands from an Islamic majority to a Christian based party. The new ruling Kadazan Party changed the region's liberal residence laws. As a result, to this day up to 58,000 Filipinos in Sabah do not have the citizenship status that would provide them with more security of residence.[151] What the Filipino Muslim case demonstrates is that although Malaysia allows refuge to be sought in

[145] Vitit Muntarbhorn says that there were between 60 000 and 80 000. Muntarbhorn, *The Status of Refugees in Asia*, 1992, p. 115. Courtland Robinson says that there has been 50 000. Robinson, *Terms of Refuge: The Indochinese Exodus and the International Response*, 1998, p. 283. The UNHCR though, which was providing financial assistance for programmes that pertained to the Filipino refugees, said that the numbers were around 90 000 at the time, UNGA, *Report on UNHCR Assistance Activities in 1984–1985 and Proposed Voluntary Funds Programmes and Budget for Executive Committee of the High Commissioner's Programme*, Executive Committee of the High Commissioner's Programme, Thirty-Sixth Session, A/AC.96/657, 5 August 1985, p. 360.

[146] McKenna, T. M. *Muslim Rulers and Rebels: Everyday Politics and Armed Separatism in the Southern Philippines* (Berkeley: University of California Press, 1998).

[147] Zolberg, A., et al. *Escape From Violence: Conflict and the Refugee Crisis in the Developing World*, 1989, p. 175.

[148] Rachagan, 'Refugees and illegal immigrants: the Malaysian experience with Filipino and Vietnamese refugees', in Ruggie, J. (ed.), *Refugees: A Third World Dilemma*, 1987, pp. 253–268; Muntarbhorn, *The Status of Refugees in Asia*, 1992, p. 115; UNGA, *Report on UNHCR Assistance Activities in 1984–1985 and Proposed voluntary Funds Programmes and Budget for Executive Committee of the High Commissioner's Programme*, Executive Committee of the High Commissioner's Programme, Thirty-Sixth Session, A/AC.96/657, 5 August 1985, p. 360.

[149] UNHCR, *Country Operations Plan, Country: Malaysia*, Planning Year 2004 (2003) p. 1.

[150] Rachagan, 'Refugees and illegal immigrants: the Malaysian experience with Filipino and Vietnamese refugees', in Ruggie, J. (ed.), *Refugees: A Third World Dilemma*, 1987, p. 253.

[151] UNHCR, *Country Operations Plan, Country: Malaysia*, Planning Year 2004 (2003) p. 2.

its territory, it does not mean that it wants to provide anything *more than* that to the population. Moreover, it simultaneously took measures to uphold the Treaty of Amity and Cooperation in its relationship with the Philippines. This is evidenced by the fact that though Malaysia allowed Sabah to provide refuge to those seeking asylum from Mindanao, it also took steps to block Libyan attempts to place the discussion of the Muslim uprising in the Philippines on the agenda of the Organization of Islamic Conference (OIC) during the 1970s.[152]

In 1975 Malaysia accepted 1,275 Cambodian Muslims who had fled the Pol Pot regime and during the Indochinese refugee crisis Malaysia continued to allow a select number of Cambodian Muslims to locally integrate. By 1992, it was estimated that 10,000 Cambodian Muslims had been allowed to settle in Malaysia, assisted by the Malaysian Muslim Welfare Organization (PEKIM) which received funding from the UNHCR and the Malaysian government. In the early 1980s, Malaysia also permitted the local settlement of a small number of Rohinga Muslims fleeing Burma and Acehnese Muslims fleeing the violence from Indonesia.[153]

Therefore, Malaysian government has allowed people to seek refuge at the risk of breaching the TAC. Malaysia has been able to strike a balance between solidarity with other Muslims and adherence to TAC. This balanced approach may not be in accordance with the 1951 Convention, but it suits Malaysia. Robinson quotes the director of PEKIM:

> I don't think this country is interested in proclaiming itself as a haven for Muslims around the world . . . The government will not accede to the Refugee Convention but it needs to recognize that selected groups are in need of protection and assistance. Sri Lankans, Burmese Rohingyas, Bosnians have a case. There are also others who are not Muslims but who say their lives are in danger. Do we treat them simply as illegals and deport them? Generally, the government does not do this but they have not recognized them as refugees either.[154]

---

152 Astri Suhrke (1993), for instance, refers to a desire by the Malaysian government to inflame the 1968 territorial dispute over Sabah between the Philippines and Malaysia through providing refugee to the Filipino 'insurgents'. Suhrke, 'The "High Politics" of Population Movements: Migration, State and Civil Society in Southeast Asia', in Weiner, Myron (ed.), *International Migration and Security*, 1993. However, as Greg Fealy (2004) points out, and as the lack of refugee status provision to the Filipino group, it seems that Malaysia still had every intention of not interfering or condemning Philippines internal matter. Therefore, it seems important to differentiate between local Sabah forces and the Malaysian government. Fealy, G., 'Islam in Southeast Asia: Domestic Pietism, Diplomacy and Security', in Beeson, M. (ed.), *Contemporary Southeast Asia: Regional Dynamics, National Differences*, 2004, pp. 136–155.

153 During the 1980s UNHCR documents such as the Weekly Notes prepared for the Protection Office in Geneva, and the UNHCR Yearly Programmes refer to these populations as receiving assistance from the Malaysian Muslim Welfare Organisation (PEKIM) and UNHCR providing funds to further that assistance. It should be noted though, that in the last ten or so years, with the acceptance of Burma into ASEAN and Indonesia's removal of martial law, Malaysia has changed its stance on the unspecified numbers of Rohingya and Acehnese Muslims which have sought refuge. Upon discovery, such people are labeled as 'illegal migrants' and arrested. UNHCR, *Country Operations Plan, Country: Malaysia*, Planning Year 2004 (2003).

154 Robinson, *Terms of Refuge: The Indochinese Exodus and the International Response*, 1998, p. 283.

How did this practice affect Indochinese refugees? The first thing to note is that the Cambodian Muslims accepted in Malaysia during the same period were not Malay—they were Cambodian. This point is emphasized to cast further doubt on the idea that Malaysia's refugee policy was racist. Though racial issues certainly played a part, they were not Malaysia's primary concern and thus do not explain Malaysia's refusal to sign the 1951 Convention and 1967 Protocol. As argued earlier, Malaysia's record was one of, if not the best, when it came to responding to the Indochinese refugees after the 1979 Conference.

Prior to the 1979 Conference, Malaysia was receiving a massive influx of Indochinese refugees: 60,000 boat people arrived in one month in early 1979.[155] Consequently, the Malaysian government did not hesitate in joining the ASEAN Joint Communiqué of 30 June 1979, which stated that no more boat people would be allowed into ASEAN territorial shores.[156] Prior to this Communiqué, Malaysia had already pushed a number of boats back into perilous waters.[157] Even after the 1979 Conference, the UNHCR Weekly Protection notes reported that Malaysia continued to practice push-backs.[158] However these were sporadic, and during the early 1980s Malaysia, in contrast to Thailand, made genuine efforts through its Task Force VII[159] to prevent the violent activities of pirates around their shores; it also encouraged fishermen to be proactive in preventing pirate attacks on boat people.[160]

After the 1979 Conference, Malaysia's level of cooperation was considered 'exemplary' until at least 1987, when Indochinese refugee numbers rose again.[161] Of course, Malaysia provided cooperation on the condition that all Vietnamese boat people were resettled in third countries. Overall, the UNHCR considered Malaysia's upholding of the agreement to continue providing temporary asylum as an attitude that was 'all the more praiseworthy in the face of confirmed and persistent reports of push off practiced elsewhere in the region by states which have assumed similar commitments as Malaysia to grant the boatpeople a temporary refuge'.[162] Therefore, Malaysia's acceptance of Vietnamese refugees was better than

155 Robinson, *Terms of Refuge: The Indochinese Exodus and the International Response*, 1998, p. 283.

156 ASEAN, *Joint Communiqué of the Twelfth ASEAN Ministerial Meeting*, Bali, Indonesia, 30th June 1979 (Jakarta: Terbatas, ASEAN Sekretariat Nasional, 1979).

157 Robinson, *Terms of Refuge: The Indochinese Exodus and the International Response*, 1998, p. 189.

158 From August 1979 to January 1982, the UNHCR Protection Division in Southeast Asia would report of the Malaysian authorities sporadically partaking in pushbacks of vessels containing boat people into international waters.

159 Task Force VII was developed to specifically deal with the Indochinese refugee problem—comprised of members from the police department, military and bureaucratic officials.

160 UNHCR, Darioush Bayandor, UNHCR Representative for Kuala Lumpur, *Report on Situation of the VNBP*, Annual Review Meeting of Vietnamese Boatpeople, 30 January 1984; 010.MLS, pp. 13–14.

161 UNHCR, Darioush Bayandor, UNHCR Representative for Kuala Lumpur, *Report on Situation of the VNBP*, Annual Review Meeting of Vietnamese Boatpeople, 30 January 1984; 010.MLS, p. 2.

162 UNHCR, Darioush Bayandor, UNHCR Representative for Kuala Lumpur, *Report on Situation of the VNBP*, Annual Review Meeting of Vietnamese Boatpeople, 30 January 1984; 010.MLS, p. 2.

other states despite the fact that there were times when the rate of resettlement was not always commensurate with the rate of arrivals.[163]

The main position taken by Malaysia was that they should not be expected to take all of those who sought asylum for permanent refuge. Malaysia argued that the Indochinese refugee problem was not one that only Southeast Asia should have to solve. Rather it was 'incumbent upon all countries... to work towards a solution of the problem, particularly through speedier resettlement and by attacking the problem at its roots'.[164] Southeast Asian states had provided asylum on humanitarian grounds to the 'influx of Indo-Chinese refugees and illegal Vietnamese immigrants' despite the 'socio-economic and political threats that their presence posed to regional and national security'.[165]

However, although Malaysia's Indochinese refugee population fluctuated, during the early 1980s the UNHCR rarely reported concern about whether or not Malaysian cooperation would continue.[166] In fact, Malaysia often took the boats that Thailand had pushed back from their shores.[167] This is not characteristic of a vehemently racist country. As indicated earlier, Malaysia had the highest number of Indochinese boat people throughout the crisis, second only to Thailand in terms of total refugee numbers, yet their provision of protection was one that the UNHCR derived most assurance from.[168] Therefore, Malaysia's response to Indochinese refugees in general cannot be characterized as one dominated by the internal politics of race. Rather, Malaysia's overriding concern was that it not be expected to provide limitless asylum. By the early 1980s, Malaysia was becoming concerned (like Western states, remaining Southeast Asian states and even UNHCR) that not all of the Indochinese seeking asylum were 'genuine' refugees. Malaysia also expressed concern in the early 1980s that this rise in 'illegal migrants' or 'economic migrants' was leading to a decrease in the provision of resettlement places and that the burden needed to be shared by all.[169] Malaysia expressed the

---

[163] UNHCR, Darioush Bayandor, UNHCR Representative for Kuala Lumpur, *Report on Situation of the VNBP*, Annual Review Meeting of Vietnamese Boatpeople, 30 January 1984; 010.MLS, p. 2.

[164] Mr Kamil, Observer for Malaysia. UNGA, *Summary Records of the 346th Session on 13 October*, Executive Committee of the High Commissioner's Programme, Thirty-Third Session, A/AC.96/SR.346, 18 October 1982, p. 7.

[165] Mr Kamil, Observer for Malaysia. UNGA, *Summary Records of the 346th Session on 13 October*, Executive Committee of the High Commissioner's Programme, Thirty-Third Session, A/AC.96/SR.346, 18 October 1982, p. 7.

[166] UNGA, *Report on UNHCR Assistance Activities in 1984–1985 and Proposed voluntary Funds Programmes and Budget for Executive Committee of the High Commissioner's Programme*, Executive Committee of the High Commissioner's Programme, Thirty-Sixth Session, A/AC.96/657, 5 August 1985, p. 360.

[167] Muntabhorn, *The Status of Refugee in Asia*, 1992, p. 114.

[168] UNHCR, UNHCR Kuala Lumpur to UNHCR, Geneva, *Incoming Cable*, 18 February 1980; HCR/KL/137, 671.1.MLS; UNHCR, UNHCR Kuala Lumpur to Legal Adviser for Asia, Hong Kong, *Incoming Cable*, 19 November 1981; HCR/KL/648; HCR/KL/MISC/1457, 671.1.MLS; UNHCR, Darioush Bayandor, UNHCR Representative for Kuala Lumpur, *Report on Situation of the VNBP*, Annual Review Meeting of Vietnamese Boatpeople, 30 January 1984; 010.MLS.

[169] Mr Kamil, Observer for Malaysia. UNHCR, *Summary Records of the 346th Session on 13 October*,

same concern as Southeast Asian states prior to the 1979 Conference that states such as United States needed to give more 'adequate attention to the boat people in Malaysia which has [sic] grown to a sizeable proportion'.[170]

Malaysia's refusal to sign the 1951 Convention was primarily instrumental. The Malaysian government continued to demonstrate a reluctance to sign the instruments for a number of reasons. First, the lack of accession allowed Malaysia to act more freely and in a way of its own choosing.[171] The Malaysian government believed that it had a sovereign right to decide how its state was run, who could enter and who could not. If the Malaysian government subscribed to the UNHCR's legal instruments, it believed that it would lose this independence. Second, the need to maintain sovereign independence in the treatment of asylum seekers becomes all the more evident when it is observed who Malaysia wished to provide permanent asylum to. Malaysia accepted fleeing Muslims according to the traditional notion of an Islamic refugee—the *muhajir*—where the Islamic faith calls upon people to accept Muslims that need to flee oppression.[172] In addition, Malay national identity has become increasingly based on the Islamic faith, in comparison to its Christian Chinese and Hindu Indian counterparts.[173] However, the government believed that it would be required to grant refugee status to all, resulting in Malaysia having to declare that its neighbors were mistreating their citizens and provide refugee protection to people that their neighbor may see as 'political terrorists'. The third reason for Malaysia's refusal to accede was that it did not wish to provide asylum to all who entered. Under this regime, not even Muslim asylum seekers were guaranteed inalienable rights. The Malaysian government afforded itself considerable room for maneuver by not acceding to international refugee law. For instance, in the case of the Filipino Muslims, approximately 48,000 are yet to be given citizenship.[174] The

---

Executive Committee of the High Commissioner's Programme, Thirty-Third Session, A/AC.96/SR.346, 18 October 1982, p. 7.

170 UNHCR, Note for the File, *Meeting with Mr Ahmad Kamil bin Jaafar*, Confidential, 28 June 1978; 78/KL/845, Folio 6, 671.1.MLS, p. 1.

171 UNHCR, UNHCR Kuala Lumpur to UNHCR, Geneva, *Incoming Cable*, 18 February 1980; HCR/KL/137, 671.1.MLS; UNHCR Kuala Lumpur to Legal Adviser for Asia, Hong Kong, *Incoming Cable*, 19 November 1981; HCR/KL/648; HCR/KL/MISC/1457, 671.1.MLS, p. 1; UNHCR, Darioush Bayandor, UNHCR Representative for Kuala Lumpur, *Report on Situation of the VNBP*, Annual Review Meeting of Vietnamese Boatpeople, 30 January 1984; 010.MLS.

172 Zolberg, A., et al., *Escape From Violence: Conflict and the Refugee Crisis in the Developing World*, 1989. Evidence of Malaysia's desire to develop a refugee understanding based on Islam is evidenced by its desire to link up with Pakistan in providing recognition of an Afghan Mujahidin Office in Kuala Lumpur. UNHCR, D Bayandor, UNHCR Representative in Malaysia, to UNHCR Headquarters, Geneva, *Set Up of Afghan Mujahidin Office in Kuala Lumpur*, 24 April 1984; 84/KL/HQ.186, 010.MLS. Pakistan (also not a member of the 1951 Convention or 1967 Protocol) often referred to its provision of asylum to Afghan refugees during this same time as being in recognition of *muhajir*, as opposed to the international instruments regarding refugees. UNGA, *Summary Record of the 333rd Meeting on 14 October 1981*, Executive Committee Meeting of the High Commissioner's Programme, Thirty-Second Session, A/AC.96/SR.333, 21 October 1981, p. 15.

173 Fealy, 'Islam in Southeast Asia: Domestic Pietism, Diplomacy and Security', in Beeson, M. (ed.), *Contemporary Southeast Asia: Regional Dynamics, National Differences*, 2004, pp. 136–155.

174 UNHCR, *Country Operations Plan, Country: Malaysia*, Planning Year 2004 (2003).

Filipinos, like the Acehnese and the Burmese Rohingya Muslims were welcomed in the 1980s when the need for labour made their presence more welcome.[175] However, as labour patterns have shifted, these groups—in spite of their shared Muslim identity—are no longer any more secure than the Vietnamese refugees. They are also now subject to arrest, detention and forced deportation.[176]

4.4 *Conclusion*

This chapter has demonstrated that the 1979 Conference did not have a profound effect on Southeast Asian state practice in relation to refugees. Southeast Asian states continued to insist that the Indochinese refugee problem was as much an international problem as a regional one. These states continued to manipulate the crisis by threatening to refuse entry to the Indochinese unless resettlement places and assistance continued to be provided. At the same time, the UNHCR's efforts to introduce a regional refugee protection regime met with ongoing opposition from Southeast Asian states. The fact that the 1979 Conference placed very little pressure on Southeast Asian states to comply with international refugee protection instruments encouraged them to continue to expect the same heightened level of assistance and resettlement numbers. As a result, in the early 1980s when Southeast Asian states were concerned that assistance could fall below the level provided in 1979–80, they had no hesitation in reverting to threats of pushbacks and refusal of temporary asylum.

The support of states such as United States, Australia and Japan encouraged Southeast Asian states to continue insisting that they would only cooperate if international assistance continued. This had the effect of undercutting the UNHCR's attempts to encourage adherence to refugee protection principles. The UNHCR had little hope of convincing Southeast Asian states that they had an obligation to sign the international refugee law instruments in a context where they continued to receive significant assistance. Thus, Southeast Asian states believed that it would not be in their interests to sign these instruments because, by and large, their demands were already being met. These states were able to insist that temporary asylum was all they would and could provide, and states such as the United States, Australia and Japan expected little more. The UNHCR's attempts to instigate refugee protection principles at the regional level failed, as did its encouragement of accession at the state level. Here again, the Southeast Asian states[177] argued that their lack of involvement in the drafting of these laws left them with no knowledge of the instruments and no desire to sign. In addition, they argued that they refused to sign

175 UNHCR, *Country Operations Plan, Country: Malaysia*, Planning Year 2004 (2003); Rachagan, 'Refugees and illegal immigrants: the Malaysian experience with Filipino and Vietnamese refugees', in Ruggie, J. (ed.), *Refugees: A Third World Dilemma*, 1987, pp. 253–268.

176 UNHCR, *Country Operations Plan, Country: Malaysia*, Planning Year 2004 (2003), pp. 1–2.

177 With the exception of the Philippines as noted in Section 4.3.3.

because they could not commit to adhering to the instruments. This demonstrates that their resistance to the instruments was articulated through the description of them as 'not applicable' to those seeking asylum in their region. The 'not applicable' argument signifies a continued impact on the perceived Eurocentric nature of the 1951 Convention and the 1967 Protocol.

Therefore, by the mid-1980s, just prior to the second increase of Indochinese asylum seekers, Southeast Asian states had successfully maneuvered their way out of any real obligation to refugee populations. They now also enjoyed the cooperation of key resettlement states in framing a different perception of those seeking asylum. At this stage we first begin to see Southeast Asian states argue that their label for Indochinese asylum seekers as 'non-genuine' refugees was legitimate in contrast to the 'genuine' refugee definition contained in the 1951 Convention. It is this development and the increasing Western states support of the Southeast Asian states position that will be the focus of Chapter 5.

Chapter 5

'Compassion Fatigue'[1] in the Mid 1980s

During the 1980s, refugee flows from Indochina continued but resettlement numbers started to fall as developed states started to suffer from what ASEAN termed 'compassion fatigue'.[2] In addition, international assistance began to be redirected towards new refugee crises in Africa and Central Asia. This prompted Southeast Asian states to argue that they should not be required to assist populations who were not *bona fide* refugees and who were better described as 'economic migrants', 'illegal migrants', or 'non-genuine' refugees. Southeast Asian states called for asylum seekers to be individually assessed and if found not to meet the 1951 Convention definition, be forcibly returned to their country of origin. This about-turn in the perception of Indochinese asylum seekers caused uncertainty about how they were to be defined and treated. In this chapter, I illustrate how Southeast Asian states continually manipulated this uncertain situation.

---

1 First used by ASEAN states to describe resettlement states reluctance to continually accept Indochinese as refugees. ASEAN, *Joint Statement by the ASEAN Foreign Ministers on Indochinese Refugees*, Singapore, 14 June 1987. http://www.aseansec.org/2484.html I am aware of the term 'compassion fatigue' being used by authors such as Susan Moeller, Luc Boltanski and Stanley Cohen who refer to the public having a dulled sensitivity towards crises that are reported by the media. However, as ASEAN states used the term 'compassion fatigue' in their responses during sessions of the Executive Committee Meetings of the High Commissioner and in ASEAN Joint Statements I have chosen to use their understanding of the term. Moeller, S. D. *Compassion Fatigue: How the Media Sell Disease, Famine, War and Death* (London: Routledge, 1998); Boltanski, L. *Distant Suffering: Morality, Media and Politics*. Translated by Graham Burchell (Cambridge: Cambridge University Press, 1999); Cohen, S. *States of Denial: Knowing about Atrocities and Suffering* (Cambridge: Polity Press, 2001).

2 ASEAN, *Joint Statement by the ASEAN Foreign Ministers on Indochinese Refugees*, Singapore, 14 June 1987. http://www.aseansec.org/2484.html

In this chapter, I argue that by the mid 1980s Southeast Asian states' became successful in claiming that Indochinese asylum seekers did not deserve *prima facie* refugee status. Acceptance of their argument by the international community further legitimised their refusal to accede to the 1951 Convention and 1967 Protocol. The 'non-genuine' refugee argument was first made in the late 1970s around the time that people began to pay traffickers to be taken out of Vietnam (see Chapter 3). However, the label commonly used then was 'illegal migrants'. It was not until the mid 1980s that Southeast Asian states began to position the 'non-genuine' Indochinese refugee in contrast to the 'genuine' refugee contained in the 1951 Convention, that many Western states and even the UNHCR began to accept the idea that Indochinese asylum seekers should not receive *prima facie* refugee status.

This chapter is divided into five sections. First, I will look at Southeast Asian states demands for Western states to adhere to the promises of resettlement and assistance made at the 1979 Conference. The continuing arrival of Indochinese refugees meant that Southeast Asian states wanted to ensure that their plight was ever present in the mind of donor and resettlement states. One way in which they effectively maintained the international community's attention was by questioning the refugee status of the boat people. The second part of the chapter looks at precisely how Southeast Asian states started to frame this argument. At this stage of the crisis, when the number of Indochinese seeking asylum begins to increase again, there was a curious lack of counter-argument by Western states and the UNHCR. In section three of the chapter, I show how this impacted on the Cambodian refugee population. The Cambodians were not protected by the UNHCR as refugees, unless they could gain access to a UNHCR camp on the Thai border, which was very difficult. Therefore, the majority remained on the border throughout the late 1970s and 1980s, being constantly displayed as evidence of Thailand's generosity and as a reminder of the need for the international community to deal with the Indochinese refugee problem. The fourth section of the chapter looks at how, by the mid 1980s, relations between the UNHCR and Thailand became increasingly strained. Thailand was affronted by the UNHCR publicly discussing the difficulty it was having in preventing pirate attacks on boat people in the Thai Gulf. This led the UNHCR to attempt to appease Thailand in order to maintain a presence there and keep the general cooperation of the Southeast Asian states. However, this need to appease was taking its toll on the UNHCR and Western states both financially and politically. In the final section of this chapter I demonstrate how Southeast Asian states succeeded in convincing key international actors that the Indochinese should not be considered *prima facie* refugees. This occurred just as the numbers started to rise again and provided the catalyst for the 1989 Comprehensive Plan of Action (CPA) (discussed in the next chapter).

5.1 *Demands for resettlement states to 'lift their game'*

A 1980 UNHCR report on the resettlement of refugees acknowledged that there had been an increase in the number of boat people since May 1980. Resettlement countries were 'urged to maintain their efforts to provide new homes for the large number of Indo-Chinese who have no alternative but to seek resettlement in third countries'.[3] At the same time, the UNHCR's Asia Regional Section received warnings from Bangkok and Indonesia of a potential new exodus of boat people from Vietnam due to 'the unresolved specifics on the Orderly Departure Programme' (see Chapter 3).[4] At the time, the Orderly Departure Programme (ODP) was causing problems because the US had no consular presence in Vietnam, which meant that negotiations needed to be done by 'middle persons'. Moreover, Vietnam's initial ODP list consisted of mainly ethnic Chinese that they wished to expel. The comparison of lists indicates why the wrangling took so long: United States provided 4,000 names of people linked to former employees of the US government before 1975; the Vietnamese provided a quite different list of 21,000 names.[5]

The UNHCR was working hard behind the scenes to ensure that Malaysia and Thailand would not force more asylum seekers arriving by boat back into international waters and onto the mercy of pirates.[6] However, Thailand, Japan and Malaysia argued that the source of the problem lay with resettlement states making the screening procedures too strict for Indochinese refugees, an argument supported by the UNHCR. Thailand, for instance, argued that 'developed countries should assume their share of responsibility in solving the problem, in particular by agreeing to resettle larger number of displaced persons within their borders'.[7] Thailand also pointed out that the UNHCR would achieve more of its objectives in Southeast Asia when the 'international community was prepared to provide it with active support and adequate financial and material resources'.[8]

Japan, which at the time was considering accession to the 1951 Convention and 1967 Protocol, insisted that the 'refugee problem in Asia, in which Japan naturally, showed the greatest interest, was seriously affecting the pace and stability of the region'.[9] The UNHCR needed to 'further improve' its operations as the financial

---

3 UNGA, *Report on the Resettlement of Refugees*, Submitted by the High Commissioner, Executive Committee of the High Commissioner's Programme, Thirty-First Session, A/AC.96/580, 15 August 1980, pp. 4, 6.

4 UNHCR, S N Chetty to Mr P. M. Moussalli, *Weekly Notes 30 May to 5 June 1980*, 5 June 1980; Folio 153, 602.3 ASIA, p. 2.

5 Robinson, *Terms of Refuge: The Indochinese Exodus and the International Response*, 1998, p. 172.

6 UNHCR, S. Bari to Mr P. M. Moussalli, *Weekly Notes 20 to 26 June 1980*, 26 June 1980; Folio 157, 602.3 ASIA, pp. 1–2.

7 UNGA, *Summary Record of the 317th Meeting on 7 October 1980*, Executive Committee of the High Commissioner's Programme, Thirty-First Session, A/AC.96/SR.317, 7 October 1980, p. 5.

8 UNGA, *Summary Record of the 317th Meeting on 7 October 1980*, Executive Committee of the High Commissioner's Programme, Thirty-First Session, A/AC.96/SR.317, 7 October 1980, p. 4.

9 UNGA, *Summary Record of the 318th Meeting on 7 October 1980*, Executive Committee of the High Commissioner's Programme, Thirty-First Session, A/AC.96/SR.318, 10 October 1980, p. 3.

and administrative burden of the refugee problem increased.[10] Malaysia wanted to alert the international community to the fact that 'problems remained' in the region.[11] The Malaysian observer, Mr Kamil, noted that the refugee problem had worsened throughout the world, and though the number of boat people had been reduced overall in Malaysia, there were still many awaiting resettlement and thus 'urged the *continued cooperation of the countries of resettlement in maintaining and, where possible, increasing the pace of intake*'.[12]

The reason for Thailand, Japan and Malaysia's concern about continuing assistance becomes clear when we consider the UNHCR's position. Discussing the UNHCR's assistance activities, Mr Zollner, the Director for the Assistance Division, pointed out that 228,000 offers of resettlement places had been received by the end of September 1980. However, this figure was not enough to cover the 'needs of "boat people", refugees in transit centres, those living in camps in Thailand, Vietnam and China, or of others arriving during the next 12 months'.[13] Furthermore, the UNHCR warned that if funding could not be provided for the 1981 Programme by 1 January 1981, the overall programme would be slashed and governments of first asylum (such as Southeast Asian states) would have 'no assurance that UNHCR could meet its financial requirements in 1981 or, what was still more serious, that the programmes scheduled for the beginning of the year would be started or others would be continued'.[14] These two statements stayed with the Southeast Asian states into the beginning of 1981 and had a negative affect on their willingness to ensure that boat people arrived safely on their shores.[15]

5.2 *Questioning the refugee status of the Indochinese*

Southeast Asian states had a history of arguing that the Indochinese asylum seekers were not refugees, but by the early 1980s their level of argumentation increased and resettlement states also became open to this argument. This happened largely

10 UNGA, *Summary Record of the 318th Meeting on 7 October 1980*, Executive Committee of the High Commissioner's Programme, Thirty-First Session, A/AC.96/SR.318, 10 October 1980, p. 4.

11 UNGA, *Summary Record of the 321st Meeting on 9 October 1980*, Executive Committee of the High Commissioner's Programme, Thirty-First Session, A/AC.96/SR.321, 13 October 1980, p. 3.

12 UNGA, *Summary Record of the 321st Meeting on 9 October 1980*, Executive Committee of the High Commissioner's Programme, Thirty-First Session, A/AC.96/SR.321, 13 October 1980, p. 3. Emphasis added.

13 UNGA, *Summary Record of the 323rd Meeting on 10 October 1980*, Executive Committee of the High Commissioner's Programme, Thirty-First Session, A/AC.96/SR.323, 15 October 1980, p. 13.

14 UNGA, *Summary Record of the 326th Meeting on 13 October 1980*, Executive Committee of the High Commissioner's Programme, Thirty-First Session, A/AC.96/SR.326, 17 October 1980, p. 11.

15 UNHCR, *Weekly Notes*, October 1980 to December 1980; 602.3 ASIA. Henry Kamm, a journalist for the *New York Times*, reported on the High Commissioner Poul Hartling's concerns with the Thailand government in particular having no concerns with how refugees were kept away from Thailand, in Robinson, *Terms of Refuge: The Indochinese Exodus and the International Response*, 1998, p. 169.

because states such as the United States, Australia and France started to suffer from resettlement 'fatigue',[16] and even some officials within the UNHCR started to question whether they were running a refugee resettlement programme or an immigration service. As a result, many Western states, including the US, began to accept the idea that Indochinese asylum seekers were not *prima facie* refugees, thus removing the need to treat them all according to the principles of international refugee law and the assumption that all Indochinese were *genuine* refugees.

Although the Southeast Asian states' response to the Indochinese refugees did not substantively change, between 1980 and 1986, the attitudes of the actors around them did. The United States, Australia and Japan started to support Southeast Asian doubts about whether Indochinese refugees were refugees at all. The UNHCR's ability to ensure protection was constantly undermined when Southeast Asian states practiced pushbacks and forced repatriations. However, divisions began to appear within the UNHCR as some staff members rebelled against the policy of satisfying Southeast Asian states' interests without demanding protection for refugees in return.[17] These officials argued that the UNHCR must be free to act independently. However, in the face of a massive rise of Indochinese refugees by 1987 and the determination of many Western states to support the Southeast Asian states' view that the asylum seekers were 'economic migrants', these UNHCR officials lost the argument.

From our discussion thus far, it is clear that by the early 1980s concern was being raised about whether people fleeing Indochina were refugees at all. In this section I will assess this emerging debate. Before we do that, however, it is important to identify who was fleeing Indochina and under what circumstances, so as to highlight how Western and Southeast Asian states justified their characterization of the majority of asylum seekers as 'economic migrants'. In 1982, Southeast Asian states were concerned with the failure to reduce the boat people population, while resettlement numbers were declining.[18] Although the ODP had begun that year in Vietnam, there were still a number of people wishing to flee the communist regime there. Kosol Sobhak-Vichitr described this desire on the part of the Vietnamese to flee their country as being due to the 'transfer of power from one party to another [and] the way of life in various aspects: social, cultural, etc. *Under such conditions, there must naturally be a number of people wishing to leave*'.[19] Vietnam had also been encouraging the expulsion of 'ethnic Chinese' since the late 1970s. There were two main reasons for this. First, the ethnic Chinese in Vietnam were considered to be

[16] United Nations Social and Economic Council, *Note on International Solidarity and Refugee Protection*, Sub-Committee on International Protection (SCIP), EC/SCP/50, 13 July 1988, p. 1.

[17] UNHCR, Mr P. M. Mousalli to High Commissioner, *Regional Protection Meeting Pattaya, Thailand, 12–14 August 1981*, 2 October 1981; Folio 263, 602.3 ASIA; Jackson, *The Refugee in Group Situations*, 1999, pp. 317–346.

[18] UNGA, *Summary Records for 1982*, Executive Committee of the High Commissioner's Programme, Thirty-Third Session, 12–18 October 1982. A/AC.96/SR.344 to A/AC.96/SR.351.

[19] UNHCR, *Round Table of Asian Experts on Current Problems in the International Protection of Refugees and Displaced Persons*, April 1980. Publication Box 4, Section One, p. 176. Emphasis added.

'fifth columnists' supporting China and were therefore not to be trusted. After the Chinese incursion into Vietnam in February 1979, this distrust multiplied. Second, ethnic Chinese comprised the wealthier segments of society. Many of them were business owners and thus belonged to the private sector which the Vietnamese authorities wanted to transform into socialized collective industries.[20] The end result was that many ethnic Chinese left Vietnam and continued to do so into the 1980s. However, there were many workers, fishermen and peasants of Chinese and Vietnamese descent from North Vietnam who also wished to leave. During the 1980s there was an increased flight of middle class ethnic Vietnamese attempting to avoid the 'reeducation camps' or relocation to Vietnam's New Economic Zones.[21] However, a number of scholars argue that these reasons for flight did not mean that they were not *prima facie* refugees, as Southeast Asian states had been arguing and as Western states were starting to agree.[22] At the same time, the UNHCR's Representative in Thailand had been raising the question of whether all Indochinese arrivals were 'genuine asylum seekers'[23] with the UNHCR's headquarters. In light of both first asylum and resettlement states' increasing reluctance to grant blanket refugee status to all arrivals, the UNHCR's Regional Office suggested that it was time to reconsider the *prima facie* refugee status afforded to Indochinese refugees to that point.[24]

The discussion about continuing the policy of offering blanket resettlement for Indochinese refugees also caused a division within the United States government. The US Ambassador to Thailand, Morton Abramowitz, strongly disagreed with the view that his country was encouraging people to leave Vietnam in order to destabilize it. Abramowitz argued that people wanted to leave and this was 'what mattered at the end of the day'.[25] However, the Immigration National Service (INS) disagreed, and by late 1981 was starting to insist that the screening of Indochinese refugees be conducted according to the US' 1980 Refugee Act.[26] The State Department agreed, and Indochinese refugees started to be screened according to the traditional requirements of the 1951 Convention—an *individual* fear

---

[20] Zolberg, A. et al., *Escape From Violence: Conflict and the Refugee Crisis in the Developing World*, 1989, pp. 164–165.

[21] Luise Druke provides quite a detailed examination of the 'push' (conditions in Vietnam that led to departure) and 'pull' (belief that there were more improved circumstances upon leaving) factors that led Vietnamese to leave. Druke, *Preventative Action for Refugee Producing Situations*, 1993, pp. 85–105.

[22] Professor Kosol Sobhak-Vichitr in UNHCR, *Round Table of Asian Experts on Current Problems in the International Protection of Refugees and Displaced Persons*, April 1980. Publication Box 4, Section One, p. 176; Greig, D. W., 'The Protection of Refugees and Customary International Law', *Australian Yearbook of International Law*, Vol. 8 (1980), pp. 108–1141; Tsyamenyi, B. M., 'The "Boat People": Are They Refugees?', *Human Rights Quarterly*, Vol. 5 (1983), pp. 349–373; Hathaway, J., 'Labelling the "boat people": the failure of the human rights mandate of the Comprehensive Plan of Action for Indochinese Refugees', *Human Rights Quarterly*, Vol. 15, No. 4 (1993), pp. 686–702.

[23] Jackson, *The Refugee Concept in Group Situations*, 1999, p. 329.

[24] Jackson, *The Refugee Concept in Group Situations*, 1999, p. 329.

[25] Robinson, *Terms of Refuge: The Indochinese Exodus and International Response*, 1998, pp. 161–162.

[26] Robinson, *Terms of Refuge: The Indochinese Exodus and International Response*, 1998, pp. 163–164.

of persecution, as opposed to the *prima facie* status that had been accorded to the original mass influx of Indochinese. As a result, the United States' intake of refugees fell from around 20,000 a month in 1981, to just 75,000 for all of 1982. This practice was soon followed by the other refugee resettlement countries such as France, Canada and Australia.[27]

As mentioned earlier (see Chapter 4), Cambodians had been harshly treated in Thailand, they had not been given the same access to refugee status as Vietnamese and were not granted similar resettlement quotas. Southeast Asian and Western states did not recognize Cambodia's Vietnamese-appointed government and thus preferred to label those fleeing as 'displaced persons'—meaning that they were expected to return to their country once the invasion ended. The situation in Laos was different again. The Laotian Hilltribe people, who had been fighting against the Laotian Communist Government since the 1970s had no desire to be resettled. Nor were they a priority with resettlement countries except for the United States.[28] In the early 1980s, the numbers leaving Laos were low though there is a dispute in the literature as to whether or not this meant that Thailand's humane deterrence policy (see below) applied to the Laotians and whether it was working. Robinson argued that it did not apply to the Laotians as there was no point threatening them with the retraction of resettlement when their main priority was repatriation, and the Thai government knew this.[29] However, Cerquone argues that humane deterrence did apply and when the Laotians refugee numbers fell as a result of this policy, the Thai government saw policies such as these as an example of what could be achieved through refugee deterrence measures.[30]

In January 1981, the UNHCR agreed to a screening procedure for all Laotians entering Thai territory in cooperation with the Thai government. This led to a marked decrease of asylum seekers from Laos in the following two years.[31] The UNHCR wanted *prima facie* recognition of refugees to be maintained as the screening procedure was enough to make Laotians weary of entry, at least, initially. This supports Cerquone's view that Laotian asylum seekers were, like the Cambodians, also receiving a harsh response from the Thailand government.[32] This no doubt also served to buoy Thailand's confidence, as the people screened and found not to be deserving of refugee status were immediately repatriated.[33] Like the Cambodian

---

27 Robinson, *Terms of Refuge: The Indochinese Exodus and International Response*, 1998, pp. 165–166.

28 Jackson, *The Refugee Concept in Group Situations*, 1999, p. 328; Robinson, *Terms of Refuge: The Indochinese Exodus and International Response*, 1998, pp. 115–116.

29 Jackson, *The Refugee Concept in Group Situations*, 1999, pp. 328–329; Robinson, *Terms of Refuge: The Indochinese Exodus and International Response*, 1998, p. 115.

30 Cerquone, J. *Refugees From Laos: In Harm's Way* (Washington: American Council for Nationalities Service, 1986), pp. 6–7.

31 Jackson, *The Refugee Concept in Group Situations*, 1999, p. 330.

32 UNHCR, I Khan to Mr P. M. Moussalli, *Weekly Notes 21 to 27 August 1981*, 27 August 1981; Folio 257, 602.3 ASIA, p. 1.

33 The UNHCR *Weekly Notes* for all of the years up to 1984 report in the Thailand section that numbers from 7 to over 400 Laotians were repatriated either weekly or monthly.

situation, the Laotian government, which was not part of the repatriation effort, was wary of those who returned. By 1984, the deterioration in the economy, the continued fighting between the Hmong (Hilltribe people) and the government, the creation of forced reeducation camps, and pressure to join the military draft led to the highest exodus of Laotians into Thailand since 1979.[34]

By the mid 1980s there was great uncertainty about how to label the Indochinese. The label afforded to this group was important because it affected how they would be protected. This is demonstrated by Southeast Asian states' refusal to call them anything but 'illegals' or 'displaced persons' so as to dispel any idea that these people ought to be granted refugee status.[35] Many Western states no longer wished to grant refugee status to all Indochinese exiles and provide resettlement places for them; so they also seemed to be moving towards accepting the idea that not all the Indochinese fleeing their home were legitimate refugees. This left the UNHCR trying to deal with the effects of reversing Western states initial demand of refugee protection for everyone fleeing Indochina (regardless of the UNHCR's inability to individually screen each person, as the 1951 Convention dictated). In addition, it seemed that even within the UNHCR there was a division between the headquarters and the regional office as to whether or not it was necessary to continue assuming that all who left Indochina had legitimate reasons for doing so under the 1951 Convention.[36]

As a result, the emphasis on solving the refugee crisis started to move towards the country of origin, as the creation already of the ODP demonstrated. This required a different assessment of those leaving, to justify the fact that they would no longer be immediately given refugee protection and may at times need to be sent back against their own will. This trend was becoming clear in the Regional Protection Meeting in Asia, during August 1981. At this meeting, it was decided that though the *prima facie* refugee definition had applied to the large-scale influx from Indochina, it was time for the UNHCR to begin conducting precise, individual assessment of those arriving in first asylum countries.[37] At the same time however, and this is where the confused role of the UNHCR starts to appear, the UNHCR was still to ensure that all those seeking asylum were given the protection owed to refugees and to prevent the forcible rejection of refugees.[38] The UNHCR was also expected to stop urging resettlement countries to provide larger quotas of resettlement places,

34 Cerquone, *Refugees From Laos: In Harm's Way*, 1986, p. 7. Robinson, *Terms of Refuge: The Indochinese Exodus and the International Response*, 1998, p. 116.

35 Greig, D. W., 'The Protection of Refugees and Customary International Law', *Australian Yearbook of International Law*, Vol. 8 (1980), pp. 108–1141; Jackson, *The Refugee Concept in Group Situations*, 1999, p. 345.

36 Jackson, *The Refugee Concept in Group Situations*, 1999, p. 329.

37 UNHCR, P. M. Moussalli to the High Commissioner, *Summary of Report on South-East Asia Protection Meeting Thailand, 12–14 August 1981*, 2 October 1981; Folio 963, 602.3 ASIA, p. 1.

38 UNHCR, P. M. Moussalli to the High Commissioner, *Summary of Report on South-East Asia Protection Meeting Thailand, 12–14 August 1981*, 2 October 1981; Folio 963, 602.3 ASIA, p. 2.

whilst simultaneously ensuring that resettlement places were indeed provided.[39] In addition, though the UNHCR was to have a protection role for the asylum seekers, when it came to repatriating refugees, the role of the UNHCR was to be 'at an acceptable minimum'.[40] These dilemmas were most clearly demonstrated by the UNHCR's response to the rapidly emerging Kampuchean refugee crisis.

5.3 *Why the Cambodians were not refugees*

In light of ASEAN states' continued reluctance to fully implement the agreement reached at the 1979 Conference, it is essential at this point to discuss the Cambodian refugee population, and what effect their presence had on ASEAN states and in particular Thailand's response to the Indochinese refugee crisis. The majority of Cambodians who attempted to enter Thai territory or remained on the Cambodia-Thai border were never given refugee status. It was this treatment of the Cambodians, and the international community's failure to demand refugee status for this population, that led to Southeast Asian states raising further questions about the veracity of the refugee claims of all those fleeing Indochina. This section therefore charts the move towards viewing Indochinese refugees as 'economic migrants' and 'non-genuine' refugees, a view which helped to further legitimise the Southeast Asian argument.

As the fighting between Vietnamese and Khmer Rouge forces increased during 1979, so too did the number of people fleeing the crisis. By October, some 200,000 Cambodians had sought asylum in Thailand with another 130,000 in the border area wanting to cross into Thailand.[41] In response, the Thai government passed a new Immigration Act. The Immigration Act determined no distinction between a refugee and an illegal migrant—all who entered Thailand without the state's permission first would, regardless of their circumstances, be considered as an illegal migrant. Therefore all who entered Thailand were technically liable for deportation.[42] Thailand granted temporary refuge to Cambodians although its generosity was sporadic at best. As I noted in Chapter 3, in June 1979 Thailand forcibly returned 40,000 Cambodians into Preah Valley, where many of the refugees were killed by land mines. Thailand practiced the same policy towards Laotians, whose numbers also rose, fell, then rose again, during this period. The Laotians

39 UNHCR, P. M. Moussalli to the High Commissioner, *Summary of Report on South-East Asia Protection Meeting Thailand, 12–14 August 1981*, 2 October 1981; Folio 963, 602.3 ASIA, p. 2.

40 UNHCR, P. M. Moussalli to the High Commissioner, *Summary of Report on South-East Asia Protection Meeting Thailand, 12–14 August 1981*, 2 October 1981; Folio 963, 602.3 ASIA, p. 3.

41 UNGA, *Office of the United Nations High Commissioner for Refugees Meeting on Refugees and Displaced Persons in South-East Asia,* Convened by the Secretary-General of the United Nations at Geneva on 20 and 21 July 1979 and Subsequent Developments, Conclusion, Thirty-Fourth Session, Agenda Item 83, A/34/627, 7 November 1979, p. 14.

42 Zieck, M. *UNHCR and Voluntary Repatriation of Refugees: A Legal Analysis* (The Hague: Martinus Nijhoff, 1997), p. 140; Muntarbhorn, *The Status of Refugees in Asia*, 1992.

were also occasionally granted temporary refuge by the Thailand government, but *refoulement* or denial of asylum often occurred as well.[43]

Thai policy towards Indochinese asylum seekers was contradictory. In September 1979, the Thai Prime Minister insisted that the Cambodians would be given temporary asylum on humanitarian grounds 'only if it is necessary'. This came to be known as Thailand's 'Open Door Policy', which lasted until 24 January 1980. Even at the announcement of the 'Open Door Policy' though, the Prime Minister emphasized the idea that the international community had primary responsibility for providing assistance to those granted temporary asylum, for his government 'would take measures *it thinks fit to deal with the refugees if the international community fails to respond*'.[44]

The treatment that Cambodian refugees received also depended upon where their asylum was based—in a Thai-run camp, a UNHCR camp or along a border area (these were the northern, central and southern areas).[45] The Khmer Rouge took control of many camps on the border and was able to control the distribution of aid. This meant that the livelihood of the majority of asylum seekers was in the hands of the Khmer Rouge.[46] The United States did very little to suppress the overt support that Thailand and China were providing the Khmer Rouge in the shape of arms and aid.[47] Therefore, the Khmer Rouge led the resistance against Vietnamese forces and held the Cambodian seat in the UN until 1982.[48] In 1982 with ASEAN assistance, a new Coalition Government of Democratic Kampuchea was formed with the Khmer Rouge still a member but no longer the only voice, and they gained UN General Assembly recognition calling for the withdrawal of Vietnamese forces in late October 1982.[49]

The Khmer Rouge continued to control most of the border camps and used them as bases for procuring supplies, launching offensives against the Vietnamese and recruiting refugees to join the resistance.[50] The UNHCR did not assume

---

43 UNHCR, S. Bari, Protection Officer to Dr E. Jahn, Acting Director of Protection, *Weekly Notes 21 to 27 September 1979*, 27 September 1979; Folio 118, 602.3 ASIA, p. 1; UNHCR, S. N. Chetty, to Mr P. M. Moussalli, Director of Protection, *Weekly Notes 18 to 24 April 1980*, 24 April 1980; Folio 147, 602.3 ASIA, p. 1.

44 UNHCR, S. Bari, Protection Officer, East Asia Regional Section and South & South East Asia Regional Section to Dr E. Jahn, Acting Director of Protection, *Weekly Notes 6 to 13 September 1979*; 13 September 1979, Folio 115, 602.3 ASIA, p. 1. Emphasis added.

45 Zieck, *UNHCR and Voluntary Repatriation of Refugees: A Legal Analysis*, 1997, p. 140.

46 Unger, 'Ain't Enough Blanket: International Humanitarian Assistance and Cambodian Political Resistance', in Stedman, S. J. and Fred Tanner (eds.), *Refugee Manipulation: War, Politics, and the Abuse of Human Suffering*, 2003.

47 Robinson, *Terms of Refuge: The Indochinese Exodus and International Response*, 1998, p. 67.

48 Unger, 'Ain't Enough Blanket: International Humanitarian Assistance and Cambodian Political Resistance', in Stedman, S. J. and Fred Tanner (eds.), *Refugee Manipulation: War, Politics, and the Abuse of Human Suffering*, 2003, p. 25.

49 Unger, 'Ain't Enough Blanket: International Humanitarian Assistance and Cambodian Political Resistance', in Stedman, S. J. and Fred Tanner (eds.), *Refugee Manipulation: War, Politics, and the Abuse of Human Suffering*, 2003, p. 27.

50 Zieck, *UNHCR and Voluntary Repatriation of Refugees: A Legal Analysis*, 1997; Robinson, *Terms of Refuge: The Indochinese Exodus and the International Response*, 1998; Unger, 'Ain't Enough Blanket:

responsibility for this border population; the Thai government insisted that the Cambodians were displaced and that the majority was not in their territory and therefore not in need of refugee assistance.[51] Until November 1979, the Thai government had been reluctant to involve the UNHCR in assisting any of the Cambodian refugees massed on the border. However, in late October 1979, it requested the UNHCR's assistance in setting up and running camps in Thai territory for the Cambodians who had successfully sought asylum there. The Thai government insisted on military supervision of the camps as some of the Cambodians fleeing the violence were believed to be combatants.[52] The UNHCR would come to run camps for Cambodians within Thailand, where these groups would be eligible for resettlement. However, despite UNHCR reporting peaks of 136,967 refugees in their camps at the beginning of 1980,[53] at the same time 750,000 Cambodians remained in limbo in the border areas.[54]

What protection did the UNHCR afford the people remaining on the border? The short answer is none as the UNHCR was not legally responsible for providing either protection or assistance to the Cambodians forced to remain on the Cambodian side of the border.[55] Nor was there any attempt by the UNHCR to become involved in protecting those massed on the border. When the UNHCR offered to be the 'executing agency' for the UN in Thailand to deliver aid and protection, they insisted the camps be moved away from the border, be demilitarized and that the UN be granted unrestricted access. These were conditions that UNHCR staff at the time knew would not be met, and Robinson refers to a UNHCR official explaining that the conditions were set because 'we did not want to go to the border'.[56] High Commissioner Hartling felt that the UNHCR was already overburdened with work and Zia Rizvi, the UNHCR's senior regional coordinator for Southeast Asia, did not want to 'jeopardize relations with the Indochinese states by getting too involved with the resistance'.[57]

Therefore, the UNHCR was reluctant to become involved in a border area that was extremely dangerous and problematic politically. The UNHCR feared that if it

---

International Humanitarian Assistance and Cambodian Political Resistance', in Stedman, S. J. and Fred Tanner (eds.), *Refugee Manipulation: War, Politics, and the Abuse of Human Suffering*, 2003.

51 Helton, A. *The Price of Indifference: Refugees and Humanitarian Action in the New Century* (Oxford: Oxford University Press, 2002), p. 80. This point is also drawn from Robinson, *Terms of Refuge: The Indochinese Exodus and the International Response*, 1998, p. 69; and Unger, 'Ain't Enough Blanket: International Humanitarian Assistance and Cambodian Political Resistance', in Stedman, S. J. and Fred Tanner (eds.), *Refugee Manipulation: War, Politics, and the Abuse of Human Suffering*, 2003, pp. 28, 33–35.

52 Robinson, *Terms of Refuge: The Indochinese Exodus and the International Response*, 1998, pp. 69–70.

53 UNHCR, S. Bari to Mr P. M. Moussalli, *Weekly Notes 4 to 10 January 1980*, 10 January 1980; Folio 131, 602.3 ASIA, p. 1.

54 Robinson, *Terms of Refuge: The Indochinese Exodus and the International Response*, 1998, pp. 72, 80.

55 Helton, *The Price of Indifference: Refugees and Humanitarian Action in the New Century*, 2002, p. 80.

56 Robinson, *Terms of Refuge: The Indochinese Exodus and the International Response*, 1998, p. 73.

57 Robinson, *Terms of Refuge: The Indochinese Exodus and the International Response*, 1998, p. 73.

got too involved in the border regions it would be drawn into protecting refugees against the Thai government and Khmer actions which could have jeopardized its wider regional strategy. In addition, the US, Thailand and UN Secretary-General Kurt Waldheim, were reluctant to permit the UNHCR to take on such responsibility for the border population. The US Ambassador to Thailand, Morton Abramowitz explained that this reluctance was due to the UNHCR having a 'mentality which saw itself as a small agency providing protection against refoulement, staffed by people who had been working for 30 years on European problems and were totally unprepared for this new thing... handling large emergencies. It was an organization not equipped to handle the responsibility it was seeking'.[58] However, it did not appear that the UNHCR was in any great rush to take this responsibility as they did not force the issue. As a result, UNICEF (United Nations Children's Fund) and the ICRC (International Committee of the Red Cross) took responsibility for assisting the border population. However, UNICEF and ICRC did not have a protection mandate for refugees or the ability to locate people that needed resettlement assistance, leaving the majority of civilians on the border vulnerable to forced repatriation, expulsion and abuse.[59]

January 1980 saw the end of Thailand's so-called 'Open Door Policy' for refugees and its replacement by the 'Humane Deterrence Policy'. At the 1981 UNHCR Executive Committee meeting the Thai delegate justified the introduction of this policy as being:

> [I]n accordance with humanitarian principles and national interest and security [and it] had been approved by the Thai Parliament. Owing to changed circumstances, his Government had recently deemed it necessary to take additional measures concerning displaced persons and illegal migrants [*note: no mention of the word 'refugee'*]. It was difficult to see why so many Laotians and Vietnamese had left their countries for Thailand, since the current situation in those countries was peaceful. Their status remained questionable because it might justifiability be thought that they had ulterior motives, namely, a desire to avoid hardship and to seek an affluent life in other countries.[60]

Japan endorsed Thailand's policy, arguing in 1982 that the decreasing number of refugees entering Thailand 'might be the result of the "Humane Deterrence Policy" of the Government of Thailand, which was understandable in the case of those persons who wished to cross the frontier for merely economic reasons'.[61] The Humane Deterrence Policy justified actions by the Thai military to prevent, by any means, all

58 Robinson, *Terms of Refuge: The Indochinese Exodus and the International Response*, 1998, p. 73.

59 Robinson, *Terms of Refuge: The Indochinese Exodus and the International Response*, 1998, p. 74; Unger, 'Ain't Enough Blanket: International Humanitarian Assistance and Cambodian Political Resistance', in Stedman, S. J. and Fred Tanner (eds.), *Refugee Manipulation: War, Politics, and the Abuse of Human Suffering*, 2003, pp. 28, 33–35.

60 UNGA, *Summary Record of the 333rd Meeting on 14 October*, Executive Committee of the High Commissioner's Programme, Thirty-Second Session, A/AC.96/SR.333, 21 October 1981, p. 4.

61 UNGA, *Summary Record of the 344th Meeting on 12 October*, Executive Committee of the High Commissioner's Programme, Thirty-Third Session, A/AC.96/SR.344, 15 October 1982, p. 10.

attempts by people on the border to enter Thai territory. Moreover, the new policy insisted that those who managed to enter and avoid bullets or expulsion were not to be allowed access to UNHCR's resettlement programme. Personal freedom was also reduced. For instance, people within the UNHCR camps were not allowed to leave those camps nor were they allowed to seek employment, entrenching the population's reliance on international aid.[62]

Of even greater concern to the UNHCR were reports that the Thai government was not only closing its open door policy, but now starting to suggest that 'a substantial part or even all Kampucheans now in *UNHCR-assisted holding centres*'[63] would be forced back into Cambodia. As a result, the UNHCR started to discuss the possibility of assisting with the voluntary repatriation of refugees to Cambodia with Thai officials. The premise behind this was that the UNHCR was not averse to repatriation as an option for the Cambodians, and that by providing assistance it would ensure that at least some of the inevitable repatriations would be voluntary. However, in spite of the agreement between the Thai government and the UNHCR, the non-voluntary repatriation of refugees outside UNHCR holding centres (usually at night when the UNHCR were not allowed to be present at the camps) occurred frequently.[64]

Neither the Vietnamese-installed Cambodian government, nor Vietnam itself agreed with the voluntary repatriation of people in UNHCR camps scheduled for June 1980.[65] This lack of agreement by the country of return, imperative for successful repatriation, did not deter either the Thai government or the UNHCR, mainly because most of the refugees would be returned to Khmer Rouge controlled areas of Cambodia (this should have been a further concern of the UNHCR).[66] The UNHCR took part in this voluntary repatriation due to a wish to ensure that, as far as possible, repatriation was voluntary. However, the UNHCR could not guarantee the safety of returnees.[67] The agenda for their return to Khmer Rouge controlled areas was made clear in a visit to Thailand by the Singapore Deputy Prime Minister, who said that it was legitimate to send refugees back to 'fight for their freedom', implying that returnees would join the anti-Vietnam coalition.[68] Of greater concern was that the UNHCR gave no information at all on whether it was safe or not for refugees to go back. Even when UNHCR officials were directly asked by refugees they were instructed to give no answer, and the supervision by

62 Zieck, *UNHCR and Voluntary Repatriation of Refugees: A Legal Analysis*, 1997, p. 145.

63 UNHCR, S. Bari to Mr P. M. Moussalli, *Weekly Notes 8 to 14 February 1980*, 14 February 1980; Folio 136, 602.3 ASIA, p. 1. Emphasis added.

64 Zieck, *UNHCR and Voluntary Repatriation of Refugees: A Legal Analysis*, 1997, p. 149; UNHCR, S. Bari to Mr P. M. Moussalli, *Weekly Notes 21 to 27 March 1980*, 27 March 1980; Folio 143, 602.3 ASIA, p. 1; UNHCR, S. Bari to Mr P. M. Moussalli, *Weekly Notes 3 to 10 April 1980*, 10 April 1980; Folio 145, 602.3 ASIA, p. 1.

65 Zieck, *UNHCR and Voluntary Repatriation of Refugees: A Legal Analysis*, 1997, p. 152.

66 Robinson, *Terms of Refuge: The Indochinese Exodus and the International Response*, 1998, pp. 74–75.

67 Zieck, *UNHCR and Voluntary Repatriation of Refugees: A Legal Analysis*, 1997, p. 155.

68 Robinson, *Terms of Refuge: The Indochinese Exodus and the International Response*, 1998, p. 76.

Thai authorities at all times ensured that this instruction was obeyed.[69] In addition, the UNHCR later noted that the Thai authorities insisted on ever higher numbers of returns, making their voluntary nature harder to judge. UNHCR officials were brusquely treated, Thai officials insisted on being present at all interviews and there was suspicion that interpreters being used for the refugees were Khmer Rouge cadre. Zieck describes the level of verification of the voluntary nature of return to Cambodia as 'confined to merely watching the refugees sign the declaration'.[70]

Between 17 and 22 June 1980, 1,612 persons left the UNHCR camps for Cambodia. On 23 June the repatriation stopped because of a resumption of border fighting at the repatriation points of Nong Chan and Sarokok.[71] The Cambodian and Vietnamese governments vehemently opposed the repatriation programme, making life even more perilous for the returnees because their recipient state did not want them. The Cambodian government stated that these returnees were nothing more than a 'human shield to hide the reactionaries who were being smuggled into Kampuchea to sabotage the PRK [Peoples Republic of Kampuchea]'.[72] As a result, Vietnamese forces responded to what they saw as an aggressive act and launched an attack on the Thai-Cambodian border area and entered Thai territory, seizing the refugee camps of Mak Mun and Nong Chan, creating 50,000 more Cambodian refugees in Thai territory and displacing 2,000 Thais from their villages.[73] UNICEF and the ICRC protested against the UNHCR's repatriation effort, which they believed had the potential to incite violence between the Vietnamese forces and Khmer militia based on the border.[74] Their concerns proved valid. The Thai military counter-attacked and in two days the death toll on the border camps was several hundred, more from Thai artillery than Vietnamese fire, Robinson argues.[75] On 26 June 1980, 124 people returned to the Sa Kaeo border area, but after that the Thai-UNHCR repatriation program ended. The ASEAN Foreign Ministers condemned the action of Vietnam and described it as 'a grave and direct threat to the security of Thailand and the Southeast Asian region'.[76]

The UNHCR refused to acknowledge any link between the repatriation movement and Vietnam's attack. The military and political atmosphere in the border area was now extremely tense, with the anti-Vietnamese coalition (including the Khmer Rouge) now having not only the financial support of Thailand, ASEAN, China and US, but political legitimacy through their seat in the UN. Moreover,

---

69 Zieck, *UNHCR and Voluntary Repatriation of Refugees: A Legal Analysis*, 1997, p. 163.
70 Zieck, *UNHCR and Voluntary Repatriation of Refugees: A Legal Analysis*, 1997, p. 163.
71 UNHCR, S. Bari to Mr P. M. Moussalli, *Weekly Notes 20 to 26 June 1980*, 26 June 1980; Folio 157, 602.3 ASIA, p. 1.
72 Zieck, *UNHCR and Voluntary Repatriation of Refugees: A Legal Analysis*, 1997 p. 165.
73 Zieck, *UNHCR and Voluntary Repatriation of Refugees: A Legal Analysis*, 1997, p. 164; Robinson, *Terms of Refuge: The Indochinese Exodus and the International Response*, 1998, p. 78.
74 Unger, 'Ain't Enough Blanket: International Humanitarian Assistance and Cambodian Political Resistance', in Stedman, S. J. and Fred Tanner (eds.), *Refugee Manipulation: War, Politics, and the Abuse of Human Suffering*, 2003, p. 43.
75 Robinson, *Terms of Refuge: The Indochinese Exodus and the International Response*, 1998, p. 78.
76 Robinson, *Terms of Refuge: The Indochinese Exodus and the International Response*, 1998, p. 78.

these states were more than willing to collectively condemn Vietnam. Attempts by UNICEF and the ICRC to reevaluate their role within this conflict were also affected by the military and political machinations. The UNICEF/ICRC Joint Mission argued that its border operation needed to be reconsidered because the border relief programme was too provocative to the Vietnamese, there was a black market trade growing in the camps, and the assistance was inadvertently strengthening the Khmer Rouge.[77] However, Robinson and Unger argue that it was precisely because of the provocative effect the border relief programme was having on Vietnam and the strengthening of the Khmer Rouge, that Thailand, ASEAN, US and China wanted it to continue.[78] UNICEF and the ICRC persisted with their relief programme, but the ICRC only provided medical assistance from that point forward and UNICEF, after many failed attempts at distributing food to everyone but the Khmer Rouge, reluctantly reverted back to providing relief through Khmer Rouge camp administrators.[79]

The events of June 1980 also served to demonstrate how easily the term 'refugee' could be manipulated. The UNHCR, which was largely taking its funds and staff for the Cambodian refugees from states such as the US, was powerless to take an independent line in the face of determined responses by Thailand and US. Moreover, the UNHCR's failure to ensure respect for basic human rights reinforced the Southeast Asian view that when they wanted to take action against asylum seekers, the UNHCR could do very little to stop them. For the remainder of 1980 and all of 1981, Thailand resumed its 'relocation' of Cambodian asylum seekers as part of its Humane Deterrence Policy. In 1980, the UNHCR said that the 'rate of resettlement has not kept up with the demand caused by the influx of refugees and the high cost of living'.[80] For Thailand, this provided a justification to reduce camp services, refuse resettlement interviews for new arrivals, and 'relocate' Cambodians. These were practices that Thailand had been engaged in before the UNHCR offered to assist them through the 'voluntary' repatriation programme. The Thai military would enter camps (even UNHCR administered camps), usually at night and take people to the border. The people on the border continued to be given the title of 'displaced' by Thailand and the UNHCR alike. Their existence was a daily struggle to survive the Khmer Rouge and incursions by Vietnamese forces whilst attempting to receive what little assistance was available after Khmer Rouge had distributed the aid to the militia first and then the refugees.[81] Robinson,

---

77 Robinson, *Terms of Refuge: The Indochinese Exodus and the International Response*, 1998, p. 79.

78 Robinson, *Terms of Refuge: The Indochinese Exodus and the International Response*, 1998, p. 79; Unger, 'Ain't Enough Blanket: International Humanitarian Assistance and Cambodian Political Resistance', in Stedman, S. J. and Fred Tanner (eds.), *Refugee Manipulation: War, Politics, and the Abuse of Human Suffering*, 2003, pp. 39–40.

79 Robinson, *Terms of Refuge: The Indochinese Exodus and the International Response*, 1998, p. 79.

80 UNGA, *Report on UNHCR Assistance Activities in 1979–1980 and Proposed Voluntary Funds Programmes and Budget for 1981*, Addendum, Executive Committee of the High Commissioner's Programme, Thirty-First Session, A/AC.96/577/Add.2, 26 September 1980, p. 15.

81 UNHCR documents for the remainder of the Cambodian dispute referred to the people on the border as just Cambodians or displaced people. Thailand referred to these people in the same

Unger and UNHCR various documents speak of the involuntary 'relocation' by the Thai military of approximately 1,600 people per month by the end of 1981 into Cambodia's border area.[82] However, it appears that the UNHCR offered no direct condemnation of these actions by the Thai military.

In the whole of 1981, the UNHCR Regional Office (RO) in Bangkok made only three public statements to Thai authorities, indicating the failure of the UNHCR to more strongly ensure the protection of refugees or prevent their *refoulement*. The first statement released by RO Bangkok was in February 1981 and stated that the Thai authorities had moved up to 5,000 Cambodians back into the border area. Even though the UNHCR had not been involved in the movement, this report ascertained that the relocations had been *voluntary*. The UNHCR only expressed concern at the pro-relocation propaganda being spread through UNHCR camps by the Thai authorities.[83] However, even if the UNHCR had actually been able to ascertain that the refugee relocations were voluntary, something that is very doubtful, what is indisputable is that the UNHCR was still allowing people to go from UNHCR protection to an 'increasingly violent no-man's-land from which, Thailand made clear, there could be no recognized return'.[84]

The second communiqué was released on 27 August 1981, when the UNHCR responded to the refusal by Thai authorities to allow any more new Vietnamese or Laotians to enter Thailand by expressing 'serious concern.... and a meeting with the authorities to discuss Thai policy regarding new arrivals, durable solution for Laotian refugees and camp consolidation'.[85] These protestations were ineffective, as evidenced by the fact that the Thai authorities continued their activities for the remainder of 1981. The final communiqué was in November 1981, the UNHCR articulated a response to the treatment of Cambodians when numerous reports emerged of Cambodians in holding centres being shot and/or beaten to death by Thai guards. The UNHCR's response consisted of 'strong protests to the authori-

---

manner as UNHCR, or when justifying the policy of humane deterrence as 'illegal migrants', The immense problem with provision assistance in Cambodian border camps is discussed by Unger. Unger, 'Ain't Enough Blanket: International Humanitarian Assistance and Cambodian Political Resistance', in Stedman, S. J. and Fred Tanner (eds.), *Refugee Manipulation: War, Politics, and the Abuse of Human Suffering*, 2003, pp. 39–40.

82 UNGA, *Report on UNHCR Assistance Activities in 1979–1980 and Proposed Voluntary Funds Programmes and Budget for 1981*, Addendum, Executive Committee of the High Commissioner's Programme, Thirty-First Session, A/AC.96/577/Add.2, 26 September 1980; UNHCR, I Khan to Mr P. M. Moussalli, *Weekly Notes 6 to 12 November 1981*, 12 November 1981; Folio 567; 602.3 ASIA, p. 1; Robinson, *Terms of Refuge: The Indochinese Exodus and the International Response*, 1998; and Unger, 'Ain't Enough Blanket: International Humanitarian Assistance and Cambodian Political Resistance', in Stedman, S. J. and Fred Tanner (eds.), *Refugee Manipulation: War, Politics, and the Abuse of Human Suffering*, 2003.

83 UNHCR, I Khan to Mr P. M. Moussalli, *Weekly Notes 20 to 26 February 1981*, 26 February; Folio 187; 602.3 ASIA, p. 1.

84 Robinson, *Terms of Refuge: The Indochinese Exodus and the International Response*, 1998, p. 80.

85 UNHCR, I Khan to Mr P. M. Moussalli, *Weekly Notes 21 to 27 August 1981*, 27 August 1981; Folio 257; 602.3 ASIA, p. 1.

ties, asking for investigations to be carried out to punish the persons responsible'.[86] However, in these later communications there was no mention of attempts to verify whether returns to either Cambodia or the border areas were voluntary or of any measures to ensure that returnees received basic protection.

What conclusion can be drawn from the failure of the UNHCR to persuade Thailand to adopt a humane response to Cambodian refugees? The UNHCR's inability to influence Thailand's behavior is the primary conclusion to be drawn from the Cambodian crisis. The UNHCR had neither the moral authority nor political authority to decide who would be considered as refugees and receive protection based on their assessment. The result was that the UNHCR was further weakened and states such as Thailand took the lead in determining who received protection and why. The ambiguous role the UNHCR had to take in order to provide some degree of protection without alienating the region's states was demonstrated yet again when there was a marked increase in the number of violent pirate attacks against Indochinese asylum seekers attempting to come ashore in 1983 and 1984. One of the direct consequences of this was a worsening relationship between Thailand and the UNHCR, which further undermined the latter's efforts to protect some of the most vulnerable asylum seekers from attacks by pirates. The following section therefore explores the often fractious debate between the UNHCR and Thailand over the piracy issue.

5.4 *Breakdown between Thailand and UNHCR over the pirate crises*

Between 1983 and 1987 the number of boat arrivals in Southeast Asia decreased, while the number departing from Vietnam via the ODP increased.[87] At the same time, the number of people held in limbo on the Cambodian border remained approximately the same—though the numbers would rise and fall depending on border incursions by the Khmer Rouge and Vietnamese forces. As discussed above, the number of Laotian asylum seekers in Thailand did not decrease in 1983 and 1984, making them the largest Indochinese refugee population in the region that year.[88] At the same time though, the numbers leaving for resettlement during this period *decreased*.[89] The number of boat people in camps in Southeast Asia also remained unchanged during this period due to the fact that people kept arriving,

86 UNHCR, I Khan to Mr P. M. Moussalli, *Weekly Notes 6 to 12 November 1981*, 12 November 1981; Folio 567; 602.3 ASIA, p. 1.

87 Druke, *Preventative Action for Refugee Producing Situations*, 1993, p. 80.

88 UNGA, *Report on the Resettlement of Refugees*, Executive Committee of the High Commissioner's Programme, Thirty-Fifth Session, A/AC.96/640, 19 July 1984, p. 6.

89 For instance, in 1985 the number of resettlement places had dropped by 17 percent since 1984. UNGA, *Report on the Resettlement of Refugees*, Executive Committee of the High Commissioner's Programme, Thirty-Sixth Session, A/AC.96/661, 26 July 1985.

but not as many were leaving.[90] The result of this was that numbers within the camps did not fall, causing great concern for Southeast Asian states.[91] This was because resettlement states made entry requirements more stringent and started to experience what the UNHCR termed 'resettlement fatigue'.[92]

A large contributor to this fatigue was undoubtedly the number of schemes and level of financial assistance required to ensure that Southeast Asian states would continue to provide temporary asylum to those who arrived by their own means and those rescued. Such schemes included the Rescue at Sea Resettlement Offers (RASRO) scheme, Disembarkation Resettlement Offers (DISERO) scheme, as well as the resettlement from camps scheme.[93] The purpose of RASRO was to ensure that boat people rescued at sea would be resettled by the flag state of the ship that rescued them. If the flag state could not accept the refugees, they would be placed on the DISERO list, where resettlement states signed up to receive the refugees that flag states could not accept. All of this was done to ensure that boat people were given temporary asylum by Southeast Asian states who insisted on temporary asylum only. With the decrease of resettlement quotas in general by resettlement states, Southeast Asian states were becoming reluctant to continually accept those rescued at sea. Both of these schemes attempted to remedy this problem and provide assurances to Southeast Asian states. Overall though, these resettlement schemes only served to increase resettlement state fatigue and Southeast Asian states became increasingly anxious about the level of the problem that they would be left to solve.

One consequence of this was that Thailand did not take overt action to prevent pirates from attacking boats carrying 'human cargo'.[94] This stands in stark contrast to Malaysia which, despite its high number of arrivals, took great efforts in the 1980s to prevent acts of piracy.[95] Thailand did not seem to have as many concerns about who prevented asylum seekers from entering their shores or how they did it. In June 1982, High Commissioner Poul Hartling organized an assessment team to provide information to Thailand and other Southeast Asian states on how to best manage the piracy problem. By 1984 the number of attacks had decreased, but the

---

90 UNGA, *Annex to the Report on the Thirty-Fourth Session of the Executive Committee of the High Commissioner's Programme*, Executive Committee of the High Commissioner's Programme, Thirty-Fourth Session, A/AC.96/631/Annex.1, 20 October 1983, p. 7; Druke, *Preventative Action for Refugee Producing Situations*, 1993, p. 80.

91 UNGA, *Summary Record of the 386th Meeting on 8 October, Executive Committee of the High Commissioner's Programme*, Thirty-Fifth Session, A/AC.96/SR.386, 11 October 1985, p. 8.

92 UNGA, *Report on the Resettlement of Refugees*, Executive Committee of the High Commissioner's Programme, Thirty-Sixth Session, A/AC.96/661, 26 July 1985.

93 UNGA, *Report on the Resettlement of Refugees*, Executive Committee of the High Commissioner's Programme, Thirty-Fourth Session, A/AC.96/624, 25 August 1983.

94 UNHCR, Michel Moussalli to Sq. Ldr. Prasong Soonsiri, *Correspondence*, 17 January 1984, 010. THA, Folio 500.

95 UNHCR, Bayandor, D., *Report on Situation of the VNBP*, Annual Review Meeting of Vietnamese Boatpeople, 30 January 1984, Kuala Lumpur; 010.MLS, pp. 12–14.

level of violence in the attacks had increased.[96] The RASRO and then DISERO was introduced to deal with the fact that boat people were not being rescued because of the problem ships had in securing temporary refuge for boat people from Southeast Asian states. But the piracy problem was one that resettlement states and the UNHCR could not solve alone; it required the proactive intervention of Thailand military and police forces in particular.

What was the attitude of the Thai government at the time? The Thai delegate at the Executive Committee meeting in 1984, Prasong Soonsiri, gives us some indication. Soonsiri spoke of a high caseload of refugees in Thailand (125,859 Indochinese, 250,000 Cambodians on their border), while the departure load for resettlement was decreasing.[97] He expressed concern about the increase of Laotian refugees on top of the heavy refugee burden that Thailand was already carrying, and lamented that Thailand 'must stand alone in continuing to accept its humanitarian responsibilities'.[98] Thailand also noted that 'among people seeking refuge in Thailand were so-called economic refugees in search of a better life in a third county. The Thai authorities believed that close interrogation would reveal which individuals were genuine refugees and which were economic refugees'.[99] Thailand was clearly setting the scene for how it perceived the refugee situation and justifying its response. For instance, the Thai delegate complained that the Western media 'frequently misreported the piracy problem in the Gulf of Thailand'.[100]

Let us now turn to look at how Thailand was framing its response to boat people in relation to the piracy problem by considering how the Thai government responded to the UNHCR's concerns about piracy in 1984. This example provides an excellent case study analysis of the relationship between Thailand and the UNHCR and helps to set the scene for the discussion in the second half of the chapter on how Southeast Asian states came to shape global perceptions of Indochinese asylum seekers during the 1980s.

On 11 January 1984, 23 refugees drowned due, the UNHCR alleged, to their 'boat being pushed off in bad seas by district and marine police officials in Southern Thailand'.[101] Prior to them being pushed back into sea, the boat people had been allowed to stay in the Tak Bai district of Narathiwat since their arrival on the 4th (this incident will hereafter be referred to as the 'Narathiwat incident').

---

96 United Nations Social and Economic Council, *Report of the United Nations High Commissioner for Refugees*, United Nations Economic and Social Council, Second Regular Session, E/1984.61, 30 May 1984, p. 11.

97 UNGA, *Summary Record of the 369th Meeting on 9 October*, Executive Committee of the High Commissioner's Programme, Thirty-Fifth Session, A/AC.96/SR.369, 12 October 1984, p. 6.

98 UNGA, *Summary Record of the 369th Meeting on 9 October*, Executive Committee of the High Commissioner's Programme, Thirty-Fifth Session, A/AC.96/SR.369, 12 October 1984, p. 7.

99 UNGA, *Summary Record of the 369th Meeting on 9 October*, Executive Committee of the High Commissioner's Programme, Thirty-Fifth Session, A/AC.96/SR.369, 12 October 1984, p. 8.

100 UNGA, *Summary Record of the 369th Meeting on 9 October*, Executive Committee of the High Commissioner's Programme, Thirty-Fifth Session, A/AC.96/SR.369, 12 October 1984, p. 8.

101 UNHCR, HICOMREF Poul Hartling to Prime Minister of Thailand, *Telecommunications Transmission Request*, 23 January 1984; 010.THA, Folio 501, p. 1.

On 11 January, armed district officials forced the people 'against their will into two boats containing 33 and 39 persons respectively'.[102] Due to the roughness of the seas, the larger boat that was being towed by the police into international waters lost its tow rope and a number of refugees fell overboard. The other boat, a fishing boat, returned and collided with the larger boat. This led to the drowning of the 23 refugees. The remaining refugees who survived were then placed in another boat, towed out to sea and they landed safely in Malaysia later that day.

The High Commissioner, Poul Hartling, wrote to Thai Prime Minster Prem Tinsulanonda of this tragedy with the request that 'your government would undertake an official enquiry into this matter to ascertain the precise course of events'.[103] The High Commissioner also asked that 'appropriate instructions could be given to the Royal Thai Navy, the marine police, the harbor department and land police as well as to governors of provinces and district officials reaffirming this humanitarian commitment by your government'.[104] In addition to this, in early 1984 the UNHCR alerted Squadron Leader Prasong Soonsiri, the Chairman of the Committee on the Suppression of Piracy to instances of violence being perpetrated against boat people and the abduction of young girls from refugee boats. One particular pirate boat was identified in at least five separate incidents in the previous year. The UNHCR requested that the Thai government identify this boat and its owners in keeping with the government's 'intention of deterring such acts as expeditiously as possible'.[105] This latter statement clearly had a double meaning which tells us at least two important things about the crisis. First it seems more of a reminder to the Thai government than a statement of fact and second, it also had a placatory tone which can be explained when the ensuing difficulties between UNHCR and Thai government is considered.

Squadron Leader Soonsiri was displeased with the UNHCR's response to a media enquiry about the Narathiwat incident because the UNHCR had provided full details—which Soonsiri had considered to be not wholly factual as the incident was pending investigation. The UNHCR knew that the Thai government (sometimes referred to in the documents as Royal Thai Government or RTG) took the UNHCR allegations very seriously and hoped that 'in future reply to such enquires (it) could be along the line that UNHCR and RTG are investigating the allegations'.[106] However, the outcome of the RTG investigation was that the 'illegal entrants'—the government report never referred to the boat people in this incident as refugees, in

---

102 UNHCR, HICOMREF Poul Hartling to Prime Minister of Thailand, *Telecommunications Transmission Request*, 23 January 1984; 010.THA, Folio 501, p. 1.

103 UNHCR, HICOMREF Poul Hartling to Prime Minister of Thailand, *Telecommunications Transmission Request*, 23 January 1984; 010.THA, Folio 501, p. 2.

104 UNHCR, HICOMREF Poul Hartling to Prime Minister of Thailand, *Telecommunications Transmission Request*, 23 January 1984; 010.THA, Folio 501, p. 2.

105 UNHCR, Michel Moussalli to Sq. Ldr. Prasong Soonsiri, *Correspondence*, 17 January 1984, 010.THA, Folio 500, p. 3.

106 UNHCR, UNHCR Bangkok to HICOMREF Geneva, *Cable*, 30 January 1984; THA/HCR/0183, 010.THA.

sharp contrast to the UNHCR's position at this time—had arrived and then after being questioned by the local Thai authorities stated a wish to proceed by boat to a third country.[107] Therefore, the marine police assisted them with their wish by hiring two boats to carry the Vietnamese back out to sea and towing them back 'safely out of the Thai territorial waters'.[108] Unsurprisingly, there was considerable doubt about this report. First of all the fact that the Thai government at no stage considered or referred to these people as refugees but as illegal entrants indicates the manner in which they were viewed and how they would have been questioned. Second, the Thai government had a history of 'turning a blind eye' and had been quoted positively inferring that such acts served to discourage boat people from attempting to enter Thailand via the Gulf.[109] The report went on to state that 'the government and the people of Thailand are profoundly disappointed and deeply regret the public disclosure of the unsubstantiated allegations, particularly in view of the good cooperation Thailand has always extended to the UNHCR and other relevant international organizations in helping Indochinese refugees in accordance with humanitarian principles'.[110]

Soonsiri then went on to remind observers that Thailand has been most generous to Indochinese refugees and that:

> (A)ccording to Thai immigration laws, illegal entrants will be arrested and dealt with in accordance with Thai legal processes. This implies that illegal entrants whether of Laotian, Kampuchean or Vietnamese origin, must be arrested and deported from Thailand immediately. *However, because of the special prevailing circumstances, the authorities have been lenient and have provided temporary shelter in compliance with humanitarian principles.*[111]

But the country most responsible, ends Soonsiri, was Vietnam. Vietnam, he argued, should provide its people with a better life in their own country so that they would stop seeking it elsewhere.[112]

The tensions continued in March with Soonsiri complaining to the UNHCR about the 'continuous accusation against Thailand during past weeks'.[113] This was in relation to UNHCR press briefings in Geneva on pirate attacks in the Gulf of Thailand. The UNHCR replied that the reporting of acts of piracy was routine, but

---

107 UNHCR, Permanent Mission of Thailand, *Press Release Statement by Squadron Leader Prasong Soonsiri on 8 February 1984*, 10 February 1984; Folio 505C, 010.THA.

108 UNHCR, Permanent Mission of Thailand, *Press Release Statement by Squadron Leader Prasong Soonsiri on 8 February 1984*, 10 February 1984; Folio 505C, 010.THA, p. 2.

109 Robinson, *Terms of Refuge: The Indochinese Exodus and the International Response*, 1998, pp. 166–169.

110 UNHCR, Permanent Mission of Thailand, *Press Release Statement by Squadron Leader Prasong Soonsiri on 8 February 1984*, 10 February 1984; Folio 505C, 010.THA, p. 4.

111 UNHCR, Permanent Mission of Thailand, *Press Release Statement by Squadron Leader Prasong Soonsiri on 8 February 1984*, 10 February 1984; Folio 505C, 010.THA, p. 5. Emphasis added.

112 UNHCR, Permanent Mission of Thailand, *Press Release Statement by Squadron Leader Prasong Soonsiri on 8 February 1984*, 10 February 1984; Folio 505C, 010.THA, p. 6.

113 UNHCR, UNHCR Bangkok to HICOMREF Geneva, *Urgent Incoming Cable*, 8 March 1984; THA/CHR/429, 010.THA, p. 1.

admitted that 'in the present atmosphere of misunderstanding it should have been avoided'.[114] Soonsiri retorted that the UNHCR gave the impression that Thailand was doing nothing against piracy as it was reported that the acts of piracy were taking place in the Gulf of Thailand. Soonsiri stated that 'he had tried to exercise restraint while UNHCR had not done the same'.[115]

The UNHCR conducted its own investigation and presented Soonsiri with a dossier about the Narathiwat incident, which Soonsiri did not want publicly discussed.[116] Soonsiri also gave no indication that he would issue instructions to provinces and districts regarding the receiving of boat people, preventing push backs and combating piracy. Soonsiri suggested that the anti-piracy programme had been funded by the international community only as 'as an excuse to slander Thailand's good name and this 'chicken-feed money' should not be accepted by Thailand'.[117] The Thai government was unhappy at the continual attacks on the good name of Thailand due to these pirate attacks and complained that the UNHCR was doing nothing about the attacks on Cambodians by the Vietnamese army in the Thai-Cambodia border region.[118] In addition, Soonsiri stated displeasure with the UNHCR and international community's lack of concern about the root causes of the flow of people form Indochina and the 'lack of progress in dealing with refugee situation in Thailand'.[119] Soonsiri referred specifically to the 'increasingly restrictive resettlement criteria, overstayers in Phanat Nikhom and.... poor resettlement performance in Khao I Dang'[120] because of states such as the USA using stricter resettlement criteria. Soonsiri threatened that overstayers who were not being accepted for resettlement 'had no future'[121] and would be sent over the border if this situation continued. In response, the UNHCR expressed displeasure with the malign and 'unfair' statements about the UNHCR in the Thai press and argued that these allegations were 'incorrect and did not reflect the true nature of UNHCR service rendered in Thailand for the benefit of refugees in close collaboration with RTG'.[122]

---

[114] UNHCR, UNHCR Bangkok to HICOMREF Geneva, *Urgent Incoming Cable*, 8 March 1984; THA/CHR/429, 010.THA, p. 1.

[115] UNHCR, UNHCR Bangkok to HICOMREF Geneva, *Urgent Incoming Cable*, 8 March 1984; THA/CHR/429, 010.THA, p. 1.

[116] UNHCR, UNHCR Bangkok to HICOMREF Geneva, *Urgent Incoming Cable*, 8 March 1984; THA/CHR/429, 010.THA, p. 2.

[117] UNHCR, UNHCR Bangkok to HICOMREF Geneva, *Urgent Incoming Cable*, 8 March 1984; THA/CHR/429, 010.THA, p. 2.

[118] UNHCR, UNHCR Bangkok to HICOMREF Geneva, *Urgent Incoming Cable*, 8 March 1984; THA/CHR/429, 010.THA, p. 3.

[119] UNHCR, UNHCR Bangkok to HICOMREF Geneva, *Urgent Incoming Cable*, 8 March 1984; THA/CHR/429, 010.THA, p. 3.

[120] UNHCR Bangkok to HICOMREF Geneva, *Urgent Incoming Cable*, 8 March 1984; THA/CHR/429, 010.THA, p. 3.

[121] UNHCR Bangkok to HICOMREF Geneva, *Urgent Incoming Cable*, 8 March 1984; THA/CHR/429, 010.THA, p. 3.

[122] UNHCR Bangkok to HICOMREF Geneva, *Urgent Incoming Cable*, 8 March 1984; THA/CHR/429, 010.THA, p. 3.

These confrontations, during the first three months of 1984, demonstrate at least three negative points about the deepening crisis. The first is that whilst prior to 1984 Thailand and the UNHCR had at least a polite relationship, now both parties were no longer keeping to polite comments about each other even in public. While the tone of Thailand's statements were not new, UNHCR's press briefings in 1984 were in marked contrast to their *lack* of press briefings when the Thai government practiced *refoulement* of Cambodian refugees in 1979. Therefore, whether these 1984 press briefings were 'unfortunate' or deliberate, they nevertheless marked a very different tone to the UNHCR's public dealings with the Thai government. Second, Thailand was constantly at pains to point out that its actions regarding the Indochinese were better than that required under Thai law. This argument directly tied in with the third point—Thailand no longer referred to the Indochinese as refugees for the sake of continued assistance.

Thai authorities repeatedly made a distinction between 'genuine' and 'non-genuine' refugees during this period. For instance, in April 1984 the Thai Prime Minister began his memo to the UN Secretary General with the opening statement '(T)he Vietnamese refugees, *be they refugees in the traditional sense or not*, have continued to impose a heavy burden on Thailand'.[123] The Thai government continually pointed out that people were leaving Vietnam because they wanted a better life, not because they were fleeing persecution. Thus, Thailand was only under a moral obligation to provide charitable and humanitarian assistance. Thailand insisted that it was under no other obligation than to provide temporary asylum. Even that, it argued, was conditional on third country resettlement. Thailand also insisted that it could not be expected to patrol the entire Gulf of Thailand in order to prevent pirate attacks. Overall, Thailand insisted that the UNHCR had primary responsibility for the welfare of asylum seekers and that it needed to exercise its mandate 'and devote its efforts towards preventing the occurrence of the problem, also at the source'.[124] Thailand claimed that they could not be held morally responsible for the safety of boat people.[125] Thus, the UNHCR should be grateful for whatever assistance Thailand directed towards those people, particularly since these people were not 'genuine' refugees.[126]

123 UNHCR, Thai Prime Minister to UN Secretary-General, *Memorandum Boat People*, 14 April 1984; HC/HCR/249, 010.THA, pp. 2–4. Emphasis added.

124 UNHCR, Thai Prime Minister to UN Secretary-General, *Memorandum Boat People*, 14 April 1984; HC/HCR/249, 010.THA, p. 4.

125 Interview of Mr Nitya Pibulsonggram, Director of Department of International Organizations with Joseph Cerquone of the US Committee for Refugees, from UNHCR, *Refugees*, No. 3 March 1984; 010.THA, p. 7.

126 UNHCR, Thai Prime Minister to UN Secretary-General, *Memorandum Boat People*, 14 April 1984; HC/HCR/249, 010.THA, p. 2.

5.5 *More listeners to Southeast Asian states by mid 1980s*

During the mid-1980s, Hong Kong, Indonesia, Malaysia, the Philippines, Singapore and Thailand were still accepting 'significant numbers' of Indochinese refugees for temporary asylum.[127] The Indonesian and Filipino Refugee Processing Centres (RPCs) had collectively provided accommodation for 21,000 Indochinese refugees in 1984 alone (those in the RPCs had already been accepted for resettlement in third countries).[128] At the same time, between 1983 and 1985 the ODP rose to its highest numbers—with a peak of 29,154 people being accepted under the ODP in 1984.[129] Overall, the numbers leaving Indochina via boat during this time also appeared to be decreasing: 27,794 arrived in the region in 1983 compared to 19,527 arrivals in 1985.[130] However, from 1983 to 1986 the number of refugees awaiting resettlement did not decrease in proportion to the number arriving.[131] In addition, there were a number of 'long-stayers'. These people were repeatedly rejected by resettlement states because they did not meet their entry criteria.[132] In 1984, the UNHCR identified the problem in saying that the resettlement rate had fallen by 49 percent compared to the last reporting period of 1983, and compared to 1981–1982, the difference was 82 percent.[133] Therefore UNHCR concluded that 'the resettlement momentum faltered'.[134]

This growing reluctance by developed states to provide resettlement numbers concomitant with the number of arrivals was of concern to the UNHCR because the decrease in departures was creating a growing resistance by states in the region towards new arrivals.[135] The UNHCR described a 'reluctance of States to assume responsibility for examining an asylum request or to admit asylum-seekers otherwise than on a purely temporary basis' that was compounded by an 'an increasing unwillingness on the part of the States to give due recognition to the special status of refugees and the *blurring of the distinction between the refugee and the ordinary*

[127] UNGA, *Report of the United Nations High Commissioner for Refugees*, Official Records Supplement No. 12, Thirty-Ninth Session, (New York: 1984), p. 29.

[128] UNGA, *Report of the United Nations High Commissioner for Refugees*, Official Records Supplement No. 12, Thirty-Ninth Session, (New York: 1984), p. 29.

[129] Druke, *Preventative Action for Refugee Producing Situations*, 1993, p. 80.

[130] Druke, *Preventative Action for Refugee Producing Situations*, 1993, p. 80.

[131] UNGA, *Report on the Thirty-Fourth Session of the Executive Committee of the High Commissioner's Programme 10–20 October 1983*, Executive Committee of the High Commissioner's Programme, Thirty-Fourth Session, A/AC.96/631, 20 October 1983, p. 41; UNGA, *Summary Record of the 408th Meeting on 9 October 1986*, Executive Committee of the High Commissioner's Programme, Thirty-Seventh Session, A/AC.96/SR.408, 21 October 1986, p. 16.

[132] UNGA, *Summary Record of the 408th Meeting on 9 October 1986*, Executive Committee of the High Commissioner's Programme, Thirty-Seventh Session, A/AC.96/SR.408, 21 October 1986, p. 16.

[133] UNGA, *Report on the Resettlement of Refugees*, Executive Committee of the High Commissioner's Programme, Thirty-Fifth Session, A/AC.96/640, 19 July 1984, p. 4.

[134] UNGA, *Report on the Resettlement of Refugees*, Executive Committee of the High Commissioner's Programme, Thirty-Fifth Session, A/AC.96/640, 19 July 1984, p. 4.

[135] UNGA, *Report on the Resettlement of Refugees*, Executive Committee of the High Commissioner's Programme, Thirty-Fifth Session, A/AC.96/640, 19 July 1984, p. 4.

alien'.[136] The problem, the UNHCR argued, was that migrants were leaving developing countries for economic betterment in developed countries in higher numbers and this had led to 'refugees being identified in the public mind with the ordinary migrant'.[137] The UNHCR's criticism was not just leveled at Southeast Asian states but also at developed states for 'confusing' the migrant and refugee in order to satisfy 'xenophobic attitudes' at the domestic level.[138] How did Southeast Asian states respond to this? The resettlement of Indochinese refugees remained the preferred solution.[139] Voluntary repatriation was attempted (see above) but remained 'elusive'[140] at this stage due to a lack of cooperation from the country of origin and asylum seekers refusing to return.

The position of the resettlement states at this stage was still divided. In the 1984 Executive Committee of the High Commissioner's Programme, Australia, US, Japan and China continued to excuse Southeast Asian states' actions and placed the emphasis on finding a solution that would reduce resettlement needs. On the other hand Denmark in particular, with the support of France and the Netherlands, expressed concern about the changing perception of the Indochinese refugees. The 1951 Convention, Australia argued in response, provided for 'such distinctions which were important safeguards for States experiencing or likely to experience a mass influx'.[141] Australia suggested that 'people with unsubstantiated claims might be required to return to their country of origin'[142] after being evaluated according to the 1951 Convention requirements. Due to this being an accepted practice towards asylum seekers, the Australian government wanted to know why the UNHCR had not already considered this as a solution to the massive outflow from Indochina. For instance, the current solution of resettlement was only serving to 'perpetuate populations displacement'. Nor was it a solution for the 260,000 Cambodians 'currently gathered along the Thai-Kampuchean border who were regarded as still being within their country of origin and therefore not refugees'.[143]

The United States completed a *volte face* when it agreed with the Australian proposal, stating that 'although all refugees were needy people, *not all needy people*

---

[136] United Nations Social and Economic Council, *Report of the United Nations High Commissioner for Refugees*, Second Regular Session, E/1984.61, 30 May 1984, p. 3. Emphasis added.

[137] United Nations Social and Economic Council, *Report of the United Nations High Commissioner for Refugees*, Second Regular Session, E/1984.61, 30 May 1984, p. 3.

[138] United Nations Social and Economic Council, *Report of the United Nations High Commissioner for Refugees*, Second Regular Session, E/1984.61, 30 May 1984, p. 4.

[139] UNGA, *Summary Record of the 368th Meeting on 8 October 1984*, Executive Committee of the High Commissioner's Programme, Thirty-Fifth Session, A/AC.96/SR.368, 10 October 1984, p. 6.

[140] UNGA, *Summary Record of the 368th Meeting on 8 October 1984*, Executive Committee of the High Commissioner's Programme, Thirty-Fifth Session, A/AC.96/SR.368, 10 October 1984, p. 7.

[141] UNGA, *Summary Record of the 369th Meeting on 9 October 1984*, Executive Committee of the High Commissioner's Programme, Thirty-Fifth Session, A/AC.96/SR.369, 12 October 1984, p. 3.

[142] UNGA, *Summary Record of the 369th Meeting on 9 October 1984*, Executive Committee of the High Commissioner's Programme, Thirty-Fifth Session, A/AC.96/SR.369, 12 October 1984, p. 3.

[143] UNGA, *Summary Record of the 369th Meeting on 9 October 1984*, Executive Committee of the High Commissioner's Programme, Thirty-Fifth Session, A/AC.96/SR.369, 12 October 1984, p. 3.

were refugees'.[144] Keeping this point in mind, the US warned that 'care must be taken not to weaken the action of the international community and the High Commissioner in favor of genuine refugees'.[145] The United States and Japan also expressed concern with the fact that regional stability in Southeast Asia was being jeopardized by the refugee burden.[146] Therefore, the United States, unsurprisingly, agreed with Thailand that the 'root causes' of the refugee flows [largely Vietnam] should become part of meeting the refugee challenge.[147]

China also agreed that the main problem was that 'none of the root causes of outflows of refugees had been eliminated'.[148] What they were proposing was that the UNHCR begin to take more interest in the situations that caused refugee flows, as opposed to simply responding to them after the fact. Other states soon joined the chorus, arguing that the UNHCR had just as much of a duty to prevent refugees as to protect them. This was quite a significant step away from the avowed non-political character of the UNHCR and constituted a direct challenge to its mandate which only extended to refugees—not 'pre-refugees'. It also demonstrates the intense struggle that the UNHCR had in keeping to its non-political mandate whilst large donors like the US used foreign assistance packages to support its wider foreign policy.

However, Denmark's stance was in complete contrast to many other resettlement states. Mr Repsdorph, the delegate for Denmark, stated that his government was increasingly concerned about:

> (R)estrictive policies pursued by some Governments with regard to the admission and treatment of asylum seekers, including various measures of so-called 'humane deterrence' [Thailand] and about the increasingly strict interpretation by many countries of relevant refugee status criteria.[149]

Denmark foresaw the erosion of refugee protection in the name of reducing obligations and, most significantly, Denmark seemed to be advocating that in large scale crises a non-restrictive interpretation of refugee principles was crucial. Denmark, France and the Netherlands also expressed concern that, as regular contributors

144 UNHCR, *Summary of the 370th Meeting on 9 October 1984*, Executive Committee of the High Commissioner's Programme, Thirty-Fifth Session, A/AC.96/SR.370, 15 October 1984, p. 13. Emphasis added.

145 UNHCR, *Summary of the 370th Meeting on 9 October 1984*, Executive Committee of the High Commissioner's Programme, Thirty-Fifth Session, A/AC.96/SR.370, 15 October 1984, p. 15.

146 UNHCR, *Summary Record of the 369th Meeting on 9 October 1984*, Executive Committee of the High Commissioner's Programme, Thirty-Fifth Session, A/AC.96/SR.369, 12 October 1984, p. 12; UNHCR, *Summary of the 370th Meeting on 9 October 1984*, Executive Committee of the High Commissioner's Programme, Thirty-Fifth Session, A/AC.96/SR.370, 15 October 1984, p. 13.

147 UNGA, *Summary Record of the 369th Meeting on 9 October 1984*, Executive Committee of the High Commissioner's Programme, Thirty-Fifth Session, A/AC.96/SR.369, 12 October 1984, pp. 6–7; UNGA, *Summary of the 370th Meeting on 9 October 1984*, Executive Committee of the High Commissioner's Programme, Thirty-Fifth Session, A/AC.96/SR.370, 15 October 1984, p. 14.

148 UNGA, *Summary Record of the 371st Meeting on 10 October 1984*, Executive Committee of the High Commissioner's Programme, Thirty-Fifth Session, A/AC.96/SR.371, 17 October 1984, p. 2.

149 UNGA, *Summary Record of the 371st Meeting on 10 October 1984*, Executive Committee of the High Commissioner's Programme, Thirty-Fifth Session, A/AC.96/SR.371, 17 October 1984, p. 5.

to the anti-piracy programme in Thailand, not enough was being done to prevent continued deaths on the high seas caused by pirate attacks.[150]

In 1985 and 1986 these discussions in the Executive Committee continued in the same manner, and the UNHCR revealed its desperation to keep states compliant with refugee protection rules. In 1985, the UNHCR asserted that more accessions to the 1951 Convention and 1967 Protocol were essential, 'especially by states in those areas of the world confronted with major ongoing refugee situations [which] will help strengthen the international legal framework' and 'also make it possible to reach the goal of universality in the foreseeable future'.[151] The UNHCR argued that the lack of accessions in certain regions had compromised the instruments' claim to universality. Therefore, the 1951 Convention and 1967 Protocol could not be considered as universal until most states in most regions of the world had accepted the instruments. Yet the UNHCR also stressed that '*non-refoulement*.... has become universally recognized' and furthermore was to be applied 'irrespective of whether or not they [asylum seekers] have been formally recognized as refugees'.[152]

The UNHCR was therefore still attempting to encourage Southeast Asian states to understand that their accession to the instruments was not only important, but essential. At the same time, the UNHCR insisted that regardless of accession, articles within the instruments, particularly those relating to *non-refoulement*, were already universally recognized and therefore constituted customary law applicable to all. The contradiction here was that while the UNHCR reminded all states, Southeast Asian states in particular, that certain principles regarding refugees should be considered customary, the lack of accessions to the instruments was also used to suggest that they were not universal. The UNHCR claim that *non-refoulement* was universal and customary, yet other aspects of the instrument (in which the *non-refoulement* article was embedded) could not be similarly regarded until all states acceded to it.

The UNHCR also responded to the increasing insistence that Indochinese asylum seekers should have their refugee status individually assessed. The UNHCR's argument was that large scale influxes did not make individual status determination feasible and therefore it was more 'imperative to resort to ad hoc arrangements for group determination based on an *objective evaluation of the circumstances obtaining in the country of origin which led to the departure of the persons concerned*'.[153] Later in 1985, the UNHCR picked up this argument again explaining that:

150 UNGA, *Summary Record of the 369th Meeting on 9 October 1984*, Executive Committee of the High Commissioner's Programme, Thirty-Fifth Session, A/AC.96/SR.369, 12 October 1984, pp. 9, 11; UNGA, *Summary Record of the 371st Meeting on 10 October 1984*, Executive Committee of the High Commissioner's Programme, Thirty-Fifth Session, A/AC.96/SR.371, 17 October 1984, p. 5.

151 United Nations Economic and Social Council, *Report on the United Nations High Commissioner for Refugees*, Second Regular Session, E/1985/62, 8 May 1985, p. 4.

152 United Nations Economic and Social Council, *Report on the United Nations High Commissioner for Refugees*, Second Regular Session, E/1985/62, 8 May 1985, p. 6.

153 United Nations Economic and Social Council, *Report on the United Nations High Commissioner for Refugees*, Second Regular Session, E/1985/62, 8 May 1985, pp. 19–20. Emphasis added.

> (E)ven though the majority of today's refugees are persons *who do not fall within the 'classic' refugee definition in the UNHCR Statute*, they have, as helpless victims of man-made disasters without the possibility of safe return, come to be recognized as persons of concern to the High Commissioner. This has been confirmed by successive resolutions of the General Assembly.[154]

The UNHCR argued that the method of determining refugee status had to be flexible enough to cope with mass influxes and other crises; there were going to be more and more people seeking asylum for reasons that did not fit the 1951 Convention's understanding, but this was not an excuse to deny them, at a minimum, temporary asylum:

> (T)he vast majority of those seeking asylum today are not persons fleeing from direct persecution or because of fear of persecution, but rather persons who have been displaced from their countries owing to situations of armed conflict, foreign aggression or occupation, or internal upheavals accompanied by serious human rights violations. There is now an increasing recognition that persons in this latter category should be protected from danger through the granting of at least temporary asylum until such a time as conditions in their country of origin permit their return.[155]

However, at this stage, resettlement in a third country remained the only option for Indochinese refugees, as local integration was still out of the question in Southeast Asia and repatriation could not be done in large enough numbers to significantly reduce the load in the asylum camps.[156] The problem with the resettlement 'solution' was that it was becoming less of an option with states no longer wanting to provide a seemingly endless quota for Indochinese refugees.[157] At the same time, the number of 'long-stayers' in the camps also continued to rise. This had a negative effect on Southeast Asian states' level of cooperation and raised concerns in the UNHCR about their continued cooperation in providing temporary asylum.[158] In 1985 therefore, the UNHCR attempted to decisively respond to the positions being taking by resettlement and Southeast Asian states by consistently emphasizing states' obligations. For instance:

> UNHCR cannot substitute for the will and determination of States to provide solutions to refugee problems. In instance where the political interests of States take

[154] UNGA, *Note on International Protection*, Submitted by the High Commissioner, Executive Committee of the High Commissioner's Programme, Thirty-Sixth Session, A/AC.96/660, 23 July 1985, p. 3. Emphasis added.

[155] United Nations Economic and Social Council, *Report on the United Nations High Commissioner for Refugees*, Second Regular Session, E/1985/62, 8 May 1985, p. 5.

[156] UNGA, *Durable Solutions*, Submitted by the High Commissioners, Executive Committee of the High Commissioner's Programme, Thirty-Sixth Session, A/AC.96/663, 25 July 1985, pp. 6–7.

[157] UNGA, *Report on the Resettlement of Refugees*, Submitted by the High Commissioner, Executive Committee of the High Commissioner's Programme, Thirty-Sixth Session, A/AC.96/661, 26 July 1985, p. 3.

[158] UNGA, *Note on International Protection*, Submitted by the High Commissioner, Executive Committee of the High Commissioner's Programme, Thirty-Sixth Session, A/AC.96/660, 23 July 1985, p. 4.

> precedence over humanitarian concerns, the effective international protection of refugees cannot be achieved. In other words, in situations where durable solutions are not offered by states, the international protection of refugees will suffer.[159]

In reality, the decision as to how Indochinese refugees would be considered and treated had already been made by Southeast Asian states. Moreover, it had been made increasingly so by the resettlement states and the states that mattered when it came to financial assistance: Japan and the United States. Financial assistance had added significance because the UNHCR at this time was facing bankruptcy.[160]

In 1985 the rate of boat people arrivals in the first six months was 9 percent less than the same period in 1984; yet the rate of departures for resettlement had dropped 17 percent.[161] However, the Laotian refugee population was increasing again, while the situation on the Thai-Kampuchean border remained problematic.[162] The UNHCR agreed that repatriation was the most desirable solution for all of these problems, but it was not the 'easiest' to achieve; thus resettlement was still the only viable option.[163] The problem, argued UNHCR, was that people seeking asylum by boat were those who did 'not qualify for ODP and could not have availed themselves of it'.[164] In addition, a UNHCR field study, conducted on recent arrivals in Hong Kong, Indonesia Malaysia, Philippines and Thailand found that at least two thirds of those seeking asylum 'had no claim to refugee status'.[165] These findings of course, played right into what Southeast Asian states had been arguing, for it was a concession by the UNHCR that most seeking asylum were not *genuine* refugees.

The UNHCR once again took ambiguous if not contradictory positions as it struggled to come to terms with the situation. In 1986 a UNHCR Joint Inspection Unit report on refugees in Southeast Asia for the period 1979–1983, found that it was the 'restrictive refugee admission policies of first asylum countries in the region that tended to obstruct, if not impede, the protection of refugees and asylum-seekers'.[166] Furthermore, the 'increasing reluctance of potential resettlement

159 UNGA, *Note on International Protection*, Submitted by the High Commissioner, Executive Committee of the High Commissioner's Programme, Thirty-Sixth Session, A/AC.96/660, 23 July 1985, p. 2.

160 UNGA, *Summary Record of the 385th Session on 7 October 1984*, Executive Committee of the High Commissioner's Programme, Thirty-Sixth Session, A/AC.96/SR.385, 9 October 1985, p. 8.

161 UNGA, *Report on the Resettlement of Refugees*, Submitted by the High Commissioner, Executive Committee of the High Commissioner's Programme, Thirty-Sixth Session, A/AC.96/661, 26 July 1985, p. 3.

162 UNGA, *Report on the Resettlement of Refugees*, Submitted by the High Commissioner, Executive Committee of the High Commissioner's Programme, Thirty-Sixth Session, A/AC.96/661, 26 July 1985, pp. 4–5.

163 UNGA, *Durable Solutions*, Submitted by the High Commissioners, Executive Committee of the High Commissioner's Programme, Thirty-Sixth Session, A/AC.96/663, 25 July 1985, p. 2.

164 UNGA, *Durable Solutions*, Submitted by the High Commissioners, Executive Committee of the High Commissioner's Programme, Thirty-Sixth Session, A/AC.96/663, 25 July 1985, p. 7.

165 Robinson, *Terms of Refuge: The Indochinese Exodus and the International Response*, pp. 176–178.

166 UNGA, 'Refugee question subject of Third Committee scrutiny in November', *UN Chronicle*, January 1986, Vol. 23, p. 3. http://web6.infrotrac.galegroup.com/itw/infomark/200/122/39895

countries to accept large numbers of refugees, or award refugee status, had narrowed the options of the UNHCR'.[167] In 1986, Mr Arnaout, Director of Refugee Law and Doctrine Division for UNHCR, also expressed concern with the lack of cooperation by asylum countries *and* resettlement countries exacerbating the refugee problem:

> The fact that most of the refugees were located in developing countries prevented several of those countries from providing them with anything more than a mere temporary refuge, and in view of the lack of durable solutions in those countries, many had been forced to seek asylum outside their region of origin…Their arrival in developed countries had provided defensive policies reflected in the adoption of restrictive measures and by phenomena which could not fail to affect the implementation of protection principles. Thus, asylum-seekers were described as economic migrants.[168]

Furthermore, Arnaout argued, the 'non-genuine' refugee argument was not always based on fact for 'a large number of asylum-seekers from developing countries came from regions where there was unrest, and the argument that they were economic migrants was not as well-founded as it might appear'.[169]

The response of Southeast Asian states was swift. In the Executive Committee, Thailand said that it had provided temporary refuge since 1975 and ten years later, in 1985, the number of '*displaced persons*' from Laos and Vietnam kept increasing.[170] Thailand's provision of temporary refuge, like the other ASEAN countries, had always been 'granted on the understanding that resettlement in third countries would be guaranteed'.[171] Therefore, argued Thailand, it was resettlement countries that needed to intensify their efforts.[172] Malaysia agreed, arguing that it was also willing to provide continued humanitarian assistance, despite the affect the last ten years had wrecked its economy, for '*illegal Vietnamese refugees…pending their resettlement in third countries*'.[173] Even the Philippines, a member of the 1951 Con-

167 UNGA, 'Refugee question subject of Third Committee scrutiny in November', *UN Chronicle*, January 1986, Vol. 23, p. 3. http://web6.infrotrac.galegroup.com/itw/infomark/200/122/39895

168 UNGA, *Summary Record of the 405th Meeting on 8 October 1986*, Executive Committee of the High Commissioner's Programme, Thirty-Seventh Session, A/AC.96/SR.405, 14 October 1984, p. 12.

169 UNGA, *Summary Record of the 405th Meeting on 8 October 1986*, Executive Committee of the High Commissioner's Programme, Thirty-Seventh Session, A/AC.96/SR.405, 14 October 1984, p. 12.

170 UNGA, 'Refugee question subject of Third Committee scrutiny in November', *UN Chronicle*, January 1986, Vol. 23, p. 6. http://web6.infrotrac.galegroup.com/itw/infomark/200/122/39895

171 UNGA, 'Refugee question subject of Third Committee scrutiny in November', *UN Chronicle*, January 1986, Vol. 23, p. 6. http://web6.infrotrac.galegroup.com/itw/infomark/200/122/39895

172 UNGA, 'Refugee question subject of Third Committee scrutiny in November', *UN Chronicle*, January 1986, Vol. 23, p. 6. http://web6.infrotrac.galegroup.com/itw/infomark/200/122/39895

173 UNGA, 'Refugee question subject of Third Committee scrutiny in November', *UN Chronicle*, January 1986, Vol. 23, p. 6. http://web6.infrotrac.galegroup.com/itw/infomark/200/122/39895 Emphasis added.

vention and 1967 Protocol for five years, argued that 'Asia had been the continent most seriously affected by the refugee question in recent times . . . the international community must go beyond mere assistance to real solutions by tackling the root causes of refugee movements'.[174] In the meantime, the Philippine delegate argued that as 'the developing countries, which all too often had to assume the economic and political burdens of refugee inflows, should be eligible for special treatment in terms of bilateral and multilateral development aid'.[175]

The resettlement states were also quick to validate their actions. Australia argued that the assessment of requests for asylum were essential for '70–75 per cent of asylum-seekers in his country were unable to substantiate their claims. His understanding was that in many other countries the rejection rate was similar or even higher'.[176] Therefore, Australia argued that 'the problems posed by a world on the move would not disappear, regardless of decisions on refugee status, but perhaps those pointed to the *need for a sharper focus on some of the practical problems of asylum and refugee status procedures and the need to streamline procedures which were often outdated*'.[177] Japan, which had resettled only 4,700 Indochinese refugees between 1981 and 1986, argued that whilst resettlement remained the principal solution, it was 'becoming increasingly difficult for the countries concerned, including Japan, to resettle Indo-Chinese refugees, and alternative durable solutions should be sought urgently'.[178] Japan suggested that voluntary repatriation had become the most desirable solution for this situation.[179]

Cambodia, then represented in the UN as 'Democratic Kampuchea',[180] of course, blamed the Vietnamese occupation for its refugee levels and insisted that only the withdrawal of foreign forces from the country would end the resistance and refugee problem.[181] China agreed with Cambodia and reminded the international

174 UNGA, *Summary Record of the 407th Meeting on 9 October 1986*, Executive Committee of the High Commissioner's Programme, Thirty-Seventh Session, A/AC.96/SR.407, 16 October 1984, p. 14.

175 UNGA, *Summary Record of the 407th Meeting on 9 October 1986*, Executive Committee of the High Commissioner's Programme, Thirty-Seventh Session, A/AC.96/SR.407, 16 October 1984, p. 14.

176 UNGA, *Summary Record of the 405th Meeting on 8 October 1986*, Executive Committee of the High Commissioner's Programme, Thirty-Seventh Session, A/AC.96/SR.405, 14 October 1984, p. 14.

177 UNGA, *Summary Record of the 405th Meeting on 8 October 1986*, Executive Committee of the High Commissioner's Programme, Thirty-Seventh Session, A/AC.96/SR.405, 14 October 1984, p. 14. Emphasis added.

178 UNGA, *Summary Record of the 407th Meeting on 9 October 1986*, Executive Committee of the High Commissioner's Programme, Thirty-Seventh Session, A/AC.96/SR.407, 16 October 1984, p. 13.

179 UNGA, *Summary Record of the 407th Meeting on 9 October 1986*, Executive Committee of the High Commissioner's Programme, Thirty-Seventh Session, A/AC.96/SR.407, 16 October 1984, p. 13.

180 As stated earlier, the Khmer Rouge still had representation on the 'Democratic Kampuchea' seat at the United Nations.

181 UNGA, *Summary Record of the 407th Meeting on 9 October 1986*, Executive Committee of the High Commissioner's Programme, Thirty-Seventh Session, A/AC.96/SR.407, 16 October 1984, p. 6.

community that it had taken 280,000 Indochinese refugees for local integration 'despite its stringent economy and heavy population burden'.[182] Not surprisingly, the country-of-origin states were also defensive. The Vietnamese delegate blamed the United States for any difficulties in the ODP—arguing that it should just 'end its practice of discriminating between refugees leaving legally and illegally'.[183] Incidentally, Vietnam was partially correct in its argument, the United States had started to introduce more stringent resettlement quotas. Nonetheless, it was unusual for a country-of-origin to openly encourage the departure of its citizens. Laos denied that it was responsible for the refugee problem, it was the 'imperialist, hegemonist and expansionist policies of interference in the internal affairs of States' that were the cause.[184] The Laotian delegate argued that the Laotian government had done 'everything possible to prevent that exodus and worked to encourage genuine voluntary repatriation'[185] despite the propaganda being spread by its neighboring country (Thailand) and economic hardship.

Of particular interest is the final statement by the head of the UNHCR Regional Bureau for Asia and Oceania at the Executive Committee meeting in 1986. Mr Homann-Herimberg said that 'the problem of Indo-Chinese asylum-seekers was still highly acute... first asylum countries were understandably anxious that a solution be found for long-stayers in the near future' because 'the arrival of boat people in ASEAN countries and in Hong Kong was likely to continue for some time'.[186] There were 150,000 people still awaiting durable solutions in Southeast Asia, and Mr Homann-Herimberg quoted the High Commissioner's response to this problem: 'the situation demanded a vigorous pursuit of all the classic solutions to refugee problems coupled with action on the question of root causes'.[187] The mention of 'root causes' here is important. Clearly, the UNHCR had begun to accept the suggestion that it address the causes of refugee flight as well as the act itself. This signaled that the UNHCR was ready to validate the return of refugees to

[182] UNGA, *Summary Record of the 407th Meeting on 9 October 1986*, Executive Committee of the High Commissioner's Programme, Thirty-Seventh Session, A/AC.96/SR.407, 16 October 1984, p. 6.

[183] UNGA, 'Refugee question subject of Third Committee scrutiny in November', *UN Chronicle*, January 1986, Vol. 23, p. 6. http://web6.infrotrac.galegroup.com/itw/infomark/200/122/39895.

[184] UNGA, 'Refugee question subject of Third Committee scrutiny in November', *UN Chronicle*, January 1986, Vol. 23, p. 6. http://web6.infrotrac.galegroup.com/itw/infomark/200/122/39895 pp. 6–7.

[185] UNGA, 'Refugee question subject of Third Committee scrutiny in November', *UN Chronicle*, January 1986, Vol. 23, p. 6. http://web6.infrotrac.galegroup.com/itw/infomark/200/122/39895 p. 7.

[186] UNGA, *Summary Record of the 408th Meeting on 9 October 1986*, Executive Committee of the High Commissioner's Programme, Thirty-Seventh Session, A/AC.96/SR.408, 21 October 1984, p. 16.

[187] UNGA, *Summary Record of the 408th Meeting on 9 October 1986*, Executive Committee of the High Commissioner's Programme, Thirty-Seventh Session, A/AC.96/SR.408, 21 October 1984, p. 16.

their country of origin as long as it was able to maintain responsibility for ensuring that conditions upon return were bearable and safe.

5.6 *Conclusion*

This chapter has demonstrated that there was an important shift in the way that both Southeast Asian states and resettlement states approached the Indochinese refugee crisis in the 1980s. From the beginning of the Indochinese crisis Southeast Asian states argued that all asylum seekers should not be considered refugees. In the early 1980s, Southeast Asian states displayed increased concern with the *prima facie* refugee status being afforded to all boat people. The seemingly endless stream of Indochinese asylum seekers had Southeast Asian states anxiously pressing Western states for continual financial assistance and resettlement. When Western states showed reluctance, Southeast Asian states argued that they too could become reluctant to provide first asylum to non-genuine refugees. At the same time, the Cambodian refugee problem was taxing Thailand's 'generosity'. The result was that Thailand refused to allow the majority of Cambodians on the border to receive UNHCR protection as refugees. The Thai government then insisted in 1985 that Laotian asylum seekers be screened for refugee status. This set in motion the insistence that Vietnamese boatpeople should also have their refugee status determined individually as opposed to *en masse*.

In addition, the UNHCR's public announcement of concern at Thailand's inability to prevent pirate attacks forced the UNHCR to desperately seek to resolve the crisis in bilateral relations, with Thailand threatening to close refugee camps. Thus, by the mid 1980s, the constant need to appease Southeast Asian states was starting to take its toll on the UNHCR and Western states, and it is here that a shift in their perception of the Indochinese refugee problem started to occur.

The most significant event at this stage of the crisis was not just the Southeast Asian states' perception of those seeking asylum, but the new framing of their arguments *within* international refugee law to suggest that the Indochinese were not genuine refugees. Moreover, this led to changes in the perceptions held of Western states and the UNHCR. Western states, in particular, were experiencing 'compassion fatigue' with the seemingly endless Indochinese crisis. Key Western states and the UNHCR were now willing to accept that not all of the Indochinese deserved refugee protection. Southeast Asian states positioned their argument within the framework of international refugee law in order to demonstrate that their refusal to accede to the documents had been carefully considered and their rejection of the instruments continued to be legitimate.

Yet when the refugee numbers rose across the region again in 1987, the position held by the actors that had been dealing with this crisis for over ten years was divided. The UNHCR was increasingly concerned with the level of 'non-genuine' refugee arrivals in the region. But the organization was reluctant to openly acknowledge this for fear of encouraging Southeast Asian and resettlement states to further reduce their level of cooperation. At the same time, both Southeast Asian states and resettlement states were becoming increasingly confident of the justification for removing *prima facie* recognition to the boat people.[188] The number of arrivals by 1989 had risen to heights not seen since prior to the 1979 Conference. In addition, the withdrawal of Vietnam from Cambodia in September 1989 paved the way to a possible solution for the Cambodian refugees on the border. There was now an opportunity to start thinking about the repatriation. In turn, the increased attempt to repatriate Cambodians and Laotians led to the thought that the same practice might be applicable to the boat people. These factors coalesced in 1989 to produce a situation conducive to the development of a new agreement on Indochinese refugees: the Comprehensive Plan of Action (CPA) and this is the subject of the next chapter.

[188] The Cambodians had never been given *prima facie* refugee status in the first place; and Laotian refugees had been screened since 1985.

Chapter 6

The 1989 Comprehensive Plan of Action

Between 1988 and 1989, the number of Vietnamese who sought asylum in Southeast Asia and Hong Kong increased by 84 per cent.[1] This was largely attributed to a temporary lapse in the Orderly Departure Programme (ODP) and the lure of resettlement in wealthy, western nations. The ODP problems were due to differences between the US and Vietnam about who could be given immediate refugee status and resettlement: the US wanted to include those who had been sent to re-education camps and the Vietnamese were not willing for these people to be placed on the lists.[2] The UNHCR attempted to mediate between the US and Vietnam in order to resolve the ODP dispute and enjoyed some success as US State Department officials were allowed to visit Vietnam for the first time since the war to be present for ODP interviews.[3] However, more and more people were prepared to pay traffickers sums of $1500 for a place in a boat; thousands were also crossing through the recently opened land border areas of Cambodia into Thailand, or continuing by boat to Malaysia.[4]

---

1 UNGA, *Overview of UNHCR Activities: Report for 1988–1989*, Submitted by the High Commissioner, Executive Committee of the High Commissioner's Programme, Fortieth Session, A/AC.96/729, 25 August 1989, p. 5.

2 United States Committee for Refugees (USCR), *Refugee Reports*, Volume 9, Number 3, 18 March 1988, pp. 3–4; Robinson, *Terms of Refuge: The Indochinese Exodus and the International Response*, 1998, p. 195.

3 USCR, *Refugee Reports*, Volume 8, Number 8, 14 August 1987, pp. 1–2; USCR, *Refugee Reports*, Volume 9, Number 3, 18 March 1988, pp. 3–4; Robinson, *Terms of Refuge: The Indochinese Exodus and the International Response*, 1998, p. 195.

4 USCR, *Refugee Reports*, Volume 9, Number 2, 26 February 1988, pp. 1–2.

Therefore, the numbers seeking asylum radically rose while Southeast Asian states and Hong Kong became increasingly frustrated with the slow resettlement rates. Moreover, the long-stayers that had been repeatedly denied refugee status but could not be repatriated remained and were joined by another seemingly endless stream of arrivals. The options for a durable solution appeared to be evaporating.[5] This final chapter will detail how the Comprehensive Plan of Action (CPA) was created by ASEAN states, Hong Kong and the UNHCR in a collaborative effort to *solve* the Vietnamese and Laotian refugee problem. A different response was formulated for the Cambodians due to their classification as displaced persons and the nature of the political situation surrounding their displacement; thus, they were not part of the CPA.[6]

In this chapter, I argue that the adoption of UNHCR guidelines for screening refugees did not represent an acceptance by the Southeast Asian states of the basic principles of the 1951 Convention and 1967 Protocol. Rather, the CPA signified that Southeast Asian states had been successful in legitimising their argument within the international legal framework. Indochinese refugees were not to be considered 'genuine' refugees according to the 1951 Convention, but ought to be seen as 'non-genuine' refugees until proven otherwise. The acceptance by Southeast Asian states of the screening process should also not be seen as tacit acceptance of the 1951 for, at the end of the process, those deemed 'genuine' refugees were *resettled elsewhere* and those deemed 'non-genuine' were repatriated—by force in many cases. The CPA therefore provides an important insight into the wider relationship between politics and international refugee law in Southeast Asia.

This chapter is divided into three parts. The first part charts the lead up to the 1989 International Conference on Indochinese Refugees organized by the UN Secretary General. In March 1989, ASEAN states had requested all interested parties meet in Kuala Lumpur to discuss a new framework to replace the failed 1979 system. As I will show, this meeting marked the beginning of the CPA. The second part of the chapter will discuss the CPA itself, focusing on what it aimed to achieve in terms of solving the refugee problem. The two central strategies of the CPA—screening and repatriation—met with a variety of responses. I will argue that both strategies also ultimately failed to persuade ASEAN states to comply with international refugee law. Indeed, if anything, the CPA institutionalized non-compliance. In the final part of the chapter, I will assess the consequences of the CPA when it was concluded in 1996.

5 USCR, *Refugee Reports*, Volume 9, Number 6, 24 June 1988, pp. 6–7.

6 The Paris Accords were a number of meetings held in Paris where the solution for the Cambodian population was to repatriate them as soon as possible. The UNHCR, for the first time, would assist some 300,000 Cambodians to repatriate. USCR, *Refugee Reports*, Volume 10, Number 10, 20 October 1989, pp. 2–4; Robinson, *Terms of Refuge: The Indochinese Exodus and the International Response*, 1998, p. 239.

6.1 *Background to the CPA*

If 1987 marked the beginning of the second major increase in the number of Vietnamese boat people from 19,527 in 1986 to 28,056 in 1987, then 1988 marked the year when panic set in.[7] The ODP had reached a practical stalemate in January 1986, with Vietnamese officials refusing to interview any applicants.[8] However, it was hoped that the resumption of the ODP in July 1987 would provide an opportunity for those leaving by boat to delay their departure and leave via the ODP.[9] In December 1988, the UNHCR attempted to encourage this process by negotiating another Memorandum of Understanding with Vietnam. This significantly expanded and accelerated the ODP and increased the role of the UNHCR by granting it access to those seeking resettlement.[10]

However, these efforts did not reduce the rate of those leaving independently. The problem was that the majority of those leaving by boat were not eligible for ODP departure.[11] Under the ODP, those eligible for departure were either people that had assisted the United States or relatives of those who had and were seeking family reunion. This was expanded at the end of 1988, when the UNHCR assisted the US in persuading Vietnam to place former re-education camp detainees within the ODP. The US had already been frustrated in its attempts to secure the departure of such people. Vietnam had blocked many requests for people wishing leave under the ODP to reunite with their families; while those in re-education camps were mainly 'off-limits'.[12] In addition, Vietnam seemed to be using the ODP mainly to rid itself of ethnic-Chinese.[13] Others chose to leave by boat because they did not qualify for the ODP; the waiting period for the ODP was too long; and/or they were not aware of the ODP procedures or how they could use them to secure departure.[14]

As a result of the continued increase in the number of asylum seekers between 1988 and 1989, several Southeast Asian states started to publicly decry the failure of the 1979 agreement and to call for new solutions. Even prior to this, in 1987, ASEAN Foreign Ministers had collectively stated 'their concern over the compassion fatigue among the resettlement countries resulting in a slowdown in the resettlement programme which would increase the residual problem of refugees in ASEAN

---

7 Druke, *Preventative Action for Refugee Producing Situations*, 1993, p. 80.
8 United States Committee for Refugees, *Refugee Reports*, Volume 8, Number 8, 14 August 1987, p. 1.
9 UNGA, *UNHCR Activities Financed by Voluntary Funds: Report for 1987–1988 and Proposed Programmes and Budget for 1989, Part II: Asia and Oceania*, Submitted by the High Commissioner, Executive Committee of the High Commissioner's Programme, Thirty-Ninth Session, A/AC.96/708 (Part II), 28 July 1988, p. 30.
10 Robinson, *Terms of Refuge: The Indochinese Exodus and the International Response*, 1998, p. 183.
11 USCR, *Refugee Reports*, Volume 8, Number 8, 14 August 1987, p. 5; Robinson, *Terms of Refuge*, 1998, pp. 177–178.
12 USCR, *Refugee Reports*, Volume 8, Number 8, 14 August 1987, pp. 1–2.
13 USCR, *Refugee Reports*, Volume 8, Number 8, 14 August 1987, p. 2.
14 USCR, *Refugee Reports*, Volume 8, Number 8, 14 August 1987, p. 5.

countries'.[15] In 1988, ASEAN expressed greater urgency and denounced the 1979 agreement as inherently unable to produce a durable solution to the problem:

> The ASEAN Foreign Ministers are seriously concerned about the continued outflow of refugees, displaced persons and illegal immigrants from Indochina and the problems this poses for the ASEAN countries. The Foreign Ministers note with particular concern the large increase in the number of Vietnamese boat people coming into the ASEAN region over the past year. The Foreign Ministers are of the view that the structures, premises and assumptions of the past are no longer capable of dealing with the Vietnamese boat people problem. The Foreign Ministers agree that a new comprehensive programme of action is needed.[16]

At the 1988 Executive Committee of the High Commissioner's Programme meetings, the ASEAN states, with the support of Australia and Japan, further expressed their discontent with the system of response set up in 1979. In addition, ASEAN states drafted a decision for the Executive Committee's consideration; this was the proposal for an international conference on Indochinese refugees. Australia was the first to support it, saying:

> A new approach to the problem in South-East Asia was in fact essential if the principles of first asylum and humane treatment of refugees were to be sustained. The consensus reached at the 1979 Meeting on Refugees and Displaced Persons in South-East Asia had been undermined. The framework for a new approach had been laid down in the call by the Foreign Ministers of the ASEAN countries for the convening of an international conference on Indo-Chinese refugees. Australia supported that initiative.[17]

Japan followed suit, arguing that that 'international efforts had thus far been concentrated mainly on the resettlement of Indochinese refugees in third countries, but that process could not continue indefinitely and it was of the utmost importance to explore more actively the possibilities of voluntary repatriation and to pursue efforts to halt the possibilities of voluntary repatriation to pursue efforts to halt the outflow'.[18] Indonesia, Malaysia and Thailand all repeatedly stressed the importance of a new conference. Thailand said that it was becoming 'increasingly apparent that the norms and principles formulated at an earlier time in one part of the world and under a particular set of circumstances could not always be applied automatically to other regions or situations';[19] the purpose of a new conference was to 'refine and

15 ASEAN, *Joint Statement by the ASEAN Foreign Ministers on Indochinese Refugees*, Singapore, 14 June 1987. http://www.aseansec.org/2484.html

16 ASEAN, *Joint Statement by the ASEAN Foreign Ministers on the Indochinese Refugees*, Bangkok, Thailand, 4 July 1988. http://www.aseansec.org/907.html

17 UNGA, *Summary Record of the 426th Meeting on 3rd October 1988*, Executive Committee of the High Commissioner's Programme, Thirty-Ninth Session, A/AC.96/SR.426, 18 October 1988, p. 6.

18 UNGA, *Summary Record of the 427th Meeting on 4th October 1988*, Executive Committee of the High Commissioner's Programme, Thirty-Ninth Session, A/AC.96/SR.427, 9 November 1988, p. 4.

19 UNGA, *Summary Record of the 427th Meeting on 4th October 1988*, Executive Committee of the High Commissioner's Programme, Thirty-Ninth Session, A/AC.96/SR.427, 9 November 1988, p. 5.

build upon the arrangements established by the 1979 International Conference on Indochinese refugees so that a new consensus could be reached on comprehensive and durable solutions to deal in a realistic yet humanitarian manner'.[20]

Indonesia and Malaysia concurred with Thailand's appraisal of the 1979 Conference's usefulness at the time, but stressed the need for change in order to meet contemporary problems. Indonesia suggested that the continued outflow of Indochinese warranted a new approach as the 'approach adopted in the past to the refugee problem was no longer adequate for the present situation, and that the refugee problem was the responsibility of the international community as a whole'.[21] Malaysia felt that their 'liberal policy and humanitarian assistance extended by countries in the region had been misinterpreted in certain quarters and the flow of refugees to Malaysia had continued unabated... such a [new] conference would be all the more valid at present, since the mechanisms agreed at the 1979 Conference were no longer adequate to cope with the situation'.[22] Obviously then, the ASEAN states were increasingly hostile to old solutions that did not solve a seemingly perpetual problem. But what was their preferred solution to the problem?

On 27 January 1988, Thailand pushed back 40 Vietnamese asylum seekers from the shores of its easternmost province of Trat. On 28 January, the Thai Ministry of the Interior announced that all Vietnamese boats heading toward Thailand would be pushed back to sea.[23] In the next month, the United States Committee for Refugees (USCR) reported that more than 550 people were pushed back from Thai waters, with at least 100 people dying in the water and another 530 people stranded on the islands off Trat with no food, water or shelter.[24] According to Robinson, at least 1,500 boats in the six weeks from the 27 January were pushed back with the death of 170 people.[25] Either way, the loss was tragic but Thailand's action had been designed to inhibit the massive new rise of boat people seeking asylum. In the first five months of 1989, Malaysia also had 'near-record levels'[26] of boat people arriving; Indonesia, Japan, the Philippines and Thailand also recorded 'unusually high arrival figures'.[27] By the end of June 1989, the number of boat

20 UNGA, Summary Record of the 432nd Meeting on 6th October 1988, Executive Committee of the High Commissioner's Programme, Thirty-Ninth Session, A/AC.96/SR.432, 13 October 1988, p. 11.

21 UNGA, *Summary Record of the 428th Meeting on 4th October 1988*, Executive Committee of the High Commissioner's Programme, Thirty-Ninth Session, A/AC.96/SR.428, 10 October 1988, p. 12.

22 UNGA, *Summary Record of the 428th Meeting on 4th October 1988*, Executive Committee of the High Commissioner's Programme, Thirty-Ninth Session, A/AC.96/SR.428, 10 October 1988, p. 16.

23 USCR, *Refugee Reports*, Volume 9, Number 2, 26 February 1988, p. 1.

24 USCR, *Refugee Reports*, Volume 9, Number 2, 26 February 1988, p. 1.

25 Robinson, *Terms of Refuge: The Indochinese Exodus and the International Response*, 1998, p. 182.

26 UNGA, *UNHCR Activities Financed by Voluntary Funds: Report for 1988–89 and Proposed Programmes and Budget for 1990*, Part II: Asia and Oceania, Submitted by the High Commissioner, Executive Committee of the High Commissioner's Programme, Fortieth Session, A/AC.96/724 (Part II), 28 August 1989, p. 2.

27 UNGA, *UNHCR Activities Financed by Voluntary Funds: Report for 1988–89 and Proposed Programmes and Budget for 1990*, Part II: Asia and Oceania, Submitted by the High Commissioner,

people registered at UNHCR camps in the region stood at 96,669—representing an 82 percent rise compared with the same period in 1988.[28]

By April 1988, Indonesia was reported to be practicing pushbacks.[29] The Thai government claimed in March that its pushbacks had been discontinued, but reports suggested otherwise.[30] As a result, the loss of life continued. The possibility of Malaysian pushbacks increased when the government stated in April that 'there is a big possibility of the government setting a one-year period, from a date to be fixed later to resettle the Vietnamese . . . starting from that date, the government will no longer adopt a soft attitude to these illegal immigrants and will turn them away'.[31] Hong Kong's rate of arrivals in the first six months of 1989 also substantially increased—to the point where an average of 300 boat people arrived each day in May and June. On 15 June, the Hong Kong government announced that all newly arrived Vietnamese would have to prove their refugee status to be eligible for resettlement, or 'face detention as illegal aliens until they could be returned to Vietnam'.[32] The British colony stated that its 'existing policy of conferring refugee status on all Vietnamese boat people means in effect an open-ended commitment, and indeed an invitation, to all Vietnamese who might be considering leaving in Vietnam by boat. We cannot allow the open-door policy to continue'.[33] Hong Kong was the first state to introduce the screening of asylum seekers. As the conditions in camps were also cramped and uninhabitable this move had two purposes. The first was to deter Vietnamese without genuine refugee claims from leaving Vietnam and the second was for Vietnam to step up its repatriation negotiations with UNHCR. Resettlement numbers had reached an all-time low and Hong Kong insisted that the only way to solve this crisis was with screening.[34]

Prior to Hong Kong's announcement, the ASEAN states had met in May 1988 at a Ford Foundation sponsored conference in Cha-Am, Thailand to discuss the continuing refugee crisis. The ASEAN delegates, along with those from Hong Kong, agreed that non-genuine refugees should be prevented from seeking asylum and that region-wide screening procedures should be established. A further proposal was that the UNHCR set up a holding centre in the region which would house asylum seekers who had been screened and rejected. This would reduce the long-stay camp population in first asylum states while the UNHCR negotiated repatriation agree-

Executive Committee of the High Commissioner's Programme, Fortieth Session, A/AC.96/724 (Part II), 28 August 1989, p. 2.

[28] UNGA, *UNHCR Activities Financed by Voluntary Funds: Report for 1988–89 and Proposed Programmes and Budget for 1990*, Part II: Asia and Oceania, Submitted by the High Commissioner, Executive Committee of the High Commissioner's Programme, Fortieth Session, A/AC.96/724 (Part II), 28 August 1989, p. 2.

[29] USCR, *Refugee Reports*, Volume 9, Number 5, 20 May 1988, p. 11.

[30] USCR, *Refugee Reports*, Volume 9, Number 5, 20 May 1988, p. 11.

[31] USCR, *Refugee Reports*, Volume 9, Number 5, 20 May 1988, p. 11.

[32] USCR, *Refugee Reports*, Volume 9, Number 6, 24 June 1988, p. 6.

[33] USCR, *Refugee Reports*, Volume 9, Number 6, 24 June 1988, p. 6.

[34] USCR, *Refugee Reports*, Volume 9, Number 6, 24 June 1988, p. 7.

ments with Vietnam.[35] The delegates also wanted 'more predictable and multi-year resettlement guarantees',[36] along with an expansion of countries prepared to offer resettlement. Most important, ASEAN states wanted a solution for those found not to be refugees. ASEAN states firmly insisted that immediate repatriation was the best option as it would not just reduce the load on first asylum camps, but would also serve as a deterrent to those leaving Vietnam because of 'economic factors'.[37] The ASEAN states wanted the emphasis to be placed on Vietnam to prevent departures as it was the 'root cause of the problem'.[38] They called for Vietnam to increase the ODP to include humanitarian and family reunion cases and to accept the return of its citizens. The introduction of screening and repatriation was seen as the most effective way of solving the crisis.

Screening was important because it meant that asylum seekers could be separated into *genuine* and *non-genuine* claimants. This demarcation meant a lot, for it determined which camp the person would be allocated to and what level of care and assistance they would receive. Hong Kong had been practicing screening of asylum seekers with UNHCR assistance since June 1988 and ASEAN states observed the success it was having in those screened and found eligible for refugee status under the 1951 Convention were immediately accepted for resettlement and those who were not could be relocated to a long-term camp. Here, their living conditions were less than welcoming so as to increase agreements for repatriation. Repatriation was the second important part of this plan for once people had been screened out, their claim to UNHCR protection was no longer valid. Technically, these people could even be involuntarily returned because their refugee claim had failed. This will be further discussed below. For now, it is important to note the intention of the proposals being made by ASEAN states.

The Cha-Am meeting set the stage for introducing the screening of asylum seekers from an agreed cut-off date after which arrivals would no longer receive *prima facie* refugee status. There would be increased resettlement speed for those screened then judged to be legitimate refugees, and immediate repatriation for those rejected refugee status. The Cha-Am conference led to the ASEAN Foreign Ministers meeting in Bangkok on 4 July 1988 calling for a 'new comprehensive plan of action'.[39] This in turn led to a decision by the UNHCR Executive Committee for a new international conference on Indochinese refugees to be convened. The UNHCR convened a meeting in Bangkok from 27–28 October 1988 to discuss the proposed new approach. The largest collection of delegates since the 1979 Conference was assembled and included Vietnam.[40] The Malaysian government

---

35 USCR, *Refugee Reports*, Volume 9, Number 6, 24 June 1988, pp. 8–9.
36 USCR, *Refugee Reports*, Volume 9, Number 6, 24 June 1988, p. 9.
37 USCR, *Refugee Reports*, Volume 9, Number 6, 24 June 1988, p. 9.
38 USCR, *Refugee Reports*, Volume 9, Number 6, 24 June 1988, p. 9.
39 ASEAN, *Joint Statement by the ASEAN Foreign Ministers on the Indochinese Refugees*, Bangkok, Thailand, 4 July 1988. http://www.aseasec.org/907.html
40 Bronee, S. A., 'The History of the Comprehensive Plan of Action', *International Journal of Refugee Law*, 5 (4), 1993, p. 538.

convened another meeting in Kuala Lumpur from 2–9 March 1989, to discuss the first draft of the Comprehensive Plan of Action (CPA). The UNHCR and ASEAN cooperated closely in preparing the draft, demonstrating how much the UNHCR had yielded to ASEAN states' wishes.

A Draft Declaration and Comprehensive Plan of Action were approved by the Meeting in Kuala Lumpur. The draft aimed to respond mainly to the Vietnamese asylum seekers, along with the Laotians. The Cambodians were not included in the CPA because their issues were 'being discussed, among parties directly involved, within a different framework and as such have not been included in the deliberations of the Conference'.[41] It must be remembered that Cambodians were never placed under UNHCR protection and thus it was not until the Paris Agreement decided on their repatriation that some Cambodians finally received refugee status (see chapter 5).

It was also in March 1989 that the Southeast Asian states collectively agreed that the cut-off date for asylum seekers' access to immediate refugee status without screening would be 14 March 1989.[42] The CPA provided a more precise formula for how the asylum seekers would be met, treated and dealt with, all according to whether or not they received the status of a refugee. There were *eight sections* in the CPA. The first was *Clandestine Departure* and the objective here was to enlist the Vietnamese and Laotian governments to prevent people leaving their country illegally. It was suggested that this was to be done through central government directing local authorities on the need to prevent departures. The media was also to alert its listeners to the dangers of clandestine departures, the introduction of status determination in asylum countries, the difficulty of resettlement and the need to consider an alternative, regular, means of departure. The second section of the CPA was the *Regular Departure Programme*, and the effort here was for the ODP to be 'fully encouraged and promoted',[43] with UNHCR and Intergovernmental Committee for Migration (ICM now International Organization of Migration) assistance in expediting and processing departures.

The third and fourth sections were an interesting combination and the product of a compromise between the UNHCR and Southeast Asian states. The third section was on the *Reception of New Arrivals* and stressed that 'temporary refuge will be given to all asylum-seekers, who will be treated identically regardless of their mode of arrival until the status-determination process is completed'.[44] It goes on

41 UNGA, *Draft Declaration and Comprehensive Plan of Action Approved by the Preparatory Meeting for the International Conference on Indo-Chinese Refugees on 8 March 1989*, A/CONF.148/2, 26 April 1989, p. 2.

42 Robinson, *Terms of Refuge: The Indochinese Exodus and the International Response*, 1998, p. 183.

43 UNGA, *Draft Declaration and Comprehensive Plan of Action Approved by the Preparatory Meeting for the International Conference on Indo-Chinese Refugees on 8 March 1989*, A/CONF.148/2, 26 April 1989, p. 4.

44 UNGA, *Draft Declaration and Comprehensive Plan of Action Approved by the Preparatory Meeting for the International Conference on Indo-Chinese Refugees on 8 March 1989*, A/CONF.148/2, 26 April 1989, p. 4.

to say that the UNHCR was to be given 'full and early access to arrivals' and 'full access to the refugee status-determination process'.[45] The fourth section was one that Southeast Asian states had been insisting was necessary for some time—*Refugee Status*. The fourth section insisted that all asylum seekers, regardless of mode of arrival and whether they arrived before or after the cut-off date, were to be given the opportunity to seek refugee status and must be considered as refugees until proven otherwise. The UNHCR's concern on this matter was illustrated in its 1989 Note on International Protection, where it states that:

> (A)dmission, coupled with acceptable conditions of stay and just treatment of refugees, remain, together, an important aspect—albeit only one—of any broadly-based approach to the refugee problem. For many refugees, even though asylum is only a temporary state and voluntary return under acceptable and safe conditions is the optimal solution, their safety and integrity will, in the first instance, rest on admission and leave to stay.[46]

What did the fourth section, *Refugee Status* propose for how asylum seekers should be screened? Screening was to be a 'consistent region-wide refugee status-determination process' which would take place in accordance with 'national legislation and internationally accepted practice'.[47] The status of an asylum seeker was to be determined by national authorities, according to the refugee criteria and procedures as set out in the 1951 Convention and 1967 Protocol. In addition, the UNHCR Handbook on Procedures and Criteria for Determining Refugee Status was to be 'an authoritative and interpretative guide in developing and applying the criteria'.[48] Therefore, the UNHCR's procedures and articles for determining refugee status were to be used by ASEAN authorities. In addition, the UNHCR was to be consulted on the development of a questionnaire for interviewing applicants and given access to the decisions made on each applicant, with the UNHCR able to advise in writing each individual of the procedure, implication of a rejected case and right to appeal when rejected. The UNHCR was also to train officials across the region in the determination process, experience which it had gained from conducting similar training exercises in Hong Kong.[49] It is significant to note at this stage that the status determination process was still a national exercise, carried out

45 UNGA, *Draft Declaration and Comprehensive Plan of Action Approved by the Preparatory Meeting for the International Conference on Indo-Chinese Refugees on 8 March 1989*, A/CONF.148/2, 26 April 1989, p. 4.

46 UNGA, *Note on International Protection*, Submitted by the High Commissioner, Executive Committee of the High Commissioner's Programme, Fortieth Session, A/AC.96/728, pp. 5–6.

47 UNGA, *Note on International Protection*, Submitted by the High Commissioner, Executive Committee of the High Commissioner's Programme, Fortieth Session, A/AC.96/728, pp. 5–6.

48 UNGA, *Draft Declaration and Comprehensive Plan of Action Approved by the Preparatory Meeting for the International Conference on Indo-Chinese Refugees on 8 March 1989*, A/CONF.148/2, 26 April 1989, p. 5.

49 UNGA, *Draft Declaration and Comprehensive Plan of Action Approved by the Preparatory Meeting for the International Conference on Indo-Chinese Refugees on 8 March 1989*, A/CONF.148/2, 26 April 1989, p. 5.

by government officials. This will be discussed further in the next section which addresses the ramifications of the screening processes in more depth.

The fifth section of the CPA focused on *Resettlement* and here it was stated that a resettlement program should be formulated specifically for the 'long-stayers' present in camps prior to the cut-off date.[50] Resettlement states were to provide multi-year commitments to resettle all Vietnamese who had arrived in camps prior to the cut-off date. A resettlement programme for 'newly determined refugees' was also to be established, with resettlement countries asked to pledge their acceptance of all those screened in as genuine refugees within a 'prescribed period'.[51]

The sixth section of the CPA was *Repatriation/Plan of Repatriation*. The phrase 'plan of repatriation' indicated that the position taken by states and the UNHCR on how repatriation should occur had not yet been fully agreed to—largely because of Vietnamese and United States resistance to non-voluntary repatriation.[52] However, the position presented in this section was that those who had been determined not to be refugees were to 'return to their country origin in accordance with international practices reflecting the responsibilities of States towards their own citizens'.[53] The section said that '*in the first instance*, every effort will be made to encourage the voluntary return of such persons'. The implication of 'in the first instance' was that after the first instance, involuntary return was acceptable. Importantly, this policy was in accordance with international practices for those considered not to be refugees.[54] The next point made in this section was that the country of origin was to accept its citizens 'within the shortest possible time',[55] in safety and dignity without fear of persecution. Then in further reference to voluntary repatriation, the section states:

> If, after the passage of reasonable time, it becomes clear that voluntary repatriation is not making sufficient progress towards the desired objective, alternatives recognized as being acceptable under international practices would be examined.[56]

[50] UNGA, *Draft Declaration and Comprehensive Plan of Action Approved by the Preparatory Meeting for the International Conference on Indo-Chinese Refugees on 8 March 1989*, A/CONF.148/2, 26 April 1989, p. 6.

[51] UNGA, *Draft Declaration and Comprehensive Plan of Action Approved by the Preparatory Meeting for the International Conference on Indo-Chinese Refugees on 8 March 1989*, A/CONF.148/2, 26 April 1989, p. 6.

[52] United States Committee for Refugees, *Refugee Reports*, Volume 10, Number 6, 16 June 1989, p. 8.

[53] UNGA, *Draft Declaration and Comprehensive Plan of Action Approved by the Preparatory Meeting for the International Conference on Indo-Chinese Refugees on 8 March 1989*, A/CONF.148/2, 26 April 1989, p. 7.

[54] UNGA, *Draft Declaration and Comprehensive Plan of Action Approved by the Preparatory Meeting for the International Conference on Indo-Chinese Refugees on 8 March 1989*, A/CONF.148/2, 26 April 1989, p. 7.

[55] UNGA, *Draft Declaration and Comprehensive Plan of Action Approved by the Preparatory Meeting for the International Conference on Indo-Chinese Refugees on 8 March 1989*, A/CONF.148/2, 26 April 1989, p. 7.

[56] UNGA, *Draft Declaration and Comprehensive Plan of Action Approved by the Preparatory Meeting for the International Conference on Indo-Chinese Refugees on 8 March 1989*, A/CONF.148/2, 26 April 1989, p. 7.

It was this passag e that called for the creation of a UNHCR holding centre; but the section stated quite clearly that repatriation, voluntary or otherwise, would be the eventual outcome for those determined not to be refugees.

The seventh section of the CPA addressed *Laotian asylum-seekers*. Though it could be assumed that much of the CPA was relevant to the situation of the Laotians in Thailand, it was nonetheless considered necessary to include a separate section on them. The majority of Laotian refugees only sought temporary asylum in Thailand and a screening process had been in place for them since 1985. The only resettlement country accepting Laotians by this stage was the United States.[57] The section announced that 'intensified trilateral negotiation between UNHCR, the Lao People's Democratic Republic and Thailand' was to continue.[58] The CPA's purpose in this regard was to give all displaced Laotians safe access to the Lao screening process as there had been reports that only the Hmong had enjoyed sporadic access to screening procedures.[59] Also, the Laotian government was required to improve its compliance in permitting those deemed not to be refugees to return home safely.[60] Finally, this section of the CPA insisted that resettlement offers for Laotian refugees remained essential.[61]

The eighth and final section of the CPA covered *Implementation and Review Procedures*. This section created an important mechanism: the Steering Committee. The Steering Committee was to be based in Southeast Asia and contain representatives from all governments making commitments to the CPA. It was to meet under UNHCR chairmanship to discuss the implementation of the CPA, provide for areas found to need improvement and deal with the implementation of status determination, repatriation and resettlement.[62] The UNHCR was placed in charge of 'continuing liaison and co-ordination with concerned Governments and intergovernmental as well as non-governmental organizations'[63] with the financial support of the donor community. The CPA was to be reviewed annually at the UNHCR Executive Committee sessions.

---

57 Robinson, *Terms of Refuge: The Indochinese Exodus and the International Response*, 1998, p. 223.

58 UNGA, *Draft Declaration and Comprehensive Plan of Action Approved by the Preparatory Meeting for the International Conference on Indo-Chinese Refugees on 8 March 1989*, A/CONF.148/2, 26 April 1989, p. 7.

59 USCR *Refugee Reports*, Volume 8, Number 3, 20 March 1987, pp. 10–11; Robinson, *Terms of Refuge*, 1998, p. 223.

60 UNGA, *Draft Declaration and Comprehensive Plan of Action Approved by the Preparatory Meeting for the International Conference on Indo-Chinese Refugees on 8 March 1989*, A/CONF.148/2, 26 April 1989, p. 7.

61 Robinson, *Terms of Refuge: The Indochinese Exodus and the International Response*, 1998, p. 223.

62 UNGA, *Draft Declaration and Comprehensive Plan of Action Approved by the Preparatory Meeting for the International Conference on Indo-Chinese Refugees on 8 March 1989*, A/CONF.148/2, 26 April 1989, p. 8. This Committee was the forum for important disputes about repatriation over the next few years, as will be discussed in the next section of the chapter.

63 UNGA, *Draft Declaration and Comprehensive Plan of Action Approved by the Preparatory Meeting for the International Conference on Indo-Chinese Refugees on 8 March 1989*, A/CONF.148/2, 26 April 1989, p. 8.

It can be seen that the CPA was devised with five (according to Robinson) or six (according to Bronee) objectives in mind: 1) to prevent clandestine departures; 2) guarantee temporary first asylum; 3) encourage the continuation of the ODP and promote its expansion in Vietnam (Robinson links this with point one); 4) establish consistent, region wide status determination processes; 5) continue the resettlement of refugees and long-stayers; and 6) repatriate rejected asylum seekers to Vietnam (and Laos).[64]

In the next section of this chapter, I will focus particularly on points four and six of the CPA. These two sections raise the question of whether or not the adoption of UNHCR guidelines for screening refugees represented an acceptance by the Southeast Asian states of the basic principles of the 1951 Convention and 1967 Protocol.

6.2 *CPA in practice: Screening and Repatriation*

The CPA was passed by all states present in Geneva at the Conference on Indochinese refugees on 13–14 June 1989. Arguably, the two most important decisions made at the conference (which had already been decided upon in prior draft meetings) was that asylum seekers should be screened and those who did not receive refugee status should be returned to their country of origin. The introduction of screening procedures by the Southeast Asian states has been described in the literature as a positive development for international refugee law. It is said to have marked a new level of compliance by Southeast Asian states with the terms for determining the refugee status of the asylum seekers according to 1951 Convention and 1967 Protocol, thus representing an affirmation of the legitimacy of these laws.[65] The repatriation of 'non-genuine' asylum seekers to their country of origin and the prevention of the continual exodus of such people through these measures has also been cited as evidence of the CPA's success in dealing with complex, enduring refugee situations.[66] It must be kept in mind though that the primary purpose of

---

[64] Robinson, *Terms of Refuge: The Indochinese Exodus and the International Response*, 1998, p. 189; Bronee, S. A., 'The History of the Comprehensive Plan of Action', *International Journal of Refugee Law*, 5 (4), 1993, p. 540.

[65] Martin, D. A., 'Refugees and Migration', in Joyner, Christopher C. (ed.), *The United Nations and International Law* (Cambridge: Cambridge University Press; The American Society of International Law, 1997), pp. 155–180; Helton, A. 'Refugee Determination under the Comprehensive Plan of Action: Overview and Assessment', *International Journal of Refugee Law*, 5 (4), 1993, pp. 544–558. It should be noted though, that Helton did argue this, but he also conceded that there were problems with states implementing the screening procedures as they should, which placed doubt on their adherence to these principles. Muntarbhorn, *The Status of Refugees in Asia*, 1992; Goodwin-Gill, *The Refugee in International Law*, 1996, pp. 282, 292.

[66] Helton, A. 'Refugee Determination under the Comprehensive Plan of Action: Overview and Assessment', *International Journal of Refugee Law*, 5 (4), 1993, p. 557; Feller, E., 'The Evolution of the International Refugee Protection Regime', *Washington University Journal of Law and Policy*, Volume 5, 2001, p. 133; Loescher, G. and James Milner, 'The Missing Link: the need for Comprehensive Engagement in regions of refugee origin', *International Affairs*, 79 (3), 2003, p. 611.

the CPA was to be 'a deterrent measure to facilitate the return of those determined by the authorities not to be refugees'.[67] The CPA was the result of Southeast Asian states successfully arguing that the majority of asylum seekers from Indochina were not genuine refugees. Therefore, this section will look at how screening and repatriation developed in relation to that objective of the CPA—to end non-genuine refugees seeking asylum. I will argue that Southeast Asian attitudes to screening procedures and repatriation did not reflect an affirmation of international refugee protection principles; the actions of Southeast Asian states were primarily geared towards ending what they saw as non-genuine refugees exploiting their charitable generosity. Therefore, the CPA did not represent regional compliance with the 1951 Convention and 1967 Protocol. Rather, the CPA only served to further demonstrate how malleable refugee protection could be in the hands of states.

On 25 and 26 May 1989, the Coordinating Committee for the International Conference on Indo-Chinese Refugees met in Geneva to discuss how the national procedures for determination of refugee status should proceed. The UNHCR consulted with each state in the region and there were a number of procedures 'currently envisaged in the countries of first-asylum'[68] that differed from state to state. The main conditions that did not change, of course, was that all states would screen refugees according to the definition of a refugee in the 1951 Convention; the UNHCR Handbook on Criteria and Procedures relating to Refugee Status was to serve as the 'authoritative and interpretative guide'.[69] The next section of this chapter will look at what procedures each state in the region took in the determination process, starting with Indonesia.

6.2.1 *Indonesia*

Indonesia had made the cut-off date for *prima facie* refugee recognition 17 March 1989. This meant that every asylum seeker who arrived on and after 18 March would be subject to the screening process carried out by P3V (the national body responsible for the administration of refugees; two-thirds were military officials).[70] The screening procedure in Indonesia was then to be carried out as follows. First of all, the UNHCR was to participate in all stages of the procedures as an adviser/observer and hold briefing sessions for Indonesian government officials involved in the determination procedure. P3V was to have 'overall responsibility for the

[67] Helton, A. 'Refugee Determination under the Comprehensive Plan of Action: Overview and Assessment', *International Journal of Refugee Law*, 5 (4), 1993, p. 556.

[68] UNGA, *Note on National Procedures for the Determination of Refugee Status*, Submitted by the High Commissioner, Co-ordinating Committee for the International Conference on Indo-Chinese Refugees 25 and 26 May 1989, A/CONF.148/4, Annex 1, p. 3.

[69] UNGA, *Draft Declaration and Comprehensive Plan of Action Approved by the Preparatory Meeting for the International Conference on Indo-Chinese Refugees on 8 March 1989*, A/CONF.148/2, 26 April 1989, p. 5.

[70] UNGA, *Note on National Procedures for the Determination of Refugee Status*, Submitted by the High Commissioner, Co-ordinating Committee for the International Conference on Indo-Chinese Refugees 25 and 26 May 1989, A/CONF.148/4, Annex 1, p. 4.

reception of asylum-seekers and will arrange for their registration on arrival and transfer to a reception centre'.[71] The UNHCR was to be informed of all arrivals and given full access to them as early as this stage. At the reception centre, P3V officials would immediately interview arrivals, with the 'UNHCR present as an observer at such interviews'.[72] The form for taking information from the arrivals was developed by UNHCR in conjunction with the Indonesian government. The initial information collected went to the 'Screening' Commission. There were five teams within the Commission—each led by an immigration officer, an official from P3V and UNHCR. These teams were to visit the reception centres, with interpreters, and conduct 'full interviews of asylum applicants, on the basis of a questionnaire developed with the assistance of UNHCR'.[73] The UNHCR was to be present and thus submit its views on each applicant. Though the Note does not specifically say, it seems that the 'Screening' Commission would then decide on each applicant's case, which was to be recorded (with the reasons for the decision) in their file. Upon receiving the decision in writing, applicants were to be informed of the reason for the rejection and seek for a review by the Appeal Board.

The Appeal Board was 'more senior than the one of the first instance, of one official each from P3V and the Immigration Department'.[74] The UNHCR was to participate on the Appeal Board as an observer/advisor.[75] The final allowance was for the resettlement states to 'advise the P3V on general issues relating to the determination process or on specific cases if they so wish'.[76] This level of advice had the potential to either increase restrictions on certain 'undesirables' or make allowances for those seeking family reunification or claiming other exceptional circumstances.

6.2.2 *Malaysia*

The Malaysian government retained its cut-off date of 14 March 1989 for those seeking asylum. The National Task Force VII (primarily made up of military, then

71 UNGA, *Note on National Procedures for the Determination of Refugee Status*, Submitted by the High Commissioner, Co-ordinating Committee for the International Conference on Indo-Chinese Refugees 25 and 26 May 1989, A/CONF.148/4, Annex 1, p. 4.

72 UNGA, *Note on National Procedures for the Determination of Refugee Status*, Submitted by the High Commissioner, Co-ordinating Committee for the International Conference on Indo-Chinese Refugees 25 and 26 May 1989, A/CONF.148/4, Annex 1, p. 4.

73 UNGA, *Note on National Procedures for the Determination of Refugee Status*, Submitted by the High Commissioner, Co-ordinating Committee for the International Conference on Indo-Chinese Refugees 25 and 26 May 1989, A/CONF.148/4, Annex 1, p. 5.

74 UNGA, *Note on National Procedures for the Determination of Refugee Status*, Submitted by the High Commissioner, Co-ordinating Committee for the International Conference on Indo-Chinese Refugees 25 and 26 May 1989, A/CONF.148/4, Annex 1, p. 5.

75 UNGA, *Note on National Procedures for the Determination of Refugee Status*, Submitted by the High Commissioner, Co-ordinating Committee for the International Conference on Indo-Chinese Refugees 25 and 26 May 1989, A/CONF.148/4, Annex 1, p. 5.

76 UNGA, *Note on National Procedures for the Determination of Refugee Status*, Submitted by the High Commissioner, Co-ordinating Committee for the International Conference on Indo-Chinese Refugees 25 and 26 May 1989, A/CONF.148/4, Annex 1, p. 5.

police and immigration officials) had 'overall responsibility for the reception of asylum-seekers and the determination process'.[77] The UNHCR though was to be present in the observer/advisory capacity in 'all stages of the process... entitled to submit its views on any particular case'.[78] In addition, like in Indonesia, the UNHCR would hold briefing sessions with Malaysian authorities on determination procedure practice.

The precise procedure for status determination procedures in Malaysia were first, within five days of the asylum seekers' arrival, they were to undergo a preliminary interview by a local official in the temporary reception centre. A UNHCR official could be present. The second interview would occur after the asylum applicant was transferred to a more permanent camp on the east coast, here they would be interviewed by the Task Force VII officials. There would also be an interviewing officer, assistant and interpreter present for the interview, the UNHCR was again able to be an observer at the interview and 'entitled to submit its views on any case or issues at this stage'.[79] The interview was based on the questionnaire formulated by UNHCR. Then, the interviewing officer would write a recommendation to be forwarded for a final decision by the senior immigration official attached to the National Task Force. The decision and its reasons would be recorded on the file. Applicants would be immediately informed of the decision in writing, and the reasons for the rejection. Applicants were able to appeal their rejection, with UNHCR assistance. The National Task Force would hear the review with the UNHCR in an adviser/observer capacity. Those granted refugee status were immediately moved to transit centres for resettlement processing. Failed applicants were moved to a separate centre pending repatriation.[80]

6.2.3 *The Philippines*

The Philippines, the only state in the region that was a signatory to the 1951 Convention and 1967 Protocol, also insisted on screening, with third-country resettlement for the successful applicants and repatriation for those found not to be refugees. The Philippine government cut-off date for *prima facie* refugee status was, like Indonesia, 17 March 1989. There were to be three stages in the screening process in the Philippines: reception, status determination and appeal. UNHCR

[77] UNGA, *Note on National Procedures for the Determination of Refugee Status*, Submitted by the High Commissioner, Co-ordinating Committee for the International Conference on Indo-Chinese Refugees 25 and 26 May 1989, A/CONF.148/4, Annex 1, p. 6.

[78] UNGA, *Note on National Procedures for the Determination of Refugee Status*, Submitted by the High Commissioner, Co-ordinating Committee for the International Conference on Indo-Chinese Refugees 25 and 26 May 1989, A/CONF.148/4, Annex 1, p. 6.

[79] UNGA, *Note on National Procedures for the Determination of Refugee Status*, Submitted by the High Commissioner, Co-ordinating Committee for the International Conference on Indo-Chinese Refugees 25 and 26 May 1989, A/CONF.148/4, Annex 1, p. 6.

[80] UNGA, *Note on National Procedures for the Determination of Refugee Status*, Submitted by the High Commissioner, Co-ordinating Committee for the International Conference on Indo-Chinese Refugees 25 and 26 May 1989, A/CONF.148/4, Annex 1, p. 6.

was always to have full access to asylum seekers and camp files. The first step in the screening process was reception. Local officials would register all arrivals and then transfer them to a transit centre for a 'confirmation interview with UNHCR and authorization from the Department of Foreign Affairs'.[81] The second step was status determination. All asylum-seekers were to be interviewed by non-governmental staff with the supervision of the UNHCR. The standard interview forms had been approved by the Inter-agency Task Force on Refugee Assistance and Administration and was based on the questionnaire drawn up by the UNHCR. The 'written results of the pre-determination interviews will be signed by the asylum-seekers and presented to the Commissioner on Immigration and Deportation (CID) for a decision'.[82] The determination of refugee status was than made by CID. When the CID official presiding over a case found it necessary or when there was a possibility of rejection, the asylum-seeker and their interpreter were to be present for follow-up questions and 'the decision-maker can assess the asylum-seeker's credibility'.[83] The third and final step in the screening process was appeal. The applicant was to receive the decision in writing, with a copy sent to the UNHCR. The basis for denial was to be stated in the letter and the applicant could appeal to the Inter-agency Task Force on International Refugee Assistance and Administration. The asylum-seeker could submit a written statement supporting the reasons for their appeal; with the UNHCR able to arrange legal counsel for the applicant and present their own comments to the Appeal Board.

6.2.4 *Singapore*

There was no entry in the CPA for Singapore as, since 1977, it maintained its policy of 'no entry' to asylum seekers from Indochina, unless an offer of third-county resettlement could be made for each entrant.[84] In addition, the resettlement country had to guarantee that the asylum seekers would be removed from Singapore's Hawkins Road camp within ninety days. Therefore, the number of asylum seekers in Singapore never reached beyond the hundreds even at the peak of boat people arrivals in 1989.[85] As for those who attempted to land in Singapore

---

81 UNGA, *Note on National Procedures for the Determination of Refugee Status*, Submitted by the High Commissioner, Co-ordinating Committee for the International Conference on Indo-Chinese Refugees 25 and 26 May 1989, A/CONF.148/4, Annex 1, p. 7.

82 UNGA, *Note on National Procedures for the Determination of Refugee Status*, Submitted by the High Commissioner, Co-ordinating Committee for the International Conference on Indo-Chinese Refugees 25 and 26 May 1989, A/CONF.148/4, Annex 1, p. 7.

83 UNGA, *Note on National Procedures for the Determination of Refugee Status*, Submitted by the High Commissioner, Co-ordinating Committee for the International Conference on Indo-Chinese Refugees 25 and 26 May 1989, A/CONF.148/4, Annex 1, p. 7.

84 Muntarbhorn, *The Status of Refugees in Asia*, 1992, p. 121.

85 UNGA, *UNHCR Activities Financed by Voluntary Funds: Report for 1988–89 and Proposed Programmes and Budget for 1990*, Part II: Asia and Oceania, Submitted by the High Commissioner, Executive Committee of the High Commissioner's Programme, Fortieth Session, A/AC.96/724 (Part II), 28 August 1989, pp. 38–39.

by boat, they were intercepted by the Singapore Navy which patrolled the area and if resettlement places were not on offer, the boat would be assisted to continue its journey to another destination. Therefore, the CPA did not affect the procedures that Singapore had adopted towards Indochinese refugees and thus there was no need to introduce screening procedures in Singapore.

6.2.5 *Thailand*

In Thailand though, the story was very different. Like Malaysia, Thailand adopted 14 March 1989 as the cut-off date for those seeking immediate refugee status; for the Laotian asylum seekers the cut-off time of January 1985 would still apply to them. The UNHCR was to be 'closely associated with the determination process and would provide appropriate training for the officials concerned',[86] with the procedure for status determination of asylum seekers in Thailand to be carried out as follows. First, district officials in the province of arrival would 'conduct preliminary interviews'[87] of all arrivals; with the UNHCR to be immediately informed of arrivals and granted access to the groups. After being held in the Holding (Screening) Centre for no more than 30 days, all asylum seekers would be 'thoroughly interviewed'[88] by a team from the Ministry of Interior (MOI). Within the team there were two officials from the Operations Centre for Displaced Persons, two assistants and two interpreters. The UNHCR was to have full access 'to observe these interviews and to present its views'.[89] The interviewers would record information on an eligibility form and make written recommendations on each case. Then the form and recommendation would be submitted to the central Board for Status Determination in Bangkok where the decision on all applicants was made. Senior MOI officials and Operations Centre for Displaced Persons of the MOI would chair the Board. Decisions were to be made within 45 days after the interview information being received and the Board recorded its majority decision on each case in writing with reasons attached in cases where a negative decision was reached. If the applicant was rejected, the UNHCR was able to institute an appeal on the applicant's behalf to the Secretariat of the Board for Status Determination. The UNHCR could present its opinion at the appeal and then the decision of the

[86] UNGA, *Note on National Procedures for the Determination of Refugee Status*, Submitted by the High Commissioner, Co-ordinating Committee for the International Conference on Indo-Chinese Refugees 25 and 26 May 1989, A/CONF.148/4, Annex 1, p. 8.

[87] UNGA, *Note on National Procedures for the Determination of Refugee Status*, Submitted by the High Commissioner, Co-ordinating Committee for the International Conference on Indo-Chinese Refugees 25 and 26 May 1989, A/CONF.148/4, Annex 1, p. 8.

[88] UNGA, *Note on National Procedures for the Determination of Refugee Status*, Submitted by the High Commissioner, Co-ordinating Committee for the International Conference on Indo-Chinese Refugees 25 and 26 May 1989, A/CONF.148/4, Annex 1, p. 8.

[89] UNGA, *Note on National Procedures for the Determination of Refugee Status*, Submitted by the High Commissioner, Co-ordinating Committee for the International Conference on Indo-Chinese Refugees 25 and 26 May 1989, A/CONF.148/4, Annex 1, p. 8.

panel would be final. Successful asylum seekers would be transferred to the Phant Nikhom camp for resettlement, while rejected cases were then sent to the Ban Thad camp 'pending repatriation'.[90]

6.3 *CPA procedures in practice*

The important question is how did the CPA procedures develop in practice? There were quite a number of changes made by the first asylum countries right after these procedures were agreed to in June 1989 at the International Conference on Indo-Chinese Refugees. But first, let us briefly look at the difference that the first year of screening made, keeping in mind that before March 1989 all who arrived were given immediate refugee status on a *prima facie* basis.

In the first five months of 1990, the number of boat people arrivals fell overall by 40 percent.[91] However, there was an increase of arrivals in Indonesia and Thailand and a shift away from the more popular arrival destinations in 1989 of Malaysia and Hong Kong. The shift can largely be accounted for by increased awareness of the 'deplorable'[92] conditions in Hong Kong camps and the continual pushback of boats by Malaysia.[93] The Malaysian authorities had been practicing such pushbacks since March 1989 and even after the 1989 Conference this activity continued, with most of the boats towed towards Indonesian waters.[94]

Robinson accounts for Malaysia's indifference to the call for first asylum provision by pointing to the government's expressed bitterness in the 1989 Conference towards resettlement states for their refusal to allow the cut-off date to be set at June 1989.[95] Malaysia, along with Hong Kong, had been bearing the highest numbers of boat arrivals since 1988 and was therefore hoping for resettlement states to accept these populations and the ones that arrived in massive numbers in the first six months of 1989. The refusal by resettlement states to take any more

[90] UNGA, *Note on National Procedures for the Determination of Refugee Status*, Submitted by the High Commissioner, Co-ordinating Committee for the International Conference on Indo-Chinese Refugees 25 and 26 May 1989, A/CONF.148/4, Annex 1, pp. 9–10.

[91] UNGA, *UNHCR Activities Financed by Voluntary Funds: Report for 1989–1990 and Proposed Programmes and Budget for 1991*, Part II: Asia and Oceania, Submitted by the High Commissioner, Executive Committee of the High Commissioner's Programme, Forty-First Session, A/AC.96/751 (Part II), 13 August 1990, pp. 1–2.

[92] In 1990, Hong Kong was accused of deliberately making camp conditions 'deplorable' through overcrowding, restriction on services, poor sanitation causing higher rates of transferable diseases in order to make people volunteer to return to Vietnam. United States Committee for Refugees, *Refugee Reports*, Volume 11, Number 3, 23 March 1990, p. 10.

[93] Helton, A. C., 'Refugee Determination under the Comprehensive Plan of Action: Overview and Assessment', *International Journal of Refugee Law*, 5 (4), 1993; Robinson, *Terms of Refuge*, 1998.

[94] Helton, A. C., 'The Malaysian Policy to Redirect Vietnamese Boat People: *Non-refoulement* as a Human Rights Remedy', *New York University Journal of International Law and Politics*, Volume 24, 1992.

[95] Robinson, *Terms of Refuge: The Indochinese Exodus and the International Response*, 1998, p. 190.

after March led Malaysia to 'cut its losses' and conduct its own first asylum policy irrespective of its commitments to the CPA.[96] This action is not surprising, for as Chapter 3 showed, after the 1978 December meeting Malaysia had refused asylum because it felt that the West was expecting too much of Southeast Asian states. Malaysia only changed its pushback policy when resettlement states agreed to a higher intake. This time around, resettlement states would make no such offer. Of even more concern to Malaysia, the asylum seekers who had been 'screened-out' were not being immediately sent back to Vietnam. When considering the generally positive position that Malaysia had adopted during the 1980s, in contrast to other ASEAN states, it is not surprising that Malaysia became frustrated with the CPA not fulfilling the repatriation requirement. As a result of its re-adoption of the pushback policy Malaysia was successful in deterring more arrivals by boat. By 1990 Indonesia had a ten-fold increase in its number of arrivals, while Malaysia's arrivals for the same year numbered only 1,300.[97] This was in contrast to 1989 when there were 20,475 arrivals in Malaysia and 4,428 in Indonesia.[98]

Further changes after the CPA came in the number of people that left via the ODP—43,177 in 1989 compared to 15,123 in 1988.[99] In the first five months of 1990, 23 300 had already left via the ODP, and the expectation was that this figure would remain high—which it did throughout the six years the CPA operated.[100] In addition, over 60 percent of those who arrived before the cut off date had been resettled by the beginning of 1990.[101] However, funding for the CPA was low; at the beginning of 1990 it was still $63 million short of its total requirement of $116 million.[102] This money was essential for it was to cover all the costs of refugee-status determination procedures in Southeast Asia: repatriation costs,

96 Robinson, *Terms of Refuge: The Indochinese Exodus and the International Response*, 1998, p. 190.

97 Robinson, *Terms of Refuge: The Indochinese Exodus and the International Response*, 1998, p. 191.

98 UNGA, *UNHCR Activities Financed by Voluntary Funds: Report for 1989–1990 and Proposed Programmes and Budget for 1991*, Part II: Asia and Oceania, Submitted by the High Commissioner, Executive Committee of the High Commissioner's Programme, Forty-First Session, A/AC.96/751 (Part II), 13 August 1990, pp. 13, 17.

99 1988 figure came from Druke, *Preventative Action for Refugee Producing Situations*, 1993, p. 80; 1989 figure came from UNGA, *UNHCR Activities Financed by Voluntary Funds: Report for 1989–1990 and Proposed Programmes and Budget for 1991*, Part II: Asia and Oceania, Submitted by the High Commissioner, Executive Committee of the High Commissioner's Programme, Forty-First Session, A/AC.96/751 (Part II), 13 August 1990, p. 2.

100 UNGA, *UNHCR Activities Financed by Voluntary Funds: Report for 1989–1990 and Proposed Programmes and Budget for 1991*, Part II: Asia and Oceania, Submitted by the High Commissioner, Executive Committee of the High Commissioner's Programme, Forty-First Session, A/AC.96/751 (Part II), 13 August 1990, p. 2; Robinson, *Terms of Refuge*, 1998, p. 198.

101 UNGA, *UNHCR Activities Financed by Voluntary Funds: Report for 1989–1990 and Proposed Programmes and Budget for 1991*, Part II: Asia and Oceania, Submitted by the High Commissioner, Executive Committee of the High Commissioner's Programme, Forty-First Session, A/AC.96/751 (Part II), 13 August 1990, p. 1.

102 UNGA, *UNHCR Activities Financed by Voluntary Funds: Report for 1989–1990 and Proposed Programmes and Budget for 1991*, Part II: Asia and Oceania, Submitted by the High Commissioner, Executive Committee of the High Commissioner's Programme, Forty-First Session, A/AC.96/751 (Part II), 13 August 1990, p. 2.

care and maintenance as well as transport costs. These financial problems reflected the UNHCR's wider budget and management difficulties and partly accounts for how the CPA developed.[103]

In 1990 the UNHCR reported that the refugee-status determination procedures were 'functioning' in Southeast Asian states, but there was still a region-wide need for more 'expeditious decisions on refugee status'.[104] In addition, further training and briefing on the 'proper application of refugee-status criteria' was being conducted in the region.[105] The single greatest concern was the inability to 'reach a consensus related to the future of those Vietnamese asylum-seekers determined not to be refugees, and, in particular, the question of their return, other than voluntary, to their country of origin'.[106] This situation represented a risk to the continued cooperation of first asylum states and thus the UNHCR stressed the necessity for a solution.[107] Repatriation will be discussed in more detail later, but suffice to say at this stage, the backlog of 'non-genuine' refugees in first asylum camps was affecting refugee-status determination procedures.

As time passed, there was greater opportunity for the process of screening in Southeast Asian states to be further analyzed and its success or lack thereof to be accounted for. By 1992/3, it had become clear that there were problems with the way the determination of refugee status was being conducted in Southeast Asia. Robinson's account of the region's screening process was that 'the most fundamental consistency across the region proved to be that each country did things differently,

[103] On 1 November 1989, High Commissioner Jean-Pierre Hocke suddenly resigned due to charges of mismanagement and misuse of funds. Exactly one year later, as the UNHCR started to recover from its financial and institutional crisis, High Commissioner Thorvald Stoltenberg suddenly resigned to become Foreign Minister of the new Norwegian Government. Sadako Ogata was appointed as High Commissioner in December 1991. She was the first woman and High Commissioner from Northeast Asia in the UNHCR's 40 year history. During her time at the post the UNHCR's budget and staff increased rapidly, but with budget expansion the UNHCR had to lose its independence and autonomy to the donor states. According to Loescher, donor interference rapidly dominated Ogata's decisions, and the expansion of the institution's focus led to a further loss of emphasis on protection. USCR, *Refugee Reports*, Volume 11, Number 11, 30 November 1990, p. 14; Loescher, *The UNHCR and World Politics: A Perilous Path*, 2001, pp. 268, 273.

[104] UNGA, *UNHCR Activities Financed by Voluntary Funds: Report for 1989–1990 and Proposed Programmes and Budget for 1991*, Part II: Asia and Oceania, Submitted by the High Commissioner, Executive Committee of the High Commissioner's Programme, Forty-First Session, A/AC.96/751 (Part II), 13 August 1990, p. 1.

[105] UNGA, *UNHCR Activities Financed by Voluntary Funds: Report for 1989–1990 and Proposed Programmes and Budget for 1991*, Part II: Asia and Oceania, Submitted by the High Commissioner, Executive Committee of the High Commissioner's Programme, Forty-First Session, A/AC.96/751 (Part II), 13 August 1990, p. 1.

[106] UNGA, *UNHCR Activities Financed by Voluntary Funds: Report for 1989–1990 and Proposed Programmes and Budget for 1991*, Part II: Asia and Oceania, Submitted by the High Commissioner, Executive Committee of the High Commissioner's Programme, Forty-First Session, A/AC.96/751 (Part II), 13 August 1990, p. 1.

[107] UNGA, *UNHCR Activities Financed by Voluntary Funds: Report for 1989–1990 and Proposed Programmes and Budget for 1991*, Part II: Asia and Oceania, Submitted by the High Commissioner, Executive Committee of the High Commissioner's Programme, Forty-First Session, A/AC.96/751 (Part II), 13 August 1990, p. 1.

some better than others and none perfectly'.[108] There are two obvious reasons for this. The first is that internally, the UNHCR did not agree on who should be considered as a refugee. In Hong Kong, a field officer was arguing that Vietnamese seeking asylum because they had family members who had been persecuted were to be 'given full and due consideration' for the 'UNHCR is in a very dangerous position right now of losing all creditability with the Vietnamese asylum seekers'.[109] By contrast, Erika Feller, who was the UNHCR's Representative in Malaysia and Regional Coordinator of Status Determination was quoted as saying that though the boat peoples' stories were not ones 'I should like to have for my children . . . but these are *not refugee* stories'.[110]

James Hathaway argued that the UNHCR failed to uphold socio-economic persecution as falling under the definition of persecution in the 1951 Convention and this was the greatest problem with the CPA.[111] Yet, socio-economic persecution had constantly caused great numbers of people in the third world to flee *en masse* perhaps more so than politically-based persecution.[112] This supports Zolberg, Suhrke and Aguayo's argument that the 1951 Convention's definition of political violence does not take into account the economic and social violence that particularly third world countries can perpetrate against their citizens.[113] But as Erika Feller's comments demonstrate, in spite of the factual and moral basis of these arguments, the UNHCR was nonetheless bound to operate within the 1951 Convention and the definition of a refugee constructed between 1949 and 1951. This meant that 'refugee-ness' was still predominantly determined by the aftermath of the Second World War in Europe and the political climate which started the Cold War.

The second problem with the screening process was that it was being done by states that had previously believed themselves to have no legal or moral obligation to the 1951 Convention and its 1967 Protocol. As a result, their screening process was strictly perfunctory, in the sense that it was done as a deterrent exercise to future asylum seekers. A humanitarian consideration of determining 'genuine' from 'non-genuine' refugees was not at the forefront of this practice. This is demonstrated in Arthur Helton's 1993 analysis of the screening process. Helton argued that when

108 Robinson, *Terms of Refuge: The Indochinese Exodus and the International Response*, 1998, pp. 202–203.

109 Robinson, *Terms of Refuge: The Indochinese Exodus and the International Response*, 1998, p. 204.

110 Robinson, *Terms of Refuge: The Indochinese Exodus and the International Response*, 1998, p. 205. Emphasis added.

111 James Hathaway quoted in Nichols, A. and Paul White, *Refugee Dilemmas: Reviewing the Comprehensive Plan of Action for Vietnamese Asylum Seekers* (Manila: LAWASIA Human Rights Committee, 1993), pp. 32, 37–38; Hathaway, J. C., 'Labelling the 'boat people': the failure of the human rights mandate of the Comprehensive Plan of Action for Indochinese Refugees', *Human Rights Quarterly*, 15 (4), 1993, pp. 686–702.

112 Zolberg, A., et al., *Escape From Political Violence: Conflict and the Refugee Crisis in the Developing World*, 1989; Hathaway, J. C., 'Labelling the 'boat people': the failure of the human rights mandate of the Comprehensive Plan of Action for Indochinese Refugees', *Human Rights Quarterly*, 15 (4), 1993, pp. 686–702.

113 Zolberg, A., et al., *Escape From Political Violence: Conflict and the Refugee Crisis in the Developing World*, 1989.

looking at the way the CPA had come to be practiced, it should be remembered that its underlying assumption was that 'most of the boat people were not refugees'.[114] Thus the CPA had been practiced as a deterrent measure which 'profoundly affected its implementation'.[115] In his state-by-state analysis, Helton found Status determination was flawed, for it was implemented 'in a way that fails to accord the benefit of the doubt to asylum seekers. . . . due to the fact that the arrangement has been imbued with migration control considerations'.[116] The next section of this chapter will look at each state's practice in the refugee screening process, and analyze how it deviated from the original state-by-state procedures set out in the CPA arrangements (described above).[117]

6.3.1 *Indonesia*

According to the UNHCR, a leaflet describing the determination of refugee status was distributed to all arrivals at the Galang camp. However, this did not 'articulate the "internationally recognized criteria" with respect to the asylum seeker's claim to refugee status'.[118] Asylum seekers were able to meet with the UNHCR Eligibility Unit in a weekly information session before their screening interview. Prior to Indonesian authorities screening the asylum seekers, the UNHCR legal consultants interviewed asylum seekers and an initial assessment of the person's claim for refugee status was forwarded to the Indonesian authorities. The P3V Committee conducted the main interview with asylum seekers and decided on their status. UNHCR legal consultants were not present during these interviews. However, the practice of 'fast-track' screening was widely practiced in Indonesia. This was where interviews were conducted for only 10–15 minutes and decisions were immediately made based on this brief interview. There were concerns that this form of status determination procedures had a 'get them in and out' mentality as opposed to a careful adjudication process.[119] When the P3V and UNHCR disagreed on the status of an asylum seeker, discussions were held jointly in order to reach a resolution. An applicant denied refugee status received a written decision, but the 'reasons for the decisions are cursory'.[120] Asylum seekers had 15 days to appeal the decision.

---

[114] Helton, A. C., 'Refugee Determination under the Comprehensive Plan of Action: Overview and Assessment', *International Journal of Refugee Law*, 5 (4), 1993, p. 556.

[115] Helton, A. C., 'Refugee Determination under the Comprehensive Plan of Action: Overview and Assessment', *International Journal of Refugee Law*, 5 (4), 1993, p. 557.

[116] Helton, A. C., 'Refugee Determination under the Comprehensive Plan of Action: Overview and Assessment', *International Journal of Refugee Law*, 5 (4), 1993, p. 557.

[117] UNGA, *Note on National Procedures for the Determination of Refugee Status*, Submitted by the High Commissioner, Co-ordinating Committee for the International Conference on Indo-Chinese Refugees 25 and 26 May 1989, A/CONF.148/4, Annex 1.

[118] Helton, A. C., 'Refugee Determination under the Comprehensive Plan of Action: Overview and Assessment', *International Journal of Refugee Law*, 5 (4), 1993, p. 547.

[119] Nichols, A. and Paul White, *Refugee Dilemmas: Reviewing the Comprehensive Plan of Action for Vietnamese Asylum Seekers*, 1993, pp. 28–30.

[120] Helton, A. C., 'Refugee Determination under the Comprehensive Plan of Action: Overview and Assessment', *International Journal of Refugee Law*, 5 (4), 1993, p. 548.

The UNHCR Durable Solutions staff would first 'counsel asylum seekers on the voluntary repatriation programme' though before they made an appeal.[121]

If the asylum seeker still wished to appeal they could do so through the UNHCR, who would forward this to the Review Committee in Jakarta, made up of government officials from the ministries of foreign affairs and immigration and the P3V. If the appeal did not present any new findings, then the denial of appeal was upheld. If there had been a misinterpretation of elements within the claim, then the appeal was sent to the Appeal Board (which consisted of the same representation as in the Review Committee, but all of a higher ranking). A UNHCR official was present at the Review Committee and the Appeal Board and able to present their views on each individual case. The UNHCR did not assist in the preparation of the appeal, but screened-in Vietnamese were at times allowed to assist those seeking an appeal. Of the 11,039 persons interviewed in Indonesia by July 1992, 3,657 received 'positive' decisions or refugee status, and 7,382 received negative decisions.[122] 1,980 persons appealed the decision and out of this number only 165 received a positive review decision[123]

The differences between the CPA and Indonesia's actual practice in relation to the screening of refugees are very noticeable. First, the UNHCR was to *participate in all stages of the procedures* and be *present as an observer at such [P3V] interviews*,[124] and yet we find that the UNHCR was not present at the most important part of the process—the interview with P3V officials.[125] Second, there was to be a Screening Commission, led by an immigration officer, an official from P3V and UNHCR to collect information from all new arrivals; yet in practice, there is no mention of the Screening Commission. Third, the Review Committee in 1992 was a *new* addition to the appeals procedure, for originally, all appeals were to go straight to the Appeal Board. Another two issues of concern were that in the screening process, UNHCR assistance was not being provided to those submitting applications and second, the UNHCR officials were advising rejected applicants to first consider voluntary repatriation as opposed to an appeal against the decision! These practices indicate not only a failure to follow the original procedures specified according to the 1951 Convention and the UNHCR Handbook on Criteria and Procedures, but also an acquiescence on the part of the UNHCR, which allowed such deviations to occur. The lack of UNHCR presence at the interviews of course enabled the development of Indonesia's 'fast tracking' interview process; the failure to implement the

121 Helton, A. C., 'Refugee Determination under the Comprehensive Plan of Action: Overview and Assessment', *International Journal of Refugee Law*, 5 (4), 1993, p. 548.

122 Helton, A. C., 'Refugee Determination under the Comprehensive Plan of Action: Overview and Assessment', *International Journal of Refugee Law*, 5 (4), 1993, p. 549.

123 Helton, A. C., 'Refugee Determination under the Comprehensive Plan of Action: Overview and Assessment', *International Journal of Refugee Law*, 5 (4), 1993, p. 549.

124 UNGA, *Note on National Procedures for the Determination of Refugee Status*, Submitted by the High Commissioner, Co-ordinating Committee for the International Conference on Indo-Chinese Refugees 25 and 26 May 1989, A/CONF.148/4, Annex 1, pp. 4–5.

125 Helton, A. C., 'Refugee Determination under the Comprehensive Plan of Action: Overview and Assessment', *International Journal of Refugee Law*, 5 (4), 1993.

Screening Commission only served to further the creation of 'fast tracking'. The addition of the Review Committee enabled quick rejection of certain applicants, and the UNHCR's lack of assistance to those denied refugee status served to prevent many appeals in the first place.[126]

Clearly, it cannot be said that Indonesia was demonstrating a willingness to embrace international refugee law. Of even greater concern is that, as boundaries were manipulated to allow the expeditious refusal of refugee status and deter potential boat people, the UNHCR was present throughout this. The UNHCR's complicity in these acts further demonstrate how malleable refugee protection appeared to Indonesia and, as Chapter 3 and 4 demonstrated, it was this malleability of refugee protection principles that enabled the region's states to manipulate the institutions and laws relating to refugees.

6.3.2 *Malaysia*

Helton found the following procedures to be in place for asylum seekers in Malaysia after March 1989. The UNHCR provided information leaflets to all recent arrivals. These leaflets covered various issues such as general information, refuge status determination, the ODP, special procedures for unaccompanied minors and voluntary repatriation. None of the leaflets addressed the definition of a refugee though, or the purpose of the interview.[127] The UNHCR also provided group, not individual, sessions for asylum seekers on the adjudication process. Military officers attached to National Task Force VII (which dealt with the Indochinese arrivals) conducted screening interviews and Malaysia is the only country where the UNHCR is present for all interviews. The interviewer and the UNHCR legal consultant together discussed the merits of each claimant and the UNHCR provided written assessments to the government authorities on every case. The UNHCR assessment and the interviewer's assessment were both sent to the National Task Force for a decision. Written notice of decisions were then hand-delivered to each asylum seeker. Like Indonesia, no reasons were provided to the asylum seeker for the decision that was made.

In practice, asylum seekers had seven days to submit an appeal. The UNHCR did not assist in this process; instead they recruited three Malaysian lawyers to advise the Review Advice Groups (an informal network set up voluntarily by university-educated asylum seekers). Appeals went to the Refugee Status Review Board, where the UNHCR was an observer and advisor on this board. As of December 1992,

[126] Going by Helton's figures on those interviewed—11,039 and those that appealed—1,980 with 1,815 of this number rejected. Helton, A. C., 'Refugee Determination under the Comprehensive Plan of Action: Overview and Assessment', *International Journal of Refugee Law*, 5 (4), 1993, p. 549.

[127] Helton, A. C., 'Refugee Determination under the Comprehensive Plan of Action: Overview and Assessment', *International Journal of Refugee Law*, 5 (4), 1993, p. 549.

15,032 persons had been interviewed for refugee status and 3,487 had been screened in as refugees; 7,362 received negative decisions.[128] The number that appealed were 5,463 with 964 accepted as refugees on review; 4,499 were rejected again.[129]

In Malaysia, out of approximately 11,000 screened by 1993, 32.14 percent were determined to be refugees. In Indonesia, by comparison, out of approximately 11,000 asylum seekers in the same period, 35.66 percent were screened in as refugees.[130] Therefore, Malaysia's screening procedure identified marginally fewer refugees as eligible for resettlement. However, Malaysia's practice of screening was more generous than Indonesia's, in the sense that UNHCR was allowed to be present for all interviews with the asylum seekers. The Malaysian government also did not deviate from its obligation to screen and follow the procedures as set out in the CPA. This observation and adherence to screening procedures needs to be contrasted with Malaysian government actions towards boat arrivals.[131] By pushing back boats after June 1989 at the alarming rate discussed earlier they *did* breach the CPA agreement to provide first asylum.[132] Thus, Malaysia's adherence to the screening procedures may indicate, in principle, an acceptance of international refuge law. However, it must be remembered that at the same time, the Malaysian government was breaching its commitment to first asylum. This practice was an act of *refoulement* against people deserving refugee protection until proven otherwise.[133]

---

128 The discrepancy in the number screened and outcome for those screened can be explained in 'decisions pending'. Helton, A. C., 'Refugee Determination under the Comprehensive Plan of Action: Overview and Assessment', *International Journal of Refugee Law*, 5 (4), 1993, p. 550.

129 Helton, A. C., 'Refugee Determination under the Comprehensive Plan of Action: Overview and Assessment', *International Journal of Refugee Law*, 5 (4), 1993, p. 550.

130 Percentages determined based on comparing the approximate number screened in Indonesia to Malaysia with a comparative total. Numbers from Helton, A. C., 'Refugee Determination under the Comprehensive Plan of Action: Overview and Assessment', *International Journal of Refugee Law*, 5 (4), 1993, pp. 549, 550 by 1995, the percentages had changed again to 31 percent acceptance rate by Malaysia and 30 percent by Indonesia, UNHCR, *Information Package on the Comprehensive Plan of Action on Indo-Chinese Refugees (CPA)*, October 1995, p. 20.

131 UNGA, *Office of the United Nations High Commissioner for Refugees: International Conference on Indo-Chinese Refugees, Report of the Secretary-Genera, Annex: Declaration and Comprehensive Plan of Action (CPA)*, Forty-Fourth Session Item 111 (c), 22 September 1989, A/44/523/Annex, Section C—Reception of New Arrivals.

132 UNGA, *UNHCR Activities Financed by Voluntary Funds: Report for 1989–1990 and Proposed Programmes and Budget for 1991*, Part II: Asia and Oceania, Submitted by the High Commissioner, Executive Committee of the High Commissioner's Programme, Forty-First Session, A/AC.96/751 (Part II), 13 August 1990, p. 13; Helton, A. C., 'The Malaysian Policy to Redirect Vietnamese Boat People: *Non-refoulement* as a Human Rights Remedy', *New York University Journal of International Law and Politics*, Volume 24, 1992l; Robinson, *Terms of Refuge: The Indochinese Exodus and the International Response*, 1998, p. 191.

133 UNGA, *Office of the United Nations High Commissioner for Refugees: International Conference on Indo-Chinese Refugees, Report of the Secretary-Genera, Annex: Declaration and Comprehensive Plan of Action (CPA)*, Forty-Fourth Session Item 111 (c), 22 September 1989, A/44/523/Annex, Section C—Reception of New Arrivals.

6.3.3 *The Philippines*

Having looked at two non-signatory countries to the 1951 Convention and 1967 Protocol, it is important to see how the Philippines practiced its screening procedures. The Philippines, though a member of the 1951 Convention and 1967 Protocol, did not wish to locally resettle asylum seekers. Therefore, they also requested the screening process and were in favor of repatriation for those screened out by the refugee status determination procedures. The Philippines practiced determination in three stages: reception, status determination and appeal.

The first action in determining refugee status was reception of the asylum seekers. Once asylum seekers were transferred to the government-administered camps they were all registered by UNHCR staff, and then interviewed by UNHCR legal consultants. The UNHCR prepared reports on each asylum seeker which served as a predetermination interview for submission to the officials from the Bureau of Immigration and Deportation (BID), who interviewed the asylum seekers and determined their refugee status. A UNHCR report was considered as non-binding in the Philippines.[134]

Before a screening interview, the second part of determining refugee status in the Philippines, asylum seekers were able to seek out UNHCR counseling four times. First on their arrival the UNHCR gave a verbal and written explanation of the CPA in Vietnamese; then two weeks after their arrival, the UNHCR registrar distributed an information leaflet; the third time the UNHCR legal consultant counseled groups before they had their individual interview and then a UNHCR legal consultant individually interviewed each asylum seeker, it is at this point that the UNHCR prepared their pre-determination report. A BID official, trained by the UNHCR, would conduct the interview with a UNHCR observer present, but the UNHCR did not interfere with the interview process as it took place. However, a BID official could ask the UNHCR officer for their views on each case. The government department that administered the camps, PFAC, then decided on each asylum seeker's refugee status according to all the information received; the decision was then mailed to each asylum seeker in writing.

Finally the appeal was the third stage of the CPA procedures in the Philippines. An appeal was to be made within 15 days of receiving the decision in writing. Three government officials from each department of Justice, Foreign Affairs and National Defence, Social Welfare and Development and the Office of the President made up the Appeals Board. The Appeals Board sent copies of all appeals that it received to the UNHCR and the UNHCR was permitted to send a written statement in support of the appeal. The UNHCR attended all appeals and was able to present its comment to the Board. The times when the UNHCR did not directly assist with appeals, a self-help group of Vietnamese asylum seekers provided advice. A UNHCR legal consultant provided supervision and advice to this group, and the

134 Helton, A. C., 'Refugee Determination under the Comprehensive Plan of Action: Overview and Assessment', *International Journal of Refugee Law*, 5 (4), 1993, p. 552.

Jesuit Refugee Service and Legal Assistance for Vietnamese Asylum Seekers provided legal assistance for the appeals. In July 1992 out of the 7,952 boat people screened for refugee status, 3,245 persons were successful and 3,622 were found not to be refugees.[135] There were 902 people that appealed and 71 had their decisions changed to refugee status, 831 did not.[136]

In the CPA, the Philippines agreed to asylum seekers being interviewed by non-government staff. In practice, interviews were conducted by BID.[137] In Helton's report there is also no mention of asylum seekers signing a written report of their interview so as to verify its accuracy. Yet, according to the CPA agreement this was meant to occur. The appeal process was the only procedure that had not changed in substance. What can be drawn from this? It is true that the Philippines had the most even and positive refugee determination process. However, the deviation from the procedures put in place for interviews and determination of refugee status do not indicate a faithful adherence to the refugee protection principles as laid out in the CPA. It can be concluded that while the Philippines was more generous than others in its processes, it also failed to be faithful to the procedures agreed to originally. Thus, it can be argued that like its neighbors, the Philippines met the basic structural requirements of the CPA but did not express any aspirations towards permanent refugee protection procedures.[138]

6.3.4 *Thailand*

In Thailand, the process was similar to the region in general. The majority of asylum seekers were rejected and the UNHCR was present only on the sidelines. Once again, the screening procedure in Thailand served the purpose of deterrence, but not always the asylum seeker. In Thailand all boat people were labeled 'illegal immigrants' until their status was proved otherwise. Upon arrival in the detention camp, asylum seekers were provided with leaflets explaining the CPA process. However, as Helton notes there was 'no explanation of the criteria upon which the refugee determination is made'.[139] Asylum seekers had no access to the UNHCR, non-governmental organizations or any other organization until their interview.

---

135 Helton, A. C., 'Refugee Determination under the Comprehensive Plan of Action: Overview and Assessment', *International Journal of Refugee Law*, 5 (4), 1993, p. 554.

136 Helton, A. C., 'Refugee Determination under the Comprehensive Plan of Action: Overview and Assessment', *International Journal of Refugee Law*, 5 (4), 1993, p. 554.

137 UNGA, *Note on National Procedures for the Determination of Refugee Status*, Submitted by the High Commissioner, Co-ordinating Committee for the International Conference on Indo-Chinese Refugees 25 and 26 May 1989, A/CONF.148/4, Annex 1, p. 7.

138 Robinson, *Terms of Refuge: The Indochinese Exodus and the International Response*, 1998, p. 209. It should be noted that there were allegations of corruption and bribery for positive refugee status made against the Philippines government. The US House of Representatives Hearing in July 1995 heard 12 'substantiated' allegations. The UNHCR's investigation cleared the Philippines government and its officials of any wrong doing. See UNHCR, *Information Package on the Comprehensive Plan of Action on Indo-Chinese Refugees (CPA)*, October 1995.

139 Helton, A. C., 'Refugee Determination under the Comprehensive Plan of Action: Overview and Assessment', *International Journal of Refugee Law*, 5 (4), 1993, p. 550.

Screening interviews were carried out by officials within the Ministry of Interior (MOI) and the UNHCR was only present as observers for approximately 20 percent of interviews. After the interview, the interviewer drafted a recommendation and sent the file to an MOI field supervisor, who then sent it to the Refugee Status Determination Committee (Screening Committee) in Bangkok. If the UNHCR was present, then their recommendation would also be sent with the file. If the UNHCR was not present at the interview, the field supervisor would send the file but not the recommendation to the UNHCR.

The UNHCR could request to the Screening Committee that a case be reopened, and could provide an oral assessment on cases where they were not present for the interview. The UNHCR and Thai authorities agreed on the determination made 'in the vast majority of the cases'[140]—something which both Helton and the UNHCR (in retrospect) said happened more often than not.[141] Screening Committee decisions on cases would be sent to the Operations Centre for Displaced Persons (OCDP) in Bangkok prior to final decision. After deliberation in Bangkok the asylum seeker would receive the decision in a letter, with 'cursory reasons for the denial'[142] and notice for seven days to appeal through the UNHCR. The Appeal Board consisted of representatives from MOI, National Security Council, Ministry of Foreign Affairs, Navy, Immigration and Marine Police. With the exception of the MOI, Helton notes, no other members on the Board had formal training in refugee law.[143] The UNHCR 'had considerable responsibility on appeals'[144] and attended all Appeal Board meetings in the capacity of observer and advisor. The UNHCR also held information sessions for appeal applicants—but it would only assist in the cases where it believed there were valid grounds for appeal.[145] As of July 1992, 6,480 of the 13,856 Vietnamese asylum seekers in Thailand had been screened. Of the 6,480 persons screened, 1,364 were found to be refugees and 5,063 were refused rejected refugee status; 886 persons went on to appeal and only 29 of these had their status changed to that of a refugee.[146]

A comparison of Thailand's practice to its procedural promises in the CPA indicates significant divergences in the determination process. The most obvious

140 Helton, A. C., 'Refugee Determination under the Comprehensive Plan of Action: Overview and Assessment', *International Journal of Refugee Law*, 5 (4), 1993, p. 551; UNHCR, *Information Package on the Comprehensive Plan of Action on Indo-Chinese Refugees (CPA)*, October 1995.

141 Helton, A. C., 'Refugee Determination under the Comprehensive Plan of Action: Overview and Assessment', *International Journal of Refugee Law*, 5 (4), 1993; UNHCR, *Information Package on the Comprehensive Plan of Action on Indo-Chinese Refugees (CPA)*, October 1995.

142 Helton, A. C., 'Refugee Determination under the Comprehensive Plan of Action: Overview and Assessment', *International Journal of Refugee Law*, 5 (4), 1993, p. 551.

143 Helton, A. C., 'Refugee Determination under the Comprehensive Plan of Action: Overview and Assessment', *International Journal of Refugee Law*, 5 (4), 1993, p. 551.

144 Helton, A. C., 'Refugee Determination under the Comprehensive Plan of Action: Overview and Assessment', *International Journal of Refugee Law*, 5 (4), 1993, p. 552.

145 Helton, A. C., 'Refugee Determination under the Comprehensive Plan of Action: Overview and Assessment', *International Journal of Refugee Law*, 5 (4), 1993, p. 552.

146 Helton, A. C., 'Refugee Determination under the Comprehensive Plan of Action: Overview and Assessment', *International Journal of Refugee Law*, 5 (4), 1993, p. 552.

discrepancy was the lack of UNHCR presence at the interviews. In 1989 it was said that the UNHCR would have 'full access to observe these interviews and to present its views', but this did not happen.[147] The other divergence was that all rejected cases were to receive reasons for their rejection of refugee status in writing.[148] By 1992 this had also changed, with the Screening Committee issuing only 'cursory reasons'[149] for denial of refugee status. However, when compared to Indonesia, Malaysia and Philippines where no reasons for denial of status were issued, Thailand represented some progress.

6.4 *Voluntary repatriation*

As the 1989 Conference, it was stated that under the CPA in the 'first instance, every effort will be made to encourage the voluntary return' of persons deemed not to be refugees.[150] However, if 'after the passage of reasonable time', voluntary repatriation was not efficiently expediting the return of asylum seekers who did not receive refugee status, then 'alternatives recognized as being acceptable under international practices would be examined'.[151] Educational and orientation programmes were also to be delivered to the failed asylum seekers aimed at encouraging their return. Though the United Kingdom issued a formal demand for the forced repatriation of Vietnamese which was seconded by Australia, it was believed to be an initiative drawn up by Hong Kong and the ASEAN states. At the 1989 Conference, all but two states agreed with the necessity for forced repatriation if the situation became too prolonged.[152] Rather ironically, these two states were the United States and Vietnam. The United States argued that 'unless and until dramatic improvements occur in [Vietnam's] economic, social and political life, the United States will remain unalterably opposed to the forced repatriation of Vietnamese asylum seekers'.[153] Vietnam concurred with the need to avoid forced repatriation; it argued that such

---

147 UNGA, *Note on National Procedures for the Determination of Refugee Status*, Submitted by the High Commissioner, Co-ordinating Committee for the International Conference on Indo-Chinese Refugees 25 and 26 May 1989, A/CONF.148/4, Annex 1, p. 8.

148 UNGA, *Note on National Procedures for the Determination of Refugee Status*, Submitted by the High Commissioner, Co-ordinating Committee for the International Conference on Indo-Chinese Refugees 25 and 26 May 1989, A/CONF.148/4, Annex 1, p. 8.

149 Helton, A. C., 'Refugee Determination under the Comprehensive Plan of Action: Overview and Assessment', *International Journal of Refugee Law*, 5 (4), 1993, p. 551.

150 UNGA, *Office of the United Nations High Commissioner for Refugees: International Conference on Indo-Chinese Refugees, Report of the Secretary-Genera, Annex: Declaration and Comprehensive Plan of Action (CPA)*, Forty-Fourth Session Item 111 (c), 22 September 1989, A/44/523/Annex, Section F—Repatriation/Plan of Repatriation.

151 UNGA, *Office of the United Nations High Commissioner for Refugees: International Conference on Indo-Chinese Refugees, Report of the Secretary-Genera, Annex: Declaration and Comprehensive Plan of Action (CPA)*, Forty-Fourth Session Item 111 (c), 22 September 1989, A/44/523/Annex, Section F—Repatriation/Plan of Repatriation.

152 USCR, *Refugee Reports*, Volume 10, Number 6, 16 June 1989, p. 8; USCR, *Refugee Reports*, Volume 10, Number 7, 28 July 1989, p. 6.

153 USCR, *Refugee Reports*, Volume 10, Number 7, 28 July 1989, p. 6.

an act would be coercion and 'coercion constitutes a violation of the Declaration of Human Rights and could only bring on unforeseeable consequences'.[154]

The progress of repatriation for those deemed 'non-genuine' refugees was to be reported in Steering Committee meetings of the CPA. The first of these was held in October 1989 and, as at the 1989 Conference, it was agreed that if no progress had been made in convincing people to return 'alternative measures including compulsory repatriation may have to be considered'.[155] At the same time, the United Kingdom was meeting with Vietnam to prepare the way for their acceptance of non-genuine refugees from camps in Hong Kong. However, Vietnam said that returnees would not be accepted unless their return was voluntary. Why, asked Vietnam, should they rush to appease Southeast Asian and Western states when there was no promise of aid?[156] The provision of aid, argued Vietnam, was an important part of repatriation as 'the problem of illegal emigration for economic reasons could be solved at its source'.[157] On 12 December 1989, Hong Kong began its first forcible repatriation of Vietnamese asylum seekers, after a repatriation agreement had been signed between Vietnam and Britain earlier that month.[158]

At the Steering Committee conference on Indochinese refugees in Geneva on 23 and 24 January 1990, the US and Vietnam reiterated their opposition to involuntary repatriation of asylum seekers until at least after July.[159] The United States had originally been 'unalterably opposed' to forced returns until after 1 July 1991, and Vietnam was opposed until after 1 October 1990. However, the remaining 27 countries at the Steering Committee conference insisted on 1 July 1990 as the deadline.[160] United Kingdom said that it would continue permitting Hong Kong officials to return non-genuine refugees to Vietnam by force if necessary, while ASEAN states started to make murmurs about refusing first asylum until the situation improved and the backlog of non-genuine refugees refusing to return voluntarily to Vietnam were removed.[161]

In a Joint Declaration of the eighth ASEAN-EC Ministerial Meeting in Kuala Lumpur on 16–17 February 1990, ministers all agreed that the 'humanitarian solution to this problem lies in the balanced and coordinated implementation of all elements of the CPA by all parties concerned'.[162] In particular, 'there must be an early implementation of the CPA as regards the repatriation of those not

[154] USCR, *Refugee Reports*, Volume 10, Number 7, 28 July 1989, p. 6.
[155] USCR, *Refugee Reports*, Volume 10, Number 6, 16 June 1989, p. 8; USCR, *Refugee Reports*, Volume 10, Number 7, 28 July 1989, p. 6.
[156] USCR, *Refugee Reports*, Volume 10, Number 6, 16 June 1989, p. 8; USCR, *Refugee Reports*, Volume 10, Number 7, 28 July 1989, p. 6.
[157] USCR, *Refugee Reports*, Volume 10, Number 6, 16 June 1989, p. 8; USCR, *Refugee Reports*, Volume 10, Number 7, 28 July 1989, p. 7.
[158] USCR, *Refugee Reports*, Volume 10, Number 12, 29 December 1989, p. 1.
[159] USCR, *Refugee Reports*, Volume 11, Number 1, 31 January 1990, p. 7.
[160] USCR, *Refugee Reports*, Volume 11, Number 1, 31 January 1990, p. 7.
[161] *Ibid.*; USCR, *Refugee Reports*, Volume 11, Number 5, 18 May 1990, p. 2.
[162] USCR *Refugee Reports*, Volume 11, Number 5, 18 May, 1990, p. 7.

qualifying for the status of refugees to the country of origin in a phased, orderly and safe manner'.[163] On the 16 May 1990, the ASEAN Foreign Ministers issued their first statement indicating just how committed they were to the larger refugee principles at stake in suggesting that if the CPA continued to be undermined by 'selective representation of its provisions' by states (mainly US and Vietnam), then countries of asylum have the 'right to take such unilateral action as they deem necessary to safeguard their national interests, including the abandonment of temporary refuge'.[164] Furthermore, they insisted that any country which opposed involuntary repatriation had a direct obligation to offer an effective intermediate solution.[165]

On 24 July 1990 the Joint Statement by the ASEAN Foreign Ministers on the Problem of Vietnamese Boat People stepped up the demand for a solution with reprisals if this warning was not heeded:

> The Foreign Ministers reaffirmed the need for the CPA to be implemented in a balanced and coordinated manner. They regretted the fact that while the CTR [Countries of Temporary Refuge, i.e. ASEAN states] have been pressured to continue to provide temporary refuge, two countries have chosen to ignore fundamental elements of the CPA. Vietnam, as the country of origin, has failed to take effective measures to prevent the clandestine departure of its citizens. Vietnam and the United States have refused to accept the involuntary repatriation of non-refugees. This position is inconsistent with internationally accepted practice, risks establishing precedents that will lead inevitably to a breakdown of the very integrity of the CPA.... *The Foreign Ministers reiterated the sovereign right of the CTR to take such actions as they deem necessary, in a more coordinated and concerted manner, to safeguard their national interests including the abandonment of temporary refuge.*[166]

In essence, the ASEAN states were arguing that as other participants in the CPA were only practicing 'selective implementation' of the CPA, they were absolved of any 'responsibility to honor their own commitments'.[167] ASEAN states therefore did not see the CPA as the stepping stone to the acceptance of wider refugee principles, but rather as a means to end the refugee problem in which everyone involved had reciprocal obligations and if one member broke it ASEAN states were not under any more of a moral or legal obligation to uphold their end of the deal. There were no 'rules' which they had to obey and no obligation unless others were also part of the solution. Southeast Asian states had witnessed how relatively easily the UNHCR and resettlement states changed their characterization of the Indochinese refugees and thus did not perceive their obligation to be any greater. As Hathaway argued in relation to the CPA, the worst part was that the 'UNHCR has been coopted into the legitimation of the tacit pact between first asylum and resettlement states

163 USCR *Refugee Reports*, Volume 11, Number 5, 18 May, 1990, p. 7.

164 USCR *Refugee Reports*, Volume 11, Number 5, 18 May, 1990, p. 7.

165 ASEAN, *Joint Statement by the Countries of Temporary Refuge* (CTR), ASEAN, Manilla, 16th May 1990.

166 ASEAN, *Joint Statement by the ASEAN Foreign Ministers on the Problem of Vietnamese Boat People*, Jakarta, 24 July 1990. http://www.aseansec.org/1205.html Emphasis added.

167 USCR, *Refugee Reports*, Volume 11, Number 5, 18 May, 1990, p. 7.

to relegate the explicit human rights mandate to the realm of pure symbolism'.[168] I agree with Hathaway in that the UNHCR's position effectively legitimised ASEAN's manipulation of the situation and exploited the indeterminacy of international refugee law. However, the UNHCR's actions did not have a negative impact on ASEAN states' perception of refugee protection principles, for their statement in July 1990 that they had a 'sovereign right of the CTR to take such actions as they deem necessary',[169] was more a re-statement of an old position (see Chapter 3) than indication of a new stance on international refugee law.

6.5 *CPA—the end result*

The actions taken to bring the CPA to a close and resolve the repatriation problem were numerous and all troubling. There are three circumstances in particular that dominated attempts to bring a close to the CPA. The first was repeated threats by ASEAN states to stop providing first asylum when the rate of voluntary repatriation slowed. This galvanized non-governmental organizations such as the USCR to request that the United States change its policy against forcible repatriation, so that more could be sent back to their country of origin. The second was the UNHCR's own efforts to bring the CPA to a 'rapid close'. This involved not only speeding up the forcible return of non-refugees, but also making conditions in the camps worse so as to encourage departures. The final act was an agreement made between Vietnam and each of the Southeast Asian states on the forcible return of Vietnamese still refusing to leave the camps.

At this stage of the CPA (1991–1992) progress was being made with the repatriation of Laotians through a tripartite agreement between UNHCR, Thailand and Laos; over 300,000 Cambodians were repatriated to Cambodia under an agreement between UNHCR, Cambodia and Thailand, in time for the 1993 Cambodian general elections.[170] However, just prior to this, the CPA's repatriation efforts experienced some difficulty; the Malaysian government conducted pushbacks on a regular basis and cited the United States refusal to allow forced repatriation as the cause.[171] Courtland Robinson, policy analyst for the USCR, testified to the US Senate Subcommittee that 'the United States must seek a new consensus on involuntary repatriation of the screen-out... with some compromise likely to be

168 Hathaway quoted in Nichols, A. and Paul White, *Refugee Dilemmas: Reviewing the Comprehensive Plan of Action for Vietnamese Asylum Seekers*, 1993, p. 32.

169 ASEAN, *Joint Statement by the ASEAN Foreign Ministers on the Problem of Vietnamese Boat People*, Jakarta, 24 July 1990. http://www.aseansec.org/1205.html

170 UNGA, *Summary Record of the 473rd Meeting on 5 October 1992*, Executive Committee of the High Commissioner's Programme, A/AC.96/SR.473, 12 October 1992, p. 7. See also USCR, *Refugee Reports*, Volume 10, Number 10, 20 October 1989 and *Refugee Reports*, Volume 11, Number 8, 24 August 1990, which both discuss the Cambodian refugee repatriation processes; the difficulties surrounding this problem and the repatriation efforts.

171 USCR, *Refugee Reports*, Volume 11, Number 5, 18 May 1990, p. 1.

needed on the length of the moratorium'.[172] This suggestion came just before the ASEAN states threatened to completely break from the CPA because of the United States and Vietnamese position on forced return. The ASEAN states argued that in their refusal to allow involuntary repatriation, the US and Vietnam were not fulfilling the CPA and this meant that ASEAN states could 'take such unilateral action as they deem necessary to safeguard their national interests, including the abandonment of temporary refuge'.[173] The Southeast Asian states were not alone in their frustration. The British government, which was responsible for the Hong Kong situation, was outspoken in saying that if the US did not want to allow involuntary repatriation then they could have the 9,000 screened-out Vietnamese in Hong Kong in a special camp in Guam.[174] By June even the Philippines, which up until then had been continuing to accept boat people rescued on international waters, refused to accept 101 Vietnamese boat people rescued by a US naval supply ship.[175]

In 1991 the United States agreed to the involuntary return of Vietnamese—but still insisted on international monitors being present at 'both ends of the mandatory return process',[176] that is the returns needed to be monitored at both the first asylum camps and in Vietnam. This still meant that involuntary repatriation would not be condoned by the largest donor to the CPA process. The United Kingdom decried this continued hypocrisy by the United States over forced repatriation, with the Member for Blackpool South, Sir Peter Blaker stating in Parliament that:

> The position of the United States is wholly illogical. It agreed to the comprehensive programme of action, as did Vietnam, but it is impeding putting that programme into practice. At the same time, it turns back, without any ceremony, boat people from Haiti, and the regime in Haiti is at least as oppressive as that in Vietnam. It turns back people from Mexico if they arrive at the border, and British people arriving at United States airports if they do not have permission to enter. The United States, like other countries, has recently been sending back Kurds from Turkey to Iraq, whether they like it or not. This is the universal practice for illegal immigrants. Therefore it is essential that the same policy should be applied in the case of Vietnamese boat people who are screened out as not being genuine refugees.[177]

In addition, there seemed to be little rationale for the United States position according to international refugee law. With the screened-out being declared 'non-genuine' refugees, the principle of *non-refoulement* and with it, the safeguard from involuntary repatriation, no longer applied to these people.[178] In 1991, the

---

172 USCR, *Refugee Reports*, Volume 11, Number 3, 23 March 1990, p. 11.

173 USCR, *Refugee Reports*, Volume 11, Number 8, 24 August 1990, p. 5.

174 USCR, *Refugee Reports*, Volume 11, Number 5, 18 May 1990, p. 8.

175 USCR, *Refugee Reports*, Volume 11, Number 6, 221 June 1990, p. 5.

176 Robinson, *Terms of Refuge: The Indochinese Exodus and the International Response*, 1998, p. 215.

177 The United Kingdom Parliament. Sir Peter Blaker, 'Vietnamese Boatpeople', *House of Commons Hansard Debates for 25 July 1991* http://www.publications.parliament.uk/pa/cm199091/cmhansrd/1991–07–25/Debate-1.html

178 Barcher, A. C., 'First Asylum in Southeast Asia: Customary Norm or Ephemeral Concept?', *New York University Journal of International Law and Politics*, Volume 24, 1992, in particular pp. 1273–1283.

UNHCR and European Community began assistance schemes for those who agreed to return to Vietnam. This was developed in order to entice more to leave the camp and had some success throughout 1992. It was however described by some as 'woefully inadequate' for encouraging higher numbers.[179]

In 1993, the Hong Kong UNHCR office drew up a paper to present at the CPA Steering Committee Meeting in Jakarta to discuss the progress of the CPA. At this stage, 44,000 Vietnamese had returned home, the screening process was near closing and the Vietnamese exodus had dramatically slowed down.[180] However, there were still tens of thousands of 'screened-out' Vietnamese refusing to leave the camps. The UNHCR paper said 'time is and has been the worst enemy of those who still remain. There is an urgent need to act'.[181] The call was for the CPA to be brought to an end quickly. The recommendations were that screening be quickly completed; new arrivals be 'summarily returned' unless an obvious basis for asylum was demonstrated; and that further agreements on the involuntary return of non-refugees should be 'promoted and implemented' between Vietnam and first asylum states.[182] The final UNHCR recommendation was that conditions in camps be sharply reduced so that 'expectations of permanence of life in detention should cease'.[183] The UNHCR endorsed cutbacks in medical and counseling assistance; freedom of movement outside the camps; elimination of income-generating activities; reduction in employment opportunities and monthly remittances from overseas; and the elimination of all educational programmes above primary school level.[184]

However, in 1989, the agreement had been that *even if* rejected asylum seekers refused to return to their country of origin there should not be any steps taken to increase their 'social outcast mentality'.[185] In essence, they should not be denied basic services that would affect their sense of normalcy in a situation where they obviously had little control. The agreement was to ensure that rejected cases maintained their dignity while they deliberated on their eventual repatriation to their country of origin. This was to be achieved via 'basic education for school-age children; Vietnamese literacy, and numeracy for adults and vocational training with emphasis on programmes to facilitate reintegration into the country of origin'.[186]

---

179 Nichols, A. and Paul White, *Refugee Dilemmas: Reviewing the Comprehensive Plan of Action for Vietnamese Asylum Seekers*, 1993, p. 34; Barcher, A.C., 'First Asylum in Southeast Asia: Customary Norm or Ephemeral Concept?', *New York University Journal of International Law and Politics*, Volume 24, 1992, p. 1285.

180 Helton, A. C., 'Refugee Determination under the Comprehensive Plan of Action: Overview and Assessment', *International Journal of Refugee Law*, 5 (4), 1993; Robinson, *Terms of Refuge*, p. 217.

181 Robinson, *Terms of Refuge: The Indochinese Exodus and the International Response*, p. 218.

182 Robinson, *Terms of Refuge: The Indochinese Exodus and the International Response*, p. 218.

183 Robinson, *Terms of Refuge: The Indochinese Exodus and the International Response*, p. 218.

184 Robinson, *Terms of Refuge: The Indochinese Exodus and the International Response*, p. 218.

185 UNGA, *Note on Departures and Repatriation*, Submitted by the High Commissioner, Co-ordinating Committee for the International Conference on Indo-Chinese Refugees 25 and 26 May 1989, A/CONF.148/4, Annex II, p. 15.

186 UNGA, *Note on Departures and Repatriation*, Submitted by the High Commissioner, Co-ordinating Committee for the International Conference on Indo-Chinese Refugees 25 and 26 May 1989, A/CONF.148/4, Annex II, p. 15.

The 1993 paper endorsed the removal of the latter two services in order to encourage voluntary repatriation. As the Jesuit Regional Services regional director for Southeast Asia said, 'it was cowardly of the UNHCR. UNHCR was obviously under international pressure for repatriation to occur—it would almost be fairer to have just told them [rejected cases] they had to go back'.[187]

In addition to the UNHCR's deterrence measures, ASEAN states began signing Orderly Return Programme (ORP) agreements with the Vietnamese government. Indonesia signed the first of these on 2 October 1993, and the other ASEAN states followed suit soon after. At this stage, neither Vietnam nor the US opposed involuntary repatriation—all the states by now had reached their limit with the 'protracted problem' of Indochinese asylum seekers.[188] The deadline for repatriation was set for 25 June 1996, and Malaysia was the first to send all its population back by the due date. Singapore followed in the next two days, and on the 30 June, UNHCR ceased all funding for the Vietnamese boatpeople. Indonesia and Thailand were not able to successfully repatriate all of their rejected cases by the deadline, but 'each moved aggressively on involuntary repatriations in the latter half of 1996'. During these operations, the UNHCR was not allowed to access the camps.

6.6 *Conclusion*

The majority of Southeast Asian states came out of the Indochinese refugee crisis without committing to international refugee law. The region's states did not feel obligated to sign the 1951 Convention or 1967 Protocol but nevertheless felt obliged to legitimate their position by framing it within the discourse of international refugee law. The CPA demonstrated their success in positing their argument that there existed 'non-genuine' refugees in the Southeast Asian region and thus the applicability of the 'genuine' refugee status to these groups, as defined in the 1951 Convention, would be wrong and an 'unfair burden' to the region.

By the end of the CPA, the UNHCR and Southeast Asian states agreed with the majority of decisions made concerning the refugee status of asylum seekers during the screening process.[189] How had the UNHCR gone from arguing *prima facie* refugee recognition for the Indochinese asylum seekers, to allowing non-signatory states of the 1951 Convention and 1967 Protocol to decide who could be given refugee status? There had been no dramatic change in the humanitarian circumstances that necessitated an abrupt change from *prima facie* refugee recognition to status screening between 1988 and 1989. Why the change in protection status for Indochinese asylum seekers, and more importantly how did this development

[187] Robinson, *Terms of Refuge: The Indochinese Exodus and the International Response*, p. 219.
[188] Robinson, *Terms of Refuge: The Indochinese Exodus and the International Response*, pp. 219–220.
[189] Helton, A. C., 'Refugee Determination under the Comprehensive Plan of Action: Overview and Assessment', *International Journal of Refugee Law*, 5 (4), 1993; UNHCR, *Information Package on the Comprehensive Plan of Action on Indo-Chinese Refugees (CPA)*, October 1995.

in refugee protection provisions affect Southeast Asian states' perception of international refugee law?

The seemingly endless arrival of boat people heightened Southeast Asia's resistance to continually accepting boat people and also increased resistance among resettlement states. As shown in Chapter 5, resettlement states started to agree with Southeast Asian states' characterization of arrivals as 'economic migrants' and 'non-genuine' refugees. The UNHCR, resettlement states and first asylum states agreed that screening would serve as an important deterrent to these 'opportunistic' migrants.

How did the UNHCR and Western states' complicity with this about turn in *prima facie* refugee status affect Southeast Asian states perception of international refugee law? As observed in Chapter 5, Southeast Asian states already doubted the uniformity of international refugee law practice and indeed its applicability to all regions—particularly developing ones. The fact that until March 1989 the Indochinese had received refugee status, seemed to demonstrate the malleability of refugee protection. The CPA created a mechanism that enabled the region to utilize elements of the 1951 Convention to justify the expulsion of asylum seekers. Though the 1951 Convention had proven to be a useful tool for dividing 'genuine' refugees from 'non-genuine', two things must be remembered when looking at why the CPA did not become permanent practice in Southeast Asia. The first is that, as Helton's analysis of status procedures in the region demonstrated, Southeast Asian states never embraced screening in the name of refugee protection but only as a deterrent measure to the Indochinese refugees.[190] Southeast Asian states' primary concern was not how to best provide refugee protection, but how to deter them. As Chang-Muy has argued, the screening procedures had no basis in law and 'have been formed in response to specific refugee caseloads, the regime for the protection of refugees in Asia remains fragile'.[191]

Second, taking Chang-Muy's point further, the 1951 Convention did not serve any purpose for Southeast Asian states outside the CPA. The only way that the UNHCR and resettlement states, in particular the United States, would agree to the resettlement or repatriation of these people was if they were individually screened. Southeast Asian states were financially assisted in the screening processes, those accepted as refugees would be resettled in another country, and those who were not were to be repatriated. As such, there was no real commitment at the domestic level to the screening process and the lack of impact on domestic politics made it easier to agree to the process and very easy to disband it after the Indochinese had left. There were few discernable political repercussions or legal commitments to refugee protection. The screening process was a 'one-off practice' to expedite a problem that many believed had gone on for too long.

190 Helton, A. C., 'Refugee Determination under the Comprehensive Plan of Action: Overview and Assessment', *International Journal of Refugee Law*, 5 (4), 1993, pp. 556–557.

191 Chang-Muy, F., 'International Refugee Law in Asia', *New York University Journal of International Law and Politics*, 24, 1992, p. 1177.

In this case the success in legitimating a practice by reference to international law reflects the law's malleability in the face of political expediency. Yet, at the same time, the CPA case also indicates that even Southeast Asian states, with their long history of rejecting international refugee law, still needed to acknowledge it and work within its framework to achieve the outcomes they desired. CPA experience suggests that the latter factor is pivotal for it refers to 'political sensibilities about what can properly be done, and how affairs should be conducted'.[192] The most significant factor that situated Southeast Asian states' argument within international refugee law was that the 'non-genuine' refugee claim resonated within the existing legal framework (leading to the creation of the CPA). However, this legal argument could only be successful if the law was open to manipulation in the first place.

Southeast Asian states' argument depended to a great degree on the framers of the international refugee instruments viewing their argument as legitimate. At this stage of the crisis, Western states had grown increasingly reluctant to provide resettlement places, while the UNHCR had become more amenable to the idea of screening out the 'non-genuine' refugees. Though Southeast Asian states had been formulating their argument that the Indochinese seeking asylum were not genuine refugees since the mid-1970s, it found greater resonance as the political preferences of outside states and institutions began to shift.

---

[192] Clark, *Legitimacy in International Society*, 2005, p. 220.

Conclusion

I have argued in this book that the majority of Southeast Asian states refused to sign the 1951 Convention and 1967 Protocol because they have never felt obliged to, and that this stemmed from two factors. First, Southeast Asian states have consistently argued that the instruments were both implicitly Eurocentric and largely irrelevant to Southeast Asian experiences. Second, during the region's largest refugee crisis, the 1975–1996 Indochinese refugee crisis, these states received material assistance and resettlement offers that covered most people who sought temporary asylum in the region. The international community's willingness to take on the Indochinese refugee burden at that time helped to absolve Southeast Asian states from any sense of obligation or responsibility.

The original basis for the rejection of international refugee law by Southeast Asian states can be found in the historical evolution of the law itself and in their initial response to the Indochinese refugee crisis. Chapter 1 demonstrates that the development of the UNHCR's Statute and the 1951 Convention were shaped by the perceived needs and experiences of European states at the end of the Second World War. During the construction of international refugee law, specific concerns were presented by India, Pakistan and China, but were marginalised. Consequently, the definition of a refugee in the 1951 Convention focused on Europeans who had fled their countries prior to 1 January 1951. This fed the perception that the 1951 Convention was Eurocentric.

Although the 1967 Protocol removed the time and geographic limits from the Convention's definition of a refugee, it did not address the wider concerns that many developing states still had about the legal framework. As discussed in Chapter 2, the 1967 Protocol failed to persuade Southeast Asian states to question their perception that international refugee law was Eurocentric. Three commonly expressed concerns were: first, that the 1951 Convention and 1967 Protocol assumed all states had the requisite bureaucratic structures to facilitate the assessment of individual cases, even in times of mass influx; second, that there was no acknowledgement of the financial burdens associated with complying with the 1951 Convention and 1967 Protocol; third, that there were differences in the causes of mass influx in developing states as opposed to developed states. While the 1967 Protocol removed the more obviously Eurocentric components of international refugee law, it failed to address these concerns or to remove the tag of perceived Eurocentrism.

In ascertaining how this situation developed, I studied the Indochinese refugee crisis from 1975 to 1996 and demonstrated that the majority of Southeast Asian states have not rejected refugee recognition procedures because of 'good neighbourliness', 'economic cost' or 'threats to social cohesion'. Southeast Asian states, such as Malaysia, have often violated the 'good neighbour' rule by taking in people fleeing their neighbouring states. There is little clear evidence that asylum seekers posed an economic threat to Southeast Asian states; nor do refugee populations lead to increased social instability (or dominate a state's reason for rejecting these people). Rather, I demonstrated that the formal rejection of the 1951 Convention and 1967 Protocol was due to the lack of a sense of obligation.

The Indochinese refugee crisis was the largest refugee crisis to affect the Southeast Asian region in the post-Second World War era. It thus provides an excellent case for analysing the relationship between Southeast Asian states, the UNHCR, Western states and international refugee law. From the beginning of this crisis, Southeast Asian states argued that the Eurocentric nature of the 1951 Convention and 1967 Protocol made the instruments inapplicable. This argument gained further currency as many of the region's states developed a strategy of 'refugee manipulation'. Many Southeast Asian states learned that they could use their rejection of international refugee law to threaten the removal of temporary asylum and force the wider international community to provide both material assistance and resettlement places. Chapter 3 demonstrated that from the beginning of the crisis, but especially by the time of the 1979 Conference, states such as Thailand and Indonesia learned that refusal to provide even temporary asylum for the Indochinese asylum seekers reaped more resettlement offers from third countries and more material assistance. By the early 1980s, as shown in Chapter 4, the manipulation of the Indochinese crisis to secure more assistance and the continued refusal to sign the international refugee law instruments had become a hallmark of Southeast Asian policy towards Indochinese refugees.

However, the refusal by the majority of Southeast Asian states to accede to the key international refugee law instruments did not mean that they did not feel a need to legitimate their policies towards the Indochinese asylum seekers. Many of the region's states used the legal framework provided by international refugee law to deny the asylum seekers' claim for refugee status. This strategy became more apparent in the later stages of the crisis when Western states and the UNHCR became less willing to provide assistance and resettlement places. In spite of the fact that the overwhelming majority of states in Southeast Asia refused to accede to the international refugee law instruments, these states sought to legitimate their policies by reference to the legal framework constituted by those instruments.

At the very outset of the crisis many Southeast Asian states argued that the Indochinese asylum seekers were not 'genuine' refugees. These arguments were largely overlooked and rejected by the international community until 1986 when key Western states and even the UNHCR first began to experience what ASEAN labelled 'compassion fatigue'. As Chapter 5 demonstrated, by the mid-1980s the 'non-genuine' refugee argument began to resonate and find wider legitimacy because of the shifting political preferences of actors like the UNHCR and resettlement states. Keen to bring the crisis to a swift end, the UNHCR and resettlement states such as the US, Australia and France began to accept the argument that Indochinese refugees were 'illegal immigrants', and not genuine refugees as they had earlier insisted. This led to the UNHCR withdrawing *prima facie* refugee status from the Indochinese asylum seekers and a concession to Southeast Asian states that the international community no longer considered them to be genuine refugees. Thus, Chapter 6 demonstrates that these actors shifted their position in the 1989 CPA to endorse a policy of forced repatriation for the 'non-genuine' refugees. The critical issue was that during the course of this transition, Southeast Asian states did not change their argument and neither did the material causes of Indochinese flight change demonstrably. What changed were the political preferences of powerful actors. The increased legitimacy of the 'illegal migrant' argument owed more to the changing political sensibilities of key states and the UNHCR than to whether Indochinese asylum seekers were 'genuine' or 'non-genuine' refugees.

Politics and International Law

The fact that Southeast Asian states did not simply reject international refugee law without explanation because it was contrary to national interests or considered irrelevant, signifies a broader relationship between politics and international law than is usually acknowledged. Southeast Asian states attempted to explain and validate their actions by reference to the instruments themselves. For instance, the majority of Southeast Asian states referred to Indochinese asylum seekers and other irregular migrant populations from past to present as 'economic migrants', 'illegal migrants' or 'non-genuine' refugees. These descriptions only make sense within a legal framework that affords the logical possibility of a 'genuine' refugee or legal migrant. The notion of a 'non-genuine' refugee only has meaning if we know what the 'genuine' refugee looks like. Thus, when Southeast Asian states claimed in dialogue with the UNHCR and other states that the irregular migrants flooding out of Indochina were 'non-genuine' refugees, they were tacitly accepting the definition of a 'refugee' (as set out in the 1951 Convention). According to most of the region's states, the definition of the refugee within that instrument did not apply to their irregular migrant populations because Indochinese asylum seekers did not have an individual fear of persecution but a generalised fear of economic hardship.

Southeast Asian states defended their refusal to accede to international refugee law by reference to the instruments they were rejecting and this casts new light on the relationship between international law and politics. The rejection of international refugee law by Southeast Asian states gained legitimacy because it was justified by reference to the existing terms—the 1951 Convention and 1967 Protocol. As Skinner suggests, the region's states would have been inhibited from refusing to accede had they not been able to legitimate their position in a way that made sense to other actors.[1] The realist argument is that international legal rules are largely irrelevant amongst the factors that shape the way states behave and as a result, states feel no need to legitimate their action by reference to prevailing norms (including international legal norms).[2] Superficially, the Southeast Asian position on international refugee law seems to support the realist claim. Closer scrutiny, however, shows that realist understandings of state behaviour fail to capture the more nuanced relationship between international law and politics. In the period 1975–1996, many Southeast Asian states legitimated their decision not to accede to international refugee law by arguing that the Indochinese asylum seekers were not 'genuine' refugees under the definition set out in the 1951 Convention and 1967 Protocol. So, rather than ignoring the law or offering spurious justifications, the region's states felt obliged to offer justifications for their actions that made sense within the legal framework. The UNHCR's decision to commence individual 'screening' of Laotians in 1985 and then the Vietnamese in 1989,[3] helped to validate Southeast Asian states' central claim: that Indochinese asylum seekers should not be afforded *prima facie* refugee status and that their claim to refugee status needed to be questioned.

This use of international refugee law suggests some new directions in considering the relationship between political argumentation and international law. There are two main schools of thought here. Critical legal theorists such as Martti Koskenniemi and David Kennedy argue that international law has an 'indeterminacy gap', that there is no determinate end to the possible justifications that a state may use within the international legal framework to justify its actions.[4] Koskenniemi see this as

[1] Skinner, Q., 'Analysis of Political Thought and Action', in Tully, J. (ed.), *Meaning and Context: Quentin Skinner and his Critics* (Cambridge: Polity Press, 1988), p. 117.

[2] For further discussion of this see, Kratochwil, *Rules, Norms, and Decisions: On the Conditions of Practical and Legal Reasoning in International Relations and Domestic Affairs*, 1989.

[3] Note that the screening and repatriation of Cambodians was done separately under the 1991 Paris Peace Accords.

[4] Koskenniemi, *From Apology to Utopia: The Structure of International Legal Argument*, 1989; Koskenniemi, 'Comments on Chapter 1 and 2', in Byers, M. and George Nolte (eds.), *United States Hegemony and the Foundations of International Law*, 2003; Koskenniemi, M., 'International Law and Hegemony: A Reconfiguration', *Cambridge Review of International Affairs*, Vol. 17, No. 3 (2004), pp. 197–218; Koskenniemi, M., 'Legal Universalism: Between Morality and Power in a World of States', in Cheng, S. (ed.), *Law, Justice, and Power. Between Reason and Will* (Stanford: Stanford University Press, 2004); Koskenniemi, M., 'International Law in Europe: Between Tradition and Renewal', *European Journal of International Law*, Vol. 16, No. 1 (2005), pp. 113–124; Kennedy, D., 'The Sources of International Law', *American University Journal of International Law and Policy*, Vol. 2, No. 1 (1987), pp. 1–96; Kennedy, D., 'A New Stream in International Law Scholarship', *Wisconsin International Law Journal*, Vol. 7, No. 1 (1988–89), pp. 1–49; and Purvis, N., 'Critical Legal Studies in Public International Law', *Harvard International Law Journal*, Vol. 32, No. 1 (1991), pp. 81–115.

largely deriving from the fact that contemporary international law is the result of the actions of powerful states in imperial times; international law was used to legitimate the instrumental power of these states.[5] Thus, critical legal scholars do not see law as secondary to power and politics. Rather each constitutes the other.[6]

In contrast, the New Haven school argues that there are limits to what can be seen as a justifiable legal argument.[7] From this perspective, there is a point where an argument becomes 'implausible'.[8] In my book, I analyse the relationship between refugee instruments perceived as Eurocentric and Southeast Asian states, and evaluate how Southeast Asian states situated themselves in relation to international refugee law. I demonstrate that it is important to look at the varied reasons for a state's rejection of the law and *not to assume that formal rejection means that states are acting outside of the process and framework of international law*. As I sought to demonstrate throughout this book, while Southeast Asian states justified their rejection of international refugee law with reference to its legal structure: they had to acknowledge the law's existence and follow its textual rules. However, the consequence of this was that there appeared to be no limit to the way in which they could interpret the law, or their obligations to the law, to justify their rejection. Thus, the rejection of international refugee law by Southeast Asian states and their justifications for doing so demonstrates the ever important and influential political contestation that shapes international law.

The Southeast Asian case shows that both the critical legal approach and the New Haven school are partially correct. Southeast Asian states were only successful in using the term 'non-genuine' refugee because they did so within the pre-existing framework embedded in international refugee law *and* because the global balance of political preferences shifted in their favour. Here, the New Haven school has a valid point—the argument about 'non-genuine' refugees had to be made within a framework that saw certain modes of argumentation as reasonable (but ruled others out). Southeast Asian states were thus not entirely free to make *any* argument in legitimating their position. However, the critical legal approach also helps explain why, during the Indochinese refugee crisis, Southeast Asian states had success in

[5] Koskenniemi, M., 'International Law in Europe: Between Tradition and Renewal', *European Journal of International Law*, Vol. 16, No. 1 (2005), pp. 113–124.

[6] Simpson, G. J., 'The Situation on the International Legal Theory Front', *European Journal of International Law*, Vol. 11, No. 2 (2000), pp. 439–464.

[7] McDougal, M., 'Some Basic Theoretical Concepts about International Law: A Policy Oriented Framework of Inquiry' in Falk, R and Saul Mendlovitz (eds.), *The Strategy of World Order*, vol. II, *International Law* (New York: World Law Fund, 1966); McDougal, M. and Harold Lasswell, 'The Identification and Appraisal of Diverse Systems of Public Order', *ibid*; McDougal, M. and W. M. Reisman, *International Law in Contemporary Perspective* (New Haven: Yale University Press, 1980); Higgins, R. *Problems and Processes: International Law and How We Use It* (Oxford: Oxford University Press, 1994); Byers, M. *Custom, Power and the Power of Rules: International Relations and Customary International Law* (Cambridge: Cambridge University Press, 1999); Reus-Smit, C., 'The Politics of International Law', in Reus-Smit, C. (ed.), *The Politics of International Law* (Cambridge: Cambridge University Press, 2004).

[8] Higgins, R. *Problems and Processes: International Law and How We Use It* (Oxford: Oxford University Press, 1994).

stretching the 'non-genuine' refugee approach to include all Indochinese asylum seekers. These states were able stretch the commonly understood meaning of refugee norms so far that they all but lost their meaning. According to critical legal scholars, this is proof of states' ability to use international law as a tool to shape political outcomes.[9] The critical legal school suggests that Southeast Asian states were only able to do this successfully in the mid to late 1980s because it suited the political preferences of powerful actors, such as the US and UNHCR. So both the critical legal approach and the New Haven school can explain aspects of the situation in Southeast Asia in the 1980s.

Migrant and Refugee Studies in Southeast Asia

In the literature on Southeast Asian refugees, there is a clear division between those who study 'migrants' (legal or illegal) and those whose object of analysis is 'refugees'. However, neither approach sufficiently acknowledges the legal and political complexity surrounding these terms in the Southeast Asian context. In the Southeast Asian context, use of the term 'migrant' or 'illegal migrant' appears to exclude the possibility that an individual may also be deserving of refugee status. However, in Southeast Asia asylum seekers do not have the opportunity to seek refugee status and this means that an individual is often forced to live in fear of being found to be an 'illegal migrant'.[10] This means almost immediate deportation, which depending on their reason for leaving their country of origin, could well be considered as an act of *refoulement*. In the Southeast Asian context, use of the term 'refugee' also needs to be carefully considered. When the literature refers to a group of people as 'refugees' in the Southeast Asia this does not necessarily signify that the host country sees these people in the same light; nor does it guarantee them better treatment according to the 1951 Convention or greater security.

Given all this, how are scholars and practitioners to think anew about their responses to refugees? This book argues that the formal rejection of international law does not signify a state's departure from the legal framework. In fact, a state may refer to the norms that frame the legal framework in order to legitimate their formal rejection of the legal texts. In other words, the impact of law on policy behaviour is not simply a matter of compliance or non-compliance, as is often suggested especially in Refugee Studies. Furthermore, the nexus between the illegal migrant, the refugee and the migrant must be understood as part of a broader discursive domain, not as words corresponding to truths. The lack of a regional mechanism to collectively deal with irregular migrants is a potentially major problem in Southeast Asia. Reliance on the UNHCR and Western states to fill regional gaps in providing access to

---

[9] Kratochwil, 'How do Norms Matter?', in Byers, M. (ed.)., *The Role of Law in International Politics*, 2000, p. 42.

[10] Communication with Diego Rosero, (then) Senior Legal Officer, UNHCR Tokyo. Date: 27 August 2003.

refugee for asylum seekers needs to be examined in further detail. In addition, we need to acknowledge the fact that in some parts of the world, individuals do not have access to the rights and protection that elements of international law seek to offer. This means that we need to remain vigilant to the justifications that can be made to deny protection. For, as this book has revealed, the cost of Southeast Asian states' success in rejecting international refugee law has been, and will continue to be, paid by those most vulnerable.

Appendix 1

Convention Relating to the Status of Refugees (189 UNTS 150)

Adopted on 28 July 1951 by the United Nations Conference of Plenipotentiaries on the Status of Refugees and Stateless Persons convened under General Assembly resolution 429 (V) of 14 December 1950

Entry into force 22 April 1954, in accordance with article 43

Preamble

The High Contracting Parties,

Considering that the Charter of the United Nations and the Universal Declaration of Human Rights approved on 10 December 1948 by the General Assembly have affirmed the principle that human beings shall enjoy fundamental rights and freedoms without discrimination,

Considering that the United Nations has, on various occasions, manifested its profound concern for refugees and endeavoured to assure refugees the widest possible exercise of these fundamental rights and freedoms,

Considering that it is desirable to revise and consolidate previous international agreements relating to the status of refugees and to extend the scope of and the protection accorded by such instruments by means of a new agreement,

Considering that the grant of asylum may place unduly heavy burdens on certain countries, and that a satisfactory solution of a problem of which the United Nations has recognized the international-scope and nature cannot therefore be achieved without international co-operation,

Expressing the wish that all States, recognizing the social and humanitarian nature of the problem of refugees, will do everything within their power to prevent this problem from becoming a cause of tension between States,

Noting that the United Nations High Commissioner for Refugees is charged with the task of supervising international conventions providing for the protection of refugees, and recognizing that the effective co-ordination of measures taken to deal with this problem will depend upon the co-operation of States with the High Commissioner,

Have agreed as follows:

CHAPTER I

GENERAL PROVISIONS

Article 1. Definition of the term "refugee"

A. For the purposes of the present Convention, the term "refugee" shall apply to any person who:

(1) Has been considered a refugee under the Arrangements of 12 May 1926 and 30 June 1928 or under the Conventions of 28 October 1933 and 10 February 1938, the Protocol of 14 September 1939 or the Constitution of the International Refugee Organization;
Decisions of non-eligibility taken by the International Refugee Organization during the period of its activities shall not prevent the status of refugee being accorded to persons who fulfill the conditions of paragraph 2 of this section;

(2) As a result of events occurring before I January 1951 and owing to well-founded fear of being persecuted for reasons of race, religion, nationality, membership of a particular social group or political opinion, is outside the country of his nationality and is unable, or owing to such fear, is unwilling to avail himself of the protection of that country; or who, not having a nationality and being outside the country of his former habitual residence as a result of such events, is unable or, owing to such fear, is unwilling to return to it.
In the case of a person who has more than one nationality, the term "the country of his nationality" shall mean each of the countries of which he is a national, and a person shall not be deemed to be lacking the protection of the country of his nationality if, without any valid reason based on well-founded fear, he has not availed himself of the protection of one of the countries of which he is a national.

B. (1) For the purposes of this Convention, the words "events occurring before I January 1951" in article 1, section A, shall be understood to mean either (a) "events occurring in Europe before I January 1951"; or (b) "events occurring in Europe or elsewhere before I January 1951"; and each Contracting State shall make a declaration at the time of signature, ratification or accession, specifying which of these meanings it applies for the purpose of its obligations under this Convention.

(2) Any Contracting State which has adopted alternative (a) may at any time extend its obligations by adopting alternative (b) by means of a notification addressed to the Secretary-General of the United Nations.

C. This Convention shall cease to apply to any person falling under the terms of section A if:

(1) He has voluntarily re-availed himself of the protection of the country of his nationality; or
(2) Having lost his nationality, he has voluntarily reacquired it; or
(3) He has acquired a new nationality, and enjoys the protection of the country of his new nationality; or
(4) He has voluntarily re-established himself in the country which he left or outside which he remained owing to fear of persecution; or
(5) He can no longer, because the circumstances in connection with which he has been recognized as a refugee have ceased to exist, continue to refuse to avail himself of the protection of the country of his nationality;
Provided that this paragraph shall not apply to a refugee falling under section A (I) of this article who is able to invoke compelling reasons arising out of previous persecution for refusing to avail himself of the protection of the country of nationality;
(6) Being a person who has no nationality he is, because the circumstances in connection with which he has been recognized as a refugee have ceased to exist, able to return to the country of his former habitual residence;
Provided that this paragraph shall not apply to a refugee falling under section A (I) of this article who is able to invoke compelling reasons arising out of previous persecution for refusing to return to the country of his former habitual residence.

D. This Convention shall not apply to persons who are at present receiving from organs or agencies of the United Nations other than the United Nations High Commissioner for Refugees protection or assistance.

When such protection or assistance has ceased for any reason, without the position of such persons being definitively settled in accordance with the relevant resolutions adopted by the General Assembly of the United Nations, these persons shall ipso facto be entitled to the benefits of this Convention.

E. This Convention shall not apply to a person who is recognized by the competent authorities of the country in which he has taken residence as having the rights and obligations which are attached to the possession of the nationality of that country.

F. The provisions of this Convention shall not apply to any person with respect to whom there are serious reasons for considering that.

(a) He has committed a crime against peace, a war crime, or a crime against humanity, as defined in the international instruments drawn up to make provision in respect of such crimes;
(b) He has committed a serious non-political crime outside the country of refuge prior to his admission to that country as a refugee;
(c) He has been guilty of acts contrary to the purposes and principles of the United Nations.

Article 2. General obligations

Every refugee has duties to the country in which he finds himself, which require in particular that he conform to its laws and regulations as well as to measures taken for the maintenance of public order.

Article 3. Non-discrimination

The Contracting States shall apply the provisions of this Convention to refugees without discrimination as to race, religion or country of origin.

Article 4. Religion

The Contracting States shall accord to refugees within their territories treatment at least as favourable as that accorded to their nationals with respect to freedom to practise their religion and freedom as regards the religious education of their children.

Article 5. Rights granted apart from this Convention

Nothing in this Convention shall be deemed to impair any rights and benefits granted by a Contracting State to refugees apart from this Convention.

Article 6. The term "in the same circumstances"

For the purposes of this Convention, the term "in the same circumstances,, implies that any requirements (including requirements as to length and conditions of sojourn or residence) which the particular individual would have to fulfill for the enjoyment of the right in question, if he were not a refugee, must be fulfilled by him, with the exception of requirements which by their nature a refugee is incapable of fulfilling.

Article 7. Exemption from reciprocity

1. Except where this Convention contains more favourable provisions, a Contracting State shall accord to refugees the same treatment as is accorded to aliens generally.
2. After a period of three years' residence, all refugees shall enjoy exemption from legislative reciprocity in the territory of the Contracting States.
3. Each Contracting State shall continue to accord to refugees the rights and benefits to which they were already entitled, in the absence of reciprocity, at the date of entry into force of this Convention for that State.
4. The Contracting States shall consider favourably the possibility of according to refugees, in the absence of reciprocity, rights and benefits beyond those to which they are entitled according to paragraphs 2 and 3, and to extending exemption from reciprocity to refugees who do not fulfill the conditions provided for in paragraphs 2 and 3.
5. The provisions of paragraphs 2 and 3 apply both to the rights and benefits referred to in articles 13, 18, 19, 21 and 22 of this Convention and to rights and benefits for which this Convention does not provide.

Article 8. Exemption from exceptional measures

With regard to exceptional measures which may be taken against the person, property or interests of nationals of a foreign State, the Contracting States shall not apply such measures to a refugee who is formally a national of the said State solely on account of such nationality. Contracting States which, under their legislation, are prevented from applying the general principle expressed in this article, shall, in appropriate cases, grant exemptions in favour of such refugees.

Article 9. Provisional measures

Nothing in this Convention shall prevent a Contracting State, in time of war or other grave and exceptional circumstances, from taking provisionally measures which it considers to be essential to the national security in the case of a particular person, pending a determination by the Contracting State that that person is in fact a refugee and that the continuance of such measures is necessary in his case in the interests of national security.

Article 10. Continuity of residence

1. Where a refugee has been forcibly displaced during the Second World War and removed to the territory of a Contracting State, and is resident there, the period of such enforced sojourn shall be considered to have been lawful residence within that territory.
2. Where a refugee has been forcibly displaced during the Second World War from the territory of a Contracting State and has, prior to the date of entry into

force of this Convention, returned there for the purpose of taking up residence, the period of residence before and after such enforced displacement shall be regarded as one uninterrupted period for any purposes for which uninterrupted residence is required.

Article 11. Refugee seamen

In the case of refugees regularly serving as crew members on board a ship flying the flag of a Contracting State, that State shall give sympathetic consideration to their establishment on its territory and the issue of travel documents to them or their temporary admission to its territory particularly with a view to facilitating their establishment in another country.

CHAPTER II

JURIDICAL STATUS

Article 12. Personal status

1. The personal status of a refugee shall be governed by the law of the country of his domicile or, if he has no domicile, by the law of the country of his residence.
2. Rights previously acquired by a refugee and dependent on personal status, more particularly rights attaching to marriage, shall be respected by a Contracting State, subject to compliance, if this be necessary, with the formalities required by the law of that State, provided that the right in question is one which would have been recognized by the law of that State had he not become a refugee.

Article 13. Movable and immovable property

The Contracting States shall accord to a refugee treatment as favourable as possible and, in any event, not less favourable than that accorded to aliens generally in the same circumstances, as regards the acquisition of movable and immovable property and other rights pertaining thereto, and to leases and other contracts relating to movable and immovable property.

Article 14. Artistic rights and industrial property

In respect of the protection of industrial property, such as inventions, designs or models, trade marks, trade names, and of rights in literary, artistic and scientific works, a refugee shall be accorded in the country in which he has his habitual residence the same protection as is accorded to nationals of that country. In the territory of any other Contracting States, he shall be accorded the same protection as is accorded in that territory to nationals of the country in which he has his habitual residence.

Article 15. Right of association

As regards non-political and non-profit-making associations and trade unions the Contracting States shall accord to refugees lawfully staying in their territory the most favourable treatment accorded to nationals of a foreign country, in the same circumstances.

Article 16. Access to courts

1. A refugee shall have free access to the courts of law on the territory of all Contracting States.
2. A refugee shall enjoy in the Contracting State in which he has his habitual residence the same treatment as a national in matters pertaining to access to the courts, including legal assistance and exemption from *cautio judicatum solvi.*
3. A refugee shall be accorded in the matters referred to in paragraph 2 in countries other than that in which he has his habitual residence the treatment granted to a national of the country of his habitual residence.

CHAPTER III

GAINFUL EMPLOYMENT

Article 17. Wage-earning employment

1. The Contracting States shall accord to refugees lawfully staying in their territory the most favourable treatment accorded to nationals of a foreign country in the same circumstances, as regards the right to engage in wage-earning employment.
2. In any case, restrictive measures imposed on aliens or the employment of aliens for the protection of the national labour market shall not be applied to a refugee who was already exempt from them at the date of entry into force of this Convention for the Contracting State concerned, or who fulfils one of the following conditions:
   (a) He has completed three years' residence in the country;
   (b) He has a spouse possessing the nationality of the country of residence. A refugee may not invoke the benefit of this provision if he has abandoned his spouse;
   (c) He has one or more children possessing the nationality of the country of residence.
3. The Contracting States shall give sympathetic consideration to assimilating the rights of all refugees with regard to wage-earning employment to those of nationals, and in particular of those refugees who have entered their territory pursuant to programmes of labour recruitment or under immigration schemes.

Article 18. Self-employment

The Contracting States shall accord to a refugee lawfully in their territory treatment as favourable as possible and, in any event, not less favourable than that accorded to aliens generally in the same circumstances, as regards the right to engage on his own account in agriculture, industry, handicrafts and commerce and to establish commercial and industrial companies.

Article 19. Liberal professions

1. Each Contracting State shall accord to refugees lawfully staying in their territory who hold diplomas recognized by the competent authorities of that State, and who are desirous of practising a liberal profession, treatment as favourable as possible and, in any event, not less favourable than that accorded to aliens generally in the same circumstances.
2. The Contracting States shall use their best endeavours consistently with their laws and constitutions to secure the settlement of such refugees in the territories, other than the metropolitan territory, for whose international relations they are responsible.

CHAPTER IV

WELFARE

Article 20. Rationing

Where a rationing system exists, which applies to the population at large and regulates the general distribution of products in short supply, refugees shall be accorded the same treatment as nationals.

Article 21. Housing

As regards housing, the Contracting States, in so far as the matter is regulated by laws or regulations or is subject to the control of public authorities, shall accord to refugees lawfully staying in their territory treatment as favourable as possible and, in any event, not less favourable than that accorded to aliens generally in the same circumstances.

Article 22. Public education

1. The Contracting States shall accord to refugees the same treatment as is accorded to nationals with respect to elementary education.

2. The Contracting States shall accord to refugees treatment as favourable as possible, and, in any event, not less favourable than that accorded to aliens generally in the same circumstances, with respect to education other than elementary education and, in particular, as regards access to studies, the recognition of foreign school certificates, diplomas and degrees, the remission of fees and charges and the award of scholarships.

Article 23. Public relief

The Contracting States shall accord to refugees lawfully staying in their territory the same treatment with respect to public relief and assistance as is accorded to their nationals.

Article 24. Labour legislation and social security

1. The Contracting States shall accord to refugees lawfully staying in their territory the same treatment as is accorded to nationals in respect of the following matters;
   (a) In so far as such matters are governed by laws or regulations or are subject to the control of administrative authorities: remuneration, including family allowances where these form part of remuneration, hours of work, overtime arrangements, holidays with pay, restrictions on home work, minimum age of employment, apprenticeship and training, women's work and the work of young persons, and the enjoyment of the benefits of collective bargaining;
   (b) Social security (legal provisions in respect of employment injury, occupational diseases, maternity, sickness, disability, old age, death, unemployment, family responsibilities and any other contingency which, according to national laws or regulations, is covered by a social security scheme), subject to the following limitations:
      (i) There may be appropriate arrangements for the maintenance of acquired rights and rights in course of acquisition;
      (ii) National laws or regulations of the country of residence may prescribe special arrangements concerning benefits or portions of benefits which are payable wholly out of public funds, and concerning allowances paid to persons who do not fulfil the contribution conditions prescribed for the award of a normal pension.
2. The right to compensation for the death of a refugee resulting from employment injury or from occupational disease shall not be affected by the fact that the residence of the beneficiary is outside the territory of the Contracting State.
3. The Contracting States shall extend to refugees the benefits of agreements concluded between them, or which may be concluded between them in the future, concerning the maintenance of acquired rights and rights in the process

of acquisition in regard to social security, subject only to the conditions which apply to nationals of the States signatory to the agreements in question.
4. The Contracting States will give sympathetic consideration to extending to refugees so far as possible the benefits of similar agreements which may at any time be in force between such Contracting States and non- contracting States.

CHAPTER V

ADMINISTRATIVE MEASURES

Article 25. Administrative assistance

1. When the exercise of a right by a refugee would normally require the assistance of authorities of a foreign country to whom he cannot have recourse, the Contracting States in whose territory he is residing shall arrange that such assistance be afforded to him by their own authorities or by an international authority.
2. The authority or authorities mentioned in paragraph I shall deliver or cause to be delivered under their supervision to refugees such documents or certifications as would normally be delivered to aliens by or through their national authorities.
3. Documents or certifications so delivered shall stand in the stead of the official instruments delivered to aliens by or through their national authorities, and shall be given credence in the absence of proof to the contrary.
4. Subject to such exceptional treatment as may be granted to indigent persons, fees may be charged for the services mentioned herein, but such fees shall be moderate and commensurate with those charged to nationals for similar services.
5. The provisions of this article shall be without prejudice to articles 27 and 28.

Article 26. Freedom of movement

Each Contracting State shall accord to refugees lawfully in its territory the right to choose their place of residence and to move freely within its territory subject to any regulations applicable to aliens generally in the same circumstances.

Article 27. Identity papers

The Contracting States shall issue identity papers to any refugee in their territory who does not possess a valid travel document.

Article 28. Travel documents

1. The Contracting States shall issue to refugees lawfully staying in their territory travel documents for the purpose of travel outside their territory, unless compelling reasons of national security or public order otherwise require, and the

provisions of the Schedule to this Convention shall apply with respect to such documents. The Contracting States may issue such a travel document to any other refugee in their territory; they shall in particular give sympathetic consideration to the issue of such a travel document to refugees in their territory who are unable to obtain a travel document from the country of their lawful residence.

2. Travel documents issued to refugees under previous international agreements by Parties thereto shall be recognized and treated by the Contracting States in the same way as if they had been issued pursuant to this article.

Article 29. Fiscal charges

1. The Contracting States shall not impose upon refugees duties, charges or taxes, of any description whatsoever, other or higher than those which are or may be levied on their nationals in similar situations.
2. Nothing in the above paragraph shall prevent the application to refugees of the laws and regulations concerning charges in respect of the issue to aliens of administrative documents including identity papers.

Article 30. Transfer of assets

1. A Contracting State shall, in conformity with its laws and regulations, permit refugees to transfer assets which they have brought into its territory, to another country where they have been admitted for the purposes of resettlement.
2. A Contracting State shall give sympathetic consideration to the application of refugees for permission to transfer assets wherever they may be and which are necessary for their resettlement in another country to which they have been admitted.

Article 31. Refugees unlawfully in the country of refuge

1. The Contracting States shall not impose penalties, on account of their illegal entry or presence, on refugees who, coming directly from a territory where their life or freedom was threatened in the sense of article 1, enter or are present in their territory without authorization, provided they present themselves without delay to the authorities and show good cause for their illegal entry or presence.
2. The Contracting States shall not apply to the movements of such refugees restrictions other than those which are necessary and such restrictions shall only be applied until their status in the country is regularized or they obtain admission into another country. The Contracting States shall allow such refugees a reasonable period and all the necessary facilities to obtain admission into another country.

Article 32. Expulsion

1. The Contracting States shall not expel a refugee lawfully in their territory save on grounds of national security or public order.

2. The expulsion of such a refugee shall be only in pursuance of a decision reached in accordance with due process of law. Except where compelling reasons of national security otherwise require, the refugee shall be allowed to submit evidence to clear himself, and to appeal to and be represented for the purpose before competent authority or a person or persons specially designated by the competent authority.
3. The Contracting States shall allow such a refugee a reasonable period within which to seek legal admission into another country. The Contracting States reserve the right to apply during that period such internal measures as they may deem necessary.

Article 33. Prohibition of expulsion or return ("refoulement")

1. No Contracting State shall expel or return ("refouler") a refugee in any manner whatsoever to the frontiers of territories where his life or freedom would be threatened on account of his race, religion, nationality, membership of a particular social group or political opinion.
2. The benefit of the present provision may not, however, be claimed by a refugee whom there are reasonable grounds for regarding as a danger to the security of the country in which he is, or who, having been convicted by a final judgement of a particularly serious crime, constitutes a danger to the community of that country.

Article 34. Naturalization

The Contracting States shall as far as possible facilitate the assimilation and naturalization of refugees. They shall in particular make every effort to expedite naturalization proceedings and to reduce as far as possible the charges and costs of such proceedings.

CHAPTER VI

EXECUTORY AND TRANSITORY PROVISIONS

Article 35. Co-operation of the national authorities with the United Nations

1. The Contracting States undertake to co-operate with the Office of the United Nations High Commissioner for Refugees, or any other agency of the United Nations which may succeed it, in the exercise of its functions, and shall in particular facilitate its duty of supervising the application of the provisions of this Convention.
2. In order to enable the Office of the High Commissioner or any other agency of the United Nations which may succeed it, to make reports to the competent

organs of the United Nations, the Contracting States undertake to provide them in the appropriate form with information and statistical data requested concerning:
(a) The condition of refugees,
(b) The implementation of this Convention, and
(c) Laws, regulations and decrees which are, or may hereafter be, in force relating to refugees.

Article 36. Information on national legislation

The Contracting States shall communicate to the Secretary-General of the United Nations the laws and regulations which they may adopt to ensure the application of this Convention.

Article 37. Relation to previous conventions

Without prejudice to article 28, paragraph 2, of this Convention, this Convention replaces, as between Parties to it, the Arrangements of 5 July 1922, 31 May 1924, 12 May 1926, 30 June 1928 and 30 July 1935, the Conventions of 28 October 1933 and 10 February 1938, the Protocol of 14 September 1939 and the Agreement of 15 October 1946.

CHAPTER VII

FINAL CLAUSES

Article 38. Settlement of disputes

Any dispute between Parties to this Convention relating to its interpretation or application, which cannot be settled by other means, shall be referred to the International Court of Justice at the request of any one of the parties to the dispute.

Article 39. Signature, ratification and accession

1. This Convention shall be opened for signature at Geneva on 28 July 1951 and shall thereafter be deposited with the Secretary-General of the United Nations. It shall be open for signature at the European Office of the United Nations from 28 July to 31 August 1951 and shall be re-opened for signature at the Headquarters of the United Nations from 17 September 1951 to 31 December 1952.
2. This Convention shall be open for signature on behalf of all States Members of the United Nations, and also on behalf of any other State invited to attend the Conference of Plenipotentiaries on the Status of Refugees and Stateless

Persons or to which an invitation to sign will have been addressed by the General Assembly. It shall be ratified and the instruments of ratification shall be deposited with the Secretary-General of the United Nations.

3. This Convention shall be open from 28 July 1951 for accession by the States referred to in paragraph 2 of this article. Accession shall be effected by the deposit of an instrument of accession with the Secretary-General of the United Nations.

Article 40. Territorial application clause

1. Any State may, at the time of signature, ratification or accession, declare that this Convention shall extend to all or any of the territories for the international relations of which it is responsible. Such a declaration shall take effect when the Convention enters into force for the State concerned.
2. At any time thereafter any such extension shall be made by notification addressed to the Secretary-General of the United Nations and shall take effect as from the ninetieth day after the day of receipt by the Secretary- General of the United Nations of this notification, or as from the date of entry into force of the Convention for the State concerned, whichever is the later.
3. With respect to those territories to which this Convention is not extended at the time of signature, ratification or accession, each State concerned shall consider the possibility of taking the necessary steps in order to extend the application of this Convention to such territories, subject, where necessary for constitutional reasons, to the consent of the Governments of such territories.

Article 41. Federal clause

In the case of a Federal or non-unitary State, the following provisions shall apply:

(a) With respect to those articles of this Convention that come within the legislative jurisdiction of the federal legislative authority, the obligations of the Federal Government shall to this extent be the same as those of parties which are not Federal States;

(b) With respect to those articles of this Convention that come within the legislative jurisdiction of constituent States, provinces or cantons which are not, under the constitutional system of the Federation, bound to take legislative action, the Federal Government shall bring such articles with a favourable recommendation to the notice of the appropriate authorities of States, provinces or cantons at the earliest possible moment;

(c) A Federal State Party to this Convention shall, at the request of any other Contracting State transmitted through the Secretary-General of the United Nations, supply a statement of the law and practice of the Federation and its constituent units in regard to any particular provision of the Convention showing the extent to which effect has been given to that provision by legislative or other action.

Article 42. Reservations

1. At the time of signature, ratification or accession, any State may make reservations to articles of the Convention other than to articles 1, 3, 4, 16 (1), 33, 36-46 inclusive.
2. Any State making a reservation in accordance with paragraph I of this article may at any time withdraw the reservation by a communication to that effect addressed to the Secretary-General of the United Nations.

Article 43. Entry into force

1. This Convention shall come into force on the ninetieth day following the day of deposit of the sixth instrument of ratification or accession.
2. For each State ratifying or acceding to the Convention after the deposit of the sixth instrument of ratification or accession, the Convention shall enter into force on the ninetieth day following the date of deposit by such State of its instrument of ratification or accession.

Article 44. Denunciation

1. Any Contracting State may denounce this Convention at any time by a notification addressed to the Secretary-General of the United Nations.
2. Such denunciation shall take effect for the Contracting State concerned one year from the date upon which it is received by the Secretary-General of the United Nations.
3. Any State which has made a declaration or notification under article 40 may, at any time thereafter, by a notification to the Secretary-General of the United Nations, declare that the Convention shall cease to extend to such territory one year after the date of receipt of the notification by the Secretary-General.

Article 45.—Revision

1. Any Contracting State may request revision of this Convention at any time by a notification addressed to the Secretary-General of the United Nations.
2. The General Assembly of the United Nations shall recommend the steps, if any, to be taken in respect of such request.

Article 46. Notifications by the Secretary-General of the United Nations

The Secretary-General of the United Nations shall inform all Members of the United Nations and non-member States referred to in article 39:

(a) Of declarations and notifications in accordance with section B of article 1;
(b) Of signatures, ratifications and accessions in accordance with article 39;
(c) Of declarations and notifications in accordance with article 40;
(d) Of reservations and withdrawals in accordance with article 42;
(e) Of the date on which this Convention will come into force in accordance with article 43;
(f) Of denunciations and notifications in accordance with article 44;
(g) Of requests for revision in accordance with article 45.

IN FAITH WHEREOF the undersigned, duly authorized, have signed this Convention on behalf of their respective Governments.

DONE at Geneva, this twenty-eighth day of July, one thousand nine hundred and fifty-one, in a single copy, of which the English and French texts are equally authentic and which shall remain deposited in the archives of the United Nations, and certified true copies of which shall be delivered to all Members of the United Nations and to the non-member States referred to in article 39.

Appendix 2

Statute of the Office of the United Nations High Commissioner for Refugees G.A. Res. 428 (V) U.N. Doc. A/1775 (1950)

CHAPTER I

GENERAL PROVISIONS

1. The United Nations High Commissioner for Refugees, acting under the authority of the General Assembly, shall assume the function of providing international protection, under the auspices of the United Nations, to refugees who fall within the scope of the present Statute and of seeking permanent solutions for the problem of refugees by assisting governments and, subject to the approval of the governments concerned, private organizations to facilitate the voluntary repatriation of such refugees, or their assimilation within new national communities.
   In the exercise of his functions, more particularly when difficulties arise, and for instance with regard to any controversy concerning the international status of these persons, the High Commissioner shall request the opinion of an advisory committee on refugees if it is created.
2. The work of the High Commissioner shall be of an entirely nonpolitical character; it shall be humanitarian and social and shall relate, as a rule, to groups and categories of refugees.

3 The High Commissioner shall follow policy directives given him by the General Assembly or the Economic and Social Council.
4. The Economic and Social Council may decide, after hearing the views of the High Commissioner on the subject, to establish an advisory committee on refugees, which shall consist of representatives of States Members and States non-members of the United Nations, to be selected by the Council on the basis of their demonstrated interest in and devotion to the solution of the refugee problem.
5. The General Assembly shall review, not later than at its eighth regular session, the arrangements for the Office of the High Commissioner with a view to determining whether the Office should be continued beyond 31 December 1963.

CHAPTER II

FUNCTIONS OF THE HIGH COMMISSIONER

6. The competence of the High Commissioner shall extend to:
   A. (i) Any person who has been considered a refugee under the Arrangements of 12 May 1926 and 30 June 1928 or under the Conventions of 28 October 1933 and 10 February 1938, the Protocol of 14 September 1939 or the Constitution of the International Refugee Organization;
   (ii) Any person who, as a result of events occurring before 1 January 1951 and owing to well-founded fear of being persecuted for reasons of race, religion, nationality or political opinion, is outside the country of his nationality and is unable or, owing to such fear or for reasons other than personal convenience, is unwilling to avail himself of the protection of that country; or who, not having a nationality and being outside the country of his former habitual residence, is unable or, owing to such fear or for reasons other than personal convenience, is unwilling to return to it.
   Decisions as to eligibility taken by the International Refugee Organization during the period of its activities shall not prevent the status of refugee being accorded to persons who fulfil the conditions of the present paragraph.
   The competence of the High Commissioner shall cease to apply to any person defined in section A above if:

   (a) He has voluntarily re-availed himself of the protection of the country of his nationality; or
   (b) Having lost his nationality, he has voluntarily re-acquired it; or
   (c) He has acquired a new nationality, and enjoys the protection of the country of his new nationality; or
   (d) He has voluntarily re-established himself in the country which he left or outside which he remained owing to fear of persecution; or
   (e) He can no longer, because the circumstances in connection with which he has been recognized as a refugee have ceased to exist, claim grounds

other than those of personal convenience, for continuing to refuse to avail himself of the protection of the country of his nationality. Reasons of a purely economic character may not be invoked; or

(f) Being a person who has no nationality, he can no longer, because the circumstances in connection with which he has been recognized as a refugee have ceased to exist and he is able to return to the country of his former habitual residence, claim grounds other than those of personal convenience for continuing to refuse to return to that country.

B. Any other person who is outside the country of his nationality or, if he has no nationality, the country of his former habitual residence, because he has or had well-founded fear of persecution by reason of his race, religion, nationality or political opinion and is unable or, because of such fear, is unwilling to avail himself of the protection of the government of the country of his nationality, or, if he has no nationality, to return to the country of his former habitual residence.

7. Provided that the competence of the High Commissioner as defined in paragraph 6 above shall not extend to a person:

(a) Who is a national of more than one country unless he satisfies the provisions of the preceding paragraph in relation to each of the countries of which he is a national; or
(b) Who is recognized by the competent authorities of the country in which he has taken residence as having the rights and obligations which are. attached to the possession of the nationality of that country; or
(c) Who continues to receive from other organs or agencies of the United Nations protection or assistance; or
(d) In respect of whom there are serious reasons for considering that he has committed a crime covered by the provisions of treaties of extradition or a crime mentioned in article 6 of the London Charter of the International Military Tribunal or by the provisions of article 14, paragraph 2, of the Universal Declaration of Human Rights.

8. The High Commissioner shall provide for the protection of refugees falling under the competence of his Office by:

(a) Promoting the conclusion and ratification of international conventions for the protection of refugees, supervising their application and proposing amendments thereto;
(b) Promoting through special agreements with governments the execution of any measures calculated to improve the situation of refugees and to reduce the number requiring protection;
(c) Assisting governmental and private efforts to promote voluntary repatriation or assimilation within new national communities;
(d) Promoting the admission of refugees, not excluding those in the most destitute categories, to the territories of States;

(e) Endeavouring to obtain permission for refugees to transfer their assets and especially those necessary for their resettlement;
(f) Obtaining from governments information concerning the number and conditions of refugees in their territories and the laws and regulations concerning them;
(g) Keeping in close touch with the governments and inter-governmental organizations concerned;
(h) Establishing contact in such manner as he may think best with private organizations dealing with refugee questions;
(i) Facilitating the co-ordination of the efforts of private organizations concerned with the welfare of refugees.

9. The High Commissioner shall engage in such additional activities, including repatriation and resettlement, as the General Assembly may determine, within the limits of the resources placed at his disposal.
10. The High Commissioner shall administer any funds, public or private, which he receives for assistance to refugees, and shall distribute them among the private and, as appropriate, public agencies which he deems best qualified to administer such assistance.
The High Commissioner may reject any offers which he does not consider appropriate or which cannot be utilized.
The High Commissioner shall not appeal to governments for funds or make a general appeal, without the prior approval of the General Assembly.
The High Commissioner shall include in his annual report a statement of his activities in this field.
11. The High Commissioner shall be entitled to present his views before the General Assembly, the Economic and Social Council and their subsidiary bodies.
The High Commissioner shall report annually to the General Assembly through the Economic and Social Council; his report shall be considered as a separate item on the agenda of the General Assembly.
12. The High Commissioner may invite the co-operation of the various specialized agencies.

CHAPTER III

ORGANIZATION AND FINANCES

13. The High Commissioner shall be elected by the General Assembly on the nomination of the Secretary-General. The terms of appointment of the High Commissioner shall be proposed by the Secretary-General and approved by the General Assembly. The High Commissioner shall be elected for a term of three years, from I January 1951.
14. The High Commissioner shall appoint, for the same term, a Deputy High Commissioner of a nationality other than his own.

15. (a) Within the limits of the budgetary appropriations provided, the staff of the Office of the High Commissioner shall be appointed by the High Commissioner and shall be responsible to him in the exercise of their functions.
    (b) Such staff shall be chosen from persons devoted to the purposes of the Office of the High Commissioner.
    (c) Their conditions of employment shall be those provided under the staff regulations adopted by the General Assembly and the rules promulgated thereunder by the Secretary-General.
    (d) Provision may also be made to permit the employment of personnel without compensation.
16. The High Commissioner shall consult the governments of the countries of residence of refugees as to the need for appointing representatives therein. In any country recognizing such need, there may be appointed a representative approved by the government of that country. Subject to the foregoing, the same representative may serve in more than one country.
17. The High Commissioner and the Secretary-General shall make appropriate arrangements for liaison and consultation on matters of mutual interest.
18. The Secretary-General shall provide the High Commissioner with all necessary facilities within budgetary limitations.
19. The Office of the High Commissioner shall be located in Geneva, Switzerland.
20. The Office of the High Commission—shall be financed under the budget of the United Nations. Unless the General Assembly subsequently decides otherwise, no expenditure, other than administrative expenditures relating to the functioning of the Office of the High Commissioner, shall be borne on the budget of the United Nations, and all other expenditures relating to the activities of the High Commissioner shall be financed by voluntary contributions.
21. The administration of the Office of the High Commissioner shall be subject to the Financial Regulations of the United Nations and to the financial rules promulgated thereunder by the Secretary-General.
22. Transactions relating to the High Commissioner's funds shall be subject to audit by the United Nations Board of Auditors, provided that the Board may accept audited accounts from the agencies to which funds have been allocated. Administrative arrangements for the custody of such funds and their allocation shall be agreed between the High Commissioner and the Secretary-General in accordance with the Financial Regulations of the United Nations and rules promulgated thereunder by the Secretary-General.

Appendix 3

1967 Protocol Relating to the Status of Refugees (606 UNTS 267)

The Protocol was taken note of with approval by the Economic and Social Council in resolution 1186 (XLI) of 18 November 1966 and was taken note of by the General Assembly in resolution 2198 (XXI) of 16 December 1966. In the same resolution the General Assembly requested the Secretary-General to transmit the text of the Protocol to the States mentioned in article V thereof, with a view to enabling them to accede to the Protocol

Entry into force 4 October 1967, in accordance with article VIII

The States Parties **to the present Protocol,**

Considering that the Convention relating to the Status of Refugees done at Geneva on 28 July 1951 (hereinafter referred to as the Convention) covers only those persons who have become refugees as a result of events occurring before I January 1951,

Considering that new refugee situations have arisen since the Convention was adopted and that the refugees concerned may therefore not fall within the scope of the Convention,

Considering that it is desirable that equal status should be enjoyed by all refugees covered by the definition in the Convention irrespective of the dateline I January 1951,

Have agreed as follows:

Article 1. General provision

1. The States Parties to the present Protocol undertake to apply articles 2 to 34 inclusive of the Convention to refugees as hereinafter defined.
2. For the purpose of the present Protocol, the term "refugee" shall, except as regards the application of paragraph 3 of this article, mean any person within the definition of article I of the Convention as if the words "As a result of events occurring before 1 January 1951 and..." and the words "...as a result of such events", in article 1 A (2) were omitted.
3. The present Protocol shall be applied by the States Parties hereto without any geographic limitation, save that existing declarations made by States already Parties to the Convention in accordance with article I B (I) (a) of the Convention, shall, unless extended under article I B (2) thereof, apply also under the present Protocol.

Article 2. Co-operation of the national authorities with the United Nations

1. The States Parties to the present Protocol undertake to co-operate with the Office of the United Nations High Commissioner for Refugees, or any other agency of the United Nations which may succeed it, in the exercise of its functions, and shall in particular facilitate its duty of supervising the application of the provisions of the present Protocol.
2. In order to enable the Office of the High Commissioner or any other agency of the United Nations which may succeed it, to make reports to the competent organs of the United Nations, the States Parties to the present Protocol undertake to provide them with the information and statistical data requested, in the appropriate form, concerning:
   (a) The condition of refugees;
   (b) The implementation of the present Protocol;
   (c) Laws, regulations and decrees which are, or may hereafter be, in force relating to refugees.

Article 3. Information on national legislation

The States Parties to the present Protocol shall communicate to the Secretary-General of the United Nations the laws and regulations which they may adopt to ensure the application of the present Protocol.

Article 4. Settlement of disputes

Any dispute between States Parties to the present Protocol which relates to its interpretation or application and which cannot be settled by other means shall be referred to the International Court of Justice at the request of any one of the parties to the dispute.

Article 5. Accession

The present Protocol shall be open for accession on behalf of all States Parties to the Convention and of any other State Member of the United Nations or member of any of the specialized agencies or to which an invitation to accede may have been addressed by the General Assembly of the United Nations. Accession shall be effected by the deposit of an instrument of accession with the Secretary-General of the United Nations.

Article 6. Federal clause

In the case of a Federal or non-unitary State, the following provisions shall apply:

(a) With respect to those articles of the Convention to be applied in accordance with article I, paragraph 1, of the present Protocol that come within the legislative jurisdiction of the federal legislative authority, the obligations of the Federal Government shall to this extent be the same as those of States Parties which are not Federal States;
(b) With respect to those articles of the Convention to be applied in accordance with article I, paragraph 1, of the present Protocol that come within the legislative jurisdiction of constituent States, provinces or cantons which are not, under the constitutional system of the Federation, bound to take legislative action, the Federal Government shall bring such articles with a favourable recommendation to the notice of the appropriate authorities of States, provinces or cantons at the earliest possible moment;
(c) A Federal State Party to the present Protocol shall, at the request of any other State Party hereto transmitted through the Secretary-General of the United Nations, supply a statement of the law and practice of the Federation and its constituent units in regard to any particular provision of the Convention to be applied in accordance with article I, paragraph 1, of the present Protocol, showing the extent to which effect has been given to that provision by legislative or other action.

Article 7. Reservations and declarations

1. At the time of accession, any State may make reservations in respect of article IV of the present Protocol and in respect of the application in accordance with article I of the present Protocol of any provisions of the Convention other than those contained in articles 1, 3, 4, 16(1) and 33 thereof, provided that in the case of a State Party to the Convention reservations made under this article shall not extend to refugees in respect of whom the Convention applies.
2. Reservations made by States Parties to the Convention in accordance with article 42 thereof shall, unless withdrawn, be applicable in relation to their obligations under the present Protocol.

3. Any State making a reservation in accordance with paragraph I of this article may at any time withdraw such reservation by a communication to that effect addressed to the Secretary-General of the United Nations.
4. Declarations made under article 40, paragraphs I and 2, of the Convention by a State Party thereto which accedes to the present Protocol shall be deemed to apply in respect of the present Protocol, unless upon accession a notification to the contrary is addressed by the State Party concerned to the Secretary-General of the United Nations. The provisions of article 40, paragraphs 2 and 3, and of article 44, paragraph 3, of the Convention shall be deemed to apply *muratis mutandis* to the present Protocol.

Article 8. Entry into Protocol

1. The present Protocol shall come into force on the day of deposit of the sixth instrument of accession.
2. For each State acceding to the Protocol after the deposit of the sixth instrument of accession, the Protocol shall come into force on the date of deposit by such State of its instrument of accession.

Article 9. Denunciation

1. Any State Party hereto may denounce this Protocol at any time by a notification addressed to the Secretary-General of the United Nations.
2. Such denunciation shall take effect for the State Party concerned one year from the date on which it is received by the Secretary-General of the United Nations.

Article 10. Notifications by the Secretary-General of the United Nations

The Secretary-General of the United Nations shall inform the States referred to in article V above of the date of entry into force, accessions, reservations and withdrawals of reservations to and denunciations of the present Protocol, and of declarations and notifications relating hereto.

Article 11. Deposit in the archives of the Secretariat of the United Nations

A copy of the present Protocol, of which the Chinese, English, French, Russian and Spanish texts are equally authentic, signed by the President of the General Assembly and by the Secretary-General of the United Nations, shall be deposited in the archives of the Secretariat of the United Nations. The Secretary-General will transmit certified copies thereof to all States Members of the United Nations and to the other States referred to in article 5 above.

Appendix 4

Final Text of the AALCC'S 1966 Bangkok Principles on Status and Treatment of Refugees

Adopted on 24 June 2001 at the AALCC'S 40th Session, New Delhi, India.

Article I

Definition of the term "refugee"

1. A refugee is a person who, owing to persecution or a well-founded fear of persecution for reasons of race, colour, religion, nationality, ethnic origin, gender, political opinion or membership of a particular social group:
   (a) leaves the State of which he is a national, or the Country of his nationality, or, if he has no nationality, the State or Country of which he is a habitual resident; or,
   (b) being outside of such a State or Country, is unable or unwilling to return to it or to avail himself of its protection;
2. The term "refugee" shall also apply to every person, who, owing to external aggression, occupation, foreign domination or events seriously disturbing public order in either part or the whole of his country of origin or nationality, is compelled to leave his place of habitual residence in order to seek refuge in another place outside his country of origin or nationality.

3. A person who was outside of the State of which he is a national or the Country of his nationality, or if he has no nationality, the State of which he is a habitual resident, at the time of the events mentioned above and is unable or unwilling due to well founded fear thereof to return or to avail himself of its protection shall be considered a refugee.
4 The lawful dependents of a refugee shall be deemed to be refugees.
5. A person having more than one nationality shall not be a refugee if he is in a position to avail himself of the protection of any State or Country of which he is a national.
6. A refugee shall lose his status as refugee if:
   (i) he voluntarily returns permanently, to the State of which he was a national, or the Country of which he was a habitual resident; or
   (ii) he has voluntarily re-availed himself of the protection of the State or Country of his nationality;
   (it being understood that the loss of status as a refugee under this sub-paragraph will take place only when the refugee has successfully re-availed himself of the protection of the State of his nationality;) or
   (iii) he voluntarily acquires the nationality of another State or Country and is entitled to the protection of that State or Country; or
   (iv) he does not return to the State of which he is a national, or to the Country of his nationality, or if he has no nationality, to the State or Country of which he was a habitual resident, or if he fails to avail himself of the protection of such State or Country after the circumstances in which he became a refugee have ceased to exist.
   (Provided that this paragraph shall not apply to a refugee who is able to invoke compelling reasons arising out of previous persecution for refusing to avail himself of the protection of the country of nationality).
   (v) if it becomes evident to the country of refuge that the refugee acquired the refugee status on the basis of false information, incorrect documents or cheating which influenced the decision of national authority to grant him refugee status.
7. A person who, prior to his admission into the Country of refuge, has committed a crime against peace, a war crime, or a crime against humanity as defined in international instruments drawn up to make provisions in respect of such crimes or a serious non-political crime outside his country of refuge prior to his admission to that country as a refugee, or has committed acts contrary to the purposes and principles of the United Nations, shall not be a refugee.

Article II
Asylum to a Refugee

1. Everyone without any distinction of any kind, is entitled to the right to seek and to enjoy in other countries asylum from persecution.

2. A State has the sovereign right to grant or to refuse asylum in its territory to a refugee in accordance with its international obligations and national legislation.
3. The grant of asylum to refugees is a humanitarian, peaceful and non-political act. It shall be respected by all other States and shall not be regarded as an unfriendly act so long as its humanitarian, peaceful and non-political nature is maintained.
4. States shall, bearing in mind provisions of Article X, use their best endeavors consistent with their respective legislation to receive refugees and to secure the settlement of those refugees who, for well-founded reasons, are unable or unwilling to return to their country of origin or nationality.

Article III
Non-refoulement

1. No one seeking asylum in accordance with these Principles shall be subjected to measures such as rejection at the frontier, return or expulsion which would result in his life or freedom being threatened on account of his race, religion, nationality, ethnic origin, membership of a particular social group or political opinion. The provision as outlined above may not however be claimed by a person when there are reasonable grounds to believe the person's presence is a danger to the national security or public order of the country in which he is, or who, having been convicted by a final judgment of a particularly serious crime, constitutes a danger to the community of that country.
2. In cases where a State decides to apply any of the above-mentioned measures to a person seeking asylum, it should grant provisional asylum under such conditions as it may deem appropriate, to enable the person thus endangered to seek asylum in another country.

Article IV
Minimum standards of treatment

1. A State shall accord to refugees treatment no less favorable than that generally accorded to aliens in similar circumstances, with due regard to basic human rights as recognized in generally accepted international instruments.
2. The standard of treatment referred to in paragraph 1 shall include the rights relating to aliens contained in the Final Report of the Committee on the Status of Aliens, to the extent they are applicable to refugees.
3. A refugee shall not be denied any rights on the ground that he does not fulfill requirements which by their nature a refugee is incapable of fulfilling.
4. A refugee shall not be denied any rights on the ground that there is no reciprocity in regard to the grant of such rights between the receiving State and the State or Country of nationality of the refugee or, if he is stateless, the State or Country of his former habitual residence.

5. States undertake to apply these principles to all refugees without discrimination as to race, religion, nationality, ethnic origin, gender, membership of a particular social group or political opinion, in accordance with the principle of non-discrimination.
6. States shall adopt effective measures for improving the protection of refugee women and as appropriate, ensure that the needs and resources of refugee women are fully understood and integrated to the extent possible into their activities and programmes.
7. States shall take appropriate measures to ensure that a child who is seeking refugee status or who is considered a refugee in accordance with applicable international or domestic law and procedures shall, whether unaccompanied or accompanied by his parents or by any other person, receive appropriate protection and humanitarian assistance in the enjoyment of applicable rights set forth in the present Principles and in other international human rights instruments to which the said States are Parties.
8. States shall give special attention to the protection needs of elderly refugees to ensure not only their physical safety, and to the extent possible, the full exercise of their rights, including their right to family reunification. Special attention shall also be given to their assistance needs, including those relating to social welfare, health and housing.

Article V
Expulsion and deportation

1. Save in the national or public interest or in order to safeguard the population, the State shall not expel a refugee.
2. Before expelling a refugee, the State shall allow him a reasonable period within which to seek admission into another State. The State shall, however, have the right to apply during the period such internal measures as it may deem necessary and as applicable to aliens under such circumstances.
3. A refugee shall not be deported or returned to a State or Country where his life or liberty would be threatened for reasons of race, colour, nationality, ethnic origin, religion, political opinion, or membership of a particular social group.
4. The expulsion of a refugee shall be only in pursuance of a decision reached in accordance with due process of law. Except where compelling reasons of national security otherwise require, the refugee shall be allowed to submit evidence to clear himself, and to appeal to and be represented for the purpose before the competent authority or a person or persons specially designated by the competent authority.

Article VI
Right of return

1. A refugee shall have the right to return if he so chooses to the State of which he is a national or the country of his nationality or if he has no nationality to the State of which he is a habitual resident and in this event it shall be the duty of such a State or Country to receive him.
2. This principle should apply, inter alia, to any person who because of foreign domination, external aggression or occupation has left his habitual place of residence, or who being outside such place desires to return thereto.
3. It shall be the duty of the Government or authorities in control of such place of habitual residence to facilitate, by all means at their disposal, the return of all such persons as are referred to in the foregoing paragraph, and the restitution of their property to them.
4. This natural right of return shall also be enjoyed and facilitated to the same extent as stated above in respect of the dependants of all such persons as are referred to in paragraph 1 above.

Article VII
Voluntary repatriation

1. The essentially, voluntary character of repatriation shall be respected in all cases and no refugee shall be repatriated against his will.
2. The country of asylum, in collaboration with the country of origin, shall make adequate arrangements for the safe return of refugees who request repatriation.
3. The country of origin, shall provide all necessary documents to expedite their return on receiving back refugees, facilitate their resettlement and grant them the full rights and privileges of nationals of the country, and subject them to the same obligations.
4. Refugees who voluntarily return to their country shall in no way be penalized for having left it or for any of the reasons giving rise to refugee situations. Whenever necessary, an appeal shall be made through national information media and through the relevant universal and regional organizations inviting refugees to return home without risk and to take up a normal and peaceful life without fear of being disturbed and punished, and that the text of such appeal should be given to refugees and clearly explained to them by their country of asylum.
5. Refugees who freely decide to return to their homeland, as a result of such assurances or on their own initiative, shall be given every possible assistance by the country of asylum, the country of origin, country of transit, voluntary agencies and international and intergovernmental organizations to facilitate their return.

Article VIII
International Co-operation on comprehensive solutions

1. Voluntary repatriation, local settlement or third country resettlement, that is, the traditional solutions, all remain viable and important responses to refugee situations, even while voluntary repatriation is the pre-eminent solution. To this effect, States may undertake, with the help of inter governmental and non-governmental organizations, development measures which would underpin and broaden the acceptance of the three traditional durable solutions.
2. States shall promote comprehensive approaches, including a mix of solutions involving all concerned States and relevant international organizations in the search for and implementation of durable solutions to refugee problems.
3. The issue of root causes is crucial for solutions and international efforts should also be directed to addressing the causes of refugee movements and the creation of the political, economic, social, humanitarian and environmental conditions conducive to voluntary repatriation.

Article IX
Right to compensation

1. A refugee shall have the right to receive compensation from the State which he left or to which he was unable to return.
2. The compensation referred to in paragraph 1 shall be for such loss as bodily injury, deprivation of personal liberty in denial of human rights, death of the refugee or of the person whose dependant the refugee was, and destruction of or damage to property and assets, caused by the authority of the State or country, public officials or mob violence.
3. Where such person does not desire to return, he shall be entitled to prompt and full compensation by the Government or the authorities in control of such place of habitual residence as determined, in the absence of agreement by the parties concerned, by an international body designated or constituted for the purpose by the Secretary-General of the United Nations at the request of either party.
4. If the status of such a person is disputed by the Government or the authorities in control of such place of habitual residence, or if any other dispute arises, such matter shall also be determined, in the absence of agreement by the parties concerned, by an international body designated or constituted as specified in paragraph (3) above.

Article X
Burden Sharing

1. The refugee phenomenon continues to be a matter of global concern and needs the support of international community as a whole for its solution and as such the principle of burden sharing should be viewed in that context.
2. The principle of international solidarity and burden sharing needs to be applied progressively to facilitate the process of durable solutions for refugees, whether within or outside a particular region, keeping in perspective that durable solutions in certain situations may need to be found by allowing access to refugees in countries outside that region, due to political, social and economic considerations.
3. The principle of international solidarity and burden sharing should be seen as applying to all aspects of the refugee situation, including the development and strengthening of the standards of treatment of refugees, support to States in protecting and assisting refugees, the provision of durable solutions and the support of international bodies with responsibilities for the protection and assistance of refugees.
4. International solidarity and co-operation in burden sharing should be manifested whenever necessary, through effective concrete measures where major share be borne by developed countries in support of States requiring assistance, whether through financial or material aid (or) through resettlement opportunities.
5. In all circumstances, the respect for fundamental humanitarian principles is an obligation for all members of the international community. Giving practical effect to the principle of international solidarity and burden sharing considerably facilitates States fulfillment of their responsibilities in this regard.

Article XI
Obligations

A refugee shall not engage in subversive activities endangering the national security of the country of refuge, or any other country or in activities inconsistent with or against the principles and purposes of the United Nations.

Article XII
Rights granted apart from these Principles

Nothing in these Articles shall be deemed to impair any higher rights and benefits granted or which may hereafter be granted by a State to refugees.

Article XIII
Co-operation with international organizations
States shall co-operate with the office of the United Nations High Commissioner for Refugees and, in the region of its mandate, with the United Nations Relief and Works Agency for Palestine Refugees in the Near-East.

NOTES MADE BY THE MEMBER STATES OF AALCO

Introductory Remarks

1. These notes, comments and reservations are an integral part of the main document of the Revised Bangkok Principles.
2. The Revised Bangkok Principles are declaratory and non-binding in character and aim inter alia at inspiring Member States for enacting national legislation for the Status and Treatment of Refugees and as a guide to deal with the refugee problems.
3. In all the Articles and paragraphs where it is referred to "**The unwillingness of the refugee to go back to his country of origin, nationality or habitual residence**", it is fully understood that this unwillingness is not a choice that the refugee can exercise on his own regardless of the consent of the country of asylum but means that the reasons of his well founded fears are still persistent and that his life or liberty if he is compelled to return would be threatened. Moreover the refugee can invoke convincing reasons out of previous persecution for refusing to return to one of the States mentioned above.
4. When the words "he" or "his" are used in the text, should be read to include "she" or "her".

Bibliography

Books and Articles

Abrar, C. R. (ed.), *On the Margin: Refugees, Migrants and Minorities* (Dhaka: Refugee and Migratory Movements Research Unit, 2000).
——, 'Legal Protection of Refugees in South Asia', *Forced Migration Review*, 10 (April 2001).
Acharya, A., *Constructing a Security Community in Southeast Asia: ASEAN and the Problem of Regional Order* (London: Routledge, 2001).
——, *The Quest for Identity: International Relations of Southeast* Asia (Oxford: Oxford University Press, 2000).
Afolayan, A. A., 'Issues and Challenges of Emigration Dynamics in Developing Countries', *International Migration*, Vol. 39, No. 4 (2001).
Ahmed, S. R., *Forlorn Migrants: An International Legal Regime for Undocumented Migrant Workers* (Dhaka: The University Press Limited, 2000).
Akehurst, M., 'Custom as a Source of International Law', *British Yearbook of International Law*, Vol. 47, pp. 1–53.
Alexander, M., 'Refugee Status Determination Conducted by UNHCR', *International Journal of Refugee Law*, Vol. 11, No. 2 (1999), pp. 251–289.
Allen, R., *A Short Introduction to the History and Politics of Southeast Asia* (New York: Oxford University Press, 1970).
Anghie, A., *Imperialism, Sovereignty and the Making of International Law* (Cambridge: Cambridge University Press, 2004), pp. 3–5, 198.
Barakat, H. I., 'The Palestinian Refugees: An Uprooted Community Seeking Repatriation', *International Migration Review*, Vol. 7, No. 2 (Summer 1973), pp. 147–161.
Barcher, A., 'First Asylum in Southeast Asia: Customary Norm or Ephemeral Concept', *New York University Journal of International Law and Policy*, Vol. 24 (1991–1992), pp. 1253–1286.
Barnett, M. and Martha Finnemore, *Rules for the World: International Organization in Global Politics* (Ithaca: Cornell University Press, 2004).
Barr, M. D., *Cultural Politics and Asian Values: The Tepid War* (London: Routledge, 2006).
Battistella, G. and Maruja M. B. Asis (eds.), *Unauthorized Migration in Southeast Asia* (Quezon City: Scalabrini Migration Center, 2003).
Beck, R. J., Anthony Clark Arend and Robert D. Vander Lugt. *International Rules: Approaches from International Law and International Relations* (New York: Oxford University Press, 1996).
Beeson, Mark (ed.), *Contemporary Southeast Asia: Regional Dynamics, National Differences* (Hampshire: Palgrave Macmillan, 2004).
Bem, K., 'The Coming of the "Blank Cheque"—Europe, the 1951 Convention, and the 1967 Protocol', *International Journal of Refugee Law*, Vol. 16, No. 4 (2004), pp. 609–627.

Bernstein, A. and Myron Weiner (eds.), *Migration and Refugee Policies: An Overview*, (London: Pinter, 1999).
Bohning, W. R., 'Conceptualizing and Simulating the Impact of the Asian Crisis on Filipino's Employment Opportunities Abroad', *Asian and Pacific Migration Journal*, Vol. 7, No. 2–3 (1998).
Boltanski, L., *Distant Suffering: Morality, Media and Politics*. Translated by Graham Burchell (Cambridge: Cambridge University Press, 1999).
Bronee, S. A., 'The History of the Comprehensive Plan of Action', *International Journal of Refugee Law*, 5 (4), 1993.
Brownlie, I., *The Rule of Law in International Affairs: International Law at the Fiftieth Anniversary of the United Nations* (The Hague: Martinus Nijhoff Publishers, 1998).
Bull, H., Benedict Kingsbury and Adam Roberts, *Hugo Grotius and International Relations* (Oxford: Clarendon Press, 1990).
Byers, M. *Custom, Power and the Power of Rules: International Relations and Customary International Law* (Cambridge: Cambridge University Press, 1999).
—— (ed.), *The Role of Law in International Politics: Essays in International Relations and International Law* (Oxford: Oxford University Press, 2000).
Byers, M. and George Nolte (eds.), *United States Hegemony and the Foundations of International Law* (Oxford: Oxford University Press, 2003).
Cass, D. Z., 'Navigating the Newstream: Recent Critical Scholarship in International Law', *Nordic Journal of International Law*, Vol. 65 (1996), pp. 341–383.
Castles, S., 'New Migrations in the Asia-Pacific region: a force for social and political change', *International Social Science Journal*, Volume 48, Issue 156, (1998), pp. 215–228.
Cerquone, J., *Refugees From Laos: In Harm's Way* (Washington: American Council for Nationalities Service, 1986).
Chan Kwok Bun, Ong Jin Hui and Chew Soon Beng (eds.), *Crossing Borders: Transmigration in Asia Pacific* (Singapore: Prentice Hall, 1995).
Chanda, N., *Brother Enemy: The War after the War* (New York: Collier, 1986).
Chang-Muy, F., 'International Refugee Law in Asia', *New York University Journal of International Law and Politics*, 24, 1992.
Chantavanich, S. and E. Bruce Reynolds, *Indochinese Refugees: Asylum and Resettlement* (Bangkok: Institute of Asian Studies, Chulalongkorn University, 1988).
Charlesworth, H. and Christine Chinkin, *The Boundaries of International Law: A feminist Analysis* (Manchester: Manchester University Press, 2000).
Chatelard, G., 'Jordan as a transit country: semi-protectionist immigration policies and their effects on Iraqi forced migrants', *New Issues in Refugee Research*, Working Paper No. 61 (Geneva: UNHCR Research Unit, 2002).
Cheng, S. (ed.), *Law, Justice, and Power. Between Reason and Will* (Stanford: Stanford University Press, 2004).
Chimni, B. S., 'The Geopolitics of Refugee Studies: A View from the South', *Journal of Refugee Studies*, Vol. 11, No. 4 (1998), pp. 350–374.
——, *International Refugee Law: A Reader* (New Delhi: Sage Publications, 2000).
——, 'Protection of Refugees in South Asia: Need for a Legal Framework', in *South Asian Forum for Human Rights Refugee Studies Project* (Kathmandu: SAFHR, 2000).
Chimni, B. S., 'Reforming the International Refugee Regime: A Dialogic Model', *Journal of Refugee Studies*, Vol. 14, No. 2 (2001), pp. 151–168.
Clark, I., *Legitimacy in International Society* (Oxford: Oxford University Press, 2005).
Cohen, S., *States of Denial: Knowing about Atrocities and Suffering* (Cambridge: Polity Press, 2001).
Crisp, J., 'Who has counted the refugees? UNHCR and the politics of numbers', *New Issues in Refugee Research*, Working Paper No. 12, June 1999, (Geneva: UNHCR Policy Research Unit).
D'Amato, A. (ed.), *International Law: Prospect and Process* (New York: Transnational Publishers, 1987).
——, 'Is International Law Really Law?', *Northwestern University Law Review*, Vol. 79 (1985), pp. 1293–1314.
Daum, Andreas W., Lloyd C. Gardner and Wilfried Mausbach (eds.), *America, the Vietnam War, and the World: Comparative and International Perspectives* (Washington, D.C.; German Historical Institute New York: Cambridge University Press, 2003).
Davies, S. E., 'Start Looking South: The Refugee Convention Fifty Years On', *International Journal of Human Rights*, Vol. 8, No. 3 (Autumn 2004), pp. 355–366.
Deutsch, K. W. and Stanley Hoffmann (eds.), *The Relevance of International Law: Essays in Honor of Leo Gross* (Cambridge: Schenkman, 1968).

Donelly, J., *Universal Human Rights in Theory and Practice* (New York: Cornell University Press, 2002).
Druke, L., *Preventative Action for Refugee Producing Situations* (Frankfurt am Main: Peter Lang. 1993).
Evans, G. and K. Rowley, *Red Brotherhood at War: Vietnam, Cambodia and Laos since 1975*, 2nd edn. (London: Verso, 1990).
Falk, R and Saul Mendlovitz (eds.), *The Strategy of World Order, Vol. II, International Law* (New York: World Law Fund, 1966).
Feller, E., 'The Evolution of the International Refugee Protection Regime', *Washington University Journal of Law and Policy*, Volume 5, 2001.
Feller, E., Volker Turk and Frances Nicholson (eds.), *Refugee Protection in International Law: UNHCR's Global Consultations on International Protection* (Cambridge: Cambridge University Press, 2003).
Fitzpatrick, D., 'Land Policy in post-conflict circumstances: some lessons from East Timor', *New Issues in Refugee Research*, (Geneva: UNHCR Research Unit, 2002).
Fitzpatrick, J. (ed.), *Human Rights Protection for Refugees, Asylum-Seekers, and Internally Displaced Persons: A Guide to International Mechanisms and Procedures* (New York: Transnational Publishers, 2002).
Forsythe, D. P., 'UNRWA, the Palestine Refugees, and World Politics: 1949–1969', *International Organization*, Vol. 25, No. 1 (Winter 1971), pp. 26–45.
Fortin, 'The Meaning of "Protection" in the Refugee Definition', *International Journal of Refugee Law*, 12 (4), 2001, pp. 548–576.
Franck, T. M., 'Lessons of the Failure of the NIEO', *International Law and Development*, (Proceedings of the Canadian Council on International Law) (1986).
——, *Fairness in International Law and Institutions* (Oxford: Clarendon Press, 1995).
——, *The Power of Legitimacy Among Nations* (New York: Oxford University Press, 1990).
——, 'Legitimacy in the International System', *American Journal of International Law*, Vol. 82 (1988), pp. 705–759.
——, 'Human Rights, Asia and the West' in J. T. H. Tang (ed.), *Human Rights and International Relations in the Asia Pacific Region* (London/New York: Pinter, 1995), pp. 13–24.
Gallagher, D., *The Era of Refugees: The Evolution of the International Refugee System* (Washington: Refugee Policy Group, 1989).
Ghosh, B., *Huddled Masses and Uncertain Shores: Insights into Irregular Migration* (The Hague: Martinus Nijhoff, 1998).
Giri, T. N., *Refugee Problems in Asia and Africa: Role of the UNHCR* (New Delhi: Manak Publications, 2003).
Goldsmith, J. L. and Eric A., Posner, *The Limits of International Law* (Oxford: Oxford University Press, 2005).
Goodwin-Gill, G., *The Refugee in International Law* (Oxford: Clarendon Press, 1996).
Grahl-Madsen, A. *The Land Beyond: Collected Essays on Refugee Law and Policy*, edited by P. Macalister-Smith and Gundmundur Alfredsson (The Hague: Martinus Nijhoff Publishers, 2001).
Greig, D. W., 'The Protection of Refugees and Customary International Law', *Australian Yearbook of International Law*, Vol. 8 (1980), pp. 108–1141.
Grieco, J. M., 'Anarchy and the Limits of Cooperation: A Realist Critique of the Newest Liberal Institutionalism', *International Organization*, Vol. 42 (1988).
Haacke, J., *ASEAN's Diplomatic and Security Culture: Origins, Development and Prospects* (London: Routledge Curzon, 2003).
Hailbronner, K., 'Non-refoulement and 'Humanitarian' Refugees: Customary International Law or Wishful Legal Thinking?', *Virginia Journal of International Law*, Vol. 26, No. 4 (1986).
Hambro, E., *The Problem of Chinese Refugees in Hong Kong* (Leiden: A. W. Sijthoff, 1955).
Hart, H. L. A., *The Concept of Law* (Oxford: Oxford University Press, 1994).
Hathaway, J, 'Reconceiving Refugee Law as Human Rights Protection', *Journal of Refugee Studies*, Volume 4, Number 2, 1991.
——, *The Law of Refugee Status* (Toronto: Butterworths, 1991).
—— (ed.), *Reconceiving International Law* (The Hague: Kluwer Law International, 1997).
——, 'Labelling the 'boat people': the failure of the human rights mandate of the Comprehensive Plan of Action for Indochinese Refugees', *Human Rights Quarterly*, Vol. 15, No. 4 (Nov 1993), pp. 686–702.
Helton, A., *The Price of Indifference: Refugees and Humanitarian Action in the New Century* (Oxford: Oxford University Press, 2002).

——, 'Refugee Determination under the Comprehensive Plan of Action: Overview and Assessment', *International Journal of Refugee Law*, 5 (4), 1993, pp. 544–558.
——, 'The Malaysian Policy to Redirect Vietnamese Boat People: *Non-refoulement* as a Human Rights Remedy', *New York University Journal of International Law and Politics*, Volume 24, 1992.
——, 'The Comprehensive Plan of Action for Indo-Chinese Refugees: An Experiment in Refugee Protection and Control', *New York Law School Journal of Human Rights*, Vol. 8 (1990), pp. 111–148.
Higgins, R., *Problems and Process: International Law and How We Use It* (Oxford: Oxford University Press, 1994).
——,'Policy Considerations and the International Judicial Process', *International and Comparative Law Quarterly*, Vol. 17, No. 1 (1968), pp. 58–84.
Hobden, S. and John M Hobson (eds.), *Historical Sociology of International Relations* (Cambridge: Cambridge University Press, 2002).
Holborn, L., *Refugees: A Problem of Our Time. The Work of the United Nations High Commissioner for Refugees, 1951–1972*, Volume 1 (New Jersey: The Scarecrow Press, 1975).
——, *The International Refugee Organization: A Specialized Agency of the United Nations Its History and Work 1946–1952* (London: Oxford University Press, 1956).
——, *The League of Nations and the Problem of Refugees: A Study of the Development of International Government and Administration in Post-War Europe* (Radcliffe College: Thesis, 1937).
Holborn, L. W., 'The Legal Status of Political Refugees 1920–1938, *American Journal of International Law*, Volume 32, Issue 4 (Oct. 1938), pp. 680–703.
Hovy, B., 'Statistics on Forced Migration', *Migration Information Source*, 1 September 2002. http:/www.migrationinformation.org/Feature/print.cfm. http://www.publications.parliament.uk/pa/cm199091/cmhansrd/1991–07–25/Debate-1.html
Hugo, G., 'Migration and Development: A Perspective from Asia', *IOM Migration Research Series*, Number 14 (Geneva: International Organization for Migration, 2003).
Iredale, R., Fei Guo and Rozario, S. (eds.), *Return Migration in the Asia Pacific* (Cheltenham: Edward Elgar, 2003).
Iredale, R., Tim Turpin and Charles Hawksley, 'Migration research and migration policy making: a study of Australia, the Philippines and Thailand', *International Social Sciences Journal*, Vol. 56, Issue 179 (2004), pp. 115–134.
Jackson, I. C., *The Refugee Concept in Group Situations* (The Hague: Martinus Nijhoff Publishers, 1999).
Jacobsen, K., 'Factors influencing the policy responses of host governments to mass refugee influxes', *International Migration Review*, Vol. 30, No. 3 (Fall 1996), pp. 655–679.
——, 'Just Enough for the City: Urban Refugees Make 'Their Own Way', *World Refugee Survey Report 2004* (Washington: United States Committee for Refugees, 2004), pp. 57–65.
——, 'The Forgotten Solution: Local Integration for Refugees in Developing Countries', *UNHCR New Issues in Research*, Working Paper No. 45 (Geneva: UNHCR, 2001).
——, 'A Framework for Exploring the Political and Security Context of Refugee Populated Areas', *Journal of Refugee Studies*, Vol. 19, No. 1 (2000), pp. 3–22.
Jacobsen, M. and Ole Bruun (eds.), *Human Rights and Asian Values: contesting national identities and cultural representations in Asia* (Richmond: Curzon, 2000).
Joly, D. (ed.), *Global Changes in Asylum Regimes* (Hampshire: Palgrave Macmillan, 2002).
Joyner, Christopher C. (ed.), *The United Nations and International Law* (Cambridge: Cambridge University Press; The American Society of International Law, 1997).
Kamm, H., 'Geneva Meeting Yields Few Pledges of Aid for Indochinese Refugees', in *The New York Times*, 17 December 1978.
——, 'While Refugees Wait Off Malaysian Coast, Talks Remain at Impasse', *The New York Times*, 18 November 1978.
Kelsen, H., *The Principles of International Law*, Edited by R. W. Tucker (New York: Holt, Rinehart & Winston, 1966).
Kennedy, D., 'Tom Franck and the Manhattan School', *International Law and Politics*, Vol. 35 (2003), pp. 414–397–435.
——, *International Legal Structures* (Baden-Baden: Nomos, 1987).
——, 'A New Stream in International Law Scholarship', *Wisconsin International Law Journal*, Vol. 7, No. 1 (1988–89), pp. 1–49.
——, 'The Politics of the Invisible College: International Governance and the Politics of Expertise', *European Human Rights Law Review*, Vol. 5 (2001), pp. 463–497.

——, 'The Sources of International Law', *American University Journal of International Law and Policy*, Vol. 2, No. 1 (1987), pp. 1–96.
——, 'Theses about International Law Discourse', *German Yearbook of International Law,* Volume 23 (1980), pp. 353–391.
Kennedy, D. and Chris Tennant, 'New Approaches to International Law: A Bibliography', *Harvard International Law Journal,* Vol. 35, No. 2 (1994), pp. 417–460.
Kent, Jonathan, 'Malaysia's Trouble with Migrants', *BBC News*, accessed: 7 April 2005. http://www.news.bbc.co.uk/1/hi/world/asia-pacific/
Khan, G., 'Citizenship and statelessness in South Asia', *New Issues in Refugee Research*, Working Paper No. 47 (Geneva: UNHCR Research Unit, 2001).
Kibreab, G., 'Displacement, host government' policies, and constraints on the construction of sustainable livelihoods', *International Social Science Journal*, Vol. 55, Issue 175 (March 2003), pp. 57–67.
Knop, K., *Diversity and Self Determination in International Law* (Cambridge: Cambridge University Press, 2002).
Koh, H. H., 'Transnational Legal Process', *Nebraska Law Review*, Vol. 75 (1996), pp. 181–207.
Koskenniemi, M., *From Apology to Utopia: The Structure of International Legal Argument* (Helsinki: Finnish Lawyers' Publishing Company, 1989).
Koskenniemi, M. *From Apology to Utopia: The Structure of International Legal Argument* (Helsinki: Lakimiesliiton Kustannus, 1989).
——, *From Apology to Utopia: The Structure of International Legal Arguments, Reissue with New Epilogue* (Cambridge: Cambridge University Press, 2005).
——, *The Gentle Civilizer of Nations: The Rise and Fall of International Law 1870–1960* (Cambridge: Cambridge University Press, 2001).
—— (ed.), *Sources of International Law* (Aldershot: Ashgate Dartmouth, 2000).
——, 'International Law and Hegemony: A Reconfiguration', *Cambridge Review of International Affairs*, Vol. 17, No. 3 (2004), pp. 197–218.
——, 'International Law in Europe: Between Tradition and Renewal', *European Journal of International Law*, Vol. 16, No. 1 (2005), pp. 113–124.
——, 'Letter to the Editors of the Symposium', *American Journal of International Law*, Vol. 93, No. 2 (1999), pp. 351–361.
——, 'The Future of Statehood', *Harvard International Law Journal,* Vol. 32 (1991), pp. 387–410.
——, 'The Normative Force of Habit: International Custom and Social Theory', *Finnish Yearbook of International Law*, Vol. 1 (1990), pp. 77–153.
——, 'The Politics of International Law', *European Journal of International Law*, Vol. 1 (1990), pp. 4–32.
Kourula, P., *Broadening the Edges: Refugee Definition and International Protection Revisited* (The Hague: Martinus Nijhoff Publishers, 1997).
Krasner, S. D., *Sovereignty: Organized Hypocrisy* (Princeton: Princeton University Press, 1999).
Kratochwil, F. V., *Rules, Norms and Decisions: On the conditions of practical and legal reasoning in international relations and domestic affairs* (Cambridge: Cambridge University Press, 1989).
Lang, H., *Fear and Sanctuary: Burmese Refugees in Thailand* (Ithaca: Cornell University Press, 2002).
——, 'The repatriation predicament of Burmese refugees in Thailand: a preliminary analysis', *New Issues in Refugee Research*, Working Paper No. 46 (Geneva: UNHCR Research Unit, 2001).
Langlois, A., *The Politics of Justice and Human Rights: Southeast Asia and Universalist Theory* (Cambridge: Cambridge University Press, 2001).
Loescher, G., *Beyond Charity: International Cooperation and the Global Refugee Crisis* (New York: Oxford University Press, 1993.
——, *The UNHCR and World Politics: A Perilous Path* (New York: Oxford University Press, 2001).
Loescher, G. and James Milner, 'The Missing Link: the need for comprehensive engagement in regions of refugee origin', *International Affairs*, Vol. 79, No. 3, (2003).
Loescher, G. and Laila Monhahan (eds.), *Refugees and International Relations* (New York: Oxford University Press, 1989).
M. Weiner (ed.), *International Migration and Security* (Boulder: Westview Press, 1995).
M. A. B., Siddique (ed.), *International Migration into the 21st Century: Essays in Honour of Reginald Appleyard* (Cheltenham: Edward Elgar, 2001).
Marrus, M. R., *The Unwanted: European Refugees in the Twentieth Century* (New York: Oxford University Press, 1985).

Martin, V., 'Myanarese Refugees in Thailand: No Freedom, No Choices', *World Refugee Survey Report 2004* (Washington: United States Committee for Refugees, 2004), pp. 82–89.
Massey, D. A., Joaquin Arango, Graeme Hugo, Ali Kouaouri, Adela Pellegrino and J. Edward Taylor, *Worlds in Motion: Understanding International Migration at the End of the Millenium* (Oxford: Clarendon Press, 1998).
McDougal, M., and W. M. Reisman, *International Law in Contemporary Perspective* (New Haven: Yale University Press, 1980).
McDougal, M., H. Lasswell and M. Reisman, 'The World Constitutive Process of Authoritative Decision', *Journal of Legal Education*, Vol. 19, No. 3 (1966), pp. 253–300.
McKenna, T. M., *Muslim Rulers and Rebels: Everyday Politics and Armed Separatism in the Southern Philippines* (Berkeley: University of California Press, 1998).
Millbank, A., 'The Problem with the 1951 Convention', *Parliament of Australia Research Paper* (2001).
Moeller, S. D., *Compassion Fatigue: How the Media Sell Disease, Famine, War and Death* (London: Routledge, 1998).
Morgenthau, H. J., *Politics Among Nations: The Struggle for Power and Peace* (New York: Alfred A. Knopf, 1978).
——, 'Positivism, Functionalism and International Law', *American Journal of International Law*, Vol. 34 (1940).
Morris, B., *The Birth of the Palestinian Refugee Problem Revisited* (Cambridge: Cambridge University Press, 2003).
Muni, S. D. and Lok Raj Baral (eds.), *Refugees and Regional Security in South Asia* (Delhi: Konark Publishers, Regional Centre for Strategic Studies, Sri Lanka, 1996).
Muntarbhorn, V., *The Status of Refugees in Asia* (Oxford: Clarendon Press, 1992).
Nadig, A., 'Forced Migration and Global Processes Report of the Eighth Conference of the International Association for the Study of Forced Migration, Chiang Mai, Thailand, 5–9 January 2003', *Journal of Refugee Studies*, Vol. 16, No. 4 (2003), p. 364.
Nardin, T., *Law, Morality and the Relations of States* (Princeton: Princeton University Press, 1983).
Newman, E. and Joanne Van Selm (eds.), *Refugees and Forced Displacement: International Security, Human Vulnerability and the State* (Tokyo: United Nations University Press, 2003).
Nichols, A. and Paul White, *Refugee Dilemmas: Reviewing the Comprehensive Plan of Action for Vietnamese Asylum Seekers* (Manila: LAWASIA Human Rights Committee, 1993).
Nicholson, F. and Partick Twomey (eds.), *Refugee Rights and Realities: Evolving International Concepts and Regimes* (Cambridge: Cambridge University Press, 1999).
O. J. Hui, Chan Kwok Bun and Chew Soon Beng (eds.), *Crossing Borders: Transmigration in the Asia-Pacific* (Singapore: Simon and Schuster/Prentice Hall, 1995).
O'Connor Sutter, V., *The Indochinese Refugee Dilemma* (Baton Rouge: Louisiana State University Press, 1990).
OECD, *International Migration in Asia: Trends and Policies* (Paris: Organisation for Economic Co-operation and Development [OECD], 2001).
Oppenheim, L., 'The Science of International Law', *American Journal of International Law*, Vol. 2 (1908), pp. 313–356.
Poole, P. A., *The Vietnamese in Thailand: A Historical Perspective* (London: Cornell University Press, 1970).
Proudfoot, M. J., *European Refugees: 1939–1952 A Study in Forced Population Movement* (London: Faber and Faber, 1957).
Purvis, N., 'Critical Legal Studies in Public International Law', *Harvard International Law Journal*, Vol. 32, No. 1 (1991), pp. 81–127.
Radley, K. R., 'The Palestinian Refugees: The Right to Return in International Law', *The American Journal of International Law*, Vo. 72, No. 3 (July 1978), pp. 586–614.
Rajagopal, B., *International Law from Below: Development, Social Movements and Third World Resistance* (Cambridge: Cambridge University Press, 2003).
Rajaram, P. K., 'Humanitarianism and Representations of the Refugee', *Journal of Refugee Studies*, Vol. 15, No. 3 (2002), pp. 247–264.
Ramcharan, P., 'ASEAN and Non-Interference: A Principle Maintained', *Contemporary Southeast Asia*, 22(1) (2000), p. 65.
Read, J. M., *Magna Carta for Refugees* (New York: United Nations Department of Public Information, 1953).
——, *The United Nations and Refugees—Changing Concepts* (Geneva: Carnegie Endowment for Peace, 1962).

Refugees International, 'Protecting Burmese Refugees in Thailand', *Asian News Tribune*, 25 January 2003. http:///www.asiantribune.com/show_news.

Reisman, W. M., 'The View from the New Haven School of International Law', *American Society of International Law Proceedings*, Vol. 86 (1992), pp. 118–124.

Reus-Smit, C. (ed.), *The Politics of International Law* (Cambridge: Cambridge University Press, 2004).

Robinson, W. C., *Terms of Refuge: The Indochinese Exodus and the International Response* (London: Zed Books, 1998).

Rogge, J. R. (ed.), *Refugees: A Third World Dilemma* (New Jersey: Lowman & Littlefield, 1987).

Ruthstrom-Ruin, C., *Beyond Europe: The Globalization of Refugee Aid* (Lund: Lund University Press, 1993).

Sassen, S., *Guest and Aliens* (New York: The New Press, 1999).

Sathirathai, S., 'An Understanding of the Relationship Between International Legal Discourse and Third World Countries', *Harvard International Law Journal*, Vol. 25 (1984), pp. 395–419.

Shaw, M. N., *International Law*, Fifth Ed. (Cambridge: Cambridge University Press, 2003).

Shiblak, A., 'Residency Status and Civil Rights of Palestinian Refugees in Arab Countries', *Journal of Palestine Studies*, Vol. 25, No. 3 (Spring 1995), pp. 36–45.

Simpson, G. J. (ed.), *The Nature of International Law* (Aldershot: Dartmouth Ashgate, 2001).

——, 'Imagined Consent: Democratic Liberalism in International Legal Theory', *Australian Yearbook of International Law*, Vol. 15 (1994), pp. 103–128.

——, 'The Situation on the International Legal Theory Front: The Power of Rules and the Rules of Power', *European Journal of International Law*, Vol. 11, No. 2 (2000), pp. 439–464.

Simpson, J. H., *Refuges: A Review of the Situation Since September 1938* (London: The Royal Institute of International Affairs, 1939).

Skinner, Q., *Liberty before Liberalism* (Cambridge: Cambridge University Press, 1998).

Skran, C., *Refugees in Inter-War Europe: The Emergence of a Regime* (Oxford: Clarendon Press, 1995).

Slaughter Burley, A.-M., 'International Law and International Relations Theory: A Dual Agenda', *The American Journal of International Law*, Vol. 87 (1993), pp. 205–239.

Snyder, F. and S. Sathirathai. *Third World Attitudes to International Law: An Introduction* (Dordrecht: Matinus Nijhoff, 1987).

Soguk, N., *States and Strangers: Refugees and Displacements of Statecraft* (Minneapolis: University of Minnesota Press, 1999).

Spegele, R. D., *Political Realism in International Relations Theory* (Cambridge: Cambridge University Press, 1996).

Stedman, S. J. and Fred Tanner (eds.), *Refugee Manipulation: War, Politics and the Abuse of Human Suffering* (Washington: Brookings Institution Press, 2003).

Stein, B., 'The Geneva Conferences and the Indochinese Refugee Crisis', *International Migration Review*, Vol. 13, No. 4, (Winter 1979).

Steiner, N., Mark Gibney and Gil Loescher (eds.), *Problems of Protection: the UNHCR, Refugees and Human Rights* (New York: Routledge, 2003).

Stoessinger, J. G., *The Refugee and the World Community* (Minneapolis: The University of Minnesota Press, 1956).

Stueck, W., *The Korean War: An International History* (Princeton: Princeton University Press, 1995).

Suhrke, A., 'Indochinese Refugees: The Impact on First Asylum Countries and Implications for American Policy', *A Study Prepared for the Use of the Joint Economic Committee Congress of the United States* (Washington: US Government Printing Office, 1980).

——, 'Indochinese Refugees: The Law and Politics of First Asylum', *ANNALS of the American Academy of Political and Social Science*, Volume 467 (May 1983), pp. 102–115.

Talbott, W., *Which Rights should be Universal?* (New York: Oxford University Press, 2005).

Thomas, C. and Peter Wilkin (eds.), *Globalization, Human Security and the African Experience* (Boulder: Lynne Rienner, 1999).

Tsyamenyi, B. M., 'The "Boat People": Are They Refugees?', *Human Rights Quarterly*, Vol. 5 (1983), pp. 349–373.

Tuitt, P., *False Images: Law's Construction of the Refugee* (London: Pluto Press, 1996).

Tully, J. (ed.), *Meaning and Context: Quinton Skinner and his Critics* (Cambridge: Polity Press, 1988).

United Nations High Commissioner for Refugees (UNHCR), *The State of the World's Refugees* (New York: Oxford University Press, 2000).

United States Committee for Refugees (USCR), *World Refugee Survey 2004* (Washington: USCR, 2004).
van Selm, J., K*hoti Kamanga, John Morrison,* Aninia Nadig, Sanja Spoljar-Vrzina, *and Loes van Willigen (eds.), The Refugee Convention at Fifty: A View from Forced Migration Studies* (Lanham: Lexington Books, 2003).
Velikonja, J., 'Postwar Population Movements in Europe', *Annals of the Association of American Geographers,* Vol. 48, No. 4 (Dec, 1958), pp. 458–472.
Vernant, J., *The Refugee in the Post-War World* (London: George Allen & Unwin Ltd, 1953).
Vijayakumar, V., 'Judicial Responses to Refuge Protection in India', *International Journal of Refugee Law,* Vol. 12, No. 2 (2000), pp. 235–243.
Vinacke, H. M., *A History of the Far East in Modern Times* (London: George Allen and Unwin, 1960).
Vincent, M. and Birgitte Refslund Sorensen (eds.), Caught *Between Borders: Response Strategies of the Internally Displaced* (London: Pluto Press, Norwegian Refugee Council, 2001).
Waever, O., Barry Buzan, Morten Kelstrup and Pierre Lemaitre (eds.), *Identity, Migration and the New Security Agenda in Europe* (New York: St Martin's Press, 1993).
Wain, B., *The Refused: The Agony of the Indochina Refugees* (Hong Kong: Dow Jones [Asia] Company Ltd., 1981).
Waltz, K., *Theory of International Relations* (Reading, London: Addison-Wesley, 1979).
Watson, J., 'A Realistic Jurisprudence', *Yearbook of World Affairs,* Vol. 30 (1980), p. 280.
Weil, P., 'Towards Relative Normativity in International Law?', *American Journal of International Law,* Vol. 73 (1983), pp. 413–442.
Weiner, M. (ed.), *International Migration and Security* (Boulder: Westview Press, 1993).
Weis, P., *The Refugee Convention 1951: The Travaux Preparatoires Analysed, with a Commentary by the late Dr Paul Weis* (Cambridge: University of Cambridge, 1995).
Weisner, L., *Victims and Survivors: Displaced Persons and Other War Victims in Vietnam, 1964–1975* (New York: Greenwood Press, 1988).
Weston, B. and Michael Weisman (eds.), *Towards World Order and Human Dignity: Essays in Honor of Myers S McDougal* (New York: Free Press, 1976).
Wheeler, N., *Saving Strangers: Humanitarian Intervention in International Society* (Oxford: Oxford University Press, 2000).
Wickramasekara, P., 'Asian Labour Migration: Issues and Challenges in an Era of Globalization', *International Migration Papers* (Geneva: International Labour Office [ILO], 2002).
——, 'Asian Labour Migration: Issues and Challenges in an Era of Globalization', *International Migration Papers* No. 57 (Geneva: International Migration Programme, International Labour Office, 2002).
Woodbridge, G., *The History of UNRRA* (New York: Columbia University Press, 1950).
Yen-Fen Tseng, Chilla Bulbeck, Lan-Hung Nora Chiang and Jung-Chung Hsu (eds.), *Asian Migration: Pacific Rim Dynamics,* Monograph 1 (Taiwan: National Taiwan University, Interdisciplinary Group for Australian Studies, 1999).
Zieck, M., *UNHCR and Voluntary Repatriation of Refugees: A Legal Analysis* (The Hague: Martinus Nijhoff Publishers, 1997).
Zolberg, A. R. and Peter M. Benda (eds.), *Global Migrants, Global Refugees: Problems and Solutions* (New York: Berghahn Books, 2001).
Zolberg, A., Astri Suhrke and Sergio Aguayo, *Escape From Violence: Conflict and the Refugee Crisis in the Developing World* (New York: Oxford University Press, 1989).

Primary Documents

ASEAN, *Joint Communiqué of the Twelfth ASEAN Ministerial Meeting,* Bali, Indonesia, 30th June 1979 (Jakarta: Terbatas, ASEAN Sekretariat Nasional, 1979).
ASEAN, *Joint Statement by the ASEAN Foreign Ministers on Indochinese Refugees,* Singapore, 14 June 1987. http://www.aseansec.org/2484.html
ASEAN, *Joint Statement by the ASEAN Foreign Ministers on the Indochinese Refugees,* Bangkok, Thailand, 4 July 1988. http://www.aseansec.org/907.html
ASEAN, *Joint Statement by the ASEAN Foreign Ministers on the Problem of Vietnamese Boat People,* Jakarta, 24 July 1990. http://www.aseansec.org/1205.html
ASEAN, *Joint Statement by the Countries of Temporary* Refuge (CTR), ASEAN, Manilla, 16th May 1990.

Asian-African Legal Consultative Organization. *Final Text of the AALCO's 1966 Bangkok Principles on Status and Treatment of Refugees*. AALCO 40th session (New Delhi: 24 June 2001), 5. http://www.aalco.org/Final%20Text%20of%20Bangkok%20Prinicpl

International Refugee Organisation, *Future International Action concerning Refugees Document GC/81*, General Council, Third Special Session, GC/SR/42, 4 July 1949.

International Refugee Organisation, *Summary Record of the Fiftieth Meeting*, General Council, Third Special Session, GC/SR/50, 7 July 1949.

International Refugee Organisation, *Summary Record of the Forty-Eighth Meeting*, General Council, Third Special Session, GC/SR/48, 4 July 1949.

International Refugee Organisation, *Summary Record of the Forty-First Meeting*, General Council, Third Special Session, GC/SR/41, 4 July 1949.

International Refugee Organisation, *Summary Record of the Forty-Third Meeting*, General Council, Third Special Session, GC/SR/43, 6 July 1949.

Rockefeller, Lawrence Finkelstein to Mr Boyd Compton, *Memorandum: Proposed Colloquium on Legal Status of Refugees*, 21 October 1964; Rockefeller Foundation Archives, Record Group 1.2, Series 200, Box 484, Folder 4143.

UN Department of Social Affairs, *A Study of Statelessness* (New York: UN, August 1949).

UN News, 'Malaysia urged by UN agency to protect refugees in crackdown on migrants', *UN News Centre*, 4 March 2005. http://www.un.org/apps/news.

UNGA, 'Refugee question subject of Third Committee scrutiny in November', *UN Chronicle*, January 1986, Vol. 23, p. 3. http://web6.infrotrac.galegroup.com/itw/infomark/200/122/39895

UNGA, *1948 Universal Declaration of Human Rights*, Resolution 217 A(III), 10 December 1948.

UNGA, *Agenda of the Sub-Committee Annex 1, Proposal concerning Refugees submitted by the Delegation of the United Kingdom*, Meetings of the Joint Sub-Committee of the Second and Third Committees, Official Records of the 1st Session, Part 1, A/C.2/7 and A/C.3/3, 22 January 1946.

UNGA, *Agenda of the Sub-Committee Annex 3a, Problem of Refugees: Speech delivered by the Representative of the Netherlands at the Fourth Meeting of the Third Committee,* Meetings of the Joint Sub-Committee of the Second and Third Committees, Official Records of the 1st Session, Part 1, A/C.3/10, 22 January 1946.

UNGA, *Agenda of the Sub-Committee Annex 5, Proposal concerning Refugees submitted by the Delegation of the United States of America*, Meetings of the Joint Sub-Committee of the Second and Third Committees, Official Records of the 1st Session, Part 1, A/C.3/20, 22 January 1946.

UNGA, *Agenda of the Sub-Committee Annex 5a, Problem of Refugees: Speech delivered by the Representative of the United states of America at the Fourth Meeting at the Third Committee*, Meetings of the Joint Sub-Committee of the Second and Third Committees, Official Records of the 1st Session, Part 1, A/C.3/13, 22 January 1946.

UNGA, *Agenda of the Sub-Committee Annex 6, 'Statutory Refugees' and 'Displaced Persons': Memorandum Submitted by the Delegation of France*, Meetings of the Joint Sub-Committee of the Second and Third Committees, Official Records of the 1st Session, Part 1, A/C.3/16, 22 January 1946.

UNGA, *Annex to the Report on the Thirty-Fourth Session of the Executive Committee of the High Commissioner's Programme*, Executive Committee of the High Commissioner's Programme, Thirty-Fourth Session, A/AC.96/631/Annex.1, 20 October 1983.

UNGA, *Background Note Dated 9 July 1979 prepared by the United Nations High Commissioner for Refugees for the Meeting on Refugees and Displaced Persons in South-East Asia*, Convened by the Secretary-General of the United Nations as Geneva 20–21 July 1979, Annex 1, A/34/627, (7 November 1979).

UNGA, *Colloquium on the Legal Aspects of Refugee Problems,* Note by the High Commissioner, Executive Committee of the High Commissioner's Programme, Thirteenth Session, 5 May 1965, A/AC.96/INFO.40, Annex 1. Rockefeller Foundation Archives, Record Group 1.2, Series 200, Box 484, Folder 4143.

UNGA, *Draft Declaration and Comprehensive Plan of Action Approved by the Preparatory Meeting for the International Conference on Indo-Chinese Refugees on 8 March 1989*, A/CONF.148/2, 26 April 1989.

UNGA, *Durable Solutions*, Submitted by the High Commissioners, Executive Committee of the High Commissioner's Programme, Thirty-Sixth Session, A/AC.96/663, 25 July 1985.

UNGA, *Note on Departures and Repatriation*, Submitted by the High Commissioner, Co-ordinating Committee for the International Conference on Indo-Chinese Refugees 25 and 26 May 1989, A/CONF.148/4, Annex II.

UNGA, *Note on International Protection*, Submitted by the High Commissioner, Executive Committee of the High Commissioner's Programme, Thirty-Sixth Session, A/AC.96/660, 23 July 1985.

UNGA, *Note on International Protection*, Submitted by the High Commissioner, Executive Committee of the High Commissioner's Programme, Fortieth Session, A/AC.96/728.
UNGA, *Note on National Procedures for the Determination of Refugee Status*, Submitted by the High Commissioner, Co-ordinating Committee for the International Conference on Indo-Chinese Refugees 25 and 26 May 1989, A/CONF.148/4, Annex 1.
UNGA, *Note on National Procedures for the Determination of Refugee Status*, Submitted by the High Commissioner, Co-ordinating Committee for the International Conference on Indo-Chinese Refugees 25 and 26 May 1989, A/CONF.148/4, Annex 1.
UNGA, *Office of the United Nations High Commissioner for Refugees Meeting on Refugees and Displaced Persons in South-East Asia*, Convened by the Secretary-General of the United Nations at Geneva on 20 and 21 July 1979 and Subsequent Developments, Initiatives Taken Since the Meeting, Thirty-Fourth Session, Agenda Item 83, A/34/627, 7 November 1979.
UNGA, *Office of the United Nations High Commissioner for Refugees: International Conference on Indo-Chinese Refugees, Report of the Secretary-Genera, Annex: Declaration and Comprehensive Plan of Action (CPA)*, Forty-Fourth Session Item 111 (c), 22 September 1989, A/44/523/Annex, Section C—Reception of New Arrivals.
UNGA, *Office of the United Nations High Commissioner for Refugees: International Conference on Indo-Chinese Refugees, Report of the Secretary-Genera, Annex: Declaration and Comprehensive Plan of Action (CPA)*, Forty-Fourth Session Item 111 (c), 22 September 1989, A/44/523/Annex, Section F—Repatriation/Plan of Repatriation.
UNGA, *Official Records of the Third Committee*, Fourth Session, 250th Meeting, 4 November 1949.
UNGA, *Official Records of the Third Committee*, Fourth Session, 257th Meeting, 8 November 1949.
UNGA, *Official Records of the Third Committee*, Fourth Session, 258th Meeting, 9 November 1949.
UNGA, *Official Records of the Third Committee*, Fourth Session, 259th Meeting, 10 November 1949.
UNGA, *Official Records of the Third Committee*, Fourth Session, 260th Meeting, 11 November 1949.
UNGA, *Official Records of the Third Committee*, Fourth Session, 262nd Meeting, 14 November 1949.
UNGA, *Official Records of the Third Committee*, Fourth Session, 263rd Meeting, 15 November 1949.
UNGA, *Official Records of the Third Committee*, Fourth Session, 261st Meeting, 12 November, 1949.
UNGA, *Official Records of the Third Committee*, Fourth Session, 264th Meeting, 15 November 1949.
UNGA, *Official Records of the Third Committee*, Fourth Session, 265th Meeting, 18 November 1949.
UNGA, *Official Records of the Third Committee*, Fifth Session, 324th Meeting, 22 November 1950.
UNGA, *Official Records of the Third Committee*, Fifth Session, 325th Meeting, 24 November 1950.
UNGA, *Official Records of the Third Committee*, Fifth Session, 326th Meeting, 24 November 1950.
UNGA, *Official Records of the Third Committee*, Fifth Session, 328th Meeting, 27 November 1950.
UNGA, *Official Records of the Third Committee*, Fifth Session, 329th Meeting, 29 November 1950.
UNGA, *Official Records of the Third Committee*, Fifth Session, 330th Meeting, 30 November 1950.
UNGA, *Official Records of the Third Committee*, Fifth Session, 332nd Meeting, 1 December 1950.
UNGA, *Official Records of the Third Committee*, Fifth Session, 337th Meeting, 6 December 1950.
UNGA, *Official Records of the Third Committee*, Fifth Session, 344th Meeting, 11 December 1950.
UNGA, *Official Records of the Third Committee*, Fifth Session, Vol. 2, New York, 1950.
UNGA, *Official Records of the Third Committee*, Twenty-First Session, 1447th Meeting, 5 December 1966, p. 416.
UNGA, *Official Records of the Third Committee*, Twenty-First Session, 1447th Meeting, 5 December 1966.
UNGA, *Official Records of the Third Committee*, Twenty-First Session, 1447th Meeting, 5 December 1966.
UNGA, *Official Records of the Third Committee*, Twenty-First Session, 1449th Meeting, 6 December 1966.
UNGA, *Official Records of the Third Committee*, Twenty-First Session, 1450th Meeting, 7 December 1966.
UNGA, *Overview of UNHCR Activities: Report for 1988–1989*, Submitted by the High Commissioner, Executive Committee of the High Commissioner's Programme, Fortieth Session, A/AC.96/729, 25 August 1989.
UNGA, *Report of the Economic and Social Council 1948–1949*, Fourth Session, Volume 5, p. 56.
UNGA, *Report of the Executive Committee of the Programme of the United Nations High Commissioner for Refugees on the Work of its Thirtieth Session*, Executive Committee of the High Commissioner's Programme, Thirtieth Session, A/AC.96/572, 8–16 October 1979.
UNGA, *Report of the United Nations High Commissioner for Refugees*, Supplement No. 11, Twentieth Session, A/6011/Rev.1, New York, 1965.
UNGA, *Report of the United Nations High Commissioner for Refugees Part Two: Report on the Sixteenth Session of the Executive Committee of the High Commissioner's Programme from 31 October–8 November 1966*, Official Records of Twenty-First Session, Supplement No. 11 (A/6311/Rev.1).
UNGA, *Report of the United Nations High Commissioner for Refugees*, Official Records Supplement No. 12, Thirty-Ninth Session, (New York: 1984).

UNGA, *Report on Report on UNHCR Assistance Activities in 1977–1978 and Proposed Voluntary Funds Programmes and Budget for 1979 Addendum 1*, Submitted by the High Commissioner, Executive Committee of the High Commissioner's Programme, Twenty-Eighth Session, A/AC.96/553/Add.1 (3 October 1978).

UNGA, *Report on the Fourteenth Session of the Executive Committee of the High Commissioner's Programme*, Official Records, Twentieth Session, 25 October–2 November 1965.

UNGA, *Report on the Resettlement of Refugees*, Executive Committee of the High Commissioner's Programme, Thirty-Fifth Session, A/AC.96/640, 19 July 1984.

UNGA, *Report on the Resettlement of Refugees*, Executive Committee of the High Commissioner's Programme, Thirty-Sixth Session, A/AC.96/661, 26 July 1985.

UNGA, *Report on the Resettlement of Refugees*, Executive Committee of the High Commissioner's Programme, Thirty-Fourth Session, A/AC.96/624, 25 August 1983.

UNGA, *Report on the Resettlement of Refugees*, Executive Committee of the High Commissioner's Programme, Thirty-Fifth Session, A/AC.96/640, 19 July 1984.

UNGA, *Report on the Resettlement of Refugees*, Submitted by the High Commissioner, Executive Committee of the High Commissioner's Programme, Thirtieth Session, A/AC.96/568, 28 August 1979.

UNGA, *Report on the Resettlement of Refugees*, Submitted by the High Commissioner, Executive Committee of the High Commissioner's Programme, Thirty-Sixth Session, A/AC.96/661, 26 July 1985.

UNGA, *Report on the Resettlement of Refugees, Submitted by the High Commissioner*, Executive Committee of the High Commissioner's Programme, Thirty-First Session, A/AC.96/580, 15 August 1980.

UNGA, *Report on the Thirty-Fourth Session of the Executive Committee of the High Commissioner's Programme 10–20 October 1983*, Executive Committee of the High Commissioner's Programme, Thirty-Fourth Session, A/AC.96/631, 20 October 1983.

UNGA, *Report on the Twenty-Eighth Session of the Executive Committee of the High Commissioner's Programme, High Commissioner's Opening Statement*, Executive Committee of the High Commissioner's Programme, Twenty-Eighth Session, A/AC.96/549 Annex 1, 4 October 1977.

UNGA, *Report on the UNHCR Assistance Activities in 1978–1979 and Proposed Voluntary Funds Programme and Budget for 1980, Observations of the Advisory Committee on Administrative and Budgetary Questions*, Submitted by the High Commissioner, Executive Committee of the High Commissioner's Programme, Thirtieth Session, A/AC.96/570, 27 September 1979.

UNGA, *Report on the UNHCR Assistance Activities in 1978–1979 and Proposed Voluntary Funds Programmes and Budget for 1980*, Executive Committee of the High Commissioner's Programme, Thirtieth Session, A/AC.96/564, 14 August 1979.

UNGA, *Report on the UNHCR Assistance Activities in 1978–1979 and Proposed Voluntary Funds Programmes and Budget for 1980, Addendum*, Executive Committee of the High Commissioner's Programme, Thirtieth Session, A/AC.96/564/Add.1, 28 September 1979.

UNGA, *Report on the UNHCR Assistance Activities in 1974–1975 and Proposed Voluntary Funds Programme and Budget for 1976, Addendum 1 Special Operations*, Submitted by the High Commissioner, Executive Committee of the High Commissioner's Programme, Twenty-Sixth Session, A/AC.96/516/Add.1, 15 September 1975.

UNGA, *Report on the UNHCR Assistance Activities in 1974–1975 and Proposed Voluntary Funds Programme and Budget for 1976, Addendum 2 Assistance to Displaced Persons from Indochina in Thailand*, Submitted by the High Commissioner, Executive Committee of the High Commissioner's Programme, Twenty-Sixth Session, A/AC.96/516/Add.2, 2 October 1975.

UNGA, *Report on the UNHCR Assistance Activities in 1977–1978 and Proposed Voluntary Funds Programmes and Budget for 1979*, Submitted by the High Commissioner, Executive Committee of the High Commissioner's Programme, Twenty-Ninth Session, A/AC.96/553, 9 August 1978.

UNGA, *Report on the UNHCR Assistance Activities in 1978–1979 and Proposed Voluntary Funds Programmes and Budget for 1980*, Submitted by the High Commissioner, Executive Committee of the High Commissioner's Programme, Thirtieth Session, A/AC.96/564, 14 August 1979.

UNGA, *Report on the UNHCR Assistance Activities in 1979–1980 and Proposed Voluntary Funds Programmes and Budget for 1981*, Addendum, Executive Committee of the High Commissioner's Programme, Thirty-First Session, A/AC.96/577/Add.2, 26 September 1980.

UNGA, *Report on the UNHCR Assistance Activities in 1984–1985 and Proposed Voluntary Funds Programmes and Budget for Executive Committee of the High Commissioner's Programme*, Executive Committee of the High Commissioner's Programme, Thirty-Sixth Session, A/AC.96/657, 5 August 1985.

UNGA, *Resolution 428 (V) Statue of the High Commissioner's Office*, 14 December 1950.
UNGA, *Summary Record of the 323rd Meeting on 10 October 1980*, Executive Committee of the High Commissioner's Programme, Thirty-First Session, A/AC.96/SR.323, 15 October 1980.
UNGA, *Summary Record of the 285th Meeting held on 5 October 1977*, Executive Committee of the High Commissioner's Programme, Twenty-Eighth Session, A/AC.96/SR.285, 10 October 1977.
UNGA, *Summary Record of the 287th Meeting held on 6 October 1977*, Executive Committee of the High Commissioner's Programme, Twenty-Eighth Session, A/AC.96/SR.287, 17 October 1977.
UNGA, *Summary Record of the 295th Meeting held on 10 October 1978*, Executive Committee of the High Commissioner's Programme, Twenty-Ninth Session, A/AC.96/SR.295, 12 October 1978.
UNGA, *Summary Record of the 305th Meeting on 9th October 1979*, Executive Committee of the High Commissioner's Programme, Thirtieth Session, A/AC.96/SR.305, 11 October 1979.
UNGA, *Summary Record of the 306th Meeting on 9th October 1979*, Executive Committee of the High Commissioner's Programme, Thirtieth Session, A/AC.96/SR.306, 12 October 1979.
UNGA, *Summary Record of the 307th Meeting on 10th October 1979*, Executive Committee of the High Commissioner's Programme, Thirtieth Session, A/AC.96/SR.307, 15 October 1979.
UNGA, *Summary Record of the 308th Meeting on 10th October 1979*, Executive Committee of the High Commissioner's Programme, Thirtieth Session, A/AC.96/SR.308, 15 October 1979.
UNGA, *Summary Record of the 317th Meeting on 7 October 1980*, Executive Committee of the High Commissioner's Programme, Thirty-First Session, A/AC.96/SR.317, 7 October 1980.
UNGA, *Summary Record of the 318th Meeting on 7 October 1980*, Executive Committee of the High Commissioner's Programme, Thirty-First Session, A/AC.96/SR.318, 10 October 1980.
UNGA, *Summary Record of the 321st Meeting on 9 October 1980*, Executive Committee of the High Commissioner's Programme, Thirty-First Session, A/AC.96/SR.321, 13 October 1980.
UNGA, *Summary Record of the 326th Meeting on 13 October 1980*, Executive Committee of the High Commissioner's Programme, Thirty-First Session, A/AC.96/SR.326, 17 October 1980.
UNGA, *Summary Record of the 333rd Meeting on 14 October*, Executive Committee of the High Commissioner's Programme, Thirty-Second Session, A/AC.96/SR.333, 21 October 1981.
UNGA, *Summary Record of the 344th Meeting on 12 October*, Executive Committee of the High Commissioner's Programme, Thirty-Third Session, A/AC.96/SR.344, 15 October 1982.
UNGA, *Summary Record of the 346th Session on 13 October*, Executive Committee of the High Commissioner's Programme, Thirty-Third Session, A/AC.96/SR.346, 18 October 1982.
UNGA, *Summary Record of the 368th Meeting on 8 October 1984*, Executive Committee of the High Commissioner's Programme, Thirty-Fifth Session, A/AC.96/SR.368, 10 October 1984.
UNGA, *Summary Record of the 369th Meeting on 9 October 1984*, Executive Committee of the High Commissioner's Programme, Thirty-Fifth Session, A/AC.96/SR.369, 12 October 1984.
UNGA, *Summary Record of the 369th Meeting on 9 October*, Executive Committee of the High Commissioner's Programme, Thirty-Fifth Session, A/AC.96/SR.369, 12 October 1984.
UNGA, *Summary Record of the 369th Session on 9 October*, Executive Committee of the High Commissioner's Programme, Thirty-Fifth Session, A/AC.96/SR.369, 12 October 1984.
UNGA, *Summary of the 370th Meeting on 9 October 1984*, Executive Committee of the High Commissioner's Programme, Thirty-Fifth Session, A/AC.96/SR.370, 15 October 1984.
UNGA, *Summary Record of the 371st Meeting on 10 October 1984*, Executive Committee of the High Commissioner's Programme, Thirty-Fifth Session, A/AC.96/SR.371, 17 October 1984.
UNGA, *Summary Record of the 385th Session on 7 October 1984*, Executive Committee of the High Commissioner's Programme, Thirty-Sixth Session, A/AC.96/SR.385, 9 October 1985.
UNGA, *Summary Record of the 386th Meeting on 8 October*, Executive Committee of the High Commissioner's Programme, Thirty-Fifth Session, A/AC.96/SR.386, 11 October 1985.
UNGA, *Summary Record of the 405th Meeting on 8 October 1986*, Executive Committee of the High Commissioner's Programme, Thirty-Seventh Session, A/AC.96/SR.405, 14 October 1984.
UNGA, *Summary Record of the 407th Meeting on 9 October 1986*, Executive Committee of the High Commissioner's Programme, Thirty-Seventh Session, A/AC.96/SR.407, 16 October 1984.
UNGA, *Summary Record of the 408th Meeting on 9 October 1986*, Executive Committee of the High Commissioner's Programme, Thirty-Seventh Session, A/AC.96/SR.408, 21 October 1986.
UNGA, *Summary Record of the 426th Meeting on 3rd October 1988*, Executive Committee of the High Commissioner's Programme, Thirty-Ninth Session, A/AC.96/SR.426, 18 October 1988.
UNGA, *Summary Record of the 427th Meeting on 4th October 1988*, Executive Committee of the High Commissioner's Programme, Thirty-Ninth Session, A/AC.96/SR.427, 9 November 1988.
UNGA, *Summary Record of the 428th Meeting on 4th October 1988*, Executive Committee of the High Commissioner's Programme, Thirty-Ninth Session, A/AC.96/SR.428, 10 October 1988.

UNGA, *Summary Record of the 432nd Meeting on 6th October 1988*, Executive Committee of the High Commissioner's Programme, Thirty-Ninth Session, A/AC.96/SR.432, 13 October 1988.

UNGA, *Summary Record of the 473rd Meeting on 5 October 1992*, Executive Committee of the High Commissioner's Programme, A/AC.96/SR.473, 12 October 1992.

UNGA, *Summary Records of the 141st to the 152nd Meetings held from 31October to 8 November 1966*, Executive Committee of the High Commissioner's Programme, Sixteenth Session, A/ AC.96/SR.141–152.

UNGA, *UNHCR Activities Financed by Voluntary Funds: Report for 1987–1988 and Proposed Programmes and Budget for 1989, Part II: Asia and Oceania*, Submitted by the High Commissioner, Executive Committee of the High Commissioner's Programme, Thirty-Ninth Session, A/AC.96/708 (Part II), 28 July 1988.

UNGA, *UNHCR Activities Financed by Voluntary Funds: Report for 1988–89 and Proposed Programmes and Budget for 1990*, Part II: Asia and Oceania, Submitted by the High Commissioner, Executive Committee of the High Commissioner's Programme, Fortieth Session, A/AC.96/724 (Part II), 28 August 1989.

UNGA, *UNHCR Activities Financed by Voluntary Funds: Report for 1989–1990 and Proposed Programmes and Budget for 1991*, Part II: Asia and Oceania, Submitted by the High Commissioner, Executive Committee of the High Commissioner's Programme, Forty-First Session, A/AC.96/751 (Part II), 13 August 1990.

UNHCR, *1951 Convention Relating to the Status of Refugees*, Geneva, 1951.

UNHCR, *1967 Protocol Relating to the Status of Refugees*, Geneva, 1967.

UNHCR, A. Dhar to UNHCR Headquarters, *Ratification by the Philippines of the Convention and Protocol*, 30 March 1976; HCR/ML/48, Folio 5, 671.1 PHI.

UNHCR, Asian Regional Section to UNHCR Geneva, *Outgoing Cable*, 2 September 1975; Folio 11, 671.1 GEN; Series 1, Fonds UNHCR 11.

UNHCR, Comment by G. L. Coles, *UNHCR Action Sheet*, 5 March 1982. Folio 281A, 602.3 ASIA.

UNHCR, Comment by S. Bari to Mr Jackson, *UNHCR Action Sheet*, 17 March 1982; Folio 283, 602.3 ASIA.

UNHCR, Country Operations Plan for each of the countries in Southeast Asia, *Planning Year 2004* (Geneva: UNHCR, 2004).

UNHCR, D. Bayandor, UNHCR Representative in Malaysia, to UNHCR Headquarters, Geneva, *Set Up of Afghan Mujahidin Office in Kuala Lumpur*, 24 April 1984; 84/KL/HQ.186, 010.MLS.

UNHCR, D. McNamara to UNHCR Headquarters, *ASEAN Law Association—1980 General Assembly*, 19 January 1981; Folio 111, 383 ASEAN Protection.

UNHCR, Darioush Bayandor, UNHCR Representative for Kuala Lumpur, *Report on Situation of the VNBP*, Annual Review Meeting of Vietnamese Boatpeople, 30 January 1984; 010.MLS.

UNHCR, David Hay-Edie, Officer-in-Charge, UNHCR Manila to UNHCR Headquarters, *Protection Programme in Philippines: Problems and Promotion*, 15 March 1982; HCR/ML/073, Folio 286, 602.3 ASIA.

UNHCR, Denis McNamara to UNHCR Geneva, *Explanatory Questions and Answers on the Convention and Protocol*, 6 November 1981; Folio 238, 671.1 GEN.

UNHCR, Dennis McNamara to UNHCR Geneva, *The Refugee Definition in Asia*, 7 June 1982; Folio 3, 671.1 ASIA.

UNHCR, Dennis McNamara, *Confidential: Discussion with Dr B Sen, Secretary General of the Asian-African Legal Consultative Committee*, 13 April 1982; 601.AALCC.

UNHCR, Deputy High Commissioner to J Asscher, *Interoffice Memorandum: 1951 Convention*, 21 March 1956; Folio 535, 16/1/3 GEN, Series 1, Fonds 11. Series 1, Classified Subject Files; Fonds 11, Records of the Central Registry; Archives of the UNHCR for Refugees (hereafter Series 1, Fonds UNHCR 11).

UNHCR, Deputy High Commissioner to Minister for Foreign Affairs of Afghanistan, *Correspondence*, 3 November 1959; Folio 849, 16/1/3 GEN, Series 1, Fonds 11.

UNHCR, Deputy High Commissioner to Primer Minister and Minister for Foreign Affairs of Federation of Malaya, *Correspondence*, 4 November 1959; Folio 852, 16/1/3 GEN, Series 1, Fonds 11.

UNHCR, E. Jahn to Mr Goundian, *Asian-African Committee*, 6 February 1970; Folio 1879, 16/1/3 GEN, Series 1, Fonds 11.

UNHCR, E. Soeprapto to Director of Protection Division, 'Mid-Annual Review of the Implementation of Programme of Work for 1975', 17 September 1975; 671.1 GEN; Series 2, Fonds UNHCR 11.

UNHCR, E. Soeprapto to Director of Protection Division, *Proposed Programme of Protection Work in Asia for 1976*, 23 February 1976; Folio 22, 602.3 ASIA; Series 2, Fonds UNHCR 11.

UNHCR, E. Soeprapto to Director of Protection Division, *Mid-Annual Review of the Implementation of Programme of Work for 1975*, 17 September 1975; Folio 48, 671.1 GEN; Series 2, Fonds UNHCR 11.

UNHCR, *Explanatory Note*, Handed to Mr Goormaghtigh of the Carnegie Endowment on 24 September 1964; Folio 24, 16/1/3 AMEND, Series 1, Fonds 11.

UNHCR, Explanatory Note, *On Special aspects of the 1951 Convention and 1967 Protocol relating to the Status of Refugees*, July 1977; Folio 1, 672.MLS.

UNHCR, F. E. Krens to UNHCR Legal Adviser in Asia, *Explanatory Questions and Answers on the 1951 Convention and the 1967 Protocol*, 4 May 1982; Folio 245, 671.1 GEN.

UNHCR, F. E. Krenz to P. M. Moussalli, *Confidential: Accession of Indonesia to the 1951 Convention and the 1967 Protocol Conversation with Mr Soeprapto*, 4 August 1981; Folio 10, 671.1 INS.

UNHCR, *Global Report 2003* (Geneva: UNHCR, 2003).

UNHCR, HICOMREF Poul Hartling to Prime Minister of Thailand, *Telecommunications Transmission Request*, 23 January 1984; 010.THA, Folio 501.

UNHCR, High Commissioner Felix Schnyder to Mr Stavropoulos, Legal Counsel, *Letter and draft Memorandum by the UNHCR on the Report of the Colloquium on Legal Aspects of Refugee Problems held in April 1965 in Bellagio, Italy*, 6 August 1965; Folio 136, Series 1, Fonds 11, 16/1/3/AMEND.

UNHCR, High Commissioner Schnyder to Mr John Goormaghtigh, *Correspondence*, 20 July 1964; Folio 16, 16/1/3 GEN, Series 1, Fonds 11.

UNHCR, High Commissioner Schnyder to Mr Stavropoulos, *Memorandum by the United Nations High Commissioner for Refugees on the Report of the Colloquium on Legal Aspects of Refugee Problems held in April 1965 in Bellagio (Como), Italy*, 6 August 1965; Folio 136, 16/1/3 AMEND, Series 1, Fonds 11.

UNHCR, High Commissioner to Assistant Secretary for Human Rights and Humanitarian Affairs, US Office of the Assistant Secretary of States, *Correspondence*, 4 October 1978; Folio 6, 100.THA. GEN—Thailand—General; Series 2, Fonds UNHCR 11.

UNHCR, I. C. Jackson to The Representative, UNHCR Branch Office for Nepal, *Accession by Nepal to the 1951 Convention and the Protocol*, 16 September 1967; Folio 4741, 16/1/3 GEN, Series 1, Fonds 11.

UNHCR, I. Khan to Mr P. M. Moussalli, *Weekly Notes 20 to 26 February 1981*, 26 February; Folio 187; 602.3 ASIA.

UNHCR, I. Khan to Mr P. M. Moussalli, *Weekly Notes 21 to 27 August 1981*, 27 August 1981; Folio 257, 602.3 ASIA.

UNHCR, I. Khan to Mr P. M. Moussalli, *Weekly Notes 6 to 12 November 1981*, 12 November 1981; Folio 567; 602.3 ASIA.

UNHCR, *Information Package on the Comprehensive Plan of Action on Indo-Chinese Refugees (CPA)*, October 1995.

UNHCR, James Read, Deputy High Commissioner to Mr Mauro Calingo, Department of Foreign Affairs, Philippines, *Correspondence*, 23 December 1952; 671.1 1951 Convention 1952–1953.

UNHCR, James Read, Deputy High Commissioner to Prime Minister and Minister for Foreign Affairs, Federation of Malaya, *Correspondence*, 4 November 1959; Folio 852, 16/1/3/GEN.

UNHCR, Leslie Goodyear, Regional Representative for Western South Asia, Bangkok to The High Commissioner, UNHCR Headquarters, Geneva, *Promotion of the Accession of the 1951 Convention and the 1967 Protocol*, 19 June 1979; Folio 8, 671.1 THA, 19 June 1979.

UNHCR, *Memorandum by the United Nations High Commissioner for Refugees on the Report of the Colloquium on Legal Aspects of Refugee Problems held in April 1965 in Bellagio (Como), Italy*, 23 September 1965; HCR/RS/31, Series 1, Fonds 11, 16/1/3 GEN.

UNHCR, *Memorandum*, Handed to Mr Goormaghtigh of the Carnegie Endowment on 24 September 1964; Fonds 11, Series 1, 16/1/3/AMEND.

UNHCR, Michel Moussalli to Sq Ldr Prasong Soonsiri, *Correspondence*, 17 January 1984, 010. THA, Folio 500.

UNHCR, Minister Permanent Delegate of Japan to the International Organisations to the Deputy High Commissioner, 3 August 1956; Folio 579, 671.1 GEN; Series 1, Fonds UNHCR 11.

UNHCR, Mollie Rule, WCC to James Read, *Correspondence*, 16 February 1953; UNHCR Archives Folio 5, 671.1 1952–53.

UNHCR, Mr E. Schlatter to United Nations Vientiane, Laos, 28 January 1967; Folio 1692, 671.1 GEN; Series 1, Fonds UNHCR 11.

UNHCR, Mr O. Goundian to E Jahn, *Report on the Asian-African Committee*, 6 February 1970; 16/1/3 GEN, Series 1, Fonds 11.

UNHCR, N. Bwakira to Director of Protection Division, *Mid-Annual Review of the Implementation of Programme of Work for 1975: ASIA*, 13 November 1975; Folio 17, 602.3 ASIA; Series 2, Fonds UNHCR 11.

UNHCR, Note for File, *Meeting with the Minister of State for Home Affairs and Law, Singapore, Professor S. Jayakumar on 7 July 1982*, Folio 50, in Folio 247A, 31 August 1982.

UNHCR, Note for the File, *Meeting with Mr Ahmad Kamil bin Jaafar*, Confidential, 28 June 1978; 78/KL/845, Folio 6, 671.1.MLS.

UNHCR, Note for the File, *Meeting with Mr Dhar, the Indian Representative to the Executive Committee on 22 October 1969*, 27 October 1969; 16/1/3 GEN, Series 1, Fonds 11.

UNHCR, O. Bayer. Protection Officer, Asia Regional Section to P. M. Moussalli, Director of Protection, *Weekly Notes 3 to 9 August 1979*, 9 August 1979; Folio 110, 602.3.

UNHCR, Otto Gobius, Asia Regional Section to UNHCR Branch Office for the Philippines, *The Philippines and the 1951 Convention and 1967 Protocol*, 7 April 1976; HCR/ML/36, Folio 6, 671.1 PHI.

UNHCR, Otto Gobius, Asia Regional Section to UNHCR Branch Office for the Philippines, *Philippines and the 1951 Convention and 1967 Protocol*, 23 April 1976; HCR/ML/48, Folio 8, 671.1 PHI.

UNHCR, Otto Gobius, UNHCR Bangkok to The High Commissioner, *Convention/Protocol—Thailand*, 17 November 1972; HCR/BKK/273, Folio 2, 671.THA.

UNHCR, Otto Gobius, UNHCR Bangkok to The High Commissioner, *Discussion with Director General for International Organizations at the Foreign Ministry*, 26 January 1973; HCR/BKK/031, Folio 3, 671.THA.

UNHCR, Otto Gobius, UNHCR Bangkok to The High Commissioner, *Discussion with Director General for International Organizations at the Foreign Ministry*, 26 January 1973; HCR/BKK/031, Folio 3, 671.THA.

UNHCR, P. M. Moussalli to the High Commissioner, *Summary of Report on South-East Asia Protection Meeting Thailand, 12–14 August 1981*, 2 October 1981; Folio 963, 602.3 ASIA.

UNHCR, Permanent Mission of Thailand, *Press Release Statement by Squadron Leader Prasong Soonsiri on 8 February 1984*, 10 February 1984; Folio 505C, 010.THA.

UNHCR, Philippe Labreveux to P. M. Moussalli, *Protection Programme for Asia*, 2 March 1982; Folio 283; 602.3 ASIA.

UNHCR, *Refugees by Numbers* (2004 Edition), www.unhcr.ch/egi-bin/texis/basics.

UNHCR, *Refugees*, No. 3 March 1984; 010.THA.

UNHCR, Regional Office Manila to High Commissioner, *Incoming Cable*, 19 June 1981; Folio 115, 383 Protection.

UNHCR, *Report of the Working Group on Current Problems in the International Protection of Refugees and Displaced Persons in Asia*, Under the Auspices of the UNHCR, International Institute of Humanitarian Law, San Remo, 19–22 January 1981 (Geneva: UNHCR, March 1981).

UNHCR, *Report on Mr de Kemoularia's visit to Malaya 12/9/59*, Excerpt from File 27/3/5—WRY/MAL; 13 November 1959.

UNHCR, *Round Table of Asian Experts on Current Problems in the International Protection of Refugees and Displaced Persons*, April 1980. Publication Box 4, Section One.

UNHCR, S. Bari to Director of Protection, *Weekly Notes for 24 to the 31 May 1979*, 31 May 1979; Folio 101, 602.3 ASIA; Series 2, Fonds UNHCR 11.

UNHCR, S. Bari to Director of Protection, *Weekly Notes for 29 June to the 5 July 1979*, 5 July 1979; Folio 106, 602.3 ASIA; Series 2, Fonds UNHCR 11.

UNHCR, S. Bari to Mr P. M. Mousalli, *Weekly Notes 12 to 18 October 1979*, 18 October 1979; Folio 121, 602.3 ASIA.

UNHCR, S. Bari to Mr P. M. Moussalli, *Weekly Notes 20 to 26 June 1980*, 26 June 1980; Folio 157, 602.3 ASIA.

UNHCR, S. Bari to Mr P. M. Moussalli, *Weekly Notes 21 to 27 March 1980*, 27 March 1980; Folio 143, 602.3 ASIA.

UNHCR, S. Bari to Mr P. M. Moussalli, *Weekly Notes 3 to 10 April 1980*, 10 April 1980; Folio 145, 602.3 ASIA.

UNHCR, S. Bari to Mr P. M. Moussalli, *Weekly Notes 4 to 10 January 1980*, 10 January 1980; Folio 131, 602.3 ASIA.

UNHCR, S. Bari to Mr P. M. Moussalli, *Weekly Notes 8 to 14 February 1980*, 14 February 1980; Folio 136, 602.3 ASIA.

UNHCR, S. Bari, Protection Office, Asia Section to E. Jahn, Acting Director of Protection, *Weekly Notes 31 August to 5 September 1979*, 5 September 1979; Folio 113, 602.3.

UNHCR, S. Bari, Protection Officer to Dr E. Jahn, Acting Director of Protection, *Weekly Notes 21 to 27 September 1979*, 27 September 1979; Folio 118, 602.3 ASIA.

UNHCR, S. Bari, Protection Officer, Asia Section to Dr E. Jahn, Acting Director of Protection, *Weekly Notes 31 August to 5 September 1979*, 5 September 1979; Folio 113, 602.3 GEN.

UNHCR, S. Bari, Protection Officer, East Asia Regional Section and South & South East Asia Regional Section to Dr E. Jahn, Acting Director of Protection, *Weekly Notes 6 to 13 September 1979*; 13 September 1979, Folio 115, 602.3 ASIA.

UNHCR, S. Chetty, Chief of Protection Section, Bangkok to Protection Section, Headquarters, *Promotion of Refugee Protection in Thailand*, 16 July 1981; Folio 10, 671.THA.

UNHCR, S. Chetty, Legal Section for Regional Representative, Bangkok to J. Colombey, Conference and Treaties Section, UNHCR, *Translation of 1951 Convention in Thai Language*, 14 April 1982; HCR/BKK/HQ/0436, 671.1.GEN.

UNHCR, S. Chetty, Legal Section for Regional Representative, Bangkok to D. McNamara, Head Legal Adviser in Asia, Hong Kong, *Promotion of Refugee Law in Thailand*, 15 February 1982; HCR/BKK/MISC/1005, 602.3 ASIA.

UNHCR, S. N. Chetty to Mr P. M. Moussalli, *Weekly Notes 30 May to 5 June 1980*, 5 June 1980; Folio 153, 602.3 ASIA.

UNHCR, S. N. Chetty, to Mr P. M. Moussalli, Director of Protection, *Weekly Notes 18 to 24 April 1980*, 24 April 1980; Folio 147, 602.3 ASIA.

UNHCR, S Tharoor to P. M. Moussalli, *Protection Programme for Asia*, 16 March 1982; Folio 286A, SIN/82/HQ/053, 602.3 ASIA.

UNHCR, Secretary of Foreign Affairs, Republic of Philippines to Deputy High Commissioner, 2 July 1956; Folio 578, 671.1 GEN—1951 Convention, 1949–1969 General; Series 1, Fonds UNHCR 11.

UNHCR, Thai Prime Minister to UN Secretary-General, *Memorandum Boat People*, 14 April 1984; HC/HCR/249, 010.THA.

UNHCR, The High Commissioner Sadraddin Aga Khan to The Minister for Foreign Affairs, Kingdom of Thailand, *Correspondence*, 15 August 1977; Folio 5, 671.THA.

UNHCR, The UNHCR Representative for Southeast Asia, *Promotion of International Protection in Southeast and East Asia*, 28 June 1974; Folio 97A, 671.1 GEN; Series 2, Fonds UNHCR 11.

UNHCR, *Trends in Refugee Status Determination 1 January—30 September 2004. Asylum Applications, Refugee Status Determination and Pending Cases in 73 Mostly Developing Countries* (Geneva: Population Determination Unit, Population and Geographic Data Section UNHCR, December 2004).

UNHCR, UNHCR Bangkok to HICOMREF Geneva, *Cable*, 30 January 1984; THA/HCR/0183, 010.THA.

UNHCR, UNHCR Bangkok to HICOMREF Geneva, *Urgent Incoming Cable*, 8 March 1984; THA/CHR/429, 010.THA.

UNHCR, UNHCR Bangkok to UNHCR High Commissioner, Geneva, *Incoming Cable*, 2 December 1981; Folio 13, 671.THA.

UNHCR, *UNHCR Global Report 2003* (Geneva: UNHCR, 2003).

UNHCR, UNHCR Kuala Lumpur to Legal Adviser for Asia, Hong Kong, *Incoming Cable*, 19 November 1981; HCR/KL/648; HCR/KL/MISC/1457, 671.1.MLS.

UNHCR, UNHCR Kuala Lumpur to UNHCR, Geneva, *Incoming Cable*, 18 February 1980; HCR/KL/137, 671.1.MLS.

UNHCR, UNHCR Legal Adviser in Asia to General Legal Section, *Explanatory Questions and Answers on the 1951 Convention and the 1967 Protocol*, 4 May 1982; Folio 245, 671.1 GEN, Series 2, Fonds 11.

UNHCR, UNHCR Representative for Southeast Asia, Bangkok, *Promotion of International Protection in Southeast Asia and East Asia*, 28 June 1974; Folio 48, 671 GEN.

UNHCR, V. Tedesco to Mr Tanner, *Correspondence*,17 April 1969; Folio 1837, 16/1/3 GEN, Series 1, Fonds 11.

UNHCR, *Visit of Dr Urrutia to Legal Division on 13 April 1966*, 18 April 1966; Folio 1602, 16/1/3 GEN, Series 1, Fonds 11.

UNHCR, W. Blatter, UNHCR Representative in Philippines to Protection Division, UNHCR Headquarters, *Philippine accession to the 1951 Convention and 1967 Protocol*, 31 March 1977; HCR/ML/34, Folio 13, 671.1 PHI.

UNHCR, W. K. McCoy to UNHCR Geneva, *Indonesia—Attitude to Convention*, 6 May 1969; Folio 1839, 16/1/3 GEN, Series 1, Fonds 11.
UNHCR, W. K. McCoy to UNHCR Geneva, *Malaysia—Attitude to Convention*, Memorandum, 15 March 1969; MAC/SEA/MAL, Folio 1829, 16/1/3/GEN, Series 1, Fonds 11.
UNHCR, W. K. McCoy to UNHCR Geneva, *Singapore—Attitude to Convention*, Memorandum, 24 March 1969; MAC/SEA, Folio 1831, 16/1/3/GEN, Series 1, Fonds 11.
UNHCR, *Weekly Notes 29 June to 5 July 1979*; 602.3 ASIA; Series 2, Fonds UNHCR 11.
UNHCR, Zia Rizvi to Deputy High Commissioner, *Incoming Cable*, 21 June 1982; Folio 118, 383 Protection.
United Kingdom Parliament. Sir Peter Blaker, 'Vietnamese Boatpeople', *House of Commons Hansard Debates for 25 July 1991.*
United Nations Development Programme, *Human Development Report 1994* (New York: Oxford University Press, 1994).
United Nations Economic and Social Council, (UNESC) *Note on Asylum*, Submitted by the High Commissioner, Executive Committee of the High Commissioners' Programme, Economic and Social Committee, Twenty-Eighth Session, EC/SCP/4, 24 August 1977.
UNESC, *Report on the United Nations High Commissioner for Refugees*, Second Regular Session, E/1985/62, 8 May 1985.
UNESC, *Note on International Solidarity and Refugee Protection*, Sub-Committee on International Protection (SCIP), EC/SCP/50, 13 July 1988.
UNESC, *Report of the International Refugee Organization* (IRO), E/1334, 1949.
UNESC, *Report of the United Nations High Commissioner for Refugees*, United Nations Economic and Social Council, Second Regular Session, E/1984.61, 30 May 1984.
UNESC, *Study on the Position of Stateless Persons*, Belgium and France: Draft Resolution, 4 August 1949, E/1447/Rev.1.
United States Committee for Refugees (USCR), *Refugee Reports*, Volume 8, Number 3, 20 March 1987.
USCR, *Refugee Reports*, Volume 8, Number 8, 14 August 1987.
USCR, *Refugee Reports*, Volume 9, Number 2, 26 February 1988.
USCR, *Refugee Reports*, Volume 9, Number 3, 18 March 1988.
USCR, *Refugee Reports*, Volume 9, Number 5, 20 May 1988.
USCR, *Refugee Reports*, Volume 9, Number 6, 24 June 1988.
USCR, *Refugee Reports*, Volume 10, Number 6, 16 June 1989.
USCR, *Refugee Reports*, Volume 10, Number 7, 28 July 1989.
USCR, *Refugee Reports*, Volume 10, Number 10, 20 October 1989.
USCR, *Refugee Reports*, Volume 10, Number 12, 29 December 1989.
USCR, *Refugee Reports*, Volume 11, Number 1, 31 January 1990.
USCR, *Refugee Reports*, Volume 11, Number 3, 23 March 1990.
USCR, *Refugee Reports*, Volume 11, Number 5, 18 May 1990.
USCR, *Refugee Reports*, Volume 11, Number 6, 21 June 1990.
USCR, *Refugee Reports*, Volume 11, Number 8, 24 August 1990.
USCR, *Refugee Reports*, Volume 11, Number 11, 30 November 1990.

Index

www.ingramcontent.com/pod-product-compliance
Lightning Source LLC
LaVergne TN
LVHW081515300926
849161LV00006B/1179
9789004163515